Michael Rouland is an historian o
Afghanistan. He has published wide
culture and national identity. Since 20
Russian, Central Eurasian and global history at Georgetown, Miami, and Stanford Universities. He is currently an historian for the US Air Force.

Gulnara Abikeyeva is a Kazakh film critic and researcher, and the author of several books on the cinema of Kazakhstan and Central Asia. She is a member of FIPRESCI (International Federation of Film Critics) and NETPAC (Network for the Promotion of Asian Cinema), and has been a jury member on a range of international film festivals.

Birgit Beumers is Professor in Film Studies at Aberystwyth University, Wales. She has published widely on Russian and Soviet cinema and theatre, and is on the Advisory Board of the *KINO* series at I.B.Tauris. She is editor of *KinoKultura* and of the journal *Studies in Russian and Soviet Cinema*.

CW00432017

Published and forthcoming in *KINO: The Russian and Soviet Cinema* Series

Series Editor: Richard Taylor

Advisory Board: Birgit Beumers, Julian Graffy, Denise Youngblood

Alexander Medvedkin: kinofile Filmmakers' Companion
Emma Widdis

Cinema and Soviet Society: From the Revolution to the Death of Stalin
Peter Kenez

Cinema in Central Asia: Rewriting Cultural Histories
Edited by Michael Rouland, Gulnara Abikeyeva and Birgit Beumers

The Cinema of Alexander Sokurov
Edited by Birgit Beumers and Nancy Condee

The Cinema of Tarkovsky: Labyrinths of Space and Time
Nariman Skakov

The Cinema of the New Russia
Birgit Beumers

Dziga Vertov: Defining Documentary Film
Jeremy Hicks

Eisenstein on the Audiovisual: The Montage of Music, Image
Robert Robertson

Film Propaganda: Soviet Russia and Nazi Germany (second, revised edition)
Richard Taylor

Forward Soviet!: History and Non-Fiction Film in the USSR
Graham Roberts

Real Images: Soviet Cinema and the Thaw
Josephine Woll

Russia on Reels: The Russian Idea in Post-Soviet Cinema
Edited by Birgit Beumers

Savage Junctures: Sergei Eisenstein and the Shape of Thinking
Anne Nesbet

Soviet Cinema: Politics and Persuasion under Stalin
Jamie Miller

The Stalinist Musical: Mass Entertainment and Soviet Cinema
Richard Taylor

Vsevolod Pudovkin: Classic Films of the Soviet Avant-Garde
Amy Sargeant

Queries, ideas and submissions to:
Series Editor, Professor Richard Taylor: rtkino@hotmail.co.uk
Cinema Editor at I.B.Tauris, Anna Coatman: acoatman@ibtauris.com

Cinema in Central Asia

Rewriting Cultural Histories

Edited by Michael Rouland,
Gulnara Abikeyeva, Birgit Beumers

I.B. TAURIS

LONDON · NEW YORK

Published in 2013 by I.B.Tauris & Co Ltd
6 Salem Road, London W2 4BU
175 Fifth Avenue, New York NY 10010
www.ibtauris.com

Distributed in the United States and Canada
Exclusively by Palgrave Macmillan
175 Fifth Avenue, New York NY 10010

Copyright Editorial Selection © 2013 Michael Rouland, Gulnara Abikeyeva
and Birgit Beumers
Copyright Translations © 2013 Richard Taylor, Michael Rouland, Birgit Beumers
Copyright Introduction © 2013 Michael Rouland
Copyright Individual Chapters © 2013 Gulnara Abikeyeva, Birgit Beumers, Daria Borisova,
Joël Chapron, Vitaly Chernetsky, Gabrielle Chomentowski, Cloé Drieu, Bauyrzhan Nogerbek,
Stephen M. Norris, Sadullo Rakhimov, Michael Rouland, Swetlana Slapke, Elena Stishova,
Gulbara Tolomushova, Eugenie Zvonkine

The right of Michael Rouland, Gulnara Abikeyeva and Birgit Beumers to be identified as the
editors of this work has been asserted by them in accordance with the Copyright, Designs and
Patents Act 1988.

ISBN: 978 1 84511 900 3 (HB)
      978 1 84511 901 0 (PB)

A full CIP record for this book is available from the British Library
A full CIP record is available from the Library of Congress

Library of Congress Catalog Card Number: available

Printed and bound in Great Britain by T.J. International, Padstow, Cornwall

KINO: THE RUSSIAN CINEMA SERIES

GENERAL EDITOR'S PREFACE

C inema has been the predominant art form of the first half of the twentieth century, at least in Europe and North America. Nowhere was this more apparent than in the former Soviet Union, where Lenin's remark that 'of all the arts, cinema is the most important' became a *cliché* and where cinema attendances were until recently still among the highest in the world. In the age of mass politics Soviet cinema developed from a fragile but effective tool to gain support among the overwhelmingly illiterate peasant masses in the civil war that followed the October 1917 Revolution, through a welter of experimentation, into a mass weapon of propaganda through the entertainment that shaped the public image of the Soviet Union – both at home and abroad for both elite and mass audiences – and latterly into an instrument to expose the weaknesses of the past and present in the twin process of *glasnost* and *perestroika*. Now the national cinemas of the successor republics to the old USSR are encountering the same bewildering array of problems, from the trivial to the terminal, as are all the other ex-Soviet institutions.

Cinema's central position in Russian and Soviet cultural history and its unique combination of mass medium, art form and entertainment industry, have made it a continuing battlefield for conflicts of broader ideological and artistic significance, not only for Russia and the Soviet Union, but also for the world outside. The debates that raged in the 1920s about the relative merits of documentary as opposed to fiction film, of cinema as opposed to theatre or painting, or of the proper role of cinema in the forging of post-Revolutionary Soviet culture and the shaping of the new Soviet man, have their echoes in current discussions about the role of cinema *vis-à-vis* other art forms in effecting the cultural and psychological revolution in human consciousness necessitated by the processes of economic and political transformation of the former Soviet Union into modern democratic and industrial societies and states governed by the rule of law. Cinema's central position has also made it a vital instrument for scrutinizing the blank pages of Russian and Soviet history and enabling the present generation to come to terms with its own past.

This series of books intends to examine Russian, Soviet and ex-Soviet films in the context of Russian, Soviet and ex-Soviet cinemas, and Russian, Soviet and ex-Soviet cinemas in the context of the political history of Russia, the Soviet Union, the post-Soviet 'space' and the world at large. Within that framework the series, drawing its authors from both East and West, aims to cover a wide variety of topics and to employ a broad range of methodological approaches and presentational formats. Inevitably this will involve ploughing once again over old ground in order to re-examine received opinions but it principally means increasing the breadth and depth of our knowledge, finding new answers to old questions and, above all, raising new questions for further enquiry and new areas for further research.

The continuing aim of this series is to situate Russian, Soviet and ex-Soviet cinema in its proper historical and aesthetic context, both as a major cultural force and as a crucible for experimentation that is of central significance to the development of world cinema culture. Books in the series strive to combine the best of scholarship, past, present and future, with a style of writing that is accessible to a broad readership, whether that readership's primary interest lies in cinema or in political history.

This multi-edited volume represents our first attempt to focus on the cinemas of the former Soviet Republics of Central Asia, with all the added political, cultural and linguistic subtleties and complications that such a study involves. As General Editor of the *KINO* Series I am personally hugely indebted to Professor Birgit Beumers for deploying her considerable contacts in the region and her enormous expertise and legendary thoroughness and efficiency to render this project in its present, publishable form.

Richard Taylor
Swansea, Wales

CONTENTS

ix   List of Illustrations

xi   Contributors

xvii   Acknowledgements

xviii   Note on Transliteration

xix   Glossary

xix   Historical geography

1   An historical introduction
Michael Rouland

Part I   At the Cinematic Cradle

33   Chapter 1   Vostokkino and the foundation of Central Asian cinema
Gabrielle Chomentowski

45   Chapter 2   Birth, death and rebirth of a nation: national narrative in Uzbek feature films
Cloé Drieu

57   Chapter 3   The various births of Kazakh cinema
Bauyrzhan Nogerbek

Part II   Cinema in the Soviet Republics of Central Asia

73   Chapter 4   Landscape and loss: World War II in Central Asian cinema
Stephen M. Norris

89   Chapter 5   Fragments from the history of Turkmen cinema
Swetlana Slapke

105   Chapter 6   Bulat Mansurov's *The Contest* in context
Michael Rouland

115   Chapter 7   Tajik cinema at the end of the Soviet era
                    Sadullo Rakhimov

127   Chapter 8   A small history of Kyrgyz cinema
                    Joël Chapron

137   Chapter 9   Re-visions of *The Sky of Our Childhood*
                    Elena Stishova

147   Chapter 10   'A Wild Kazakh Boy': the cinema of Rashid
                    Nugmanov
                    Vitaly Chernetsky

Part III   The Era of Independence

163   Chapter 11   Cinematic nation-building in Kazakhstan
                    Gulnara Abikeyeva

175   Chapter 12   Aesthetic influences in young Kazakh
                    cinema
                    Eugénie Zvonkine

187   Chapter 13   Growing up: children in Central Asian
                    cinema
                    Birgit Beumers

199   Chapter 14   Kyrgyz cinema: an attempt at eternal
                    breakthrough
                    Gulbara Tolomushova

211   Chapter 15   A view from Moscow: myths and realities
                    of the Uzbek film boom
                    Daria Borisova

221   Chapter 16   Contemporary Tajik cinema in context:
                    on Djamshed Usmonov
                    Seth Graham

Part IV   Reference Section

237   Film-makers' Biographies
       Gulnara Abikeyeva

271   Appendix: Filmography

287   Index

LIST OF ILLUSTRATIONS

Page   **Chapter 1**

40   Poster for Viktor Turin's *Turksib* (1929)
42   Still from Alexander Razumny's *Kara-Bugaz* (1935)

Page   **Chapter 2**

48   Still from *Behind the Vaults of Mosque* (1928) by Kazimir Gertel
54   Still from *Alisher Navoi* (1947) by Kamil Yarmatov

Page   **Chapter 3**

60   Poster for *Amangeldy* (1938), directed by Moisei Levin
66   Poster for *Poem about Love* (1954), directed by Shaken Aimanov

Page   **Chapter 4**

77   Still from Shukhrat Abbasov's *You are Not an Orphan* (1963)
80   Still from Shaken Aimanov's *Land of the Fathers* (1966)

Page   **Chapter 5**

93   Still from *The Decisive Step* (1965) by Alty Karliev
97   Still from *Daughter-in-Law* (1972) by Khodjakuli Narliev

Page   **Chapter 6**

110   Poster for Bulat Mansurov's *The Contest* (1963)

Page   **Chapter 7**

118   Still from Bension Kimiagarov's *The Legend of Rustam* (1970)

Page   **Chapter 8**

129   Still from *The First Teacher* (1965) by Andrei Konchalovsky
130   Still from Aktan Arym Kubat's *Beshkempir: The Adopted Son* (1998)

Page   **Chapter 9**

139   Poster for Tolomush Okeev's *The Sky of Our Childhood* (1966)

Page   **Chapter 10**

153 Still from Rashid Nugmanov's *The Needle:* Moro in the desert
158 The settlement of the 'Children of the Sun' in *The Wild East,*
     constructed for the filming on the south shore of Lake Issyk
     Kul in Kyrgyzstan. Courtesy of www.yahha.com

Page   **Chapter 11**

165 Poster for Sultan Khodjikov's *Kyz-Zhibek* (1969–70)
168 Poster for Amir Karakulov's *A Woman Between Two Brothers*
     (1991)

Page   **Chapter 12**

179 Still from the film *Swift* (2007) by Abai Kulbai
184 Still from the short film *113th* (2007) by Talgat Bektursunov

Page   **Chapter 13**

190 Poster for Serik Aprymov's *Aksuat* (1998)
196 Still from Aktan Arym Kubat's *The Chimp* (2001)

Page   **Chapter 14**

204 Still from Marat Sarulu's *Song of Southern Seas* (2008)
209 Still from Talgat Asyrankulov and Gaziz Nasyrov's *Birds of
     Paradise* (2006)

Page   **Chapter 15**

214 Still from Rustam Sagdiev's film *The Unexpected Bride* (2006)

Page   **Chapter 16**

230 Still from Djamshed Usmonov's *To Get to Heaven First You Have
     to Die* (2006)

The editors would like to thank Kazakhfilm and Mentai
Utepbergenov for permission to use stills and posters to illustrate
this volume.

CONTRIBUTORS

Gulnara Abikeyeva is a Kazakh film critic and researcher. Since 2005 she has been artistic director of the International Film Festival Eurasia in Almaty. She was editor-in-chief of the film magazines *Asia-kino, Territoriya Kino*, has produced TV programmes on cinema, and taught film history and film theory at the Kazakh Academy of the Arts. From 2001 to 2002 she was a Fulbright scholar at Bowdoin College; she has lectured at several universities in North America. She is the author of six books on the cinema of Kazakhstan and Central Asia: *New Kazak Cinema* (1998), *Cinema of Central Asian: 1990–2001* (2001), *The Heart of the World: Films from Central Asia* (2003) and *Nation-Building in Kazakhstan and other Central Asian States, and How This Process is Reflected in Cinematography* (2006) and others. *Cinema of Central Asia: 1990–2001* was awarded the White Elephant Award of the Guild of Russian Film Critics. As a member of FIPRESCI and NETPAC she has been a jury member on a range of international film festivals.

Birgit Beumers is Professor in Film Studies at Aberystwyth University, Wales. She completed her D.Phil at St Antony's College, Oxford and held appointments at Cambridge and Bristol. She specializes in contemporary Russian culture and has published widely on cinema and theatre. Her most recent publications include *A History of Russian Cinema* (2009) and, with Mark Lipovetsky, *Performing Violence* (2009), as well as *Nikita Mikhalkov* (2005), *PopCulture Russia!* (2005); she has edited *24 Frames: Russia* (2007), *The Post-Soviet Russian Media* (2009, with S. Hutchings and N. Rulyova), *Alexander Shiryaev, Master of Movement* (2009, with D. Robinson and V. Bocharov), *Directory of World Cinema: Russia* (2010) and (with Nancy Condee) *The Cinema of Alexander Sokurov* (2011). She is currently working on Russian animation. She is editor of the online quarterly *KinoKultura* and of the scholarly journal *Studies in Russian and Soviet Cinema* that appears three times a year.

Daria Borisova graduated from the theatre and film department in the faculty of History and Philology of the Russian State University of Humanities (RGGU) in 2001. From 2003 to 2009 she worked for the Confederation of the Unions of Film-makers of the CIS and the

Baltics, which allowed her to acquire some firsthand knowledge of the national cinematographies in the post-Soviet space. Her special interest is in the cinema of Central Asia. From 2009 to 2012 she worked in the cinema section of the *Kultura* newspaper in Moscow; since 2012 she has been a film reviewer for *Nezavisimaia gazeta*.

Joël Chapron studied Russian at the Sorbonne before enrolling at the Paris University of Interpreters and Translators (ESIT) to become a conference interpreter. In 1995 Unifrance, an organization for the promotion of French cinema abroad, appointed him as Central and Eastern European manager. For over 15 years he has drawn up a shortlist of films from the former Soviet Union and Eastern Europe for Cannes, and he has been doing the same for the Locarno Film Festival since 2006. Following several years as researcher at the Culture and Communications Laboratory at Avignon University, he was appointed associate professor in September 2009. Chapron has written numerous articles on film-making in Eastern Europe, both for the French and foreign press, and a history of French cinema in Russia. He is on the editorial board of the *Larousse Dictionary of Cinema*, which was published in 2011.

Vitaly Chernetsky is Associate Professor of Russian and Director of the Film Studies Programme at Miami University. His recent publications include the monograph *Mapping Postcommunist Cultures: Russia and Ukraine in the Context of Globalization* (2007), an annotated Ukrainian translation of Edward Said's *Culture and Imperialism*, which he also co-edited (2007), a translation of Yuri Andrukhovych's novel *The Moscoviad* (2008), a special issue of the online journal *KinoKultura* on Ukrainian cinema, which he guest-edited (2009), as well as articles on cultural theory, literature, film and translation studies. He is the current president of the American Association for Ukrainian Studies.

Gabrielle Chomentowski holds a doctorate in Political Sciences from the Paris Institute of Political Science, where she lectures in Russian history and political science. She defended her thesis on 'The Friendship among Peoples through Soviet Cinema: The Policy of Nationalities in the USSR from 1928 to 1941' in 2009, after graduating in Russian language and history from the Sorbonne and the Institute of Oriental Languages (INALCO). She has written articles about Soviet propaganda in Soviet films of the 1960s in *Contrebande* 16 (2007), the myth of Moscow in cinema in *Théorême* 10 (2007), and conformity and accusation in Kozintsev and Trauberg's *Alone* (1931) in *Dissidences* 9 (2010).

Cloé Drieu is a research fellow at the Centre National de la Recherche Scientifique in Paris, and at the Centre d'Études Turques, Ottomanes, Balkaniques et Centrasiatiques (CETOBAC). She specializes in the history of Central Asia, with a particular interest in the interwar period, which she studied through the lens of Uzbek cinema for her PhD dissertation (2008). Since 1998 she has carried out fieldwork in archives in Uzbekistan, Tajikistan and Russia, funded through the French Institute of Research (Ministry of Foreign Affairs) in Tashkent. She has experiences in the film industry as production assistant and still photographer on Darejan Omirbaev's *The Road* (2001), and as artistic manager of the Festival des 3 Continents in Nantes where she curated a programme of Central Asian film-concerts (2009). She lectures at the National Institute of Oriental Languages and Civilizations. Her current research focus is on Central Asia during World War I and the revolts of 1916. She has published several articles in scholarly journals.

Seth Graham is Lecturer in Russian at the School of Slavonic and East European Languages, University College London, where he teaches courses on Russian literature, film and cultural studies. He previously taught at Stanford University and the University of Washington, Seattle. He is the author of *Resonant Dissonance: The Russian Joke in Cultural Context* (2009) and co-editor of *Uncensored? Reinventing Humor and Satire in Post-Soviet Russia* (2008). He has published several articles and book chapters on Russian and Central Asian cinema, and is co-editor of the online film journal *Kinokultura*. He is currently writing a monograph about Russian film genre since 1991.

Bauyrzhan Nogerbek is a film scholar and professor of art. In 1967 enrolled at VGIK and, after graduation as film historian, worked as editor-in-chief of the animation association and from 1971 to 1981 was a member of the editorial board at the film studio Kazakhfilm. He was Secretary of the Kazakh Union of Cinematographers (1981–5), and Senior Researcher at the Auezov Research Institute for Literature and Art (1985–99). From 1999 to 2001 he was

Pro-Vice-Chancellor of the Zhurgenov Theatre and Film Institute and head of the theatre and cinema section at the Committee for Culture in the Ministry. He has organized the faculty of cinema and television at the Zhurgenov National Academy of Arts. Since 1993 leads a course on film history, with the first students graduating in 1997. He is the author of several books, including on Kazakh animation (*Kogda ozhivaiut skazki*, 1984); a book on Kazakh cinema (*Kino Kazakhstana*, 1998) and a textbook on the history of Kazakh cinema (*Istoriia kazakhskogo kino*, 2005); a book on the history of Kazakhfilm Studio (*Na ekrane Kazakhfil'm*, 2007); and a study of folk themes in Kazakh cinema (*Ekranno-fol'klornye traditsii v kazakhskom igrovom kino*, 2008). He has published numerous articles, reviews and essays, many of which have been translated into other languages. At present, Nogerbek is head of the Arts Faculty and teaches film history at the Kazakh National Arts University in Astana.

Stephen M. Norris is Associate Professor of History at Miami University (OH). He is the author of *A War of Images: Russian Popular Prints, Wartime Culture, and National Identity, 1812–1945* (2006) and *Blockbuster History in the New Russia: Movies, Memory, and Patriotism* (2012). He is currently working on a book about the Soviet cartoonist, Boris Efimov.

Sadullo Rakhimov is a cultural and film historian. In 1974 he graduated from the faculty of Russian philology of the Tajik National University. In 1983 he defended his thesis in Moscow, specializing in aesthetics. In 2007 he defended his professorial *Habilitation* on philosophical aesthetic ideas of zoroastrianism. He is a member of the Tajik Union of Film-makers, and of the Confederation of Film-makers' Unions of the CIS and Baltics. For more than 10 years he was the head of the studio Tajikfilm. In 1997–8 he was Deputy Chairman of the Television and Radio Committee of the Tajik Government. Since 1999 he has worked in the Institute of Philosophy, Politics and Law of the Academy of Sciences of the Tajik Republic, where he is Head of the department of philosophy of culture. He has published *Luch ekrana* (2004), *Iz istorii esteticheskikh vozzrenii tadzhikskogo naroda* (2005), *Estetika zoroastrizma* (2006), and his articles have appeared in academic editions, encyclopaedias and periodicals nationally and internationally. He has also scripted numerous documentaries. For over 10 years he has been the art director of the IFF Didor.

Michael Rouland is an historian of Russia, Central Asia and Afghanistan. He is the author of *Music and the Making of the Kazakh Nation, 1920–1936* and has published widely on Central Asian cinema, culture and national identity. Since 2003, he has taught courses on Russian, Central Eurasian and global history at Georgetown, Miami, and Stanford Universities. He is currently an historian for the US Air Force, where he writes on international air power history and theory, Central Asia and Afghanistan, as well as specialized research topics. In recognition of his work, he has received awards from the Department of the Air Force, US Central Command, NATO, and the Office of the Secretary of Defense.

Swetlana Slapke holds a PhD and has taught the cultural history of Turkic peoples at Humboldt University, Berlin. She then worked for the second state television channel (ZDF) as consultant, editor and director of documentary films and television reports on Central Asia. Subsequently she was Programme Director of the Asian-Pacific Film Festival in Berlin and member of the artistic council of the Cottbus Film Festival for East European Cinema. Currently she is the general director of the agency 'Eurasia Global Connecting', which engages in cultural exchange, support and distribution of joint film projects, and the organization of the Eurasian Film Days in Germany. She is a member of the board of the German–Russian Festival in Berlin, where she supervises the film department and is responsible for the Russian film programme at the festival. She is the author of articles about the culture and cinema of Central Asia, and recently especially about the history of Turkmen cinema.

Elena Stishova is a film critic and film historian, a member of the Russian Film Academy NIKA and of the professional organization FIPRESCI. She has been a correspondent for the news agency ITAR-TASS and for *Nezavisimaia gazeta*, while also teaching courses at the State Institute for Cinematography. She has been on the editorial staff of the journal *Iskusstvo kino*, where she heads the section on Russian cinema. For some eight years, Stishova edited, with Konstantin Shcherbakov, the journal *Kinoforum* which was a unique publication on the cinema of the CIS and Baltic States, which was shut down due to lack of funding. She has studied gender issues in Russian cinema, and participated in the first electronic encyclopaedia on the history of feminism in Russia.

Richard Taylor is Emeritus Professor of Politics at Swansea University in Wales. He is the author of numerous articles and books on Soviet cinema, including *The Politics of the Soviet Cinema, 1917–1929* (1979, reprinted 2008), *Film Propaganda: Soviet Russia & Nazi Germany* (1998) and studies of Eisenstein's films, *The Battleship Potemkin* (2000) and *October* (2002). He has also co-edited *The Film Factory: Russian & Soviet Cinema in Documents, 1896–1939* (1988, 1994), *Inside the Film Factory: New Approaches to Russian & Soviet Cinema* (1991, 1994) and *Eisenstein Rediscovered* (1993) with Ian Christie, and *Stalinism and Soviet Cinema* (1993) with Derek Spring. He has edited and part-translated the British Film Institute edition of Eisenstein's writings in English, re-published by I.B.Tauris, London in 2010, and is General Editor of the *KINO* series of studies of Russian and Soviet Cinema for I.B.Tauris.

Gulbara Tolomushova graduated as a film scholar from the State Institute of Cinematography, Moscow and is a researcher at the Aitmatov Institute for Literature and Languages at the Kyrgyz National Academy of Sciences. She is a member of FIPRESCI (International Federation of Film Critics and Film Press) and NETPAC (Network by Promotion of the Asian Cinema), of the Kyrgyz Union of Film-makers (deputy chair from 2004 to 2010) and of the Central Asian PEN Club. She has written numerous articles published in the national and international press and she has lectured on Kyrgyz cinema. She is the author of *Territoriia Kinostan: kyrgyzskoe kino v litsakh* (*Territory Kinostan: Faces of Kyrgyz Cinema*, 2009). She is an advisor for the festival of documentary cinema on human rights, Bir Duino.

Eugénie Zvonkine is Senior Lecturer in cinema at the University of Paris 8. She has programmed Central Asian films for various festivals for many years: she has curated Kazakh Retrospectives at AsiaticaFilmMediale in 2005 and, covering films from 1938 to 2011, for the Asian Film Festival in Vesoul, France. She regularly presents papers on Central Asian cinema at national and international conferences and has written articles and reviews for *KinoKultura*. Her PhD thesis on Kira Muratova led to article publications (among others, in Studies in Russian and Soviet Cinema) and is forthcoming in monograph form.

ACKNOWLEDGEMENTS

This volume has been in the making for several years: we would like to thank all the contributors for their patience during this book's development. We are indebted to Richard Taylor, who is not only a generous and talented translator, but also our distinguished series editor. Without the patience, the support and the understanding of Philippa Brewster at I.B. Tauris this project would never have come to fruition.

This volume would not have come together without the inspiration of the Eurasia International Film Festival in Almaty and Astana, and without the kind invitations that have been issued on several occasions to the two non-Kazakh editors of this volume – and here thanks go to the head of Kazakhfilm, Ermek Amanshaev and the founder of the Eurasia Festival, Sergei Azimov. We would like to thank in particular Gulbara Tolomushova, for her enthusiasm for all things on reels and for promoting Kyrgyz cinema; Aktan Arym Kubat, Ernest Abdyjaparov, Marat Sarulu and Altynai Koichumanova. There has been huge support from colleagues from Tajikistan, especially Sadullo Rakhimov and Safar Khokdodov, who organize the Didor Festival in Dushanbe. In Moscow, Daria Borisova and Elena Stishova have offered invaluable encouragement.

In addition, Michael Rouland would personally like to thank Vladimir Padunov, who provided early encouragement, the late Richard Stites, and Natalie Rouland, who read each version of this manuscript and supported its progress through the years.

Birgit Beumers would personally also like to thank Rustam Ibragimbekov and Galina Peshkova; and Sergei Zemlianukhin and Miroslava Segida for making available their invaluable sources of information. Finally, a huge thank you goes to Joël Chapron and Martina Malacrida for their staunch support, in their festival work and beyond, of cinema from the region.

NOTE ON TRANSLITERATION

Transliteration from the Cyrillic to the Latin alphabet is a perennial problem for writers on Russian subjects. We have opted for a dual system: in the text we use the Library of Congress system (without diacritics), but we have departed from this system (a) when a Russian name has a clear English version (e.g. Maria instead of Mariia, Alexander instead of Aleksandr); (b) when a Russian name has an accepted English spelling, or when Russian names are of Germanic origin (e.g. Yeltsin instead of Eltsin; Chaliapin instead of Shaliapin; Eisenstein instead of Eizenshtein); (c) when a Russian surname ends in -ii or -yi this is replaced by a single -y (e.g. Dostoevsky instead of Dostoevskii), and all Christian names end in a single -i, (e.g. Grigori); (d) when 'ia' or 'iu' are voiced (at the beginning of a word and when preceded by a vowel) they are rendered as 'ya' or 'yu' (e.g. Daneliya, Yuri) – with the sole addition of the name Asya to avoid confusion with the continent, Asia. In the scholarly apparatus we have adhered to the Library of Congress system (with diacritics) for the specialist.

However, there is a further complication to the transliteration for this volume. Many names have been transliterated from the four Turkic languages of the region, and from Tajik (Farsi), into Russian during the Soviet era. Their spelling in international film databases is often determined by the Russian transliteration. So, in those cases where film-makers have been known largely during the Soviet era (in their 'Russianized' version), we have adhered to that spelling; where, however, film-makers have been known largely during the post-Soviet era and have used a direct transliteration of their names, we have chosen that spelling, e.g. Yolkin Tuichiev, but Zulfikar Musakov instead of Zulfiqor Musoqov; Kamil Yarmatov instead of Komil Yermatov; Nabi Ganiev rather than Nabi G'aniyev. In order to avoid confusion, we have followed that same rule in the filmography. And we have used the adjectives Tajik and Kyrgyz throughout, except where Kirghiz is part of an historical place name (Kirghiz SSR).

GLOSSARY

aul – village (Turkic), term used in the Caucasus region

kishlak – settlement (Turkic), term used in Turkmen and Uzbek cultures

jailoo – summer camp (Kyrgyz)

mahalla – urban neighbourhood (Uzbek)

dutar (*dutor, doutar*) – long-necked two-stringed lute (Tajik, Uzbek)

dombira (*dombura*) – long-necked two-stringed lute (Kazakh)

ASSR – Autonomous Soviet Socialist Republic

SSR – Soviet Socialist Republic

TsOKS – Central United Film Studios

VGIK – All-Union State Institute for Cinematography

HISTORICAL GEOGRAPHY

From the Revolution to the mid-1930s several developments took place that changed the political and ethnic landscape of Central Asia. Initially, Soviet Central Asia included the Turkestan ASSR (1920), the Bukharan People's Soviet Republic (1920), the Khorezm People's Soviet Republic (1923) and the Kirghiz ASSR (1920). In 1924, national delimitations formed the states we know today, but several names and categories changed.

Kara-Kirghiz Autonomous Oblast formed in 1924; Kirghiz in ASSR 1926; Kirghiz SSR in 1936

Kazakh lands formed part of the Kirghiz AO/ASSR (1920–5), in 1925 – Kazakh ASSR, after 1936 – Kazakh SSR

Tajik ASSR formed in 1924 within the Uzbek SSR; Tajik SSR formed in 1929

Turkmen SSR formed in 1924

Uzbek SSR formed in 1924

Alma-Ata: Verny (1867–1921); Alma-Ata (1921–93); then Almaty

Ashgabat: Ashgabat (1881–1919); Poltoratsk (1919–27); Ash-khabad (1927–91), then reversed to Ashgabat

Astana: Akmolinsk (1824–1961); Tselinograd (1961–92); Aqmola (1992–8); then Astana (capital since 1997)

Bishkek: Bishkek (1825–62); Pishpek (1862–1926); Frunze (1926–91); renamed Bishkek in 1991

Dushanbe: named Stalinabad from 1929–61

AN HISTORICAL INTRODUCTION

Michael Rouland

Without doubt, the history of cinema in Central Asia has followed an unusual path, reflecting the interests of Soviet nation-building, ideologically infused internationalism, rampant exoticism, and neo-traditionalist fantasy as the century progressed. Along the way, some truly excellent and world-renowned films have been produced in places overlooked, until the 'war on terror' evoked memories of the 'Great Game' rivalry between the Russian and British Empires (1813–1907). This introduction offers an historical context for the following collection of texts. Film has been inextricably linked with the emergence and recent success of Central Asian states to forge their national identities and share them with the world, and cinema has provided an historical record of the unique and fascinating journey of these now independent states over the course of the twentieth century.

From the arrival of film projectors at the end of the nineteenth century through the dynamic, pre-war years and until the collapse of the Soviet Union, cinema in Central Asia benefited from significant Soviet investment and suffered from its ideological control. This was particularly the case in the 1920s, when the expansion of the cinematic landscape was immense. Soviet officials recognized the importance of communicating new ideologies in the myriad languages of the Soviet Union. But they also initiated a scheme to develop new cadres of film professionals under the guidance of the Moscow establishment that remained in place throughout the Soviet era. Most of the leading directors of today share that experience. Yet the relationship between Russian and Central Asian directors was paradoxical due to conflicting ideas of identity and authority. The two groups were enmeshed but beholden to official interests in the growth of cinema.[1] The success of Soviet imperialism was manifest in the success of the Soviet film project.

Defining Central Asia has always been a difficult task, further complicated by the physical and political geography of the region as a natural, cultural, and historical bridge between Europe and Asia. For the purpose of this volume, we have chosen to focus on the five former Soviet republics of Central Asia: Kazakhstan, Kyrgyzstan, Tajikistan, Turkmenistan and Uzbekistan. There is no doubt that their cultural and historical bond is unique and important, particularly as it relates to cinema.

This volume adopts a broad chronological framework, with particular focus on thematic and professional developments. The first part consists of three chapters about the advent of cinematic production in Central Asia, dealing with the formation of the studio Vostokfilm, designed to enhance the filmic representation of Central Asia; the relationship between the centre and the periphery in the emergence of Uzbek cinema; and the birth of the film industry in Alma-Ata, closely linked to the history of the central studios in the city while evacuated during World War II. The second part discusses the representation of the impact of the war in cinema, and investigates efforts to promote autonomous film studios and their success in the 1960s and 1970s. The chapters in this section survey the main developments in Turkmen, Kyrgyz and Tajik cinema, and offer in-depth readings of some outstanding films and film-makers of postwar cinema in Central Asia, that frame the rise and decline of the national film studios in the five republics: Bulat Mansurov's *The Contest* (1963) and Tolomush Okeev's *The Sky of Our Childhood* (1966) mark the rise of poetic cinema in Central Asia; and Rashid Nugmanov's *The Needle* (1988) and his later films mark the end of the era of Soviet-supervised national film production. The third part examines the cinema of the post-Soviet era and the impact of independence on film production. The chapters investigate the rise of Kazakh national cinema and the emergence of a new generation of film-makers in Kazakhstan; the developments in Kyrgyz cinema, where the short film offered an avenue for the emergence of new talent; the arrival of a new, very young hero on the Central Asian screen; the Uzbek 'film boom'; and the work of the Tajik-born film-maker Djamshed Usmonov that serves as an example both for the fate of Tajik cinema and for a film-maker's successful migration.

Although the individual Soviet film studios located in the five republics functioned independently, there is no doubt that film professionals were well acquainted with each other, often had been trained together in Moscow and knew each others' films. Rather than a study of each respective national film studio, this collection is deliberately eclectic to provide a range of views and perspectives on cinema in Central Asia.

Early Cinematic Encounters: Soviet Ethnography

The history of cinema in Central Asia can be traced back more than a century: the first films were screened in Tashkent in 1897. Predominantly Russian communities across Central Asia patronized travelling film exhibitions and set up local theatres at the turn of the century. Uralsk had a cinema in 1904; the 'Mars' theatre opened in Verny (now Almaty) in June 1910. Since there was no electricity in the city then, the cinema was lit with gas lamps.[2] In the Russian Empire, there was a rich cinematic culture developing in non-Russian regions as well. In Ukraine, Yevgeni Bauer, Petr Chardynin, Nikolai Saltykov and Mikhail Verner were beginning to turn Odessa into a cinematic centre; and Vladimir Barsky, Ivan Perestiani and Amo Bek-Nazarov established another hub in Tiflis.

In Central Asia, Khudoibergan Divanov, a photographer and the first recorded film-maker in Uzbekistan, took filmic images of Khorezm with a Pathé camera in the spring of 1900.[3] The future revolutionary Alibi Djangildin brought a film camera back to Kazakhstan after his European travels at the turn of the century. Despite the little research on the early history of cinema in Central Asia, it is clear that the region quickly took part in the global adoration of the new invention: cinema.

With many subjects involving Central Asia, however, the 1910s tend to disappear in the annals of World War I, local revolts against labour conscription in 1916, then Revolution and civil war, which did not end until the early 1920s. Therefore the history of cinema in Central Asia of the 1920s becomes much more important. When the civil war ended and the last Russian rebels who occupied parts of

Central Asia had been vanquished, Soviet officials began to devise a plan to govern their vast territories. In Central Asia, cinema was viewed as an effective means to inculcate and educate the population with images of modernity. Red caravans and agitation trains began to arrive with new lessons on history, politics and hygiene. They brought film cameras as well as screens for their travelling movie theatres with messages from the Red Army and Bolsheviks. Thus, the new epoch in the region's cinema coincided with a new era in state-building and state control.

In March 1923, the photo department of the Turkestan People's Committee for Enlightenment formed the Turkestan State Committee for Cinematography. The latter then established ties with the State Committee for Cinematography (Goskino) in Moscow to distribute films.[4] The Turkestan State Committee for Cinematography also set up documentary film production facilities in Alma-Ata, Poltoratsk-Ashkhabad and Tashkent by the mid-1920s. Since there were inadequate funds to build a film studio in Central Asia, two studios were assigned to help the region: the film factory North-West Cinema (Sevzapkino) in Leningrad and Proletarian Cinema (Proletkino) in Moscow. Goskino also agreed to distribute films in Tashkent and Samarkand.

On 1 July 1925 officials converted the Ishankul mosque in Tashkent into the film studio 'Shark Yulduzi', or 'Stars of the East', thereby creating the first Central Asian film studio. In 1926, the Bukhara-Russian Film Joint Stock Company (*Bukharo-russkoe kinotovarishchestvo*), which had been founded two years earlier, was converted into the first Uzbek Cinema Association.[5] The same year two Russian cameramen from Leningrad's Sevzapkino, Sergei Lebedev and Boris Bashem, founded the Turkmen Film Studio (*Ashkhabad kinofabrika*).

Typical of the Soviet cultural project in remote regions, officials stressed local backwardness. At the same time, new images of 'everyday life' were captured to underscore the vitality of the Soviet project as well as the implicit need for transformation. For the first time, film viewers in remote villages of the steppe, desert and mountain regions could see images of the Revolution and feel that they were part of the historical process.

Film was an important vehicle for propaganda for the Soviets. Lenin expressed its particular significance for Central Asia: 'We need to pay special attention to organize movie theatres in the villages and in the East, where it will seem new and where it will be particularly successful.'[6] Thus, cinema had the power to shape minds as well as depict a contemporary mindset. Even foreign journalists commented on the significance of Soviet cinema; for example, the Moscow correspondent of the *New York Times*, Robin Kinkead, wrote:

> The Bolsheviki realize that the cinema is one of the best instruments for pounding new ideas into stubborn heads. Past masters of the art of propaganda in writing and speech, they are making full use of the screen to teach their people what's what in the Communist lexicon.[7]

A new generation of internationally renowned directors surfaced, led by Sergei Eisenstein with *The Strike* (1924), *The Battleship Potemkin* (1925) and *October* (1927), in which the masses became the protagonists.

In Central Asian cinema of the early Soviet era, however, two cinematic tendencies quickly emerged: one that celebrated local exoticism for the Soviet viewer, as *The Minaret of Death* (1925), *The Leper* (1928) and *The Last Bey* (1930); and another that served to educate and inculcate socialist values in the Central Asian viewer, such as *The Muslim Woman* (1925) and *The Second Wife* (1927). The tension between these two opposing trends remained throughout the Soviet period, but it was most vivid in the 1920s. The involvement of Russian film-makers in the early film production in Central Asia is a crucial issue for an understanding of the relationship between centre and periphery discussed by Cloé Drieu in her chapter.

The Minaret of Death put ideology second to an entertaining Orientalist yarn that enjoyed great commercial success in the Soviet Union. In the film, the daughter of the Khivan khan, Djamal and her foster sister Seleha, are captured by a bandit along the road. Then they face a series of travails and encounters with heroes and villains. First, the bandit's jealous wife, Gul-Saryk, helps them to escape dressed as boys. Then, they meet Sadyk (played by Oleg Frelikh), who falls in love with Djamal along the road home to Khiva. But after they arrive home, the emir of Bukhara captures the city and takes Djamal again. Soon she is made the prize of a *kok-boru* competition,[8] which Sadyk wins. But her prize is not honoured since the emir's son has also fallen in love and decides to keep her for his harem. Then, the emir and his son struggle, and the latter emerges as the new emir. Finally, Sadyk raises a popular army of his own to rescue the women and bring justice to the land. This film connects early Central Asian cinema to the Soviet adventure genre of the 1920s and the popularity of Hollywood films, such as Raoul Walsh's *The Thief of Bagdad* (1924).

Given the history of veiling women in Central Asia, films that depicted the emancipation of women became a key element of Party policy and were actively promoted by the Women's Department (*Zhenotdel*),[9] which had launched a campaign focused on health, education, and work, and often highlighted aspects of everyday life that the Soviets wanted to change. In this context, Dmitri Bassalygo's *The Muslim Woman* was more important than *The Minaret of Death*. The film was released to coincide with the first Party Conference in Uzbekistan, where women's rights were a focal point for revolutionary change. Still, filmic accuracy was an issue, since European actors played the leading roles; on request, officials did not release the film in Bukhara until later in the 1920s. It tells the story of two women: an emancipated Soviet woman and a traditional Central Asian female character. The heroine, Saodat, was a symbol for Uzbek women while the traditional woman faced the choice in the end to shed the burdens of a repressive society. Two other, early films followed the same formula: Mikhail Averbakh's *The Veil* (1927), an unsuccessful film starring Suleiman (Saib) Khodjaev as an engineer, showed the same contrast between two Uzbek women; and Doronin's *The Second Wife*, the debut film of Nabi Ganiev as an actor, again contrasted the emancipated and traditional heroine. The theme of the emancipation of women as represented on screen is discussed both by Drieu and Gabrielle Chomentowski in their chapters.

A genre that remained popular throughout the Soviet era was the Central Asian adventure film, building on the exoticism of the landscape and exploring the feats of revolutionary heroes. Kazimir Gertel's *Behind the Vaults of the Mosque* (1928) was the first Uzbek revolutionary film. A Tsarist officer takes the bride of Umar (played by Kamil Yarmatov) as payment for his father's overdue taxes. The officer tries to convert Gulasal by dressing her as a Russian woman, but she ultimately rejects him. In the end Umar learns that she has been faithful and they join the Revolution as she returns to traditional dress and veil. Oleg Frelikh's *The Covered Wagon* (1928) was an Uzbek film about the civil war in Kyrgyzstan, starring Nabi Ganiev in the comic role of Baimat. The film was designed to instruct audiences not to steal from the Soviet authorities. Gertel's *Jackals of*

Ravat (1927) was one of the most popular and hugely successful early Uzbek films, outlining the early struggle against the *basmachi*[10] and instructing audiences to turn in their enemies.

Collectivization was a particularly dominant theme during the first Five-Year Plan (1928–32), as is evident in Alexander Vladychuk's *White Gold* (1929) and Yuli Raizman's *The Earth Thirsts* (1930), embracing subjects like 'white gold' (cotton) and irrigation projects in the Karakum Desert.

Documentary films were common across the region, and the initiative of *kulturfilmy*, discussed by Chomentowski in her chapter, bears witness to an ethnographic interest in the new territories. The first documentaries on Kazakh material, as discussed in this collection by Bauyrzhan Nogerbek, were entirely political in their orientation. Several documentaries were also made from the unused footage filmed by Yakov Tolchan for Dziga Vertov's documentary *A Sixth Part of the World* [*Shestaia chast' mira*, 1926], which constructed an impressive image of the new Soviet colonial conquests.[11] Early Turkmen documentaries were shot by Sergei Lebedev and Boris Bashem, as discussed by Swetlana Slapke in her chapter. In October 1929, the first Tajik film screening took place at the Third Extraordinary Congress of Soviets, which officially declared the formation of the Tajik Soviet Socialist Republic: *The Arrival of the First Train to Dushanbe*, a primitive short film that illustrated the arrival of Soviet power in the region. Later Kazakh documentaries followed the same pattern, as Nogerbek shows in his chapter. The themes of these documentary films were entirely programmatic: explaining official policies towards land redistribution, the establishment of the party system, and new technologies introduced by the Soviets.

Groups of film professionals were sent from Leningrad and Moscow to capture the new expanses and entertaining exoticism of the new territories. Vladimir Shneiderov, who visited Central Asia in the late 1920s, understood his travels as filmic tourism, whilst hoping to provide a Soviet response to Robert Flaherty's cinematic adventurism in *Moana* (1926). Shneiderov later wrote in his memoirs: 'The task of our film group was to make expeditionary film that was scholarly and popular... to expose the nature of the region, life and everyday life of its people.'[12] He shared film images of the Soviet conquest of the Pamir in a film titled *Pedestal of Death* (1928), which offered a unique view of life at the time in Osh and the Alai region.

The 1920s ended with one of the most important Soviet films of the era, shot in Central Asia in a educational, documentary style as *kulturfilm.*[13] Viktor Turin's *Turksib* (1929) begins with the phrase, 'Turkestan in Central Asia is a land of burning heat', before explicating the importance of its relationship with Russia. The exchange of European technology for natural resources was the foundation of Soviet efforts to help Central Asia from its 'backwardness'. Similar films, such as Mikhail Kalatozov's *Salt for Svanetia* (1929) and Dziga Vertov's *Three Songs for Lenin* (1934), represented the predominant Soviet view of remote village life. These early masterpieces of Soviet cinema flash images of the 'Soviet East' as a backward place in need of rapid industrialization. Whether through the delivery of wheat, salt or the emancipation of women, Soviet power brings salvation with an ethnographic lens. Yet these films also reveal a mutual dependence among diverse Soviet peoples for their collective survival in a time of hardship and deprivation.

During the 1920s, there were no national cinemas in the region, but rather pan-Central-Asian film movements. The first generation of Central Asian film-makers began to study film in the second half of the 1920s. They were first involved as consultants, assistant directors, second cameramen and actors, but by the late 1930s they began to change the history of cinema in the region.

Building a 'Soviet' Cinema in the 1930s

The 1930s were devoted to the development of the cinematic infrastructure in Central Asia. Beginning in 1930, the graduates of the All-Union State Institute for Cinematography (VGIK) in Moscow began to arrive in Central Asia, but this time they stayed in the region: Mikhail Averbakh, Mikhail Bystrytsky and Dmitri Poznan; others came from the Leningrad Institute of Performing Arts, such as Nikolai Klado, Klimenti Mints, Alexander Razumovsky and Grigori Jagdfeld. Unpopular film-makers from the centre, or those who had fallen out of favour with Soyuzkino, were dispatched to the republics, including Lev Kuleshov to Tajikistan and Yevgeni Ivanov-Barkov to Turkmenistan, while others – including Yevgeni Cherviakov, Mark Donskoi and Yuli Raizman – worked for Vostokkino in Central Asia. The films of these film-makers during the 1930s are considered as the origin of cinema in the region; their new ventures coincided with the construction of new cinemas to screen them.

Technical limitations forced film-makers outside and on location to capture the local landscapes: deserts, rivers and mountains. Thus scripts were less important than the visual experiences in these early Central Asian films. One of the first great films from the region,

Nabi Ganiev's *The Rise* (1931), scripted by Klado, had been shot entirely in Uzbekistan by an Uzbek director: its symbolic title deals with the transformation of the local cotton industry. The film details the struggle between Komsomol activists and saboteurs in a cotton factory. Another important film, Raizman's *The Earth Thirsts* (1930), describes the efforts of four young Komsomol activists, who arrive in a small village in the Karakum Desert to build a water pipeline.[14] A struggle ensues when the local *bey*, Aman Durdy, wants to maintain control over the limited water resources. Just emerging from the era of silent films, *The Earth Thirsts* used music by Reinhold Glière and ambient noise in a semi-documentary style.

Not surprisingly, there were ample films about de-veiling and the emancipation of women. In Ashkhabad, Oleg Frelikh made *The Daughter of a Saint* (1931) in documentary style about a man who brings his wife to an imam who then takes her as a concubine. She bears a daughter, and her mother sends her to the city when the imam wants to marry her. Ultimately, the heroine becomes a worker in a Soviet factory and when the father finds her in the dormitory he is ashamed of her dress. The generational conflict is poignant here as she chooses to reject her traditional family for the Soviet family.

The redistribution of land and property was another theme of the early 1930s. Mikhail Karostin's *The Freeze* (1931) describes class struggle in an *aul*. After the Revolution, a local village chief tries to preserve his wealth while the poor hero tries to protect his own livestock during a natural disaster. *Accursed Trails* (1935) also depicted the redistribution of wealth and the collectivization in Kazakhstan.

International themes were also important in Central Asia. The first Tajik feature film, Liudmila Pechorina's *When Emirs Die* (1932) addressed collectivization and class struggle in Tajikistan through the conflict of emirs, *basmachi* and revolutionaries. The film was a project of the Culture Ministry to show local audiences that they could be a part of the screen stories. The film's title refers to the rise and fall of the Tajik emir of Afghanistan, who was briefly considered an ally of the Soviets. Yarmatov's *The Emigrant* (1934) deals with class struggle in a village and controversies with Pan-Islamism and Muslims, who fled across the border. Mikhail Verner's *Living God* (1934) provided a critique of the Ismailism and the Aga Khan, the 'living god', and their ties to British colonialism.

Like documentaries, feature films of the early 1930s provided a valuable glimpse at daily life and the real frustrations of property redistribution in Central Asia. They also illuminated the weak influence of Soviet power in remote villages. Alexander Ledash-chev's *I'll Be Back* (1935) was the first Turkmen film to address the Revolution and the struggle for life when the water runs dry. It was initially made as a silent film and given sound in 1936. *Seven Hearts* (1936), directed by Nikolai Tikhonov, dealt with the discovery of oil in Turkmenistan. Filmed with natural light and a simple script, Nabi Ganiev's *Djigit* (1935) was the first Uzbek sound film, detailing the local struggle with the *basmachi*.

The rise of Socialist Realism in the films of the late 1930s and early 1940s changed form and content of cinema in Central Asia. Characters became standard, and 'nationalism' was labelled a dangerous trait. Nevertheless, film images in Central Asia remained distinctly local. In addition to the varying landscapes, the local themes differed: cotton in Uzbekistan, oil in Turkmenistan and livestock for the Kyrgyz and Kazakh peoples. Moreover, sound films began to use their native languages by the end of the 1930s: Alexander Usoltsev-Garf's *The Oath* (1937) was made in Uzbek and Alexander Makovsky's *Umbar* (1937) in the Turkmen language.

Other important films from the era touched on the themes of tragic heroism, sacrifice and social transformation. Mikhail Romm's *Thirteen* (1936) recounted a tale of nine demobilized Red Army soldiers, a border commander, his wife and an old geologist who find a fortress of *basmachi*. It is a tale of heroism, where almost everyone perishes in the end. Kamil Yarmatov's *Friends Meet Again* (1939) was an adventure film about the civil war in Tajikistan, where a group of military surveyors work along the border and defend the new and unexplored Soviet territories as they encounter a band of *basmachi*. Originally a Turkmen project, the film became a key moment for the Tajik film industry, with local music and actors. *Asal* (1940), directed by Mikhail Yegorov and Boris Kazachkov, depicted a textile worker who moves from Tashkent to Moscow. Moisei Levin directed the two Kazakh films before the war: *Amangeldy* (1938) was a Leningrad film production, with a script by Kazakh and Russian writers; *Raihan* (1940), on the other hand, addressed the emancipation of Kazakh women. With the help of the young communist, Raihan escapes to the city and becomes a livestock expert. When she returns to her native village later, however, she encounters feudal values again and only escapes death with the help of local herders. Ivanov-Barkov and Kazachkov's *The Procurator* (1941) was produced by the Ashkhabad Film Studio and released at the onset of the war. It was based on the real-life story of Yazgul Bergenova, her rise from obscurity to a respected government post.

Following a decade of Soviet construction in Central Asia, both real and metaphorical, there was a moment of euphoria at the end of the 1930s. New cultural centres were built to accompany the factories and massive agricultural centres that began to appear across the region. Despite the human costs, the successes of the first and second Five-Year plans resulted in an obsession with the statistical proof of progress. The numbers of film theatres, film studios, and films produced were a part of this project. Therefore, the late 1930s had dual tendencies: one that violently suppressed perceived nationalism and another that celebrated national transformation along socialist lines. By 1940, however, a more defensive stance emerged with the growing fear of Germany and a shift to Russian patriotism became obvious. Officials quickly and effectively began to position Russian culture as an example to lead the more 'backward' cultures of Central Asia to socialism. This trend would delay the development of cinema in Central Asia for the next 20 years.

The War: Interlude or Engagement?

For many reasons, this era represents an interlude that anticipates later trends in the cinema of Central Asia. It was a transitory moment from the ethnographic era of the 1920s and 1930s to the experimental phase of the 1960s. Russian directors still played a key role, but local themes began to assume greater significance. During World War II, writers, artists, and film-makers descended on Central Asia to escape the front lines. The major Soviet film studios were evacuated to Alma-Ata, Tashkent, Ashkhabad, and Stalinabad (now Dushanbe), as well as Frunze (now Bishkek) and Samarkand to maintain cinematic production and support the war effort. While the war was an opportunity for Central Asian film-makers and technical assistants to work with the most talented Soviet directors, it also ended their own opportunities to make films. Kamil Yarmatov and Nabi Ganiev, who were the most important Central Asian directors of the time, became assistants to Russian directors and their talents were largely ignored.

The three major Soviet film studios Lenfilm, Mosfilm and VUKFU (Kiev) evacuated to Alma-Ata in 1942 and created TsOKS, the Central United Film Studio. Another group from the Kiev Film Studio moved to Ashkhabad, while the Soviet Children's Film Studio moved to Stalinabad. Sergei Eisenstein, Vsevolod Pudovkin, Grigori

Alexandrov, Sergei Yutkevich, Grigori Kozintsev, Leonid Trauberg, Fridrikh Ermler, Abram Room, the Vasiliev 'Brothers', Boris Barnet and composer Sergei Prokofiev all moved to Central Asia, where TsOKS produced some of the most important Soviet films of the war,[15] as discussed by Stephen Norris and Nogerbek in their contributions.

Although there were limited opportunities to produce films on local themes during the war, there were a few films that were distinctively Central Asian. For example, Adolf Minkin and Semen Timoshenko made a film concert, *To the Sounds of the Dombïra* (1943), with some of the most important Kazakh musicians of the era, including excerpts from the Kazakh operas *Er Targyn* and *Kyz Zhibek*. In Turkmenistan, Mered Atakhanov directed *The Magic Crystal* (1945) with fragments from the national operas *Abadan* and *Zohre and Tahir*, as well as the ballet *Aldar Kose*. For the Tajiks, Klimenti Mints made *Tajik Film Concert* (1943) as a documentary of recent Tajik music and theatre.

In Uzbekistan, Yakov Protazanov directed *Nasreddin in Bukhara* (1943). It was a successful comedy that blended Russian cinematography and Uzbek humour. This was his last film in an illustrious career in Russian and Soviet cinema. Ganiev's *Tahir and Zuhra* (1945) illustrated the fifteenth-century legend, comparing the upheaval of the Chingisid invasions to Hitler's Germany. Initially, the project was designed to film a theatrical production, but it evolved into an independent work. Ganiev made the film during the war and it quickly entered the canon of Soviet and world cinema. The use of music was particularly interesting, and the composer, Alexander Kozlovsky, integrated Uzbek folk arrangements into the score. The theme of friendship with Russians was also common: *Songs of Abai* (1945), directed by Yefim Aron and Grigori Roshal, based on Mukhtar Auezov's historical biography, opera, and play. His screenplay centres on the call to action of Abai (Kalybek Kuanyshpaev), seeing the suffering of the young lovers, Azhar (Amina Umurzakova) and Aidar (Shaken Aimanov) who have been separated by customary law.

From Conformity to Experiment: The Postwar Period

After the war, a period of film famine (*malokartin'e*) commenced and Central Asia was no less affected than the rest of the Soviet Union. Nevertheless, several classics from the late 1940s and early 1950s are worth singling out. Ganiev continued Protazanov's work with *The*

Adventures of Nasreddin (1946), his only comic film. The wit and humanism of Nasreddin (played by Razzak Khamraev) are on display through his comic engagement with the feudal world. Yarmatov's *Alisher Navoi* (1947) was a triumph for Uzbek cinema: he himself described this as his 'crowning' film.[16] The official Soviet reviews applauded the film for its sensitive treatment of historical details, presenting neither exoticism nor backwardness but a constructive path to the present.[17] The first postwar contemporary Uzbek drama was Ganiev's *Daughter of Fergana* (1948), which described the fate of a young girl, a cotton picker. Ganiev told a story of socialism in everyday Uzbek life, using bright and cheerful colours against gloomy and malicious characters. Djabbar-ata (played by Asad Ismatov) is not a typical, positive character for the era: he realizes the importance of socialism on his state farm, but does not entirely shed his old beliefs about women.

The last Turkmen film before the studio was destroyed in the 1948 Ashkhabad earthquake was Ivanov-Barkov's *The Distant Bride* (1948). After losing his family in the war, Zakhar, a Don Cossack, arrives in Turkmenistan and hopes that his fiancée, Guzel, is still waiting for him in a nearby village. By a turn of fate, the postman never delivered his letter so she does not know that he will come.

Yefim Aron's *Golden Horn* (1948) and Yefim Dzigan's *Dzhambul* (1952) were the only feature films in Kazakhstan for a seven-year span. *Dzhambul* was the first Kazakh feature film in colour, based on the life of the famous Kazakh and Stalinist bard. Although he was a controversial figure and well into his eighties when he became famous for his pro-collectivization poems, the film was overwhelmingly positive towards the 'revolutionary hero' and bard.

After the war, Bension (Boris) Kimiagarov returned from VGIK, where he had studied with Sergei Eisenstein. Kimiagarov played a formative role at Tajikfilm as a documentary film-maker since the studio did not produce feature films at the time. Kimiagarov and Lidia Stepanova's full-length documentary, *Tajikistan* (1945), was sent to the Venice Film Festival where it won a bronze medal.[18]

While the 1950s were an era of 'film famine', there were signs that Central Asian cinema was gearing up for considerable change. The postwar artistic malaise would not last, as Khodjakuli Narliev recalled: 'In the 1950s we had a very strong student movement. The Ministry of Culture sent, literally, train cars full of students to Moscow schools every year. When these students came back, a growth spurt occurred in all the industries.'[19] This new cohort of film graduates, along with the end of late-Stalinist cultural repression, provided the conditions for a transformative era in cinema in Central Asia. During the 1950s film-makers began to employ the Socialist Realist mantra and pan-Soviet images of modernity alongside nationalist themes and epics, and began to experiment with feature films on contemporary subjects. Thus, by the late 1950s, there was a growing diversity of subjects in Central Asian cinema that anticipated the burgeoning of the 1960s.

In Kazakhstan Shaken Aimanov experimented with genres and quickly became an influential director. His first film, co-directed with Karl Gakkel, *Poem about Love* (1954), was a filmic interpretation of the opera *Kozy Korpesh and Baian-Sulu* that relied heavily on the stage production. However, it was important as the first independently produced Kazakh film. Aimanov's later film *Our Dear Doctor* (1957), a musical comedy about a doctor who organizes a concert for a patient's birthday in a sanatorium, achieved a new level of popularity for Kazakh cinema and established Aimanov as the pre-eminent Kazakh director. One of the most interesting historical films of the era was Mazhit Begalin's *His Time will Come* (1958), an historical biography about Chokan Valikhanov that stressed the conflict of modernizers and traditionalists. In Kyrgyzstan, theatre and epic legends maintained their influence on cinema. Vasili Pronin's *Saltanat* (1955), produced in Kyrgyzstan by Mosfilm, featured an emancipated woman (Baken Kydykeeva) in a plot modelled on Ivan Pyriev's musical comedy *The Kuban Cossacks* (1949). Co-productions of the central studios (Mosfilm, Lenfilm) with Frunze's Kirgizfilm were common throughout the 1950s.

After a 12-year hiatus, Tajikfilm produced one feature film in 1955: Kimiagarov's debut *Dokhunda* (1956), based on a story about a man who loses everything in the Revolution, written by Sadriddin Aini and adapted for the screen by Viktor Shklovsky. Other popular Tajik films of the time included Tahir Sabirov's *Son, Time to Get Married* (1959), a popular comedy about the trials of everyday life and the conflicting values of generations; and Kimiagarov's *The Fate of the Poet* (1959), which explored the life of the ninth-century poet Rudaki.

In the mid-1950s, the Turkmenfilm Studio was rebuilt after the earthquake and began to make films again. Rafail Perelshtein's *The Shepherd's Son* (1954) portrayed a man from the village who goes to the city and becomes a surgeon. Jointly directed films were a common feature: with Khangeldy Agakhanov, Perelshtein made then musical comedy *The Cunning of Old Ashir* (1955) about life on a Turkmen collective farm with a famous soundtrack by the popular Azerbaijani singer Rashid Behbudov (1915–89) and Ivanov-Barkov made the civil war drama *Extraordinary Mission* (1957) with Alty Karliev.

Uzbekistan had the most active studio in Central Asia during the 1950s: Tashkent Film Studio and Mosfilm co-produced *Downfall of the Emirate* (1955), directed by Vladimir Basov and Latif Faiziev, about the foreign influences on the Bukhara emirate in 1920 while Mikhail Frunze and Valerian Kuibyshev organized the revolutionary underground. Yarmatov demonstrated his versatility as director with *Avicenna* (1956), a biopic about the Persian polymath, who lived in Bukhara during the tenth century, and which focused on the conflict between science and religion. Yuldash Agzamov's *You're My Delight* (1958) was the first Uzbek musical comedy about government officials travelling around the country to learn about the Uzbek folk culture. Agzamov's *Furkat* (1959) was a biopic about Zakirdjan Khalmukhamedov, who wrote satirical poems about backward traditions and unjust rulers while championing Russian influences. Perhaps the most influential comedy of the era was Shukhrat Abbasov's *The Whole Neighbourhood is Talking About It* (1960), a musical comedy that revealed the clash of generations between those who lived in high-rises and those who stayed in the traditional *mahallas*, or neighbourhoods.

Poetic Cinema in the 1960s

Central Asia experienced a profound cultural awakening during the 1960s and a new generation of directors revolutionized the cinema of the region with commercial and artistic successes. The early 1960s continued to reveal the versatility of Central Asian film-makers to satisfy both the ideological demands of officials in Moscow and the growing domestic demand for cinema. It was a time of historical adventures, light comedies, contemporary dramas and the emergence of a new kind of 'poetic cinema'.

Historical films remained popular in Central Asia and continued to focus on the events of the Revolution and civil war that established Soviet power in the region. Thus, this genre remained a bastion of the Russian world view as well as Russian directors. Perelshtein's *A Man Sheds his Skin* (1959), which was set in the 1920s and 1930s, described the construction of socialism in Tajikistan through the romance of an American engineer and a Russian girl. Agakhanov's *Ten Steps to the East* (1960) was an historical adventure set in the

Turkmen fortress of Kum-Basan-Kala. Alexander Davidson and Abdusalom Rakhimov's *Zumrad* (1961) illustrated the emancipation of a Tajik woman. Vladimir Motyl's *Children of the Pamir* (1962) described one of the first Soviet schools in the Pamir where Soviet ideology confronted poverty and shortages. Through education, the local children learn about the world and about the death of Lenin. Melis Ubukeev's *White Mountains* (1964) portrays the struggle for Soviet power in 1918 and the migration of young people to the cities, while Kimiagarov's *Hasan Arbakesh* (1965), based on a poem by Mirza Tursonzoda, depicts the clash of civilizations, traditional and Soviet, after the civil war and provides a glimpse of 'the bright future'.

Two comedies in particular are noteworthy: Ali Khamraev's *Where are You, My Zulfia?* (1964) was a story of young and comic love, with the Uzbek understanding that 'Yor-Yor' is a wedding song. Bakhtiyar falls in love with a young woman he sees on television, so he and his father travel around Uzbekistan to find her. It is very much a travelogue of Uzbekistan, but only when they return to their new home in Tashkent do they learn that she lives there too. Aimanov's *Aldar-Kose* (1964) is a comic film based on a Kazakh folk hero, the beardless trickster, who directs humour against the wealthy and powerful. Both films indicate flexibility in the genre, as well as the interests of native film-makers to shed the Russian language and share stories particular to the region.

In the early 1960s a new trend towards 'poetic cinema' inspired the entire Soviet Union.[20] Bulat Mansurov's *The Contest* (1963), discussed later in this volume, was the first film to announce this poetic trend. The film was a melange of music, historical legend, and cinematic beauty shot in monochrome by cinematographer Khodjakuli Narliev. *The Contest* had an ethereal style that joined philosophical parables of the past with experimental use of the camera to capture the unique beauty of the Central Asian landscape. Narliev, who would become the most important film-maker in Central Asia during the 1970s, remarked that '*The Contest* represented something totally new for the cinema of Central Asia as a whole.'[21] This influence lasted well beyond the 1960s, as Narliev remarked in a later interview on the subject: 'Nearly 20 years after the opening of *The Contest*, I see many discoveries made by Mansurov repeated and prolonged by Uzbek, Kyrgyz, and Turkmen directors.'[22]

With the formal establishment of film studios in each of the five Central Asian republics during the 1960s, the politics of national cinema tended to entrench differences between the republics.[23] However, an aesthetic revolution appeared across Central Asian cinema, as noted by Narliev, despite the politics of individual republics or common ideologies of socialism. A generation of film-makers who studied together after the war, and found themselves in a region that had just begun to exercise political autonomy as Leonid Brezhnev encouraged local officials to oversee local issues, created films that internalized a search for identity and truth as well as a visual paradigm for Central Asia. Three films reflected the vitality and importance of Central Asian cinema: Elyor Ishmukha-medov's *Tenderness* (1966); Shaken Aimanov's *Land of the Fathers* (1966), discussed by Stephen Norris; and Tolomush Okeev's *Sky of Our Childhood* (1966), which is discussed in this volume by Elena Stishova.

Broadly speaking, Italian Neorealism and the French New Wave impacted on Soviet cinema during the Thaw, and for film-makers from Central Asia this was most evident in Elyor Ishmukhamedov's *Tenderness*. The film reflected the joy of a summer in Tashkent, through stories of young love. Teenagers growing up in the postwar era viewed the world in a radically new way and their perceptions became a popular theme for cinema. Ishmukhamedov's urban youth dramas demonstrated the universality of Central Asian teenagers, showing them in the same frame as other Soviet youth. There was an internationalist tone to the film as well: its final scene evoked Federico Fellini's *Nights of Cabiria* [*Le notti di Cabiria*, 1957] and its music was a blend of Uzbek, Russian, French, Japanese and Italian songs.

In Aimanov's *Land of the Fathers* the central character, an *aksakal* (a 'white beard' or village elder, played by the award-winning actor Elubai Umurzakov), and his grandson go on a journey to a place near Leningrad where the *aksakal*'s son has died during the war. The famed Kazakh writer Olzhas Suleimenov wrote the screenplay about the sacrifice of war and bonds between grandfather and grandson when the middle generation is lost. The characters sought to honour the Kazakh tradition of returning the dead to their homeland, but they discovered that the son and father had been buried with other soldiers in a mass grave, and their cause is futile.

Okeev's first feature film *Sky of Our Childhood* provided a poetic and autobiographical film about the conflicts of nomadic and urban life. It is a story of a child who returns to mountain pastures to learn about the fading tradition of nomadic life. Okeev wrote the film as a cinematic memorial to a fading culture and it was part of a broader movement to encourage the discovery of Central Asia's past.

In the late 1960s a plethora of films from Central Asia contributed to a veritable golden age of cinema, which also saw a number of contemporary dramas and historical heroes on the screen. The youth themes dominated in contemporary films, such as Khamraev's *White, White Storks* (1966) about a young love prevented by old traditions and values and Ishmukhamedov's *Lovers* (1969), which explored the relationship of two young Russians in Tashkent.

Historical adventures and revolutionary heroism continued to proliferate in the cinema of Central Asia, but the heroes became more complex and lessons less clear. Yarmatov's trilogy about the Revolution – *Storm over Asia* (1965), *Horsemen of the Revolution* (1968) and *Death of the Black Consul* (1970) – delivered a complex account of the struggle for Soviet power in Central Asia against emirs and Russian counter-revolutionaries alike. Yarmatov argued that he wanted to place the individual into the historical process.[24] Mansurov's *The Slave Girl* (1968) provided another ambiguous story about the early years of Soviet power: based on Andrei Platonov's *Takyr*, it is the story of a former Austrian prisoner of war, Stefan, who helps the Red Army root out the local *basmachi*. When he is decommissioned, he becomes a marginal figure in a remote Turkmen village, entertaining the children as a clown and with puppet shows. Although the villagers distrust him, they accept him until he begins to share his views on the need for social transformation.

More nuanced images of the early Soviet past were presented as well. Bolotbek Shamshiev's *Gunshot at the Mountain Pass* (1968) depicts a horse-thief in pre-Revolutionary Kirghizia with vivid images of a multi-ethnic Kyrgyz past, including noble princes, Russian settlers and merchants from China. Conventional revolutionary narratives remained: Mered Atakhanov's *Path of the Burning Wagon* (1967) told of the establishment of socialism in Turkmenistan through the struggle of religious authorities and *basmachi* on one side, and Komsomol groups and collective farms on the other. Shukhrat Abbasov's *Tashkent – City of Bread* (1967) tells the story of a young Russian who leaves for Tashkent during the civil war to avoid mass starvation in the Volga region. He works hard, and returns to Russia to rebuild the country. Aimanov's *The End of the Ataman* (1970) offered a truly entertaining revolutionary hero in a film with intrigue, spies and a mission to bring down the White Army.

Men were not the only heroes of the revolutionary era, and films in the 1970s began to show the heroism of women with increasing frequency. Okeev's *Fire Worship* (1971) was a biopic of Urkuia Salieva, the first Kyrgyz female collective farm chair in the 1920s who was brutally murdered at the age of 24. Khodjakuli Narliev's *When a Woman Saddles a Horse* (1974) detailed the work of Aina Kulieva, head of the Turkmen Women's Department during the 1920s. The heroism of a female soldier during World War II was on display in Mazhit Begalin's *Song about Manshuk* (1969), based on the true story of Manshuk Memedova, who was awarded the order 'Hero of the Soviet Union' posthumously. Arguably the most famous Central Asian film, Narliev's *Daughter-in-Law* (1972), revealed the heroism of women on the home front. This film-poem, analysed in Swetlana Slapke's chapter, about a woman waiting for her husband to return from the war, is one of the most beautiful films ever made in Central Asia.

Coming of Age: The 1970s and 1980s
The 1970s linked the Thaw of the 1960s with the stagnation under Brezhnev. Central Asian film institutions finally had enough qualified directors, but few opportunities were available to the emerging generation of film professionals. Three trends from the preceding decades became further entrenched and had political consequences.

The first trend of the cinema of the 1970s was the screen adaptation, bringing national literature, epics and biographies to the screen. Sultan Khodjikov's *The Silk Maiden* (1970) transferred the famous tale in vivid colours. Kimiagarov directed a visually striking trilogy of films based on Ferdowsi's eleventh-century epic tale, *Shahnameh* or *Book of Kings: The Legend of Rustam* (1970), *Rustam and Suhrab* (1971) and *The Legend of Siyavush* (1976). Anvar Turaev made a new film account of the legendary trickster Nasreddin in *First Love of Nasreddin* (1977). In order to avoid Russian and Soviet influences, historical biopics delved ever deeper into the past. Shukhrat Abbasov's *Abu Raihan Biruni* (1974) was a biopic about the Persian scholar and scientist from Khorezm in the tenth and eleventh centuries. Ishmukhamedov's *Youth of a Genius* (1982) imagined the youth of Avicenna; Yarmatov's *Alone among the People* (1973) recalled the poetess Nadira from the early nineteenth century in a tale of intrigue about her struggle against the emir of Bukhara through the power of word and song. Films based on recent literature were popular as well. Okeev's *The Fierce One* (1973) was based on Mukhtar Auezov's novel *Kokserek*, about a boy who raises a wolf and then learns of its growing brutality to match mankind. Chingiz Aitmatov continued to provide literary sources for Central Asian cinema in Okeev's *The Red Apple* (1975) and Shamshiev's *The White Ship* (1975) and *The Early Cranes* (1979).

The second trend of the 1970s grew from the surprising popularity of Vladimir Motyl's *White Sun of the Desert* (1969), a comedy about the Revolution and civil war in Central Asia that was shot in Turkmenistan. A new genre of films, called 'Easterns', was the Soviet answer to John Wayne and the Hollywood 'Western'. The key difference here was that the 'unruly natives' were telling stories about their own revolutionary past. Ali Khamraev was the undisputed master of the genre, and Suimenkul Chokmorov was his star. His *Extraordinary Commissar* (1970) revealed Turkestan in the 1920s, with enemies at every side and a partnership between Russians and Uzbeks. *The Seventh Bullet* (1972) covered the same period, but this time a gang of *basmachi* cross the border to terrorize unprotected towns, and militia commander Maksumov vanquishes them. *Without Fear* (1972) again explored the 1920s when the chaos of de-veiling erupted in a village, affecting communists, mullahs, women and men alike. Shamshiev's entry into the genre was *Red Poppies of Issyk-Kul* (1971), which portrayed the smuggling of opium and conflicts along the Soviet border.[25]

The third trend resulted from a form of penance when Central Asian film-makers were encouraged to make films for children, because the officials feared that their ideas strayed too far from dominant ideologies. Kakov Orazsiakhedov's *The Naughty Brothers* (1972) was a musical comedy about the Djapbaki brothers, who were popular characters from Turkmen folklore. Designed for children, it was a tale about everyday life that introduced important comic folk elements to Turkmen cinema. Gennadi Bazarov's *Apple of My Eye* (1976) described the strained relationships in one family when the son, Erkin (Bolot Beishenaliev), leaves for Moscow. Abdulla Karsakbaev's *Alpamys Goes to School* (1976) tells the story of two boys in a Kazakh village and the value of education.

Two important films touched on controversial issues for their time. Okeev's *Ulan* (1977) revealed a darker side of Soviet officialdom in a story about a senior official suffering alcoholism, and Narliev's *Jamal's Tree* (1980) offered a multifaceted and poetic drama of a small village between the mountains and desert, along the railroad. In the centre of the village stands a tree that represents the dreams of a multiethnic community of Turkmen, Uzbeks, Russians and Georgians while moral and ethical dilemmas abound.

Perestroika: New Waves and New Crises

A new generation of Central Asian film-makers appeared in the late 1980s, provoking a shift in popular consciousness. The fact that these film-makers were young accounts for their awareness of the impending cultural shift while infusing it with a harsh satirical perspective. Their bleak films resonated with a stratum of society yearning for change. In particular Rashid Nugmanov's *The Needle* (1988), Serik Aprymov's *The Last Stop* (1989), Djanik Faiziev's *Who is This?* (1989), Bakhtiyar Khudoinazarov's *Bro* (1991) and Darejan Omirbaev's *Kairat* (1991) brought an unprecedented sense of disillusionment combined with deep-seated irony to the Soviet screen.

It is difficult to assign these films to a single cinematic movement, but it is certain that Central Asian cinema underwent a meaningful transformation. Many scholars have given this group the moniker of a 'New Wave'. Forrest S. Ciesol argued that:

> everyone loves a good 'wave' in film-making. It invariably distracts us from the otherwise tenuous state of world cinema. It is unlikely, however, that even the most forward-looking among us would have predicted that the next wave would be from Soviet Kazakhstan.[26]

The term 'New Wave' was first used during the Moscow International Film Festival in 1989 as a label for recent Kazakh films. Ludmila Pruner offered her estimation of the new Kazakh films: 'The cosmopolitan air of the New Wave was the product of the fusion of Asian values with the Russian aspiration towards a western lifestyle.'[27] The 'New Wave' essentially emerged from a course of Kazakh students which Sergei Soloviev had selected at the Film Institute (VGIK), including Rashid Nugmanov, Serik Aprymov, Ardak Amirkulov, Amanjol Aituarov, Talgat Temenov and Darejan Omirbaev, who had other aspirations than joining Western culture,[28] but reflected the momentous change in Soviet society and its political and cultural collapse.

Nugmanov's *The Needle* created a new hero for Soviet audiences, as explored by Vitaly Chernetsky in his chapter in this volume. Moro is a solitary individual, jobless, without family, and of an ambiguous

Asiatic ethnicity. This is a Soviet film with a Central Asian perspective that diagnoses weariness with the status quo. The film layers various genres and media – from cartoons, television and radio – to reflect the onslaught of visual discourses; this playful experimentation reflects the protagonist himself, played by the famed Leningrad musician and Soviet rock star Viktor Tsoi. His fame brought intense interest to *The Needle* and 9 million viewers to Soviet theatres.

If we can speak of any uniformity in this late Soviet film movement which expanded across Central Asia, it lies in its pessimism. Aprymov's *The Last Stop* described life languishing at the edges of the Soviet Empire. His hero appears on a quiet Saturday evening with nothing to do. He has just been demobilized from the Soviet Army and finds his hometown listless and lost. There he observes, in a disjointed narrative, the village poverty, rampant drunkenness and a suicide for no apparent reason. Ultimately he must leave to find his life and job somewhere else.

Faiziev's *Who is This?* is a road movie about three young men, an Uzbek, a Russian and a Jew, who get into trouble on their way to cotton-picking in the countryside. This was a task required of vast segments of the Uzbek society, yet the film also revealed the ruin and decay of the countryside. The fields are contaminated, there is disorder everywhere and the locals are despondent. The film uncovered the sham of socialism and the farce of sending young children to the countryside to pick cotton in order to bolster production, and it was banned in Uzbekistan. Another dark film of the era discussed in Sadullo Rakhimov's chapter is Bakhtiyar Khudoinazarov's *Bro*, which anticipated the Tajik civil war in a simple story of two young men travelling to meet their father. As they journey, they find a nation on the precipice. The images were sympathetic and rich in documentary realism, and they illuminated the depressing reality of regional rivalries and political entrenchment as poverty proliferated.

Omirbaev's *Kairat* told a story of dislocation when Kairat travels to study at a college in Alma-Ata. From the moment he embarks on his journey across the steppe and a rock shatters his window, his feelings of frustration and indifference resonate. In an allegorical context, *Kairat* struggles with the rapidly shifting space of Kazakhstan in the late 1980s and early 1990s, the growing divisions between rural life and the Westernization in Kazakh cities that came with *perestroika* and the growing inequity of everyday life. Visually and thematically, there are echoes of the French New Wave in

Omirbaev's work that turned the film into a tragic romance and showed loneliness through jump cuts and the eye of the director-*auteur.*

Independence and Internationalism

After the collapse of the Soviet Union and the new independence of the five Central Asian republics, national cinemas began to develop quite differently. While deep-rooted Soviet traditions remained, new influences and models for cinema appeared as each of the republics faced different political challenges. The 1990s were a decade of political and cultural consolidation as well as burgeoning nationalisms. Thus, it is better to address the republics individually.

Tajikistan confronted an era of civil war and exiles. Bakhtiyar Khudoinazarov emigrated to Germany, Djamshed Usmonov to France, and Mairam Yusupova to Russia, while Saif Rakhimzodi was killed on his doorstep. Like Khudoinazarov's *Bro,* Yusupova's *The Time of Yellow Grass* (1991) gave a glimpse of the Tajik countryside before the devastation of civil war. Blending documentary style and fiction, her film confronted questions of tradition, family and Islam within the context of the eroding Soviet project. In a small Tajik mountain village a dead body is found and the villagers do not know what to do with this stranger. After the civil war, and facing extreme poverty at a time when heroin and opium trafficking dominated the economy, it took the country several years to rebuild its film industry. Still, with ample external funding, two of the most important films of the region were made in the 1990s. Usmonov's *The Flight of the Bee* (1998), co-directed by Boung-Hun Min, offered a view of the new Tajikistan through a story of a village history teacher and his struggle against the new values of the marketplace and the enduring importance of community, centred on the construction of a public toilet. Usmonov's films are the subject of Seth Graham's chapter in this volume. Khudoinazarov's *Luna Papa* (1999) is a film cast against the barren landscapes of Central Asia to evoke a post-modern and post-apocalyptic view of modern Tajik life. Khudoinazarov assembled an international cast and worked with production groups from seven countries, which compliment his parodic blending of traditional, Soviet and post-Soviet values in the film.

The cinematic situation in Turkmenistan was no better during the 1990s. At the end of the Soviet era, the new Turkmen government took complete control of Turkmenkino and quickly shifted its focus to Saparmurat Niyazov's *Ruhnama,* or *The Book of the*

Soul, a treatise on Turkmen history and culture. In 1998 the studio was shut down. The founders of Turkmen cinema – Khodjakuli Narliev, Maya-Gozel Aimedova, Bulat Mansurov and Usman Saparov – all left for Russia. Saparov remarked at the time: 'I think that there is no cinema in Turkmenia today. It is my great regret. This art form has been crossed off from the list of the existence [sic].'[29] President Niyazov's rejection of European cultural influences included symphonic music, opera and ballet as well. Despite these restrictions, two particularly important films were made in Turkmenistan before 1998. Saparov's *Little Angel, Make Me Happy* (1992) was a remarkable film about German immigrants to Turkmenistan who faced unspeakable repression during World War II, a theme and a film discussed by Stephen Norris in this volume. Murat Aliev's *Night of the Yellow Bull* (1997), which was immediately banned, reveals subtle insights into the experiences of postwar Ashgabat and the 1948 earthquake, the world that defined the personality of the future president of Turkmenistan. This film may yet prove to be a seminal example of its era: it evokes a profound psychological study of those who survived the dual tragedies of the 1940s and of those who remained in Turkmenistan during the 1990s.

Kyrgyzstan, once a model of economic development, suffered constant budgetary restrictions in the 1990s. By default, the film industry ceased to produce films, with the sole exception of Aktan Abdykalykov (Arym Kubat) with his coming-of-age trilogy of films: *The Swing* (1993), *Beshkempir: The Adopted Son* (1998) and *The Chimp* (2001), which brought critical and international success to Kyrgyz cinema. *The Swing* is a film about young love and rivalries in a Kyrgyz village. The full-length feature *Beshkempir* was one of the first Central Asian films to enjoy international distribution. *Beshkempir*, which means 'five women', is an allegory for the five nations of Central Asia that share the upbringing of the young orphan. The first scene depicts *bikese salu* where the women swaddle the orphan, taking him into the community and protecting him. This moment foreshadows the central crisis of the film, and of the era. As the republic most dependent on the Soviet economy, Kyrgyzstan found itself in a cultural and economic crisis after independence. Despite the challenges, this film offers a positive ending and optimism for the future. The last film of the trilogy, however, reveals a deeper tension between the carefree and romantic world of the teenager and the alcohol-infused and smoke-filled world of adults. *The Chimp* is set in a wasteland, where young boys wait until they are drafted into the army and face the harsh responsibilities of adulthood. Joël Chapron and Gulbara Tolomushova offer insights into the Kyrgyz cinematic project of the 1990s in their chapters.

Limited state funding and the collapse of the local market also hampered Kazakh cinema in the 1990s. Despite these challenges, several acclaimed directors of the Kazakh 'New Wave' were able to locate sources of international funding to make their films. Omirbaev continued his own trilogy about the central character of *Kairat*. In *Cardiogram* (1995), the protagonist from the village finds himself in a resort where a tension exists between Kazakh speakers from the villages and Russian speakers from the city. Omirbaev's greatest international recognition came with *Killer* (1998), which won the competition of 'Un Certain Regard' at Cannes in 1998. The hero is now a chauffeur who becomes entangled in an accident and incurs a debt that he repays by turning into a contract killer. The film reveals the psychological fear of a world spinning out of control. Aprymov also made a trilogy out of his 'New Wave' masterpiece, *The Last Stop*. In contrast to the hero leaving the village, the protagonist of *Aksuat* (1998) wants to remain in his village despite the corruption and oppression. Finally, *Three Brothers* (2000) takes the viewer to an abandoned airbase where the three boys become the target of a military practice exercise. Gulnara Abikeyeva discusses the rise of Kazakh cinema from the 1990s onwards in her chapter as a way of constructing a national identity, while Birgit Beumers explores the presence of children and teenagers on the screen in Kazakh, Kyrgyz and Uzbek cinema in the context of projecting hope for the future.

The Uzbek film industry was a source of optimism during the 1990s as the government continued to support cinema in Soviet style. Uzbek film officials introduced a Bollywood-style system that reified the domestic film market while undermining access to foreign films. One of the best Uzbek films of the decade, Yusuf Azimov's *Before Dawn* (1994) uncovered the stark realities of life in Uzbek villages as Soviet power eroded in the 1970s and 1980s. It is the story of hard work in a family that decides to breed silkworms; it is a testament to the all-encompassing labours of the Soviet system. Yusup Razykov, film-maker and head of the Uzbek Film Studio from 1999 to 2004, also took a hard look at the Soviet past in *Orator* (1998). Revisiting the subject of Soviet Uzbekistan of the 1920s, Razykov offers a thoughtful film, free from the ideological constraints of earlier periods, that captures the difficult negotiations between Islamic tradition and Bolshevism. It is a satire on the conflict between the Shari'a provision for multiple wives and the Bolshevik desire to empower women told through the life of a person trying to accommodate both worldviews. Alongside social and historical critiques designed for international audiences, Uzbek cinema also produced films for a growing domestic audience, creating one of the most profitable markets in Central Asia during the 1990s.

New Millennium, New Markets?

At the end of the twentieth century, only Uzbekistan produced films for its own market. While Kazakh and Kyrgyz films garnered numerous awards at international film festivals, audiences at home could not find their films. Tajik and Turkmen films were virtually non-existent. The 1990s were a difficult decade of transition, political uncertainty and economic collapse; and cinema in Central Asia reflected this reality. Domestic film industries were further constrained by the availability of cheap, often illegal Hollywood and Russian films. This situation would change during the 2000s, when new state investment in film production and the development of an infrastructure changed the situation, at least in some republics. For the first time in the history of cinema in Central Asia, the paths of the respective republics diverged in meaningful and profound ways. Tajik directors looked towards Iranian cinema; the Uzbeks viewed Indian cinema as a model; and the Kazakhs made partnerships with Russia.[30]

Tajikfilm Studio shifted to video production, allowing for a new generation of film-makers to emerge. Seth Graham's study of Djamshed Usmonov exemplifies this transformation. At the same time, Mohsen Makhmalbaf, Iran's controversial and internationally renowned film-maker, moved to Tajikistan where he made two films: *The Silence* (1998) and *Sex and Philosophy* (2005). When asked why he went to Tajikistan, he responded:

> It's a Persian-speaking country which is high in colour and poetry. To me, this country feels like a lost half of Iran. For several decades, the people of [Tajikistan] were forced to speak Russian, but despite it all, they continued to speak Persian in secret to preserve their cultural identity. They had no textbooks and their only written references were the works of the poets. That's why their everyday language these days is close to poetry. They have rediscovered their roots but what's surprising is that they sometimes recite prayers drinking wine or spout poems![31]

In Uzbekistan, several independent studios emerged in the new millennium alongside the stalwart Uzbekfilm Studio, thus offering ample opportunities to produce commercial cinema for an energized domestic audience. Zulfikar Musakov's *Boys in the Sky* (2002) and *Boys in the Sky 2* (2004) were genuine blockbusters, exploring the trials and antics of adolescence in the lives of four boys living in Tashkent. The films provide a fascinating glimpse into contemporary Uzbek pop culture, with its melange of adorations for Michael Jackson, action films, pornography, stolen cars, and Coca-Cola. Popular Uzbek films tend to highlight the ruptures between the rich and poor, the city and village, such as Ayub Shahobiddinov's *The Other* (2008) and Jahongir Poziljonov's *Rich Guy* (aka *Boyvacha*, 2008), with the lead role played by a star from the Uzbek pop music group Bojalar. Commercial Uzbek cinema has deep connections to the aesthetics of music videos; and young directors are famous for their contributions to Uzbek MTV,[32] as is highlighted by Daria Borisova in her chapter.

Awash with petrodollars, Kazakhstan has become one of the most interesting and inconsistent film scenes of the region, as is highlighted by Eugénie Zvonkine, who explores the work of a new, young generation of Kazakh film-makers in the new millennium. On one side, the traditional masters of Kazakh cinema have continued to make important films with international support: Amir Karakulov's *Don't Cry!* (2002), a study of the bonds of unrelated women from different generations; Aprymov's *The Hunter* (2004), a mystical exploration of core, Kazakh values; and Omirbaev's *Shuga* (2007), a modern take on Leo Tolstoy's *Anna Karenina*. At the same time, Ermek Amanshaev, head of Kazakhfilm since 2008, has sought to promote a closer relationship with the government, to bolster a domestic market, and to foster a new generation of film-makers.

Kazakhfilm has increasingly turned to Russia and the global market for export. A pivotal example is the international project *The Nomad* (2005), directed by Sergei Bodrov, Ivan Passer and Talgat Temenov. With a massive budget, this film delved deeply into Kazakh history to create an imagined imperialist project with a Hollywood cast. There have been numerous recent Kazakh and Russian co-productions that received international attention and distribution: Gulshad (Guka) Omarova's *Schizo* (2004) and *Native Dancer* (2008), Sergei Bodrov's *Mongol* (2007), Sergei Dvortsevoi's *Tulpan* (2008) and Rustem Abdrashev's *Gift to Stalin* (2008). Another trend has been the connection to Hollywood through the Kazakh-born director and producer Timur Bekmambetov, who gained prominence with his blockbusters *Night Watch* (2004) and *Day Watch* (2006) in Russia, and who maintains his connections to the Kazakh film industry. Similarly, Yegor Konchalovsky, son of Andrei Mikhalkov-Konchalovsky and the actress Natalia Arinbasarova, has been enlisted for major film projects at Kazakhfilm, such as the film *Return to A.* (2011). Finally, Ermek Tursunov's *Kelin* (2009) made the shortlist of Academy Award nominations for Best Foreign Film in 2010.

More uncertainty remains in Kyrgyz cinema, despite its international acclaim: Ernest Abdyjaparov, Aktan Abdykalykov (Arym Kubat) and Marat Sarulu have placed Kyrgyz cinema firmly on the map of international film festivals, but there is little state funding (or a commercial market) to sustain domestic film production. Sarulu's *My Brother, Silk Road* (2001) tells a story of two young boys who travel along a railway track that crosses the allegorical Silk Road. Abdyjaparov's *Village Authorities* (*Saratan*, 2004) is a poignant, witty, and entertaining film about everyday life and the possible paths for Kyrgyzstan, while *Pure Coolness* (2007) depicts love in the neo-traditionalist age of bride-stealing. A girl from the city, Asem, falls in love with Murat; but fate intervenes and she marries the pastoral herder, Sagyn. These films are discussed and contextualized by Gulbara Tolomushova and Joël Chapron in this volume.

In 2007 the Turkmen Studio reopened under the new name of Oguz Khan Turkmenfilm. Although film-makers have not been able to travel to promote their films abroad, there are signs of a revival after a long hiatus. Still, it is clear that politics dictate the scripts and messages of the films. Oraz Orazov's *Melody of the Soul* (2007) describes four stories of love and loyalty from Saparmurat Niyazov's *Ruhnama: Book of the Soul.* Basim Agaev's *It's Called Life* (2008) interweaves a story of two women in a hospital: one loses her child and the other gives birth to twins, and gives up one of her children to the first mother. It is a story about community, as well as a gesture to document the new technologies of the central Ashgabat hospital. Durdy Niyazov's *Repentance* (2008) relates the staged confessions of a former drug addict who has been released from prison and asks his mother for forgiveness.[33]

Cinema in Central Asia remains fragmented, with a variety of models for the regional industry, from the international co-production model in Kazakhstan, to funding for short films in

Kyrgyzstan, to catering only for a domestic market in Uzbekistan. As interest in the cinema of Central Asia continues to expand, this volume hopes to provide a background for what should become a truly 'bright future'.

Notes

1   See Cloé Drieu and Jean Radvanyi, 'L'Héritage paradoxal du cinéma soviétique en Asie centrale', *CEMOTI* 39–40 (2005): 159–66.
2   Sergei Kuzmichev offers an account in *Novyi fil'm* 10 (1973).
3   See Ato Akhrorov, *Tadzhikskoe kino* (Dushanbe, 1971), pp. 46–7.
4   Films that were distributed include: Aleksandr Khanzhonkov's *Alcoholism and its Consequences* (1913); Iakov Protazanov's *Father Sergius* (1917); Ivan Perestiani's *Arsen Dzhordzhiashvili* (1921); Aleksandr Panteleev's *The Miracle Worker* (1922); Aleksandr Sanin's *Polikushka* (1922); Ivan Perestiani's *Little Red Imps* (1923); and Lev Kuleshov's *Extraordinary Adventures of Mr West in the Land of the Bolsheviks* (1924).
5   R. Abul'khanov, 'Bukharo-russkoe kinotovarishchestvo', *Iz istorii kino* 5 (1962): 53–70.
6   Aleksandr Gak, ed., *Samoe vazhnoe iz vsekh iskusstv: Lenin o kino* (Moscow, 1963), p. 42.
7   Robin Kinkead, 'The Screen in Moscow', *New York Times* (26 June 1932): X2.
8   *Kok-boru*, or *buzkashi*, is a Central Asian team sport played on horseback where the riders try to grab a headless sheep or goat carcass and take it clear of the other team, or place it into a scoring circle or container. The term literally means 'grey wolf,' a symbol of the Turkic people.
9   See Douglas Northrop, *Veiled Empire: Gender and Power in Stalinist Central Asia* (Ithaca NY, 2004).
10 A group associated with a series of indigenous anti-Bolshevik uprisings in Central Asia during the 1920s and 1930s.
11 See Elena Kolikova and Birgit Beumers, eds, 'Eurasia as a filmic assemblage', *Studies in Russian and Soviet Cinema*, 4.3 (2010): 321–44.
12 Vladimir Shneiderov, *Puteshestvie s kinoapparatom* (Moscow, 1952), p. 8.
13 *Kul'turfi'lm* (also *kul'turfi'lma*), or culture film, played a particularly import role in Soviet cinema as a popular genre of educational films. See Denise J. Youngblood, 'The Fate of Soviet Popular Cinema during the Stalin Revolution', *Russian Review* 2 (1991): 148–62.
14 Several years later, acclaimed US director King Vidor made a film on the same theme and with the same images: *Our Daily Bread* (1934).
15 Between 1942 and 1944 TsOKS produced, including Vera Stroeva, *Son of a Soldier*; Grigorii Roshal', *Batyrs of the Steppe* (1942); Konstantin Iudin, *Antosha Rybkin* (1942); Boris Barnet, *Priceless Head* (1942); Abram Room, *Tonya* (1942); Vsevolod Pudovkin and Iurii Tarich, *The Murderers are Coming* (1942); Leonid Trauberg, *The Actress* (1943); Fridrikh Ermler, *She Defends the Motherland* (1943); Dmitrii Vasil'ev and Vsevolod Pudovkin, *In the Name of the Fatherland* (1943); Grigorii Kozintsev and Leonid Trauberg, *Young Fritz* (1943); Boris Ivanov and Aleksandr Stolper, *Wait for Me* (1943); Georgii and Sergei Vasil'ev, *The Front* (1943); Abram Room, *The Invasion* (1944); and Sergei Eisenstein, *Ivan the Terrible, Part I* (1944).
16 Kamil Iarmatov, *Vozvrashchenie* (Moscow, 1980), pp. 242–58.
17 See *Sovetskoe kinoiskusstvo* 14 (1948).

18   Kimiagarov followed this success with a series of documentaries: *In the Pamir Mountains* (1947), *Sadriddin Aini* (1949), *Land of Youth* (1950), *Soviet Tajikistan* (1951), *On the Pamirs* (1952) and *Four Songs about Tajikistan* (1954).

19   Gul'nara Abikeeva, *Kino Tsentral'noi Azii, 1990–2001* (Almaty, 2001), p. 157.

20   See Patrick Bureau, 'Andrei Tarkovsky: I Am for a Poetic Cinema,' in John Gianvito, ed., *Tarkovsky Interviews* (University Press of Mississippi, 2006), pp. 3–5; and John Orr, 'A Cinema of Poetry,' in John Orr and Olga Taxidou, eds, *Post-war Cinema and Modernity: A Film Reader* (New York, 2000), pp. 133–141.

21   El'ga Lyndina, 'La poésie unit les hommes' in Jean Radvanyi, ed., *Le Cinéma d'Asie centrale soviétique* (Paris, 1991), p. 93.

22   Gönül Dönmez-Colin, 'Turkmen and Uzbek Film-making', *Aus dem Herzen der Welt: Das Kino der zentralasiatischen Republiken* (Vienna, 2001), p. 61.

23   See Sylvie Dallet, 'Historical Time in Russian, Armenian, Georgian and Kirghiz Cinema', in Anna Lawton, ed., *The Red Screen* (London, 1992), pp. 303–14, for a good discussion of the progress in nationality cinema from the static forms of the Stalinist era.

24   Kamil Iarmatov, 'O vremeni i o sebe', *Iskusstvo kino* 10 (1972): 31–2.

25   See Sergei Lavrent'ev, *Krasnyi vestern* (Moscow, 2009) for more information on the genre of Soviet adventure films in the 'wild east'.

26   Forrest S. Ciesol, 'Kazakhstan Wave', *Sight and Sound* 1 (1989/1990): 56.

27   Ludmila Z. Pruner, 'The New Wave in Kazakh Cinema', *Slavic Review* 4 (1992): 791.

28   The workshop made the film *The White Pigeon* [*Belyi golub*, 1985], which won a special jury prize at the Venice Film Festival in 1986.

29   Gulnara Abikeyeva, *The Heart of the World: Films from Central Asia* (Almaty, 2003), p. 77.

30   For an overview of the developments in Central Asia, see Gul'nara Abikeeva and Birgit Beumers, eds, 'Special Feature: Central Asia', *Studies in Russian an Soviet Cinema*, 4.2 (2010): 187–254.

31   Venice International Film Festival 1998, press booklet.

32   See David MacFadyen, *Russian Culture in Uzbekistan: One Language in the Middle of Nowhere* (London, 2006).

33   See Gul'nara Abikeeva, 'Kino i kul'turnye vliianiia v Tsentral'noi Azii', *Neprikosnovennyi zapas* 4 (2009) at http://magazines.russ.ru/nz/2009/4/ab17.html (accessed 18 March 2012).

PART I

AT THE CINEMATIC CRADLE

1

VOSTOKKINO AND THE FOUNDATION OF CENTRAL ASIAN CINEMA

Gabrielle Chomentowski

The story of Vostokkino is a little-known episode at the beginning of Soviet cinema. Vostokkino, meaning 'eastern cinema' or 'Oriental cinema', was a film trust launched by Soviet officials and intellectuals from the Scientific Oriental Association in Moscow in 1926; it emerged from a department within the State Committee for Cinematography (Sovkino).[1] The studio was intended to represent the eastern peoples of the Soviet Russia, to spread Soviet propaganda among the 'Oriental population', and to introduce them and their way of life to the rest of the Soviet Union. In Soviet vocabulary of the time, the concept of 'Oriental population' corresponded to that of 'backward' people within the hierarchy of cultural and industrial development.

The creation of Vostokkino reflected the nationalities policy and transformations in cultural politics in the Soviet Union during the mid-1920s: in response to the wide diversity of peoples in Russia and to their quest for the expression of national identity, in 1923 the Bolsheviks implemented a policy to promote non-Russian nationalities in various spheres (labour, education, culture). This coincided with an explosion of artistic and cultural projects in all parts of the former Russian Empire: in regions as far as Tatarstan,

Chuvashia and Uzbekistan, local intellectuals and artists decided to make their own films based on local tales or events, such as the Revolution. However, in the mid-1920s the Communist Party began to increase its control over cultural developments as it grew suspicious about such cultural activities: as a result, politicians proposed to share the financial burden with private firms and the regions.[2] Created as a joint-stock company, Vostokkino had to unify all local projects and promote non-Russian artists in cinema. For two key reasons Vostokkino's goals have been overlooked.

First, Vostokkino was short-lived, operating from 1928 to 1935, during a tumultuous period in Soviet history. At the time of its inception, Stalin had just succeeded in marginalizing his adversaries in the Politburo. The first Party Cinema Conference in March 1928 confirmed a new stage in Party control over the industry. Moreover, cinema was included in the First Five-Year Plan, which determined Vostokkino's budget and production schedule, as well as its content. By 1936, the authorities were phasing out the formerly semi-private firms such as Vostokkino or Mezhrabpomfilm, and Stalin tightened central control over the industry.[3]

Second, Soviet officials accused Vostokkino of being a front for nationalism and corruption. Above all, Vostokkino appeared to the authorities as anachronistic: Soviet nationality policy no longer celebrated 'difference' through indigenization (*korenizatsiia*), or what Terry Martin calls 'affirmative action'; on the contrary, the mid-1930s were marked by a policy of assimilation and centralization.[4] As a result, officials liquidated the trust, seized its films, and in some cases destroyed them. The authorities subsequently imprisoned, exiled, or executed many of Vostokkino's artists and managers, and Vostokkino disappeared from official catalogues and Soviet film histories.

Since the collapse of the Soviet Union, historians of the former Soviet republics as well as foreign researchers have focused on the 'national' cinemas of each republic, while neglecting regional or all-Union developments in the film industry. As Vostokkino's film-makers were not natives of Central Asia but Russian, Jewish, Ukrainian or Belorussian, the story of Vostokkino has been neglected in the recent historiography.

Vostokkino made important contributions to the development of cinema in Central Asia. Representatives of Vostokkino were the first to organize film screenings in this area and establish a cinema infrastructure, a process known as *kinofikatsiia*.[5] Vostokkino worked with local organizations to buy, sell and rent film reels and projection equipment for both travelling and fixed-location cinemas. It also published books and newspapers about cinema in local languages. From its inception, Vostokkino sought to foster closer relationships between 'Oriental' Soviet peoples and 'Oriental' peoples outside the USSR. Ultimately, the organization trained Soviet nationals of the east to become directors, cameramen, scriptwriters, actors and so on. Thus, directors' assistants, cameramen and actors in Vostokkino films were generally natives of Tatarstan, Bashkortostan, Kazakhstan, Kirghizia, Tajikistan and Turkmenistan. With this experience, several native Central Asians became film-makers in their own right.

Cinema in the East

In 1925, the Azeri politician Nariman Narimanov, citing Lenin's statement that 'of all the arts, cinema is the most important, especially for eastern peoples', argued that pictures were more useful among 'Oriental' peoples than among Europeans.[6] He claimed that 'in the Orient, where people are not used to thinking with logic but in images, cinema is the only tool of propaganda'.[7] Such ideas were widely shared in the Soviet government concerning Central Asians.[8] Taking advantage of cinema's properties as apparently universally intelligible, effective, mass-produced, direct means of communication, the Soviet regime distributed its propaganda films among all 'backward' peoples, but especially among 'eastern nationalities'.[9]

At the same time when Narimanov espoused his ideas, a group of young film-makers from Moscow and Leningrad set out to view firsthand the consequences of the Bolshevik Revolution in Central Asia. In the mid-1920s actors and directors, including Oleg Frelikh, Kazimir Gertel, Cheslav Sabinsky, Mikhail Doronin, Rakhil Messerer and others, arrived in Bukhara to work in the first Soviet cinema studio in Central Asia, Bukhkino (Bukhara Film Studio). Bukhkino was the product of an agreement signed on 12 April 1924 between the newly established Bukharan Republic and the Leningrad studio, Sevzapkino. Under this agreement, the studio produced one feature film, *The Minaret of Death* (1925), and several newsreels. The directors from Russia also worked for the Moscow studio, Proletkino, which produced *The Muslim Woman* (1925). To legitimize Soviet rule in Central Asia, these films explored an important aspect of Soviet policy in the east: the emancipation of Muslim women. Subsequent films produced by the Uzbek studio, Uzbekfilm, described this *hujum,* or 'all-out assault', for the emancipation of Muslim women conducted by the Soviet regime. The films denounced traditional roles of women in Eastern societies, as is obvious from Mikhail Doronin's *The Second Wife* (1927) and Oleg Frelikh's *The Daughter of the Saint* (1931).[10] They depicted arranged marriages, payoffs between the bride's father and the fiancé, and obligatory veiling, as for example Mikhail Averbakh's *The Veil* (1927). These films were released in a significant number of prints for this time: 50 copies. And they were distributed in Central Asia and across the Soviet Union. Yet, as Adrienne Edgar writes, 'at the height of the campaign to emancipate women in the late 1920s, Soviet secret police reported complaints by Central Asians that "the Russians" were trying to destroy Islam, communalize wives, and destroy the Muslim family'.[11] Despite the intentions of emancipatory films, some native Central Asian men beat their wives or attacked actresses after watching them.[12] To avoid this violence, Jewish or Russian actresses, such as Rakhil Messerer or Olga Tretiakova,[13] played the 'Oriental' women in these movies.

The Bolsheviks feared that films about the Soviet east stood in opposition to the 'modernist' idea of the Revolution. While directors hoped to condemn traditions, the Bolsheviks perceived these movies as exoticizing the East and promulgating imperialism. They criticized that most of the heroes were interpreted by Russian actors rather than by local ones:

> In Cinema we have noticed a lack of people familiar with the Orient who create Oriental films. We must make note of two unwanted tendencies: the first one is to perpetuate the old traditions of portraying the Orient in film, that is the creation of a stereotyped Orient in cinema with piquant stories that remind us of *A Thousand and One Nights.* Such a description of the Orient is just fine for western films. [But] it provides nothing for the Russian workers-peasants or eastern audiences. This tendency appears in *The Minaret of Death.* The second tendency is the inclusion of overly strong propaganda. For example, Bassalygo's film *Muslim Woman* [...]. Obviously, cinema development for Oriental people has to be in the hands of the Oriental people.[14]

To address these problems, Communist officials decided to offer an alternative to 'exotic' films and create a cinema enterprise that would represent all the 'Oriental' nationalities of the Soviet Union.

Its aims would be to educate these populations through film and to train members of these nationalities to become film-makers, directors and cameramen. The Bolsheviks hoped that these future film-makers could effectively represent the East, which they clearly knew better than anyone else. This project took the form of a joint-stock company, and the Communist Party leadership of each national territorial entity could become shareholder; the project was called 'Vostokkino'.

Activities of Vostokkino in Central Asia

The press announced Vostokkino's official establishment in 1926, but the organization effectively began to work only two years later, after the first shareholders' meeting in Moscow on 26 March 1928. The shareholders were representatives from each autonomous republic and each district in the Russian Federation (RSFSR),[15] including the north Caucasus, the Volga territories, northern Siberia, the Far East, Buryatia, Kazakhstan and Kirghizia.[16] Anatoli Lunacharsky, the People's Commissar of Enlightenment, also tried to convince other Central Asian republics to become shareholders in the organization. He argued that it would permit the Soviet government 'not to scatter cinema interests of Oriental peoples, but on the contrary to unify them in a single studio'.[17] But Uzbekistan [and with it, Tajikistan][18] rejected this idea, arguing that the republic already possessed a vibrant cinema industry. It is not clear whether Lunacharsky made the same proposal to Turkmenistan, which had already had a film bureau since 1926. Despite these refusals, however, Vostokkino produced several films about Uzbekistan and Turkmenistan.

Vostokkino had contacts with all the distribution outlets in the Russian Federation, including film distribution offices in Frunze (now Bishkek) and Alma-Ata (now Almaty). The organization arranged film screenings not only in cities but also in rural areas, with trucks hauling the equipment from village to village. Bringing cinema to the nomadic population was one of the central activities of the enterprise. Although Vostokkino's capital investment was not huge, its impact was quite significant: villagers and nomads in far-flung rural areas could watch films for the first time.

Vostokkino was therefore crucial to the 'cinefication' of the Soviet east. The growth of cinema in Kazakhstan, an area where interest was great from the beginning, demonstrates the achievements of Vostokkino's activities. In 1929 the local authorities counted

12 cinemas in a country with a population of 6.5 million – that is one cinema (itinerant or permanent) for every 52,003 Kazakh people.[19] By 1937, there were 40 stationary and 160 mobile cinemas, among them 71 equipped for sound.

Vostokkino also acquired 13 cinemas that NEP-era corporations had established. Most of the permanent theatres were situated in administrative centres, but also in smaller towns in both the south and north of the Kazakh Republic. Vostokkino built an immense, thousand-seat cinema in Alma-Ata, and later followed other large venues in Karaganda and Akmolinsk (now Astana).

At the beginning of 1930, Vostokkino had four production studios in Yalta (Crimea), Alma-Ata (Kazakhstan), Kazan (Tatarstan) and Verkhne-Udinsk (Buryatia). These studios not only served their republics, but also had to contribute to the development of cinema in surrounding areas. The Alma-Ata Studio therefore had to serve not only Kazakhstan but also Kirghizia, the Karakalpak Autonomous Region, and other regions from Siberia to Central Asia. The Alma-Ata Studio regularly produced newsreels, called 'The Latest News' [*Poslednie izvestiia*]. Vostokkino did not have a central production base, and most of the time the film organization worked outdoors, in the open air, or used the facilities of a large republican studio, such as Mosfilm or the Ukrainian Photo and Cinema Administration (VUFKU).

As we have already mentioned, one of Vostokkino's missions was to train people of 'Eastern' nationalities to become film-makers and thereby allow for the *korenizatsiia*, or indigenization, of the film industries in the various republics.[20] In several 'Eastern' republics, Vostokkino organized courses for directors, scriptwriters, technicians and actors. Similarly, a fixed number of places at Moscow's VGIK were reserved for members of national minorities. In various Vostokkino departments, such as Kazakhstan, promising local photographers were invited to learn how to use a film camera to make newsreels. In Alma-Ata several native writers took screen-writing lessons. The well-known Kazakh writers Sabit Mukanov and Ilyas Dzhansugurov, for example, worked as 'ethnographic consultants' for film-makers on native customs; they also participated as scriptwriters for several Vostokkino projects, including *Secret of Karatau, Accursed Trails, The Freeze*, and *Song of the Steppes*. Dzhansugurov and many others native scriptwriters were executed during the Great Terror in 1937, and their names disappeared from the credits of the films on which they had worked.

In 1928, a new wave of Russian film-makers arrived in Central Asia. Some of them were already experienced directors, including Yevgeni Ivanov-Barkov, Vladimir Yerofeev, Yefim Aron, Alexander Razumny, Yuri Leontev and Yuri Zheliabuzhsky; others were just beginning their careers, such as Mark Donskoi and Vladimir Legoshin. Vostokkino employed various native actors to play character 'types' or symbolic local characters. The Kazakh actor Khakim Davletbekov launched his career in the film *The Freeze* (1931) and continued in subsequent Vostokkino films. Theatre actors, such as those of the Ashkhabad theatre company, also had the opportunity to work in film.

Film Production

Most of the films produced in the 1920s and early 1930s were not feature films, but short ethnographic and propaganda films (*kul'turfil'my* and *agitfil'my*), documentaries, newsreels and shorts. During one of the early Vostokkino meetings, the shareholders declared that the trust's principal activity was to make feature films. Due to a lack of funds, however, documentary films remained predominant in Vostokkino's production before 1932. To make a *kulturfilm*, Vostokkino needed just two people (a director and a cameraman), some film stock and a camera. To make a feature film, on the other hand, the organization had to pay actors, support staff, purchase decorations and costumes, and so forth. On Vostokkino's limited budget, therefore, smaller productions were far more common. In 1932, a single studio, Soyuzkinokhronika, was designated as the sole producer of newsreels and documentaries. From this point onward, Vostokkino would produce only feature films. The expenditure for such films led to a complex financial situation, since Vostokkino's budget was insufficient for the creation of subtitles or dubbed sound versions in the different languages of the eastern peoples. This might also explain why the Soviet authorities decided to phase out the programme.

The most famous Vostokkino production, Viktor Turin's *Turksib*, received worldwide acclaim when it was released in 1929. The film historian Jay Leyda wrote that 'Turksib was a popular and immediate success abroad and a surprise at home, both to the makers of *kulturfilmy* and of studio-films, especially when this modest film was received with enthusiasm wherever it was shown.'[21] *Turksib* first depicted life in the steppe: cotton fields and sheep-shearing. The heat and aridity of the steppes contrasted with the Siberian cold. Over

Figure 1.1 Poster for Viktor Turin's *Turksib* (1929).

thousands of kilometres from Central Asia to Siberia, workers joined to build a railway, a formidable challenge. Then, the film showed the railroad under construction from Siberia to Tashkent, and how friendly labourers of all nationalities worked together. The film overlooked the fact that, during the construction of the railroad, ethnic relationships were very strained and that Kazakh workers were victims of Russian 'pogroms'.[22] However, this film's most important contribution was to depict Kazakhs ethnographically, as few film-makers had done before in such a poetic and aesthetic way.

Owing to this success, Kazakhstan remained in the focus in most *kulturfilmy* produced by Vostokkino in subsequent years. Approximately ten films depicted life in Kazakhstan at the end of the 1920s and the beginning of the 1930s. One showed collectivization among sheep-herders, while another demonstrated wheat hoarding by *kulaks*, the Soviet term for those who 'exploited' peasants; both were written by Sergei Vitkin in 1929 and 1930 respectively.[23] Alexander Lemberg's *Golden Shores* revealed the achievements of Soviet Kazakhstan in comparison with the tsarist era. Vostokkino also produced documentary films about Turkmenistan, as with the film *Carpets* by Mikhail Verner; or about Uzbekistan, as with the film *Faraway in Asia*, which was the first Vostokkino documentary to have sound and that was made by the famous 'ethnographic film-maker' Vladimir Yerofeev with the young cameraman Roman Karmen.[24]

Over seven years Vostokkino produced 50 feature films for almost all the 'eastern' areas of the Russian Federation. The majority of these films have disappeared, either because of bad conservation or because they were forbidden and burned. The most famous Vostokkino feature films are: Oleg Frelikh's *Zelim-Khan* (1929), depicting Russian–Chechen relations in the north Caucasus; Yuli Raizman's *The Earth Thirsts* (1930) consecrating the 'friendship of the peoples' in Turkmenistan; Mark Donskoi's *Song of Happiness* (1934) about the social rise in the Mari District; Alexander Razumny's *Kara-Bugaz* (1935); and Ivan Pravov and Olga Preobrazhenskaya's *Accursed Trails* (1935) set in Kazakhstan.

These feature films were the first examples of national cinema in the Central Asian republics. *The Song of the Steppes* (1930) was the first feature film produced by Vostokkino for the tenth anniversary of the Kazakh Republic. The second Kazakh feature film, *The Freeze*, was written by Sergei Yermolinsky and produced by Mikhail Karostin; falling somewhere between a documentary and a feature film, it depicted the effects of the famine on the Kazakh population in the late 1920s. According to the official summary,[25] the film showed the starvation of entire herds of cattle in the cold weather and the subsequent suffering of the human population. In fact, much of the famine in Kazakhstan was due to the collectivization of agriculture and the forced settlement of nomadic Kazakh herdsmen. Consequently, the Soviet regime disapproved of the film's depiction of the topic. *Song of the Steppes* and *The Freeze* disappeared soon after they were completed, and to this day no copies of the films have been located. Alexander Dubrovsky and Gabriel El-Registan produced *The Secret of Kara-Tau* in 1932 where they told the story of rubber cultivation in Kazakhstan. *Accursed Trails* related the story of collectivization in a little Kazakh village where Russian settlers and

Figure 1.2 Still from Alexander Razumny's *Kara-Bugaz* (1935).

poor, native Kazakhs lived together. This film did not examine typically Kazakh themes, but rather the class struggle among Russian settlers.

Vostokkino's most interesting films in terms of plot and cinematography are undoubtedly *The Earth Thirsts* and *Kara-Bugaz*, both concerning the access of the Central Asian population to clean water. *The Earth Thirsts* was one of the first Soviet sound films and also one of the first films to describe socialist construction in a non-Russian region of the Soviet Union. The action took place in Turkmenistan, with actors representing different nationalities: Jewish, Russian, Georgian and Turkmen. Five years later, the film-maker Alexander Razumny adapted Konstantin Paustovsky's novel *Kara-Bugaz* to make a film on a similar topic. Set in the Garabogazkul region on the border of Kazakhstan and Turkmenistan – with the highest salt concentration in the world – the film tells the story of the local population slowly dying of thirst. In this film, the film-makers made no departure from the colonial representation of the East: Russian characters bring modernity and knowledge to eastern-nomadic peoples, who are played by the Ashkhabad theatre troupe.

Despite the best intentions of Vostokkino's *auteurs*, the organization's activities were heavily criticized for bad management.

Some politicians complained in 1931 that the Kazakh department of Vostokkino did not do enough to train indigenous film-makers. Some Vostokkino workers from Kazakhstan complained that agitators stole cameras and money. A report even stated that in 1930, erotic and 'bourgeois' films were shown in Kazakhstan and Kirghizia. On a number of occasions native film-makers or 'ethnographic consultants' complained of being badly treated by Russian film-makers. Their testimonies demonstrate that, two years after Stalin took power, the Party's ideological control was still not uniform and ethnic relationships remained tense. However, since Vostokkino created the Kazakh department in Alma-Ata in 1930, the organization built a laboratory, an editing suite, a rig for cartoon-making and a room for subtitling. Many artists and writers who were natives from former Turkestan profited from this situation.

In the 1920s and 1930s Central Asia had an overwhelmingly rural population and a generally low level of economic development. The high cost of audiovisual equipment meant that cameras and projectors were very rare. For these reasons as well as others the peoples of Central Asia did not create the first films in the region, but rather cinema came to them through the efforts of adventurous film-makers from Russia. The Vostokkino story demonstrates that by the end of the 1920s cinema had already become an important part of cultural life in Central Asia. Vostokkino could even be considered a tool of cultural imperialism. Nevertheless, even if Vostokkino films were not truly 'national', they were a first step towards national cinema.

Notes

1   Among these intellectuals, the most dynamic were the scholars of the Oriental Association in Moscow, directed by Mikhail Pavlovich Vel'tman. The association had already created an Oriental Section of Cinema in 1925.
2   In 1929 Vostokkino was controlled by the following shareholders: Central Committee of Bashkiria, Crimea, Daghestan, Kazakhstan, Buryatia, Chechnia, Kalmuks, Karachaevo-Cherkessia, Kabardino-Balkarya, Ossetia, Yakutia, Chuvashia, Kirghizia, Narkompros of Russia, Mezhrabpomfilm, Sovkino, Azgoskino.
3   In 1926 Vostokkino was organized as a shareholding company. In March 1930 the organization was transformed into an industrial trust: it marked the end of NEP (New Economic Policy) and the end of private initiatives. Two years later, in March 1932, Vostokkino became a state trust, Vostokfilm. The organization was liquidated on 8 August 1935.
4   Terry Martin, *The Affirmative Action Empire: Nations and Nationalism in the Soviet Union, 1923–1939* (Ithaca NY, 2001).

5   *Cinefication* (*kinofikatsiia*) is a mix of Russian words *kino* and *elektrifikatsiia*. This word refers to the electrification policy in the Soviet Union and to the famous dictum by Lenin: 'Communism equals Soviet power plus the electrification of the whole country', which means the set-up of a cinema infrastructure (projectors, cinemas, etc). *Cinefication* and *electrification* policies were closely linked: electricity was a prerequisite to show a film.

6   'Lenin o kino', *Kino-zhurnal* 2 (1925): 3. The article is inspired by a note Lenin wrote in January 1922.

7   Nariman Narimanov, 'Organizatsiia v vostochnom kino', *Sovetskoe kino* 2–3 (May–June 1925): 16–17.

8   In general, Soviet leaders believed in the power of images for all 'backward' peoples, Central Asian and Russian alike. Nadezhda Krupskaya, Lenin's wife, who in 1925 also served in the Commissariat of Enlightenment, said that 'very often peasant as worker thinks thanks to images and not through abstract ideas', in *Sel'skokhoziaistvennaia propaganda*, 1923.

9   Officials referred to the 'backwardness' of the Soviet east generally in relation to its level of economic development in comparison with European Russia, but all too often this criterion was used to qualify 'Oriental' peoples' social or cultural development as well.

10 Oleg Frelikh also made *The Covered Wagon* and *The Leper* in Uzbekistan.

11 Adrienne Edgar, 'Bolshevism, Patriarchy, and the Nation: The Soviet "Emancipation" of Muslim Women in Pan-Islamic Perspective', *Slavic Review* 65.2 (2006): 252–72 (p. 266).

12 For example, the first Uzbek actress Iouldachkhozhdaeva Nurkhon was killed by her brother in 1929. Marianne Kamp, *The New Woman in Uzbekistan: Islam, Modernity and Unveiling under Communism* (Seattle, 2006).

13 Rakhil' Messerer (1902–93) acted in *Valley of Tears*, *The Second Wife*, and *The Leper*. She was arrested in 1937 as a wife of 'people's enemy' (*vrag naroda*). Ol'ga Tret'iakova acted in *The Muslim Woman*. She was arrested in 1937 and died in the Gulag.

14 A. Skachko, 'Kino dlia vostoka', *Kino-zhurnal ARKa* 10 (1925): 3.

15 There were 16 ASSRs: Bashkiria (Bashkortostan), Buryatia, Dagestan, Kabarda-Balkar, Kalmykia, Karelia, Komi, Mari, Mordovia, Northern Ossetia, Tatarstan, Tuva, Udmurtia, Chechnya-Ingushetia, Chuvashia and Yakutia. Autonomous oblasts were Adyghea, Gorno-Altai, Jewish, Karachai-Cherkessia and Khakassia.

16 Kirghizia and Kazakhstan were autonomous republics at this time in the RSFSR. Kazakhstan became a Vostokkino shareholder in 1928 and Kirghizia in 1929.

17 'Letter from the Secretary of the RSFSR Narkompros to the Sovnarkom President of Uzbekistan, 5 March 1926'. GARF f. 3316, op. 20, d. 859, l. 1.

18 From 1924 to 1929, Tajikistan was an autonomous republic of Uzbekistan.

19 For comparison, in 1930 Uzbekistan had 111 cinema and Turkmenistan 48. TSGA Kaz, f. 1165, op.2. d.4, l.1.

20 On the policy of *korenizatsiia* see Martin, *The Affirmative Action Empire.*

21 Jay Leyda, *Kino: A History of Russian and Soviet Film* (London, 1960), p. 260.

22 Matthew Payne, *Stalin's Railroad: Turksib and the Building of Socialism* (Pittsburgh, 2001).

23 *Sheep Farming* [*Ovtsevodstvo*, 1929] and *Bread* [*Khleb*, 1930], scriptwriter Sergei Vitkin, film-makers unknown.

24 Other *kul'turfil'my* produced by Vostokkino include *Ten Years of Kazakhstan, Turksib is Open; Today or Tomorrow.*

25 RGALI, f. 645, op. 1, d. 361, l. 57.

2

BIRTH, DEATH AND REBIRTH OF A NATION: NATIONAL NARRATIVE IN UZBEK FEATURE FILMS

Cloé Drieu

T he birth of Uzbek cinema coincided with that of the Uzbek
Republic itself: 1924 marks the ethno-territorial delimitation of
the Uzbek Soviet Socialist Republic, as well as the beginning of the
filming of *The Minaret of Death* at the newly-created film studio in
Bukhara (from 1920–4 capital of the Bukharan People's Soviet
Republic). This chapter explores the process of nation-building
throughout the 1920s and 1930s, relying on fiction films produced
between 1924 and 1937, and taking into account the entire process
of film-making (context of production, message and reception).
These films reflect how a new political and cultural community was
imagined, shaped and reshaped by Soviet policy on nationalities, but
they also offer a peculiar angle on the development of the power
relationship between the centre (Moscow) and the periphery
(Uzbekistan). In Central Asia and elsewhere in the Soviet Union, this
interwar period generated radical changes that find their reflections
on the silver screen. Accordingly, the films are considered as a 'total
social fact': not only as a political and cultural product, but as a
microcosm of state and society, which – in the Uzbek case – revealed

itself as 'loci for contact' or 'negotiation' during the 1920s, or as 'loci of resistance', 'conflict' and 'crisis' during the 1930s.[1]

Since the first years of Soviet power, cinema had embodied the idea of modernity, conferring upon itself a special place among the tools for political and ideological communication. Artists, especially film-makers, provided an indispensable link between the power and the people, or what Lenin had called the 'gear and screw'[2] – that could be a vehicle for ideological norms of behaviour and thinking. However, during the Tsarist period fictional narratives, literary or theatrical, were already a favourite domain for the Muslim reformist *élite* (*jadids*) to convey messages about the need for modernization, education, laicization and women's emancipation in Central Asia. With the Bolshevik Revolution, fiction turned further into politics, and artists had to surrender to the central state and its ideology, culminating in the 'Sovietization' of Central Asia in the late 1930s – a time when the Soviet political and cultural elites were 'purged'. But between 1924 and 1934, the Uzbek Republic benefited from cultural autonomy, originally conceded by the central Soviet authorities for pragmatic reasons and in accordance with its 'policy on nationalities'. However, the case of Uzbekistan is unique in Central Asia, since it is the only republic to have established national film production as early as 1924 and to have brought forth the first national film-makers: Suleiman Khodjaev (1892–1937); Nabi Ganiev (1904–54), considered the father of Uzbek national cinema; and, to a lesser extent, Kamil Yarmatov (1903–78) in Tajikistan, who played an important role at the Uzbek Studio after World War II. In the other Central Asian republics indigenous film-makers took hold of the camera only after 1945; until then they worked and trained with Russian film-makers invited to the local film studios.

The First Film Studios: Symbolic Cultural Domination (1924–8)

Bukhkino, the first film studio, was created in April 1924 at the initiative of the government of the Bukharan People's Soviet Republic under a cooperation agreement between the studio Sevzapkino and the Commissariat of Enlightenment.[3] The Turkestan Republic, at that time part of the Russian Soviet Federation (RSFSR), and later the Uzbek SSR, did not have its own film studio, but only an umbrella organization, Turkgoskino, which dealt with film distribution and programming. The development of a film studio and cinematographic infrastructure allowed the Republic of Bukhara, and later the Uzbek SSR, to reach a new level of development and modernity. In an article published in *Yer Yuzi* (the first cultural magazine published in Central Asia), an anonymous writer congratulates Soviet Uzbekistan, because the region was now able to produce 'incredible and unheard things', as well as obtaining the possibility to 'unveil the mysteries of the Orient'.[4] Symbolically, cinema offered the possibility of 'worldwide communication', gathering information about the whole world as well as talking about Central Asian regions and their peoples.

However, the republic did not yet have the skilled workforce in order to produce films, so the local studios had to invite film-makers, mainly of Russian origin, to work in Uzbekistan. Their films revealed in the first instance the perception of the Russian film-makers of Central Asia and of its 'indigenous peoples'. Films such as *The Minaret of Death* (1925) by Viacheslav Viskovsky and *The Muslim Woman* (1925) by Dmitri Bassalygo conveyed an orientalist and exotic vision comparable to contemporary European accounts, such as *The Thief of Bagdad* (dir. Raoul Walsh, 1924) with Douglas Fairbanks Jr and *The Sheik* (dir. George Melford, 1921) with Rudolph Valentino. Motivated not by a search for realism or political goals, film-makers like Bassalygo were influenced by foreign cinema and sought to represent a 'stylized Orient' (*uslovnyi vostok*) in their films, rejecting the involvement of indigenous people in the production: Bassalygo rejected the first script of *The Muslim Woman,* originally commissioned by the Women's Department (*Zhenotdel* – a political organization in charge of women's emancipation), clearly inspired by the everyday life of local women and intended for local audiences for educational purposes. However that may be, these first 'Oriental films' (*vostochnye fil'my*) were successful within the Soviet Union and abroad. In 1928 *The Minaret of Death* was sold to 29 countries (more than Eisenstein's *Battleship Potemkin,* 1925).[5] Despite their 'Oriental' and 'exotic' qualities, films produced in Central Asia were successful in Uzbekistan. Notably the screening of *The Minaret of Death* increased local attendance by 40 per cent, according to an official report.[6]

Politically motivated critics of these first films were particularly vociferous and called for more realism that would give birth to a specific discourse of domination. Films such as *The Second Wife* (1927) by Mikhail Doronin, *Behind the Vaults of the Mosque* (1928) by Kazimir Gertel or *The Leper* (1928) by Oleg Frelikh were less exotic (no harem, belly-dancing, Arab-type horsemen), but they sharply discriminated against Central Asians, who were portrayed as

Figure 2.1 Still from *Behind the Vaults of the Mosque* (1928) by Kazimir Gertel.

aggressive and threatening people, or even compared to animals through parallel montage. These films had much in common with the genre of *cinéma colonial* produced in France at the time,[7] and failed to convey proper political messages. A striking example of this failure is *The Leper*, where the heroine's unveiling leads to an illegal relationship and ultimately death instead of delivering a message of emancipation. The reception of such films was negative among politicians as well as local audiences, but corresponds to a period of transition when the New Economic Policy (NEP, 1921–8) allowed a free market regulated by the laws of supply and demand and stimulated private film production. During this period, films largely served to advertise the east to Russian audiences in Leningrad or Moscow rather than convey the advantages of communist values of liberation to the Central Asian peoples.

Time for Change: Towards a National Appropriation of Cinema (1928–33)

The years 1927–8 were a specific turning point with consequences for Uzbek cinema and its role in nation-building: it was the beginning of the Cultural Revolution, a decisive moment in the construction of the Soviet national identities – when the first national Uzbek film was produced. Moreover, the first Party Conference on Cinema Affairs in March 1928 confirmed the use of cinema as a tool for political propaganda from the centre. All these – at first sight contradictory – trends could coexist, because the links between local communists in the new Uzbek state and the central Party apparatus were still missing. However, Uzbek political and cultural elites managed to find ways to establish political legitimacy through Soviet ways of life. Thus, films produced in Uzbekistan between 1927 and 1931 made local and central ideologies coincide as far as the social aspects of the Soviet policy of modernization were concerned (e.g. secularization, emancipation), or, on the contrary, these films offered viewpoints that diverged from the centre in their representation of the Uzbek nation.[8]

A specific contradiction in the construction of Soviet identity was highlighted in the film *Jackals of Ravat* (1927) by Kazimir Gertel. Even if no Uzbek film-maker was involved, it was nevertheless considered the first 'Uzbek national movie' – on the basis of citizenship rather than ethnic principles. Indeed, the film's nationality was determined by three criteria: production, reception and representation. Released in 1927, the film was produced in a national-type film economy (financing, choice of the subject and censorship), and the Uzbek political or cultural elite remained the decision maker of their own cultural policy. Second, in terms of reception, some important local intellectuals, such as the novelist Abdullah Qodiri (1894–1938), welcomed the film as the 'first Uzbek' movie.[9] And third, the representation of the Uzbek community or nation is particularly eloquent: the predominantly Russian Red Guard advocated freedom and helped the Uzbeks organize an indigenous, modern and socialist society, but at the end of the film they return to their homeland. Having provided 'political education' that the previously colonized people lacked, they leave. This concept of Soviet power as a temporary political guide was viewed negatively by Russian critics from the central censorship committee (Glavrepertkom), who reckoned that the representatives of Soviet power were almost absent and 'lacked consistency' in their portrayal.[10] Thus, two concepts of Soviet Uzbek nation-building emerged: on one hand, Soviet power represented by the Red Guard as a force of liberation and modernization, who trust the communist Uzbek people; and on the other hand, Soviet power as a perennial referent of order and centralism.

The Veil (1927) by the young Moscow film-maker Mikhail Averbakh is an example of 'political convergence' on the policy of women's emancipation, although the film itself was a flop in Uzbekistan. Produced with the support of the Association for

Revolutionary Cinema (ARK) – symbolizing the indirect involvement of the Party in Uzbek film production – the film was not well
understood by female spectators, as is obvious from numerous
reviews published in the local press, who bemoaned the lack of
consideration for the local psychological background.[11] Taking
advantage of *avant-garde* editing techniques and debates over
cinema, Averbakh was completely disconnected from vernacular
female expectations and women's level of cinematographic literacy.
While Averbakh tried through his heroine Lola to symbolize the
difficult but necessary path of martyrdom towards emancipation,
women and critics demanded agit-films depicting the large
emancipation campaigns (*hujum*) with precise details: How was the
campaign organized? Who stands against it and what did the mullahs
and imams do? What is to be done and where can women go if they
want to shed their *chachvon* and *paranji*?[12] These questions were not
answered in the film.

During the 1920s only film-makers from outside the Uzbek SSR
were actively engaged in making such films. The situation changed
in 1931, when the first indigenous film-makers took hold of the
camera. Until this national appropriation of film-making, production took place in the context of economic centralization on a
union-wide scale, with the creation of the organization Soyuzkino in
1930. Consequently, the cultural and economic autonomy of each
Soviet republic came to an end. In the case of Uzbekistan, the
government did not entirely oppose the process of centralization –
it was considered an important step for greater efficiency – but
demanded permanent representation on the new organization's
board of directors, which was unfortunately not granted. Along with
economic centralization, the Party initiated a 'political cleansing'
within political, social, economic and cultural structures in order to
increase the role of Party members and to remove 'anti-Soviet
elements'. At the Uzbek film studios, the first 'purge' (1930–1) led
to the eviction largely of accounting staff and revealed many
structural problems in the management. However, this 'purge'
continued into the late 1930s and grew increasingly violent. Some
Uzbek film-makers, as well as their non-Uzbek compatriots, were
repressed.[13]

Nationalist Cinematographic Expressions (1931–6)
In this context Suleiman Khodjaev and Nabi Ganiev began their
careers as film-makers. Ganiev's early productions tackle the

contemporary theme of the nascent Uzbek proletariat and the construction of Soviet Uzbekistan (e.g. *The Rise*, 1931), or support the Soviet anti-religious campaigns. However, the filmic discourse against Muslim fasting conveyed by a film such as *Ramazan* (1933) was particularly ambiguous because the director constantly uses stories within the story. The cinematographic and narrative constructions subvert what should have been a clear propaganda film, which should convey a simple message that could be instantly and clearly understood by the audience. Instead, many characters in the film have dual identities (a positive and a negative one) that blur the emergence of a positive hero who could serve as a model for socialist behaviour. Another example of such ambiguity was *Djigit* (1935), an Uzbek version of the famous Russian film *Chapaev* (1934) by the Vasiliev 'Brothers'. The Uzbek film-maker completely ignored the political message embedded in this classical film: the leading role of the Party was totally overlooked, and Ganiev was much more inspired by the formal and narrative aspects of *Chapaev* as well as some exotic ideas of earlier Uzbek-made films.[14]

Khodjaev's cinematic language was quite different, and his only feature film *Before Dawn* (1933) can be qualified as 'nationalist' and 'militant' because of its treatment of the anti-colonial uprising of 1916 against military conscription in Central Asia, thus trying to give birth to a founder-myth of the Uzbek nation.[15] Moreover, Khodjaev relied on archival and press sources for the script, which therefore conveys a sense of authenticity to an event that is largely seen as 'the earthquake that swung Turkestan into the twentieth century'.

The revolts in Central Asia were of particular interest for the new generation of Soviet historians, who considered them as anti-colonial and spontaneous events that played a decisive role in the awakening of the people's consciousness of their exploitation through the Tsarist regime and the bourgeoisie. Thus, they ascertained a psychological and historical predisposition and a symbolic link with the October Revolution and the victory of the proletariat. But on the other hand, the reference to these revolts enabled Central Asian artists, such as Khodjaev, to interpret the uprising as the birth of a nationalist consciousness and show it as the starting point of the struggle for national liberation, when official historians tried to interpret them merely in terms of class struggle.

The film depicts the revolts and their repression by the Tsarist army, conveying strong anti-Russian feelings with an emphasis on the violence, domination, oppression and segregation – the kind of discourse that was still possible in the early 1930s, when Soviet historiography allowed the denunciation of the Russian Empire and its policy under the influence of the eminent Marxist historian Mikhail Pokrovsky (1868–1932). Several scenes, as well as onscreen intertitles, showed violence. One of them, which did not appear in the final cut but in the published script, was taken from the Central Archives – a military order to the chief of the punitive expedition:

> I propose to you to show the native vermin all the craziness of the revolt, not to allow them to go back home for the night, to leave them without any food supply and to let them starve – from the steppes to the mountains. I require from the Regiment's chief calm and resoluteness, and I categorically order to inculcate in the soldiers the belief that the sole of one old Russian boot is more worthy than the lives of thousand indigenous bastards [*svolochi*].[16]

This was a clear allegation against the imperial power of using famine as a weapon. The scenes that followed this intertitle symbolized this brutality: an imperial soldier targets a 'Sart chicken'[17] (a black small chicken), but – using the subjective camera angle – targets in fact the spectator. But instead of killing the animal, the soldier shoots a young orphan, who had lost his mother in the assault. The film-maker frequently uses subjective camera positions to emphasize violence and to encourage the spectator's identification with the main character.

Finally, in an act of 'cinematographic martyrdom', Khodjaev, who played a leading role in the film (he symbolizes the revolutionary and proletarian fraternity between Uzbeks and Russians as he prepares an uprising against the local bourgeoisie with a Russian worker) appeared himself dying on screen. This was a prophetic scene, since he was sentenced to death during the Red Terror of 1937, but it also symbolizes the sacrifice of the first local Communist elites who had believed in the Revolution. Moreover, his screen presence allowed an updating of the filmic discourse and its 'translation' into the realities of 1933–4, denouncing Soviet domination. Trying to ascertain the true intention of the film-maker, one might refer to what Edward Allworth considered one of the basic 'creative rules' in Uzbek culture at that time: to avoid the representation of violent anti-Russian feelings.[18] Khodjaev did not play 'the game' any more. In a certain branch of Central Asian literature, which Khodjaev knew, dissimulation was a way out for writers trying to 'evade reality' while suggesting it.[19] The emphasis on violence is particularly indecorous, especially considering that the contemporary audience had experienced traumatic events since 1915, including famine, civil war, the uprising of 1916, but also the pangs of collectivization and the political repression of the 1930s. Even if it is hard to assess whether the film represents an act of resistance, it is possible to read it as a proof of complete disillusionment with Bolshevik ideology, and a final statement on a specific, autonomous cultural path of Uzbekistan within the Soviet Union. In a sense, the film-maker appropriated the discourse of class struggle, but for nationalist purposes.

Before Dawn was completed at a time when the historical perception of the Russian Empire was changing: the Russian imperial past was re-evaluated positively, and the film was censured. Khodjaev was arrested in 1934 and accused of nationalism. His arrest was the result of a denunciation, alleging that he would have preferred Stalin to perish instead of Sergei Kirov (who was murdered in December 1934). Khodjaev was shot in 1937 in a camp near Tashkent.

Conclusion: Towards National Dispossession (1937–40)

After the disappearance of these two Uzbek film-makers – Ganiev was imprisoned in 1937 for two years, but continued film-making after World War II – a new period began with the first Uzbek sound film, *The Oath* by Alexander Usoltsev-Garf (1937). Shooting started in 1934, but was hampered by many delays, including the destruction of new sound equipment in a fire (an 'accident', according to the press). The action of the film takes place in 1926, and thus offers a retrospective assessment of the Soviet construction project in Uzbekistan. In the film Uzbeks participated only as actors (the 'national form'), while the crew (director, scriptwriter) were Russian. The story itself illustrates the victory of Bolshevism shown as an ideology of salvation (the 'socialist content'). This ideology was embodied by the main character, a Russian Bolshevik – a figure added by the director to the draft of the first script written by an Uzbek novelist[20] – 'rescues' Uzbek society by implementing Soviet policies and land reforms. *The Oath*, released in Uzbekistan in July 1937, turned out to be a roaring success at a time when massive waves of arrests began. A few months later, key intellectuals were repressed. After 1937, Uzbek film-makers did not make any films before the outbreak of World War II, while Russian directors made two: *Azamat*

(1939) by Arnold Kordium and *Asal* (1940) by Mikhail Yegorov and Boris Kazachkov.

After the dramatic events of the late 1930s and the development of Soviet national cultures, what really remained of the national imagination that had taken shape in the 1920s and the early 1930s? If we consider that the Soviet Union restored its Russian imperial past and largely destroyed the idea of self-determination at the end of the 1930s, could 'national' really exist within this regime on the eve of World War II? Could 'national' only be a form, as in *The Oath*? Certainly not at this particular moment.

However, in the long term *The Oath* and other films participated in Soviet 'ethnophilia' and consolidated an intertwined ethnic and national identity with a strong idea of a Soviet supra-national citizenship, especially after the mobilization for the war. During the period under discussion, the image of the Orient as conveyed in films shifted from a 'stylized Orient', imaginary and exotic as in *The Minaret of Death* or *The Muslim Woman*, to a more precise 'cinematographic ethnoscape'.[21] The idea of Uzbek ethnicity had been mainly revealed as early as 1928 with the first sound experience, and consequently language, in *Jackals of Ravat*, for which the ethno-musicologist Viktor

Figure 2.2 Still from *Alisher Navoi* (1947) by Kamil Yarmatov.

Uspensky wrote the score, collected and 'saved' Uzbek songs which were being 'bastardized' by 'foreign elements'.[22]

But the positive and attributive definition of 'Uzbekness' had given way to the intensification of the notion of 'otherness' (i.e. 'Tajikness'). For instance, just after the war, in the film *Alisher Navoi* (1947) by Kamil Yarmatov the reference to the Chaghatay language (equivalent to 'ancient Uzbek') was presented as the basis for national identity, but this time firmly directed against the Persian language (Tajik).[23] Two poets, Navoi and Jami, argue over the best language for poetry. Navoi, as a spokesman of the Turkic language (Chaghatay), asserts that the 'language of the mother' (Uzbek) was a popular one and could therefore unify 'the people and the earth'. Navoi continued, 'a people will be able to understand its destiny, when its language will be mature. Language unifies people and unifies forces'. The 1950s and 1960s were a period when the most important biographical films were produced; they offered the audience a retrospective proof of the ethnic ancestors of the 'nation'. *Alisher Navoi*, as a part of a large propaganda system along with education at schools, literature, music and so on, revealed the search for 'rediscovering' and 'authenticating' pre-existing collective myths, symbols, and traditions. At first glance, the message in the film praised Uzbekness and Uzbek language. However, Yarmatov was also the founding father of Tajik cinema. Admiring Navoi, Yarmatov could not disassociate his significance from other Persian poets, such as Ferdowsi and Hafez, and thus reaffirmed the common Turko-Persian cultural heritage.[24] In this sense, artists reinvested the national imagination by form and content, and could oppose through their creations the formative Soviet national policies that urged for a rigid (and impossible) convergence of state, territory, ethnicity and language.

Notes

1   Mette Hjort, Scott MacKenzie, 'Introduction', *Cinema and Nation* (New York, 2000), p. 4.
2   Volkov attributes the term 'gear and screw' as used by Stalin to Lenin's 1905 article 'Party Organization and Party Literature'; see Solomon Volkov, *Shostakovich and Stalin* (London, 2004), p. 59. [Editors' note].
3   Uzbek Central National State Archive (f. 20, op. 1, d. 547, pp. 23–4). Report on Bukhkino, September 1924. After the ethno-territorial delimitation the Soviet People's Republic of Bukhara and Khiva were included in the Uzbek SSR.
4   'Uzbekistonda kinokartinkachilik boshlanghichi' ['The beginning of the film production in Uzbekistan'], *Yer Yuzi* 6 (5 March 1926): 12.

5   E. Kaufman, 'Nashi kino-fil'my za granitsei', *Vecherniaia Moskva*, 1 June 1928.

6   Uz RMDA 95/1/625 p. 13: report of the People's Commissariat of Workers' and Peasants' Inspection (NK RKI) on cinematographic activity in Uzbekistan [no date; mid-1926].

7   See, for example, David Henry Slavin, *Colonial Cinema and Imperial France, 1919–1939: White Blind Spots, Male Fantasies, Settler Myths* (Baltimore, 2001); Abdelkader Benali, *Le Cinéma colonial du Maghreb* (Paris, 1998).

8   Cloé Drieu, 'Cinema, Local Power and the Central State: Agencies in Early anti-religious propaganda in Uzbekistan', *Die Welt des Islams* 50 (2010): 532–58.

9   Abdullah Qodiri, 'Ravat qashqirlari' ['Ravat's Jackals'], *Qyzyl Uzbekiston*, 28 April 1927.

10   Gosfilmofond 1/2/1: 1050 ('Ravat's Jackals'), Protocol No. 1830, 11 February 1927.

11   'Châchvân', *Yer Yuzi*, 27 October 1927: 12; 'Ob otvetrabotnikakh, divane, kartine "Chachvan" i kinoprokate', *Pravda Vostoka*, 14 December 1927: 2; Shirbek, 'Châchvân kartinkasi toghrisidâ', *Qizil Uzbekiston*, 31 October 1927: 3; Skniga, 'Chadra', *Komsomolets Vostoka*, 21 August 1928.

12   The *chachvon* is a veil made from horse hair, and the *paranji* is a tunic worn over the woman's head and covering her body.

13   See, for the Soviet Union, Jamie Miller, 'The purges of Soviet cinema', *Studies in Russian and Soviet Cinema* 1.1 (2007): 5–26; Miller, *Soviet Cinema: Politics and Persuasion under Stalin*, London, 2010), pp. 71–90.

14   For a more detailed portrait of Ganiev, see Cloé Drieu, 'Nabi Ganiev, cinéaste ouzbek sous Staline: l'idéologie à l'épreuve de la diffraction nationale', *Dissidences* 9 (2010). Available online at www.dissidences.net/complements _vol9.htm (last accessed 18 November 2010).

15   See also Cloé Drieu, 'Interdit aux Sartes, aux chiens et aux soldats: la Russie coloniale dans le film *Tong Oldidan* de Suleyman Khodzhaev, Uzbekfilm, 1933', *Cahiers d'Asie centrale* 17/18 (2010): 509–39. Available online at http://asi ecentrale.revues.org/index1302.html (last accessed 18 November 2010).

16   Suleiman Khodzhaev, *Tong Oldidan* (*Pered rassvetom*) (Moscow, 1933), p. 61.

17   The term 'Sart' indicates the sedentary population of Central Asia. During the early years of Soviet power, this term was considered pejorative. 'Uzbek' then was preferred.

18   Edward Allworth, *Uzbek Literary Politics* (London, 1964), pp. 62–3.

19   Khodjaev was a close friend of Abdullah Qodiri and worked for the theatre troupe Turan before the Revolution.

20   The film-maker recognized that the intrusion of the Russian Bolshevik in the script was particularly difficult: in this respect, he mentioned that the final version was accepted 'with the bayonet'; Usoltsev-Garf, 'Kak sozdalas' *Kliatva*', *Pravda Vostoka*, 15 July 1937.

21   Anthony Smith, 'Images of the Nation', in Hjort and MacKenzie, p. 55. His concept of 'ethnoscape' differs from that proposed by Arjun Appadurai, *Après le colonialisme: Les conséquences culturelles de la globalisation* (Paris, 2005).

22   Viktor Uspensky wrote also the score for *Djigit*.

23   See also Cloé Drieu, 'Alisher Navoi: prix Staline 1948. Cinéma et politique des nationalités,' in Kristian Feigelson, ed., 'Caméra politique: cinéma et stalinisme', *Théorème* 8 (Paris, 2005), pp. 119–27.

24   Kamil Iarmatov, *Vozvrashchenie* (Tashkent, 1987), p. 161.

3

THE VARIOUS BIRTHS OF KAZAKH CINEMA

Bauyrzhan Nogerbek

O n 12 September 1941, shortly after the outbreak of World War
II, the Council of People's Commissars (Sovnarkom) resolved
to establish a national film studio in Alma-Ata. Previously, there had
been a newsreel studio there, founded in 1935 on the basis of the
Soyuzkinokhronika Trust that had been operating in Kazakhstan
since 1933, producing a special programme titled *Soviet Kazakhstan*
as well as supplying footage for the all-Union editions of the weekly
news programmes.[1] However, the Sovnarkom Resolution 'On the
organization of a Kazakh film studio in Alma-Ata' primarily reflected
the interests of one of the studios evacuated to Kazakhstan: the
Leningrad Film Studio, Lenfilm. The goals of this resolution were
first 'to accept the proposal of the Committee for Cinematography at
the Council of People's Commissars of the USSR on the organization
of a studio at Alma-Ata'; and second, 'to temporarily accommodate
the evacuated Leningrad Film Studio on the base of the Alma-Ata
Studio'.[2] The subsequent paragraphs proposed immediate solutions
to issues of Lenfilm's production and accommodation. Mosfilm and
other cinema organizations, such as the Central Newsreel Studios,
were also evacuated to Kazakhstan. Finally, two months later, on 15
November 1941, the evacuated studios formed the Central United
Film Studio, or TsOKS (*Tsentral'naia ob"edinennaia kinostudiia*). Thus,

the Alma-Ata Film Studio practically began its activity as part of TsOKS, and its first steps were directly related to the evacuated studios.

The Bolshevik Party and the Soviet government quickly realized the importance of ideological education in the spirit of communism and took significant steps in the development of a film distribution network in Kazakhstan. From the 1920s onwards, documentary chronicles were filmed in Kazakhstan, showing the hardship of the steppe people, their savage lifestyle and their illiteracy. The thesis was always the same: only the Great October Revolution and the Bolshevik Party brought culture, education and freedom from colonial oppression to the steppe. Most of the 'scenes of everyday life' were staged. Indeed, today it is easy to spot the cameraman on screen in these scenes of Kazakh nomadic life.

Efforts to produce films in Kazakhstan were made in the 1930s, when official newsreels entitled *The Latest News* [*Poslednie izvestiia*] were released. These were filmed by Russian film-makers from Moscow. The purpose of the newsreels was to promulgate the socialist transformation of the steppe. The political reality remained outside the perspective of these documentary chroniclers: the bloody Red Terror, or Goloshchekin's 'Little October',[3] which caused a famine that killed millions of Kazakhs, reducing the population by half; and repeated waves of repression, depleting the intelligentsia. Documentary cinema was indeed politically engaged.

Realizing the importance of mythologizing history, Soviet ideologues attached great importance to making films about Bolshevik revolutionaries, Red commanders, and those defending the ideals of the Revolution. After the success of *Chapaev*, film-makers were called upon to create films about national heroes – local Chapaevs – in the republics: the Ukrainian *Shchors*, the Bashkir *Salawat Yulayev*, and the Kazakh *Amangeldy*.[4] At various levels of social and individual consciousness, the total politicization of all spheres of Soviet man extended from the personal-familial to collective-industrial to spiritual-national and ethno-cultural interests. For the sake of political and ideological demands of the Stalin era, and contrary to the facts, the films made in the Union republics by film-makers from Moscow and Leningrad were declared in the media as 'the first-borns of national cinema', so that the average viewer's interest in ethno-cultural issues would be satisfied. Such 'firsts' usually portrayed historical-revolutionary topics.

The most pervasive cinematic myth of the birth of Kazakh cinema was *Amangeldy*, produced by Lenfilm with the assistance of Kazakh writers and artists. Assertions that *Amangeldy* was 'the first Kazakh film' originated with its screen premiere, but were prepared by the media in advance. From 1931 onward, the Kazakh press had lamented that 'Kazakhstan does not have its own cinema',[5] and implored, 'Let's make Kazakh films like *Chapaev*'.[6] By 1937, the assessment of the future of national cinema became even more defined, using the term, 'first': 'The film about Amangeldy is the first feature-length film on Kazakh life and continues the tradition of Soviet cinematic masterpieces such as *Chapaev* and *We are from Kronstadt.*'[7]

The perception that *Amangeldy* was the first Kazakh feature film was rigidly re-enforced through the following decades, right up until 1980, when a Kazakh publishing house released the book *Amangeldy: The Firstborn of Kazakh Cinema* to mark the fortieth anniversary of the first Kazakh sound film on a revolutionary theme.[8] Without doubt, the myth of *Amangeldy* as the debut of Kazakh cinema stemmed from the ideology and policies of a particular historical time. The modern film historian's distance allows us to see clearly that Lenfilm's *Amangeldy* was a political film, following the traditions of early Soviet agitation films, biopics of Bolshevik revolutionaries, and the work of the Vasiliev 'Brothers'. In a sense, *Amangeldy* intentionally replicated the ideologically motivated symbol of the national avenger: a natural rebel, who served the Revolution.

Amangeldy was produced in 1938 in response to an official request from state and Party. The Kazakh government appealed to the centre with a request for a film about the popular hero, Amangeldy Imanov, the leader of a national uprising in 1916. The regime was in dire need of myths, and the heroic biography of Amangeldy perfectly suited this purpose: the request was granted.

While the Soviet press described *Amangeldy* as the first feature film in Kazakh history, this view does not correspond to historical reality. Cinematic evidence from the 1920s and 1930s shows that plenty of documentary films were made by film-makers from Leningrad and Moscow on Kazakh material,[9] including the famous documentary *Turksib* (1929) by Viktor Turin for Vostokkino,[10] which – according to the film historian Georges Sadoul – 'enjoyed great success in the West and influenced the development of British documentary film'.[11]

Vostokkino's arm in Alma-Ata had been opened in 1929, principally to produce the newsreel *The Latest News*. The section

Figure 3.1 Poster for *Amangeldy* (1938), directed by Moisei Levin.

released two films on the Turksib (Turkestan-Siberian Railway) and
several short documentaries: *The Co-operative in the Village* [*Kooper-
atsiia v aule*], *The New Capital* [*Novaia stolitsa*], *First Anniversary of the
Kazakh ASSR* [*Godovshchina KASSR*], *Red Soldier* [*Kzyl Asker*] and *On
Summer Pasture* [*Na dzhailau*], and embarked on feature films in the
1930s.

To mark the tenth anniversary of the Kazakh Autonomous
Republic, Moscow's branch of Vostokkino released the film *The Song
of the Steppes* (1930). The film was commissioned by the state to
illuminate the significant changes in the social, economic, and
cultural life of the republic. It relates the story of a former hired
labourer (*batrak*) who becomes a statesman. In keeping with the
cinematic models of the time, the film showed the 'liberation of the
East'. It was intended as a documentary with elements of fiction, but
according to the film historian Kabysh Siranov, 'the image of Kazakh

workers, first shown on screen, turned out to be a failure'.[12] In the essay 'The Cinema of Kazakhstan', written for a four-volume history of Soviet cinema, Siranov only mentions the films *The Song of the Steppes* in connection with the scriptwriter Sabit Mukanov.[13]

The Song of the Steppes has not been preserved, and there are different possible reasons, including the versions of the destruction of the copies and its negatives during the Stalinist repression, as the film was associated with the Kazakh writer Beimbet Mailin who was purged in 1937 as an 'enemy of the people'. Siranov provides the following information on the lost film:

> It was the kind of film marked by the virtues and vices of cinematography at the time. The action in the films transcended the customary pavilion shots and portrayed the vast expanses of the republic as a component of the people's struggle. Wide-angle shots of the movement of vast human masses prevailed. The slow and detailed story about the fate of several characters gave way to the impetuous flow of historical events, which submerged individual people's fates.
>
> At that time Soviet cinematography employed an artistic technique where the wide-angle shot was substantially brighter than the blurred, fading and eventually disappearing faces. Such compositional laxity, a weak story line, and the absence of characters was justified with reference to the rules of the 'epic', and films were divided into those with characters and destinies, which were drawn carefully and lovingly against a pale historical background, and those where the historical events eclipsed the fates of individuals.
>
> The authors of *Song of the Steppes* tried to combine organically the general with the particular, history with individual fate, but they could not achieve this with all the force of the cinematic expression that we see in other films of the period.[14]

Vostokkino produced *The Freeze* (1931) and *The Secret of the Karatau* (1932), while Mosfilm made *Accursed Trails* (1935) based on ideologically relevant themes: 'the awakening of class consciousness among the Kazakh workers', 'the acquisition of the rich mineral resources of the Kazakh steppe', 'the difficulties of the collectivization of agriculture, of the insidious machinations of beys and kulaks, and of the selfless struggle of the poor for a new life'.[15] Despite the regular production of documentaries on Kazakh material, the birth of the national film industry was delayed for many years.[16]

In the autumn of 1941 the Alma-Ata Studio was absorbed into TsOKS and – although films were produced on Kazakh themes during the war – there was no separate independent national cinema production unit in the republic. The actual process of organizing Kazakh film production took off in 1944 after the dissolution of TsOKS, the departure of Mosfilm and Lenfilm, and the consolidation of the local newsreel studio and feature film studios into one complex in Alma-Ata, the studio that was later named Kazakhfilm.

Thus, Kazakh national cinema was 'born' periodically during the early Soviet period: it emerged *institutionally* in the form of various studios and trusts, and *creatively* in collaboration with Moscow and Leningrad film-makers during the 1920s and 1930s in documentary and fiction films. Soviet Party officials profited every time they reported to Moscow on the birth and success of Kazakh national cinema. This repeated 'birth' of Kazakh cinema is easily explained: the film industry, as well as public and private lives of Soviet people, was forcibly politicized in favour of socialist myths, legends, and revolutionary tales. For each anniversary, the formation of the national film studios was highlighted again. Thus the attempt to embellish Kazakh cinema history led to these 'multiple births'.

The recurring births of Kazakh cinema were also reflected in its own historiography as well as in Soviet film history. The critic Kabysh Siranov credited Turin's documentary *Turksib* to Kazakh cinema, while Russian and foreign film historians attributed it to Russian film history. According to Siranov's logic, if the feature film *Amangeldy* – about a Kazakh hero and made by Leningrad film-makers – was the first Kazakh feature film, then the documentary *Turksib* of the All-Russian joint-stock company Vostokkino and concerning socialist construction in Kazakhstan can also be attributed to the history of Kazakh cinema. The question arises about the exact time and title that marks the birth of Kazakh national cinema. Here, we must define the criteria for national film production.

The release of a film is connected to an entire production industry, including creative professionals as well as technical personnel, producers, managers, economists, lawyers, psychologists and others. Thus the definition of national cinema should include two essential components: a local base of film production and national cadres. From this angle, the history of national cinema takes a completely different shape than the ideologized reading of Kazakhstan's film history.

In the 1920s and 1930s, none of the above factors required for the development of a national cinema existed in Kazakhstan. In 1938, when *Amangeldy* was made, there was no film studio for feature films; there was no production base and no national cadres of film professionals. So talking about the birth of the Kazakh national cinema during this period is premature. Moreover, during those years artists and writers were subjected to repressions in connection with the intensification of the class struggle, and the film-makers grouped around the Vostokkino trust were no exception. The first Kazakh film staff – the dramatist and scriptwriter Beimbet Mailin and the poet and essayist Ilyas Dzhansugurov, head of the script department of Vostokkino – were executed as 'enemies of the people' even before the first Kazakh feature appeared on the screens.

The Alma-Ata Newsreel Studio continued to shoot enthusiastic images of the 'victory of socialism' on the Kazakh steppe against the backdrop of bloody terror, mass hunger and poverty, which killed half the population of Kazakhstan. Despite the forced collectivization, the Soviet State machine continued to arrange festivals of literature and art and develop national culture. Facing a skilful campaign of deception, rejoicing at the successes in building socialism, it is quite natural that people eagerly received *Amangeldy* as the first Kazakh feature film, albeit created by Russians. This emphasis has distorted the image of the emergence and development of Kazakhstan's national cinema.

In the 1960s Siranov suggested the following periodization of Kazakh cinema: in the first phase (1928–37) Kazakhstan did not have its own film industry, yet the central studios created *Mutiny* (1928), *Turksib, The Song of the Steppes, The Freeze,* and *Accursed Trails* – all based on Kazakh themes. These films accelerated the birth of Kazakh national cinema and laid its foundation. In the second phase (1938–45), a technical base was formed and the first films made with the effective assistance of Russian film-makers: *Amangeldy, Raihan* (1940), and *Songs of Abai* (1945). Prominent Russian luminaries took an active part in the creation of Kazakh cinema and the formation of professionals; this period could be called the period of technical and creative training. The third phase (1946–52) was a time of stagnation: in seven years only two feature films were released, *Golden Horn* (1948) and *Dzhambul* (1952). In ideological and artistic terms the films were much weaker than those of the previous period. The sharp decline in feature film production in Kazakhstan was closely linked with the period known as film famine (*malokartin'e*) in Soviet cinema. It was not until the fourth phase (1953–66) that creativity returned to Kazakh cinema with Shaken Aimanov's *Poem about Love* (1954), followed by two films released in 1954, *The Daughter of the Steppe* and *The Djigit Girl*. But the most intensive and fruitful work of cinematography in Kazakhstan began after the historic Twentieth Party Congress in 1956.[17]

However, this system lacks objectivity, because Siranov does not take into account such critical factors as the national staff and the technical base, which leads to methodological confusion and ambiguity. He shifts the emphasis away from production and towards staff, whilst neglecting documentary films altogether. It would appear that Siranov surrendered to the dominant official narratives of the time, since the comparison of films made by Lenfilm (*Amangeldy, Raihan*) and by the Alma-Ata Studio (*Songs of Abai*) is methodologically flawed. Objectively, it would be more correct to start Kazakh film history with *Songs of Abai* – a film created by Russian cinematographers but at the Alma-Ata Studio, on the basis of a Kazakh story and with Kazakh actors.

On the other hand, *Amangeldy* should be placed alongside *Mutiny, Song of the Steppes, The Freeze, The Secret of Karatau* and *Raihan*, created by Russian film-makers with the assistance of Kazakh artists, literary consultants and screenwriters, but at a time when there was no professional base of directors and cameramen in Alma-Ata. Therefore, in these early films, we can only talk about the pre-history of Kazakh cinema through contacts and cooperation between Kazakh and Russian film-makers. Noting the greater role of Russian cinema in the formation of Kazakh national cinema, Shaken Aimanov suggests three stages of the development of film art: the creation of chronicles; the production of films based on Kazakh material; and the third, marked by *Poem about Love*:

> The great masters, Grigori Roshal, Yefim Dzigan, Mikhail Levin, Pavel Bogoliubov, and Yefim Aron came to our help. Yefim Yefimovich Aron forever linked his creative life with Kazakhstan. Regardless of our boundless gratitude for their support, these occasional performances do not define the true birth of national cinematography. It is difficult for visitors to penetrate our national character, and especially to register the remarkable changes that occurred during this rapidly passing time. Visitors are unwittingly enthralled by the picturesque exoticism of steppe life. Even the best films of

that time suffered from a certain superficiality... In cinema, the first swallow makes spring.

Therefore, in 1953, director Karl Gakkel and I inaugurated an important stage with *Poem about Love*. Frankly, it was a weak film, and not quite a film, but a film-play based on *Kozy-Korpesh and Baian-Sulu* by Gabit Musrepov. Nevertheless, it was our third birth, because we created it with our own energy. This was the beginning of national cinema.[18]

Aimanov advanced the idea of a third birth of Kazakh cinema, intuitively sensing the incompleteness, vulnerability, and scholarly bias of the proposition that *Amangeldy* is the first Kazakh film. The true birth of the Kazakh cinema had less to do with drama, themes and content than with the professionalization of film directing. And here we must agree with Aimanov. In the modern cinematic process, directing alone determines the authorship of the film, and he was the first Kazakh director.[19]

In the historiography of Soviet cinema there has been a trend to diminish and disregard human resources and technical foundations. At the forefront of cinematographic evaluation was the question of revolutionary and political relevance: *Mutiny*, relating the struggle against *basmachi* and *Amangeldy*, the 'Kazakh *Chapaev*', were chosen as ideological examples. The official policy intentionally blurred and merged the multifaceted, multilingual cultures of the Russian Empire into a single, monolithic Soviet art governed by principles of *narodnost* (nationality) and *partiinost* (party-mindedness).

Siranov adhered strictly to the traditional thematic approach in the canonization of *Mutiny*: first, the feature film was shot on revolutionary material in Kazakhstan, and second, Russian film-makers contributed to the birth of Kazakh cinema. Certainly, in the context of Siranov's principle, *Amangeldy* could also give the illusion of the birth of Kazakh national film. In addition to the revolutionary themes, the national cadres of playwrights (Gabit Musrepov, Beimbet Mailin), composer (Akhmet Zhubanov) and actors (Yeliubai Umurzakov, Sholpan Dzhandarbekova, Serke Kozhamkulov) played a key role in the film's creation. But there was no technical base, which is the fundamental link with the Alma-Ata Studio, a link fulfilled in *Songs of Abai*. Yet *Poem about Love* seems the most acceptable candidate for the first Kazakh film, organically combining all three factors: cinematic theme, material and technical base, as well as the film crew. Thus, 'the first-born'

Figure 3.2 Poster for *Poem about Love* (1954), directed by Shaken Aimanov.

of Kazakh national cinema follows this system of classification and chronology:

(1) Theme – *Mutiny* [1928];
(2) Theme and partial crew – *Amangeldy* [1938];
(3) Theme, base and partial crew – *Songs of Abai* [1945];
(4) Theme, base complete crew – *Poem about Love* [1954].

In this system the source and origin of the theme, the production base, the crew and most importantly the director serve as main factors for the definition of national cinema. Based on this system, the birth of Kazakh national cinema excludes the works of Russian film-makers: *Mutiny, Turksib, Song of the Steppes, Amangeldy,* or *Songs of Abai,* and selects the modest directorial debut of Shaken Aimanov in *Poem about Love* as the beginning of Kazakh cinema.

This 'rejuvenation' of Kazakh cinema, setting its birth in 1953 rather than 1938 or 1928, changes the perspective on its history and periodization. The history of feature film production can be divided into four major parts. First, the late 1940s and early 1950s, see the formation of the production base at the Alma-Ata Film Studio after the disbanding of TsOKS; this was a time of the active involvement of Kazakh intellectuals in cinema, which resulted in *Songs of Abai, Golden Horn, Dzhambul, Poem about Love* and *Daughter of the Steppes* Second, in the late 1950s, the founders of the Kazakh national cinema Shaken Aimanov, Mazhit Begalin and Sultan Khodjikov brought directorial leadership to feature-length and documentary films. Third, the 1960s and 1970s saw the development of Kazakh national cinema and the peak of creativity of Aimanov, Begalin, Khodjikov, as well as Abdulla Karsakbaev, alongside a shift to non-totalitarian cinema. Fourth, the late 1980s and 1990s marked the collapse of the Soviet Union and the emergence of Kazakh sovereignty, which brought about the birth of a new young cinema, the Kazakh 'New Wave' of Ardak Amirkulov, Serik Aprymov, Amir Karakulov, Abai Karpykov, Rashid Nugmanov, Darejan Omirbaev and Talgat Temenov; the heyday of directors from the so-called 'middle' generation, including Satybaldy Narymbetov, Kalykbek Salykov, Bolat Sharipov and Ermek Shinarbaev led to the birth of 'producer's' cinema.

Thanks to TsOKS, Alma-Ata became the centre of Soviet cinema for a few years, producing 80 per cent of Soviet films during the war. Directors Sergei Eisenstein, Vsevolod Pudovkin, Leonid Trauberg, Grigori Kozintsev, Dziga Vertov, the Vasiliev 'Brothers', Ivan Pyriev, Yuli Raizman, Grigori Roshal, Alexander Ptushko, Yakov Poselsky and Esfir Shub worked at the joint studio. A talented array of cameramen assisted them: Eduard Tisse, Andrei Moskvin, Anatoli Golovnia, Leonid Kosmatov, Boris Volchek, Alexander Galperin and Boris Gorbachev. Actors, such as Boris Babochkin, Boris Chirkov, Nikolai Cherkasov, Mikhail Zharov, Vera Maretskaya, Vasili Vanin, Nikolai Kriuchkov, Marina Ladynina, and Pavel Kadochnikov joined them as well. And set designers Grigori Shpigel, Yevgeni Yenei and Nikolai Suvorov participated in the wartime film effort. In total, about 3,000 film professionals were evacuated to Alma-Ata:

The teachers of the first Kazakh film-makers were Eisenstein, Pudovkin, Kozintsev and Trauberg, Ermler, Roshal and Stroeva, Shklovsky, Shub. Around the Central Studio and Script Studio, then located in Alma-Ata, Kazakh writers congregated. The work of Auezov, Tazhibaev, Musrepov, Mukanov, and other prominent writers was inseparable from the history of cinematography in Kazakhstan, not only in the sense that they acted as script writers and that their works were portrayed. Not all the Kazakh writers were scriptwriters, but of course they all helped create the intellectual atmosphere in which the labour of the artist bears fruit.[20]

It is also worth mentioning that in those war years, VGIK was also evacuated to Alma-Ata. It occupied two large buildings and included a scriptwriting workshop run by the top writers and dramatists of Soviet cinema, such as Mikhail Bleiman, Sergei Yermolinsky, Boris Chirkov, Alexei Kapler, Manuel Bolshintsov, Nikolai Erdman, Mikhail Volpin, Iosif Prut, Nikolai Kovarsky and Mikhail Papava and others. During World War II, the capital of Kazakhstan became a virtual Mecca of multinational Soviet cinema, and it gave a new impetus to the development of Kazakh themes in the work of Russian film-makers. Literary scripts and outstanding screenwriting formed the basis of TsOKS films as well as Kazakh national cinema. TsOKS provided the technical foundation for the Alma-Ata Film Studio, which began to operate independently after the departure of Lenfilm and Mosfilm in 1944. Moreover, the presence of TsOKS drew the writer Mukhtar Auezov and the actor Shaken Aimanov from literature and theatre to the new medium of film, preparing the ground for their later contribution as founders of Kazakh national cinema.

Translated by Michael Rouland and Birgit Beumers

Notes

1   Kabysh Siranov, 'Nachalo bol'shogo puti', *Ocherki istorii kazakhskogo kino* (Alma-Ata, 1980), pp. 47–9.
2   Tamara Smailova, ed., *Kino Kazakhstana: kinospravochnik* (Almaty, 2000), p. 308.
3   Filipp Goloshchekin (1876–1941), revolutionary who was involved in the murder of the Romanovs in 1918; from 1924–33 First Secretary of the Communist Party in Kazakhstan, and in this role responsible for collectivization and the forced settlement of the nomads, leading to a famine (*asharshylyk*) that reduced the Kazakh population by almost a million. He also initiated the 'Little October' (1926–7), designed to reinforce the control of the centre and destroy small units of management.
4   Vasilii Chapaev (1887–1919), Red commander in World War I and the civil war; film by the Vasil'ev Brothers, 1934; Nikolai Shchors (1895–1919),

Ukrainian Red commander during the civil war; film by Alexander Dovzhenko, 1939; Salawat Yulayev (1754–1800), national hero of Bashkortostan; film by Iakov Protazanov, 1940; Amangeldy Imanov (1873–1919), leader of the popular uprising against tsarism in October 1916; fought for the establishment of Soviet rule in Kazakhstan. The film *Amangeldy* was released in January 1939.

5   N. Blagin, 'Kazakhstan eshche ne imeet svoei kinematografii', *Sovetskaia step'* (9 July 1931).

6   I. Kabulov, 'Sozdadim fil'my ravnye Chapaevu', *Kazakhstanskaia pravda* (17 February 1935).

7   Iurii Feliks, 'O kinop'ese Amangel'dy', *Kazakhstanskaia pravda* (29 April 1937).

8   Andrei Nazarov, ed., *Amangel'dy: Pervenets kazakhskogo kino* (Alma-Ata, 1980).

9   The Central State Archive of Film and Photo Documents and Records of the Republic of Kazakhstan holds documentaries dating from 1925. See *Kino letopis'*. Vyp. 1. TsGA KFDZ (Alma-Ata, 1988).

10 *Kino letopis'*. Archive No. 1417, p. 6.

11 Zhorzh Sadul' (Georges Sadoul), *Vseobshchaia istoriia kino*, vol. 4 (Moscow, 1982), p. 472.

12 Kabysh Siranov, *Kinoiskusstvo Sovetskogo Kazakhstana* (Alma-Ata, 1966), p. 43.

13 Kabysh Siranov, 'Kino Kazakhstana', *Istoriia sovetskogo kino, 1917–1967*, vol. 2 (1931–41) (Moscow, 1973), p. 485.

14 Kabysh Siranov, *Kazakhskoe Kinoiskusstvo* (Alma-Ata, 1958), pp. 5–6.

15 Siranov, *Kinoiskusstvo*, pp. 341–2.

16 In 1935, the Alma-Ata Newsreel Studio was established and the Soyuzkinokhronika division in Kazakhstan began to produce a special film magazine, *Soviet Kazakhstan*, while also filming documentaries for the All-Union film magazine: Kabysh Siranov, 'Nachalo bol'shogo puti', pp. 47–9.

17 Siranov, *Kinoiskusstvo*, pp. 325–6.

18 Mark Berkovich, *Kadry neokonchennoi lenty* (Alma-Ata, 1984), pp. 140–1.

19 Similarly, Tolomush Okeev's masterpiece *The Fierce One* is considered a Kyrgyz film, made by a Kyrgyz director – albeit on the basis of Kazakh literature (Mukhtar Auezov) and filmed at Kazakhfilm Studio.

20 Il'ia Vaisfel'd, *Zavtra i segodnia* (Moscow, 1968), p. 11.

PART II

CINEMA IN THE SOVIET REPUBLICS
OF CENTRAL ASIA

4

LANDSCAPE AND LOSS: WORLD WAR II IN CENTRAL ASIAN CINEMA

Stephen M. Norris

O n the eastern edge of Almaty's Panfilov Park stands an
impressive monument to World War II. Dedicated to the 28
soldiers of a Kazakh infantry company who died during the 1941
defence of Moscow, the memorial encapsulates the Soviet era
memory of the war as a black-and-white struggle between good and
evil. At the same time, Almaty's memorial and similar ones that dot
Central Asian landscapes represent a Moscow-centric version of
the war – what is significant here is that Kazakh soldiers fought for
the Soviet homeland, protecting mother Moscow from the fascist
invaders. For most Central Asians, the war is an event that has
meaning, but not necessarily in the way the monument captures it. If
we know little about Ivan's war – as Catherine Merridale asserts in
her remarkable study of the average Soviet soldier[1] – we know even
less about Ivan's Central Asian comrades and their families back
home. The monument in Almaty is suggestive, but it does not
capture the experiences of Central Asian citizens who lived during
the war and did not travel to its fronts.

A second Central Asian monument provides a different version
of the war's meaning. Built in 1982 as a centrepiece to Tashkent's

Friendship of Peoples Square, the statue dedicated to the blacksmith Shaahmed Shamahmudov memorializes one of the most popular stories of Uzbek participation in the Great Patriotic War. Shamahmudov and his wife worked in Tashkent during the war and adopted 15 orphans between 1941 and 1943. The orphans came from different Soviet republics and therefore the blacksmith's actions perfectly encapsulated both Uzbek ideas about hospitality and the Soviet version of ethnic relations. The Tashkent monument is unusual in that it provides a localized version of the war's importance and how the defence of the Soviet motherland had specific Tashkent connections.

These sites of memory narrate a story that Central Asian cinematic narratives about the war have also told. The connections between film, memory, Soviet culture and Central Asian forms of nationhood are deep. Central Asia contributed to the war effort in part by hosting the evacuated film studios from Moscow, particularly Mosfilm. Relocated to Alma-Ata, Soviet directors worked at the Central United Film Studios (TsOKS). Local film-makers and studio employees benefitted from working with the giants of Soviet cinema, among them Sergei Eisenstein and Fridrikh Ermler. These contacts gave birth to the Central Asian 'national' film traditions that began to appear and flourish during Khrushchev's Thaw.

Given the centrality of the war, its subsequent monumentalization across the Soviet Union, and the encounters with Soviet film-makers during the war, it is not surprising that Central Asian directors attempted to capture the conflict's significance in their work. In this cultural endeavour, Central Asian film-makers initially followed an already established, Moscow-centric narrative of the war.[2] *She Defends the Motherland* (1943) was filmed in Kazakhstan after Mosfilm evacuated there and presents the ongoing war as a defence of Russian civilization, establishing in the process a vision of war that stressed the role of the USSR's largest ethnic group, the Russians. Vasili Pronin's *Son of Tajikistan* (1942) was the only wartime film made in the Soviet Union that focused on a Central Asian soldier, but it too presented his story in a Moscow-centric narrative. In it, a young soldier named Gafiz rushes to the front to defend his socialist motherland. Along the way, he comes to view the foreign landscape in which he fights as 'his'. Although he has never seen the sea before, when he reaches it in battle he refers to it as 'my sea' and then 'our sea', taking possession of the Soviet landscape for himself and for all his Central Asian comrades. In this embrace of the Russian land,

Gafiz's experiences are similar to most of the monuments that inscribed the war's meaning in stone throughout Central Asia – the Kazakh soldiers in Panfilov Park also defended 'their' Soviet land.

Yet the visions of war memorialized in Pronin's film did not conform to the memories Central Asian film-makers wanted to portray in their works. The question facing these artists was an important one: how to capture the experience of a far-off war, however important it was, for domestic audiences? In other words, what would define a *Central Asian* World War II film and therefore the Central Asian experience of the war? In most cases, film-makers from the Thaw-era Uzbek director Shukhrat Abbasov to the post-Soviet Uzbek director Zulfikar Musakov have attempted to depict the losses at the front embodied in the Almaty monument. Yet they also have moved beyond the Soviet wartime narrative and focused on the landscapes of these losses by setting their films in Central Asian locales and delving into the social and cultural ramifications of wartime suffering at home. Here they did not accept Gafiz's view of what constituted the homeland. Instead, they focused on how the war impacted Central Asian localities, therefore cinematically exploring what the Tashkent monument expressed. While Central Asian landscapes were not visibly ruined like the Western parts of the USSR, Central Asian film-makers have posited that the war scarred the land internally, emotionally, and just as definitively as elsewhere in the Soviet Union.

The four films analysed here represent films from two important periods in Central Asian cinema and its war narratives: the era of the Thaw and the post-Soviet era. Both Shukhrat Abbasov's *You are Not an Orphan* and Shaken Aimanov's *Land of the Fathers* appeared in the 1960s, when cinema in Central Asia first enjoyed recognition throughout the USSR. That it did so in the midst of the cultural thaw unleashed by Nikita Khrushchev's 1956 secret speech provided significant political and social contexts to the appearance of films from Central Asia on Soviet screens. Usman Saparov's *Little Angel, Make Me Happy* and Zulfikar Musakov's *Motherland* hit cinemas after the collapse of the Soviet Union, when film-makers across the former Soviet landscape have used their films to articulate ideas about the past in radically changed political and cultural contexts. All four films, despite the different political contexts in which they appeared, represent the war as an experience that has shaped Central Asia's history. At the same time, the contexts in which each film appeared shaped the narratives they told: Thaw-era films stressed shared suffering among Soviet citizens and how Central Asians responded to the war while the post-Soviet films articulate specific national responses to the war and how Central Asian nations suffered under both Soviet and Nazi ideologies.

'This is Your House': The Soviet Wartime Experience as Uzbek Family Values

Shukhrat Abbasov's film *You are Not an Orphan* (1963) represents the first significant Central Asian war film and in many ways established the parameters for those that followed. Set in Tashkent, *You are Not an Orphan* follows the fortunes of the Mahkamov family, a fictionalized version of the Shamahmudov story. While their son Batyr is fighting at the front, the Mahkamovs have opened their home to the orphans of the war, providing shelter to 14 children who collectively represent an ethnic pastiche of Soviet nationalities. Among their 'children' are Vania, Kolia and Marina (all Russians); Renat (a Tatar boy); Liana (a Moldovan girl); Dzidre (a Baltic girl); Sarsenbei (a Kazakh boy); and Abram (a Jewish boy). The wartime Mahkamov house therefore symbolizes the 'brotherhood of peoples' the USSR represented, but with a Central Asian twist – Uzbek, instead of Russian, family values predominate.

You are Not an Orphan places the war within the landscape of urban Uzbekistan, where even in Tashkent the conflict takes its toll. Fatima, the mother, spends countless hours in line trying to obtain the food that her 'family' needs, just as she and her husband spend time counselling their children about what they have witnessed and experienced. The war as it is depicted in Abbasov's Uzbekistan is one dominated by work, shortages, and dislocation. Mahkamov is forced to spend long hours in his blacksmith's job in order to supply the front but also to earn enough to feed the orphans in his home. Fatima supervises the children's education and keeps the family together, an effort that sends her to a hospital after she faints from exhaustion. In Fatima's travels around Tashkent, she also sees the war as it appears in Uzbekistan: busy railroad stations taking soldiers to the front and depositing the wounded or refugees, posters extolling Soviet citizens to do everything for the war effort, and the emotional costs of the war in the form of death notifications. The fighting may be far away, but the war is still tangibly experienced in the homes of Tashkent.

The film's poignancy unfolds through the individual stories about the 14 orphans. When asked by a Russian woman if all of them

Figure 4.1 Still from Shukhrat Abbasov's *You are Not an Orphan* (1963).

had lost their parents, Renat replies in an all-too-worldly matter-of-factness that 'not all, but some like Abram saw the Germans shoot their parents. My Mom died, then they brought my father's death notification'. Other children, such as Dzidre, live in hope that her parents will reappear and reclaim her. The woman who asks Renat about the children's fate has come to Tashkent in hopes of finding her daughter named Dzidre, but when she sees the girl at the Mahkamovs, she realizes that it is 'not the right Dzidre'. In the most emotionally gripping scene, 'our Dzidre' rushes out of a film to meet her mother, only to encounter some other woman looking for another orphan by the same name. Dzidre's adopted sister can only conclude 'it's hard here – it's war'.

It is Abram's story that offers the most revolutionary aspect of Abbasov's cinematic narrative. Because the Soviet myth of the Great Patriotic War posited that its citizens all suffered equally, acknowledgement of Jewish suffering in the Holocaust was not widespread. Abram's story and his fears provide some sense of how Soviet Jews experienced the war: he has seen his family shot in front of him and he fears that his new family will meet the same fate. When the children are talking about the war instead of studying, Vania tells his adopted father that the fascists will shoot him if they arrive in Tashkent because he has taken Abram into his home. When asked how he arrived at this conclusion, Vania states 'fascists hate Jews'. Mahkamov assures Vania that the fascists 'don't have the guts' to get to Uzbekistan and that 'they hate everybody', but the scene adds incredible nuance to the monolithic Soviet myth of the war.

As the film ends, Batyr arrives home on crutches with another orphan, a German boy named Gustav. Abram immediately tries to avenge his parents and attacks the boy, calling him 'a damned fascist'. Gustav, frightened by the hostile reception, runs away. The Mahkamovs find him and reassure the boy that the other orphans do not mean harm but they 'have been through a great deal in their lives'. Gustav has also gone through a lot, and the Uzbek family welcomes him, stating that 'this is your house'. Just as their *mahalla*, or community, has fit the orphaned brotherhood of peoples within it, so too does it have room for one more, even a German.

'They All Died Together': Central Asian Soldiers and the Motherland

Three years after Abbasov's film appeared, Shaken Aimanov's *Land of the Fathers* furthered Central Asia's ideas about the war. Like its predecessor, the film explores the losses experienced by young and old: in this case, a Kazakh boy named Bayan and his grandfather, Aksakal. *Land of the Fathers* also dissolves the distance between the front and the Central Asian home, embedding the experience of the former within the landscape of the latter.

Bayan is also an orphan. The film opens with him explaining that 'it was the first summer after the war. My father had died near Leningrad. My grandfather decided to bury him in his native land. Before we set off, we made father a grave'. With this simple yet poignant beginning, the film connects a single loss in the war to the Kazakh land, where Bayan and Aksakal are digging a grave. The remainder of the film acts as a reversal of Grigori Chukhrai's masterpiece *Ballad of a Soldier* [*Ballada o soldate*, Mosfilm 1959], which follows a young Russian soldier's journey from the front to his home. Although Alesha (the soldier) makes it, we learn at the beginning of the film that he never returns home again and lies buried in an unmarked grave. If Alesha's journey dissolves the distance between home and front and vividly depicts the individual costs of war, so too does Bayan's journey, this time taking him from the home to the front and through the prism of the war's continued costs.

As the landscape of Kazakhstan unfolds from their train, Bayan and Aksakal encounter other people affected by the war. Vitali and his daughter-in-law Sofia are headed from Kazakhstan, where her husband died, back to Leningrad, where they resided before the war. Both Sofia and Vitali are academics and both specialize in Central Asian studies – she is an expert in Turkic languages, he is an archaeologist who studies ninth century Central Asian sites. The relationship between these believers in science and progress and the traditionalist Kazakh Aksakal, who values the land and its timelessness, drives their conversations and pits Bayan in the middle. For Vitali, national values are irrelevant, as 'there is no "your land, my land", for our land is a common, huge land'. Aksakal, on the other hand, insists that 'a person must know his land, the fire side, the camping ground, the house where he was born, where the bones of his ancestors are'. Much like *You are Not an Orphan* revises the idea of the 'friendship of peoples' to articulate a view that the traditional Uzbek *mahalla* can replace Russian culture as a means to organize different ethnicities, here the Kazakh idea of homeland serves as a means to connect Soviet citizens to older, pre-socialist ideas about history.

Land of the Fathers also acknowledges the extreme losses and suffering of other ethnic groups in the Soviet space. Aksakal encounters a Chechen stowaway on the train, a victim of Stalin's 1942 violent expulsion. The Chechen is headed back to his homeland and the conversation between two old Muslims is a revelation for Soviet cinema and revolutionary for what it acknowledges about religion and history during the war:

– Are you a Muslim?
– Yes, I am Chechen.
– Where are you riding?
– There, on the roof.
– Why travel like this? At your age you have to sleep on the floor.
– I am a highlander, used to living up high. The air is cleaner there. And it is closer to Allah. They took us on this road, for a long time. I remember – 20 days. 14 more days until we reach the Caucasus. Once I go through the city, no one will find me in the mountains.
– Why are you going there alone? All your people are here.
– I am getting old. It's about time to die. I would rather die in my motherland.

Figure 4.2 Poster for Shaken Aimanov's *Land of Our Fathers*.

In this character and in Aimanov's cinematic narrative, there is a space for losses that exceed even those of Bayan and Aksakal. The Chechen has not just lost his family, but also his homeland because of Stalin's wartime policies.

Bayan has been told that he will only become a man if he can return his father's body to their homeland, and it is Bayan who ultimately arrives in Nosakino, the tiny village where his father died. The beautiful Kazakh landscape has long since disappeared, replaced by the burned-out buildings and scarred Russian country-side that still dot the landscape a year after the war ended. Enduring taunts for being 'a gypsy', Bayan eventually meets and befriends a Russian boy, Vasili, who has also lost his father in the same battle.

Vasili takes Bayan to the mass grave that marks the death of 1,000 Soviet soldiers who fought at Nosakino and states simply that 'they all died together'. Bayan locates his family name, Mukhamedn, and places a Kazakh scarf below the monument for 'these holy people'. Ultimately, he decides not to bring his father's body home, allowing him to rest with his other comrades. In making this decision, Bayan does – like the Mahkamovs – bring a Central Asian stamp to the soldiers who died at the front. These two Thaw-era films, as Gulnara Abikeyeva has argued, used the family, mothers, and fathers as symbols of Central Asian national identities.[3] The Thaw not only witnessed the birth of a Kazakh national cinema and an Uzbek national cinema (as well as other Central Asian national cinemas), it also provided the context for Central Asian film-makers to revisit wartime narratives and to provide national myths and symbols out of them. The collapse of communism would provide a new generation of Central Asian film-makers with a renewed opportunity to redefine nationhood and locate it within specific symbols of the Central Asian landscape. Once again the war served as the means to accomplish this task.

'We Know No Other Way of Burying a Human Being': Germans, Turkmens and the War

Perhaps the most revolutionary reworking of the Soviet wartime narrative comes in Usman Saparov's film *Little Angel, Make Me Happy* (1992). Again the plot revolves around an orphan of the war, but this time it involves a German boy named Georg. His family, the Franks, are members of the German community who first settled in Turkmenistan in the late nineteenth century. The war has made them and their fellow Central Asian Germans into enemies and the film opens with Soviet policemen deporting the Franks and other families to Siberia. Georg and the German children are spared this violence and are to be raised in state orphanages that will instil 'proper' Soviet values.

Saparov spares few in his depiction of Soviet power and the xenophobia that war brings. He has stated in an interview with Gulnara Abikeyeva that he got the idea for the film in the early 1990s when Turkmenistan and its remaining German population experienced another wave of emigration, this time to Germany and Russia.[4] With these present conditions as a pretext, Saparov provides a vision of another wave of refugees that affected the Turkmen nation.

Georg resists the Soviet officials who want to take him to an orphanage and instead lives with his Aunt Lisa, who escaped the deportations because she is pregnant. Georg and his cousins wander about the deserted German village, trying to forage for food and abandoned by virtually everyone – by the Turkmens who live across the river, by his family, and by the Soviet state, which has created these harsh conditions. Throughout Georg's journeys into this nightmarish world the war and the Soviet government have created, he is taunted by Turkmen children who only mouth the words of hatred they hear around them: 'fascist spawn', 'vermin', '*Leberwurst*'. When Lisa gives birth, she attempts to feed her two children and Georg with her breast milk, for no other sustenance is to be found. Eventually Lisa dies from starvation and the children drag her body to the cemetery. Only there do they find help from their Turkmen neighbours.

One of Georg's best friends, Orazka, is equally caught in this cycle of ethnic hatred the war has unleashed. Ordered by his mother not to play with Georg, Orazka is commanded 'not to hang around those Germans'. Georg has gone from a playmate to an enemy, a Turkmen to a German, in a space of weeks. Eventually Orazka's family joins fellow Turkmens fleeing from these village wartime conditions. They pack up their yurt and other belongings and 'go to a Turkmen village'. Much like the Chechen in *Land of the Fathers*, both Georg and Orazka have lost family and their home to the war, a result of the ethnic particularism inherent in the Stalinist system.

Although Saparov does not spare the Turkmen residents from his vision of a village torn apart, he does offer redemption in the form of the village elder, Nepes-Aga. He has lost a son in the war, but Nepes-Aga helps Georg whenever he can, allowing the boy to participate in Turkmen prayers as a means to get food. When another wounded soldier who has disguised himself as Nepes-Aga's dead son is offended by the presence of the German at the prayers for Turkmen dead, the elder tells him 'you can't blame a child'. Even this help has its limits. When Nepes-Aga attempts to take Georg and other Germans to a Turkmen school and orphanage, he is refused and told that they are 'Germans' and there is no place for them. In this landscape of war, ethnicity ultimately defines everything.

Georg's losses are also the most severe. After his Aunt Lisa dies, his German friend Yashka contracts measles and dies from it, emaciated from the wartime depravations and unable to resist the disease. Again Georg has to witness the burial and the arguments over what to do with a dead German boy. When Yashka's body is wrapped in a sheet and a Soviet flag, the local Party chairman asks Nepes-Aga 'you are burying a German with such honours? Don't you understand the political implications?' The elder responds, 'we know no other way to bury a human being. He's an enemy? He's just a child.' The Soviet official has the last word: 'we'll see who's an enemy and who's a friend'. Even dead German boys, killed from the neglect of the Soviet wartime system, can bring political ramifications to anyone who helps them.

The opening and closing scenes bookend the radical narrative of the landscape and loss in *Little Angel, Make Me Happy*. The film opens with Georg and his fellow German-Turkmens signing a children's song in German, establishing the idea both visually and acoustically that this film will focus on the German experience of war and that the ubiquitous Nazi beasts of Soviet propaganda might have had innocent members who suffered in the war. The song spins a folkloric tale about 'little angels' that appear around Easter to bring gifts to children who have made nests for them. Throughout the film, Georg cares for a nest in a nearby tree and looks for the gifts the little angel will bring. The last scene, after Yashka's and Lisa's funerals, sees Georg again climbing up the tree, now completely alone and abandoned. He waits for an angel that will never come.

'Are You Jewish? No, I am Uzbek': Reframing Suffering in the War Film

Saparov's film appeared just after the breakup of the USSR and suggested that Soviet persecution defined the Turkmen experience as much as wartime suffering. Zulfikar Musakov's film *Motherland* (2006) carried this idea even further and presents a history where Uzbeks suffered more than anyone in the twentieth century for they were doubly victimized by Soviets and Nazis alike.

The film follows the story of two Uzbek boys, Hamid and Kurban, who grow up best friends, love the same girl, and go off to fight in the war together. Initially the history of the two boys is told romantically, at an Uzbek village largely untouched by Soviet power where boys chase girls and fight over them. Gunafsha, the object of desire, loves Kurban and professes her feelings for him just before the Soviet recruiters come for both boys. At the front Hamid loses an arm while Kurban is captured by Germans after heroic resistance where all his comrades perish. Kurban is taken to a concentration camp and has to endure sadistic German guards, starvation and a spiritual crisis. In the midst of this hell, Kurban copes because his sense of home, his Islamic faith, and his Uzbek identity sustain him. When German guards throw scraps of bread to the inmates, all but Kurban fight over them. A German SS guard asks Kurban: 'Are you Jewish?' He replies, 'No, I am Uzbek.'

Kurban's sufferings only increase after the war, when he is 'liberated' by Soviet soldiers. Because he has been captured, Kurban is an enemy in the eyes of the Stalinist state and he is sent to the Gulag. There he endures much of the same sadism and mistreatment that he had lived through under the Nazis. In this narrative, Kurban's experiences conform to Vasili Grossman's view that the two totalitarian states shared violent tendencies towards their enemies. In the Gulag, Kurban meets one sympathetic Russian guard who treats him like a human. While working one day, Kurban meets Gunafsha, who has been sent to the camps by Hamid, now an NKVD officer. The Russian guard allows the two to talk and both share their tales of suffering, one at the hands of Nazis and Soviets, the other at the hands of her own people (in this case, the spurned lover, Hamid). Gunafsha eventually dies in the camps, unable to reunite with her true love, Kurban. In these extremes, Kurban again displays his strong faith and sense of identity. When his abilities to survive draw the attention of his Russian guards, they ask him, 'Are you Jewish?' Again he replies, 'No, I am Uzbek.'

Kurban's wartime and postwar experiences encapsulate a new cinematic narrative of loss. If films such as *You are Not an Orphan* and *Little Angel, Make Me Happy* recognized the suffering of other groups at the hands of Nazis and Soviets, *Motherland* places Uzbek suffering above that of Jews and other outsiders in Central Asia. Musakov's film asserts a post-Soviet version of history that claims Central Asian suffering as a central aspect of the twentieth-century experience ('we' suffered at the hands of Nazis and Soviets alike) while also reclaiming Uzbek identity as the source of a renewed moral code ('we' survived because we remained true to our real culture). Kurban survives all the suffering because he remains faithful to his love of home, his love for a 'real' Uzbek woman, and his love for his own culture. 'I am Uzbek' becomes his response to the twin suffering, but also a reclamation of Uzbek values. By contrast, Hamid has lost his sense of Uzbek identity by becoming one of the victimizers. This choice powerfully illustrates the loss that permeates the film: Kurban loses his friend, his love, and eventually his homeland to the Soviet state and its violent practices.

Motherland operates on two temporal levels: the story of Kurban, Hamid and Gunafsha that revolves around the war; and the story of Kurban's return to Uzbekistan after communism's collapse. This second tale allows Musakov to focus on the contemporary landscape and issues of identity that Kurban must face. As the film opens, we see Kurban living in the United States, where he has sought refuge from the losses he endured during and after the war. His son is thoroughly Americanized but wants to visit his father's homeland. Kurban sneaks on the same plane with him, and the two engage in an ongoing dialogue about identity and home. Kurban, it emerges, does not want to see contemporary Tashkent but wants to confront Hamid, also alive and living back in their village. When the two former friends meet, Hamid asks for forgiveness but Kurban dismisses him, calling him 'a bastard'. Hamid may live in the physical landscape of Uzbekistan, but Kurban maintains a more authentic Uzbek identity.

Back in Tashkent after this encounter, Kurban's son asks him what his homeland means to him. Gazing out across the horizon, Kurban answers: 'the sky, the earth, the river, the field, and the past'. What Kurban has lost becomes here connected with the landscape around him – although Kurban has had to leave, he has preserved a vision of home that allowed him to survive the horrors of the previous century. On the return flight to New York, Kurban dies. When a passenger asks his son if the dead father and his son are Americans, the son replies: 'No, I am Uzbek.'

Conclusion: The Real War and the Reel War

The urban look of Tashkent. The mountains of Kazakhstan. The villages and rivers of Turkmenistan. The sky and earth in Uzbekistan. Each of the four films locates itself within the landscape of a Central Asian place and uses this locale to provide audiences with scenery that they too can recognize as familiar. In this respect, these films from Central Asia provide national flavours to their stories about the past, visually mapping out a landscape and marking it as a homeland with a history. Kurban's comment about what the motherland means to him may be the most explicit example of this cinematic mapping, but it is no different than the Mahkamov house, the stares of Bayan and Aksakal at the mountains of Kazakhstan, or the look of the Turkmen village inhabited by Georg and Orazka. One common feature of the Central Asian war film is what Simon Schama has argued is a vital means of articulating nationhood – inscribing landscapes with a mystique, particularly a historic one.[5]

Yet the importance of these wartime landscapes adds further mystique, for these landscapes are invested with loss, the losses of World War II. Each of these films personalizes the war in a manner that moves beyond the impersonal nature of Soviet war memorials. *You are Not an Orphan* is based on the true story of the Tashkent blacksmith Shaahmed Shamahmudov and his wife Bahri Akramova. While it provides an historical truthfulness, the film also frames itself in much larger terms that encompass all Uzbeks who lived, sheltered, fought, died, or lost someone in the war. The film proved so popular that it helped to contribute to the 1982 monument dedicated to the Tashkent blacksmith. Bayan's and Aksakal's journey from rural Kazakhstan to the Soviet heartland provides an equally personal story that connects the losses experienced by Kazakhs with the deaths at the front. *Land of the Fathers* invokes specifically Kazakh ways of understanding death and therefore provides comfort and a familiar culture to mourn for all Kazakhs who experienced wartime loss. The two post-Soviet films also provide a similar sense of familiarity. *Little Angel, Make Me Happy* fuses the losses both Germans and Turkmen experienced in the war with the losses both groups experienced after communism, when large numbers of the remaining Germans in Turkmenistan emigrated. Kurban's story provides the fitting end to the fusion of landscape and loss as a means of articulating nationhood – when his son claims he is Uzbek at the end, the audience knows what values, locales, and histories this claim represents. The landscapes of all four films are therefore invested with historical meaning, for it is the *mahalla*, the mountains, the village and the rivers that Uzbeks, Turkmens, Kazakhs, Germans and other Central Asians have died fighting for.

At the same time, the increasingly nationalist and anti-Russian narrative of twentieth-century suffering captured in Musakov's film has found increasing favour in contemporary Uzbekistan. Soviet versions of the war, particularly those articulated in Abbasov's film, are under fire from Islom Karimov's government. To drive the point home, Karimov and his city government officials renamed the Friendship of Peoples Square to Independence Square. The message was clear – Uzbekistan was free from Russian imperial ventures and free from Russo-centric (or Moscow-centric) narratives about Uzbekistan. To complete this new version of Uzbek identity, on 14 April 2008 the Tashkent municipal government removed the statue of Shamahmudov and his orphans.

Notes

1 Catherine Merridale, *Ivan's War: Life and Death in the Red Army, 1941–1945* (New York, 2006).
2 For a discussion of the war film, see Denise Youngblood, *Russian War Films: On the Cinema Front, 1914–2005* (Lawrence, 2006).
3 Gul'nara Abikeeva, *Natsiostroitel'stvo v Kazakhstane i drugikh stranakh Tsentral'noi Azii i kak etot protsess otrazhaetsia v kinematografe* (Almaty, 2006), esp. pp. 189–246.
4 Gulnara Abikeyeva, *The Heart of the World: Films from Central Asia* (Almaty, 2003), pp. 76–7.
5 Simon Schama, *Landscape and Memory* (New York, 1995).

5

FRAGMENTS FROM THE HISTORY OF TURKMEN CINEMA

Swetlana Slapke

Film is the communion of minds and peoples.

(Khodjakuli Narliev)

The first stage in the creation and development of Turkmen national cinema began in the mid-1920s and lasted until the late 1940s. It goes without saying this was the most difficult stage, because laying the foundations for cinema in a country where there were no national cadres, where there were no cinemas or even the profession of actor or director as such, not to mention a technical base, was no easy task. The first Turkmen documentary, *The Proclamation of the Turkmen Soviet Socialist Republic* [*Provozglashenie Turkmenskoi SSR*, 1925], was made by cameramen from the Leningrad Studio (Sevzapkino), Sergei Lebedev and Boris Bashem. A year later, the Ashkhabad Film Factory was created, later reorganized as Turkmenfilm Studio, which began by making documentary films, topical newsreels, and propaganda shorts with catchy agitational titles such as *For Elections to the Soviets* [*K perevyboram sovetov*] or *Celebrating the Tenth Anniversary of the October Revolution in Ashkhabad* [*Prazdnovanie 10-i godovshchiny Oktiabr'skoi revoliutsii v*

Ashkhabade]. These agit-films called on Muslim women to abandon the veil and fight for the eradication of illiteracy. Specialist agitators showed these films in the villages, accompanying them with educational lectures.

Propaganda and ideological tendentiousness remained important distinguishing features of the early works of Turkmen cinema, principally documentary films, in this early period. In 1929 Alexander Vladychuk directed the first feature-length documentary film, *White Gold* about collectivization in Turkmenistan and, a year later, Yuli Raizman shot the first feature film, *The Earth Thirsts*. During the 1930s various directors and cameramen began working in the studio: Vladimir A. Lavrov, Djavanshir Mamedov, Nikolai Mikhailovich Kopysov, Djuma Nepesov and Shadurdy Annaev laid the foundations of Turkmen documentary film-making.

A pivotal event in the history of Turkmen cinema in the 1930s was the first sound feature film, *I'll Be Back* (1935) by Alexander Ledashchev, a pupil of Vsevolod Pudovkin, based on Oraz Tachnazarov's epic drama, *Labourer* [*Batrak*] about the trials of a young labourer, Kurban. This gifted and well-meaning film made an indelible impression on the audience, mainly because it was the first feature film in their lives and about their lives. The film's release was arranged like a national holiday with organized columns of spectators and music from a military brass band.

In 1939, the Turkmenfilm studio was established; it was small but not bad for that period and it had the necessary equipment. The first film shot at the new studio was *Dursun* (1940) by Yevgeni Ivanov-Barkov. The activity of this director, who had witnessed the beginnings of Russian Soviet cinema, had enormous significance for the subsequent development of Turkmen cinema. After his successful film, *Judas* (1929), he had suffered quite a long creative hiatus until he was invited to Ashkhabad to make *Dursun*, which marked his artistic revival and became a milestone in the development of Turkmen national cinema. This was because Ivanov-Barkov, in his search for veracity and authenticity, not only in the settings but also in the heroes' characters, painstakingly studied his new living raw material, Turkmen popular traditions and the particular characteristics of local daily life. The Russian actress Nina Alisova, the leading lady of *Dursun*, had in turn to be given a hand to familiarize herself with a cultural milieu with which she was unfamiliar, as she had previously played a Russian girl in Yakov

Protazanov's *The Girl without a Dowry* [*Bespridannitsa*, 1937]. She later wrote about this:

> To play the role of Dursun properly, I had to study a life that was new to me, the particularities of the national milieu. I spent many days in the villages, in different families, and there I came across more than one prototype of my Dursun.[1]

This obviously helped her because she really did succeed in creating a convincing and authentic image of a Turkmen woman. In this respect it was simpler for the actor Alty Karliev,[2] who played her husband Nury, although his role was more complex and many-sided. The essence of the great conflict in the film lay in the struggle between the new, personified by the wife, a member of the Communist Party's Youth League, the Komsomol, and the old remnants of society, embodied by her husband, Nury, although he was generally a kind man. It was important not to depict him as a straightforward traditional oriental male despot. The whole drama of the increasingly complex plot lies in the fact that, while he loves his wife, he is unable to understand and accept her new behaviour and convictions. Karliev managed to do this brilliantly and he was right to consider this as one of his best and favourite roles. The director's great achievement was that he was the first to employ, apart from Alisova, only Turkmen actors who had no experience of working in cinema but who justified his faith in them.

However, Ivanov-Barkov's later films – *The Procurator* (1941), *The Distant Bride* (1948), *The Beloved's Scarf* (1956), *Extraordinary Mission* (1957) – were not comparable artistically with *Dursun*. *The Distant Bride* stands out among them: it was the first film to be made at the studio after the war, a musical comedy, which had an enormous success on its release right across the Soviet Union and became one of his most famous films. Although some remarkable actors, including Karliev and Aman Kulmamedov, appeared in the film, it suffered as a whole from being schematic and superficial, concealed beneath a wealth of ethnographic material and oriental colour.

In the autumn of 1941, the Kiev Film Studio was evacuated to Ashkhabad and during the Great Patriotic War Ukrainian directors continued to make feature films there. A new generation of young Turkmen film-makers had a wonderful opportunity to learn their skills directly from outstanding Ukrainian directors, as the two studios had combined their efforts, jointly making feature films and newsreels. During this period, the overall professional – and especially technical – competence of Turkmen film-makers noticeably improved.

In 1948, however, a major earthquake in Ashkhabad destroyed the Turkmenfilm building and the studio's activities were suspended for several years. In the interim the nearest studios in Baku, Tashkent and Alma-Ata produced only a small number of documentary films and newsreels on Turkmen topics. This terrible blow marked a forced end to the initial period of the development of Turkmen national cinema.

The second stage may provisionally be reckoned to start in the middle to late 1950s when the newly reconstructed Ashkhabad studio started producing feature films again with Rafail Perelshtein's *The Shepherd's Son* (1954) and *The Cunning of Old Ashir* (1955). The indisputable founder of Turkmen national cinema was the actor and director Alty Karliev, whose name was given to the Turkmenfilm Studio in 1974. He graduated from the Turkmen Drama Studio in 1921 and Baku Theatre College in 1931, later working as an actor at the Ashkhabad Drama Theatre. His first appearance on screen was in 1939, when he gave an expressive performance as Kelkhan, the lead in *Soviet Patriots* (1939). Among the graphic characters created by Karliev on screen – profound, spirited, fascinating and reflecting precisely national colour – we should note in particular the previously mentioned role of Nury in *Dursun,* and the prankster Aldar Kose in *The Magic Crystal* (1945), which brought him all-Union recognition. He came into cinema with no special training or skills, learning these from the older Russian and Ukrainian directors in the course of events. In 1957 Karliev teamed up with none other than Ivanov-Barkov to make Turmenfilm's first colour film, the adventure film *Extraordinary Mission* about the exploits of the agent Mergenov during the civil war. His second film, made jointly with Viktor Ivanov, was *Ayna* (1960), which addressed the fate of a Komsomol activist in the complicated years of collectivization. Unfortunately the dramaturgy in these films was not very convincing or persuasive, so that Karliev's relatively weak debut as a director gave no reason to suppose that in his next film, *The Decisive Step* (1965), he would emerge as an experienced master.

This epic film, based on Berdy Kerbabaev's classic novel of Turkmen Soviet literature may rightly be considered the peak of Karliev's work as a director. The storyline follows a young Turkmen labourer in search of love and justice in an era of historic changes in

Figure 5.1 Still from *The Decisive Step* (1965) by Alty Karliev.

the life of the Turkmen people. The lead role was beautifully played by Baba Annanov, who managed to create a vivid, emotional character with recognizable national traits. Profound national colour and the precise reproduction of the details of the traditional Turkmen way of life defined the style and rhythm of the film. Music played a major part in this film. The great composer Nury Khalmamedov succeeded in writing a diverse and versatile score, encompassing both Turkmen folk motifs and European symphonic music, creating an organic whole that was accessible and intelligible to the simple Turkmen audience.

This film, typical of traditional adventure films, did not gain all-Union recognition, but it achieved, what we might call, cult status in Turkmenistan. People saw it over and over again and know the film's notable quotes and songs by heart. The lead actors, Baba Annanov and Artyk Djallyev, became real people's artists – household names. Karliev's last two films *Magtymguly* (1968), the first attempt to make a film about the great eighteenth-century Turkmen poet and philosopher Fragi (Pyragy) Magtymkuly, and *The Secrets of Maqam* (1974), about the life and work of the legendary Turkmen singer and performer Karkara,[3] were popular, although dramaturgically and stylistically they could not repeat the success of *The Decisive Step*.

Nonetheless, Karliev played an enormous role in the development of Turkmen cinema, providing a link between the old cinema of the 1940s and 1950s – filmed in the Turkmen studio predominantly by Russian and Ukrainian directors – and the new generation of the 1960s and 1970s, represented mainly by Turkmens. It was evidently a matter of great satisfaction to him in the last years of his life to know that he was passing the baton on to the talented and safe hands of the new star of Turkmen cinema, Khodjakuli Narliev, and that he had lived to see the flowering of Turkmen cinema and its international recognition.

A new generation in Turkmen cinema emerged in the 1960s with the first Turkmen graduates of VGIK: Khodjakuli Narliev, Yazgeldy Seidov, Kurban Yazhanov, Murad Kurbanklychev, Mukhamed Soiunkhanov and others. The arrival of these young, talented and professionally highly trained specialists provided a powerful impetus for the further development of Turkmen cinema. These were the effects of the Thaw even in Turkmenistan, allowing many directors to express their individual inner world. Both the creative atmosphere governing the studio and the courage with which the Turkmenfilm management encouraged young directors to make films, helped them to realize their audacious and, for that time, unusual creative ideas. First and foremost, that period gave Turkmen cinema a remarkable director, Bulat Mansurov, who made his first film, *The Contest* (1963), essentially his student diploma work. This brilliant debut film was the first triumph of Turkmen cinema and a landmark event.

Thus the attention of the all-Union and world audience was drawn for the first time to a Turkmen cinema that was purely national in form and profoundly humanistic in content. Mansurov proved to be a subtle, passionate and distinctive director with an original view of the world, a poetic and imaginative vision: 'It is equally important to speak the language of modern cinema, as it is to have an excellent knowledge of the ancient culture of the East.'[4] The film was based on Nurmurat Sarykhanov's *Shukur-bakhshi*, a novel dealing with real events surrounding the creative competition between the famous Turkmen *dutar* player Shukur-Bakhshi and the Persian court musician Ghulam-Bakhshi (where *bakhshi* is the attribute used to designate the role of the popular singer). But the plot, fairly widely known in the Orient, was only a backdrop, although a very beautiful one, for the profound story of the tragic fate of the Turkmen people and their search for truth and justice.

Shukur rejects war and violence as a way to solve problems and differences and so he sets out for neighbouring Persia to gain a musical victory over the enemy and to arouse warm feelings in him through his own music. The basic idea of the film concerned the conflict between good and evil and the all-conquering power of an art closely linked through its historical roots with the people, giving it strength and wisdom. For the director it was important to show, not so much a contest between two musicians, as two totally opposite characters, reflecting two polar-opposite world views. He succeeded and, what is more, in a stylistically almost impeccable way, doubtless facilitated by the delicate, attentive and emotional style of Khodjakuli Narliev's camerawork and the surprisingly multifaceted, deeply philosophical and profoundly tragic music of the great Nury Khalmamedov, which later became a classic. 'In the film the music is woven organically into the fabric of the plot and becomes its core, defining the basic dramatic conflict, action and rhythm',[5] explained Valeri Fomin. It was a surprisingly bold and rather risky decision by Mansurov to invite the non-professional actors Aman Khandurdyev (Shukur) and Khodjan Ovezgelenov (Ghulam) to play the leading roles. It is difficult to believe that they were non-professionals when you see how naturally, profoundly, precisely and convincingly they live in character and the virtuosity with which they play the national instrument, the *dutar. The Contest*, an utterly bold, experimental and innovative film, became a reference point, not only for the director, but also for the whole of Turkmen cinema, which was gradually able to progress towards the making of profound and complex films of high artistic value. Chingiz Aitmatov was shaken by the film at the time and wrote:

> In many respects *The Contest* forced me to look at cinema anew, it forced me to think about many things... The film-makers touched on a number of topical problems of the past and present. I would say that this is a film about the eternal duel between good and evil, war and peace.[6]

Mansurov's later films made at Turkmenfilm – *Quenching the Thirst* (1966), based on Yuri Trifonov's novel about the friendship between the peoples who worked together to build the Karakum canal, and *The Slave Girl* (1968), based on Andrei Platonov's tale of the emancipation of the young Jamal from slavery and how this liberates her sense of her own worth – invariably elicited deep interest from audiences and the wider public, although these films did not attain the same creative heights as the director's fulminating debut. It is difficult to overestimate the historic significance of *The Contest* in the development of Turkmen cinema. Mansurov was a pioneer, the first swallow of Turkmen cinema, opening a door to Europe, to broad international recognition, a door that paved the way a decade later for Khodjakuli Narliev and Maya-Gozel Aimedova.

The 1970s and 1980s were years of prosperity, breakthrough and international recognition for Turkmen cinema, largely thanks to the work of Khodjakuli Narliev, the well-known master of Soviet cinema, a director, cameraman, actor and writer of documentary and feature films. Among the overwhelming majority of people, Turkmen cinema at that time was, despite the presence of other talented Turkmen directors, associated first and foremost with Narliev's name. For more than two decades, from 1976 to 1998, he headed the Union of Cinematographers of Turkmenistan and was both formal and informal leader of Turkmen film-makers. In that post Narliev did a great deal for the further development and modernization of cinema in Turkmenistan and he achieved a noticeable improvement in the material and technical base of the Turkmenfilm studio and increased the number of films made in the republic. Narliev's creative biography is highly indicative of his dedication, versatility, desire and ability to learn new things, his creative courage and inexhaustible work ethic. It is probably these qualities, together with his enormous talent that provided the basis for, and the guarantee of, the success of his work.

After graduating from the camerawork faculty of VGIK (the workshop of Boris Volchek) in 1960, Narliev quickly and successfully passed his practical training. Starting as a cameraman at Turkmenfilm, he became actor, scriptwriter and director; moreover, he was perhaps the only Soviet film-maker who received the highest grade in two specialisms, cameraman and director. Khodjakuli Narliev first became known as the cameraman on Mansurov's *The Contest, Quenching the Thirst* and *The Slave Girl.* In these films he demonstrated surprisingly mature craftsmanship and his own distinctive style, distinguished by fine observation, organic fluency and expressiveness. Narliev's directorial debut, the feature film *Man Overboard* (1969), dealt with the moral conflict of a young fisherman Sapar, who could not save his friend Murad. Despite a certain straightforwardness, the film wins you over with its sincerity,

Figure 5.2 Still from *Daughter-in-Law* (1972) by Khodjakuli Narliev.

its well-chosen cast and the director's clearly expressed moral position.

Narliev's second feature film, *Daughter-in-Law* (1972) may be regarded as his true debut, not least because it was the first film in which Maya-Gozel Aimedova appeared – his favourite woman who was to become his eternal muse. It was this film that launched the personal and creative duo of Aimedova-Narliev and from then on their work and life have been inextricably linked to one another. Furthermore, it was in this film that Narliev laid the foundations of his subtle, restrained and noble style, full of inner dignity. This film is based on his own recollections of his early childhood. In his village there really was a young woman who accompanied her husband to war soon after their wedding and, after his death, stayed to live with her father-in-law forever. Although the main character, Ogulkeik, is young and beautiful and is expected to re-marry, and her father-in-law agrees and even tries to persuade her to do so, she refuses because she is the sort who loves once and wants to remain faithful and to love forever. This film is amazingly beautiful. Both nature and people seem to be located outside time, although both time and the living conditions of the characters in their social context are clearly indicated. That is probably why this film, like Narliev's other works, seems even now to be as relevant and topical as they were then. As the film scholar Gulnara Abikeyeva has so accurately noted:

> In fact, the picture is much broader, it presents the basic ethno-cultural codes of the nation and conveys the traditional Turkmen way of life: from the close connection with nature and his ability to survive in the desert, to the type of family relationships.[7]

The film's principal theme concerns the loyalty and devotion of a woman, which was a topical issue in postwar Turkmenistan, where there were still many widows who had lost their husbands in the war and did not want to re-marry, despite the repeated efforts of those around them, who condemned their refusal to re-marry, as they apparently did not fully conform to the mentality of Turkmen society at that time, according to which, as with some Caucasian peoples, the widow was expected to remain faithful to her dead husband. That is why this film was, in the director's own words, balsam for their souls.

When a Woman Saddles a Horse (1974), an historical-revolutionary drama, was dedicated to Ene Kulieva, the head of the first Women's Section (*Zhenotdel*) of Soviet Turkmenistan. Artykgul, the Turkmen activist who is the heroine of the film, fearlessly and enthusiastically promoted the new way of life and the prototype for her was the director's mother's first cousin once removed, who had been a revolutionary and had played an active part in the eradication of illiteracy, the education and emancipation of Turkmen women, and who had a good reputation amongst the people. Narliev managed to show how difficult it was to be a pioneer, an innovator, especially a disempowered Oriental woman in Islamic society. This film is also interesting because in it the traditionalist Narliev seems to contradict himself. Here he clearly emphasises that his attitude towards popular traditions depends on their being good, always on their being appropriate and he clearly outlines his own position. In his film he reveals and exposes the stagnant and reactionary elements that unfortunately also exist in any traditional structure. Even he, a man whose work is profoundly national in form and spirit, nonetheless understands the need for change in the life of both people and society at certain stages of development and welcome them if they are designed to benefit people.

We may assert with confidence that *Jamal's Tree* (1980) is a hymn to a mother and in her person to all Turkmen women. The basis for the idea of this film is 'Oriental' wisdom: the idea that, if a person was born into the world, he should not pass away simply like that, without leaving behind good deeds and visible footprints. For good reason the traditions of many peoples involve the construction of a house, the birth of a son, and the planting of even a single tree, but to do this in the arid desert is akin to an act of heroism. Nevertheless, Jamal managed to grow a small sickly shoot into a big strong tree in the middle of the boundless desert by riding on his ass every day to the end of the world to water it. For her, it was not just a tree, but also the embodiment of all life on earth. Even when she herself dies saving her husband, her tree is still alive, a symbol of life and love. Jamal nurtured her tree, continuing the good tradition of her people, thus demonstrating the great strength of spirit and faith of a simple Turkmen woman.

This film clearly resonates with his *Daughter-in-Law*: the same everyday lives of ordinary people living in the desert far from civilization, following the traditional customs of their ancestors; the same sparse dialogues, the same minimalism and intimacy of events; and, finally, the same actress. Here it is quite obvious that she has a precise notion of what the mother should be: the custodian of the home, giving life to everything that is living. The prototypes of Narliev's heroines have always been protagonists from his real surroundings: first and foremost, the woman as Mother, like the collective image of the mother, which is so dear to him and which, in one way or another, is present in all his female characters.

Much of what Narliev depicts in his films is influenced by memories of his childhood, which was dominated by the muted colours of the desert landscape with its endless sand dunes. This probably explains his attachment to black and white and an almost documentary style. He usually chooses his themes and subjects from those that are general to humanity – birth, motherhood, love, loyalty, death – and that is perhaps why his films at times evoke a sense of the eternity and the infinity of existence. He has managed surprisingly well to relate such complex phenomena in a language that is intelligible to people of different ages and different nationalities. In his films Narliev has preferred open endings, leaving the audience with a certain understatement, an 'aftertaste' and plenty of leeway for their own further reflection and their own imagination.

In the 1980s and 1990s some highly reflective films appeared in Turkmen cinema, imbued with a sense of uncertainty and hopelessness. Narliev's films, however, despite their tragic subject matter, forced people to think seriously about the meaning of life and always left them with a belief that things would get better and a hope for the future. Narliev's cinematic language is a special, very figurative and poetic language, which corresponds to the dull but expressive beauty of the desert and the restrained and dignified mentality of its people. His heroes are characterized by a profound inner absorption: they are unhurried, taciturn and capable of maintaining their dignity and humanity – even in the most difficult circumstances. They live according to centuries-old traditions and seem as eternal as the boundless desert that surrounds them. The nature in his films is always recognizable as a distinctly Turkmen landscape, almost devoid of signs of civilization: the national space of daily life is re-created in the almost complete absence of contemporary attributes, despite the relevance of what is happening.

Western journalists have compared Narliev with Fellini, and in personal conversations Tolomush Okeev and Chingiz Aitmatov have called him the 'Turkmen Fellini'. Indeed, if we look closely at his films, especially *Daughter-in-Law, When a Woman Saddles a Horse* and *Jamal's Tree*, we can see from where this comparison comes. The same subjects, uncomplicated at first glance, the same details of the life and daily grind of ordinary people, described in detail and with great affection, the same multiple layers and unobtrusive philosophy, hidden beneath the apparent simplicity of an unpretentious plot.

Narliev made *Fragi, Deprived of Happiness* (1984) at the request of the republican leadership for the 250th anniversary of Magtymguly, the eminent poet and philosopher known as the 'conscience' of the Turkmen people, and whose sayings and moral criteria have been the guideline for their life and actions. Narliev approached the film with apprehension, considering himself still insufficiently mature to tackle the enormous legacy left by the great poet, whose person and work symbolized the nation's spirituality and morality. Moreover, he had already witnessed the failed attempt by Alty Karliev, who in his Film *Magtymguly* (1968), despite the use of the wonderful actors Khommat Mullyk and Mukhammed Cherkezov, failed to produce a convincing image of the great philosopher. Bearing this in mind, the level of responsibility was too great for Narliev, he was very afraid of making a mistake and disappointing his people, who revered Magtymguly as a national idol. Nevertheless, he dared to show the great poet's early years, the story of his tragic and unhappy love for his sweetheart Mengli. In this film, as always, the theme of personal love was closely intertwined and interleaved with love for the homeland, for the people. The two-part film proved an enduring success and was well received by Turkmen critics and the general public, although – apparently because of the specific nature of the material – it was not widely acknowledged outside the republic.

Narliev's last film for the time being was *Mankurt* (1990), a screen version of the novel about the Turkic legend of the *mankurt* by Chingiz Aitmatov, *The Day Lasts More than a Hundred Years* (1980),[8] filmed at the Turkmenfilm Studio with the participation of film-makers from Turkey and Libya. It is important to note that Aitmatov himself suggested a screen version of his novel to Narliev, the director he thought most suited to make the film. Indeed, the great writer's thoughts on 'mankurtism' closely accorded with Narliev's own ideas on the role of ancestors and to his inner world view. Aitmatov's deeply philosophical and multilayered work about an existence deprived of the memory of ancestors, of one's roots, of the mother who gave one life, losing honour and conscience, appealed to Narliev with its relevance to all periods. The young Turkic warrior Elaman became a captive, was subjected to the cruellest tortures in captivity and became a *mankurt*, and completely lost his memory: he raised his hand against the most sacred thing, killing his own mother, here transformed into an image of the Primeval Mother, the source of life on earth. The two main themes of the film – deprivation and loss of memory and the loss of one's individual character and identity, including national identity – are very convincingly depicted. There is also a third, no less important theme for Narliev: the theme of motherhood and the unending and all-destroying love of a mother for her child. This love can 'move mountains', but even it is unable to return his lost memory to her son. It is impossible to forget the heart-rending cry of the mother when she realizes this, stunningly performed – no, not performed, but lived and experienced by the equally stunning Maya-Gozel Aimedova. In his film, Narliev tried to apply the legend in the context of the history of his people and seemed, involuntarily, to anticipate subsequent developments in his own country.

The late Turkmenbashi, as the leader Niyazov was titled, could not accept this open reference to his own person and *Mankurt* was banned from distribution. Despite the fact that the film was based on the ancient legend of a barbaric method of depriving captives of their memory to turn them into submissive and mindless slaves, like zombies, which had no direct relation to the present day, those in power at the time saw a hidden threat, a warning to both the leader and the people. 'I simply wanted the younger generation to know the true history of their people and not to become *mankurts*', Narliev spoke with pain and bitterness of the history of the making and banning of his programmatic and unfortunate film.[9] The path of this film, which is such a landmark work for the director, to the audience has been equally long and difficult, but it had still not lost its relevance when its grand premiere was held at the East–West Festival in Baku only in September 2007, a decade and a half after it had been made.

In 1999 Narliev and his family moved to Moscow, and he was naturally full of energy and a desire to carry on his work in cinema. With his talent and skill Narliev could of course make more than one good film in Russia but, despite his interest in Russian reality, he has continued to live with the pain of his long-suffering people and has wanted to make a film about what he understands and what means most to him. The question of cultural identity and bilingualism has been very close to Narliev, and has preoccupied both him and his friend Aitmatov, who wrote in Russian and Kyrgyz, but usually only about his – the Kyrgyz – people. Narliev has been the same. Perhaps that is why it took years, even a whole decade, for him to understand and accept the sad fact that his exile was not a short *intermezzo* but a prolonged condition and that, in spite of everything, he had to go on making films.

The last surge of interest in Turkmen cinema occurred from the mid-1980s to the mid-1990s when, on the crest of *perestroika*, films dealing with current affairs and social criticism were commonplace. Documentary films increased particularly rapidly in this period and dared to examine hitherto forbidden taboo issues, including suicide and, more accurately, the self-immolation of Turkmen women. This second Thaw for Turkmen cinema ended unfortunately in the mid-1990s, not so much as a result of the collapse of the Soviet Union but because of the ideological crackdown by former President Niyazov. He outlawed all forms of art that had no relationship to traditional Turkmen folklore. Thus, culture, science and art in Turkmenistan were condemned to extinction. The Union of Cinematographers was dissolved and film-makers were accused of lacking patriotism. Because of the harsh censorship and political persecution most Turkmen cinematographers either lost their jobs or were forced to emigrate, among them the most distinguished representatives of Turkmen cinema. Those few who remained in Turkmenistan lost their jobs or were forced in effect to act as a mouthpiece for the Great President on television; they therefore practically disappeared from world cinema.

Among the few who have remained in the country and have tried, despite all the obstacles, to go on making films, it is worth singling out the work of the director and actor Kerim Annanov, the son of People's Artist Baba Annanov, who is revered by everyone in Turkmenistan. This talented, and at the time still young, director had to experience the widest possible range of pressures from the Niyazov regime in various guises: both as director, as producer and as head of Turkmenfilm in the 1990s. He is firmly inscribed in the history of Turkmen cinema due to the sad fact that, even under Niyazov in 1999, he managed to make the last Turkmen feature film of any value, *Legend* (1999), which maintained the high standards of Soviet cinema, in terms of both technical achievements and quality, before film production in Turkmenistan was almost completely halted.

Unfortunately, even this film, shot in the new, independent Turkmenistan, met the fate of other forbidden films. Although the director sought above all to avoid censorship and ideological confrontation by deliberately departing from the present to shoot an historical picture, the president apparently detected an allegorical or direct comparison with Narliev's *Mankurt*, because these two films really are united by the search for the roots, the historical memory and the spiritual strength of their people. This film, as far as we know, has remained 'on the shelf', not finding its way to a Turkmen or, more importantly, an international audience. After this picture film production in Turkmenistan virtually ceased and Turkmen audiences had to satisfy themselves with television screenings of a few old 'authorized' Soviet, Turkmen and Indian films or to resort to aid of the video market.

The only, and very occasional, cinematic activity in the years of Niyazov's rule was the organization of days of Turkish, Russian, Indian or French cinema, usually on the initiative of those countries' diplomatic representations. Since Niyazov's death in 2006 and the coming to power of the new President Berdymukhammedov the cultural situation in Turkmenistan has noticeably improved. Many cultural institutions have been re-established, many absurd prohibitions have been abrogated – and this includes the screening of the classics of world, Soviet and Turkmen cinema. The restoration of the best Turkmen films has begun at Turkmenfilm. Both the return and repair of old cinemas devoted to entertainment have begun and the construction of new contemporary multiplexes is planned.

In autumn 2008, after a prolonged interlude, an international film festival was held in Ashgabat under the slogan: 'Turkmenistan and International Cinema'. The situation in Turkmenistan is gradually improving, and there is hope that many of the film-makers who were at one time forced to leave their country, might return to their homeland to revive the former glory of Turkmen cinema.

Translated by Richard Taylor

Notes

1 Ivan Repin and Bairam Abdullaev, *Turkmenskoe kino* (Ashkhabad, 1974), p. 13.
2 Karliev considered this to be one of his best and favourite roles.
3 First female Turkmen performer and singer of ballads, probably early nineteenth century.
4 Valerii Fomin, *Peresechenie parallel'nykh* (Moscow, 1976), p. 156.
5 Repin and Abdullaev, pp. 30–1.
6 Ch. Aitmatov, 'Muzyka, perekovavshaia mechi na orala', *Sovetskaia kul'tura* (3 October 1964).
7 Gul'nara Abikeeva, 'Dve epokhi i desiat' fil'mov', *Kinoforum* 4 (2006): 4–11 (p. 10).
8 A *mankurt*, in Turkic legend, is someone who has forgotten his motherland, language, and history and can therefore be enslaved by others.
9 Author's interview with Narliev, Moscow, June 2009.

6

BULAT MANSUROV'S *THE CONTEST* IN CONTEXT

Michael Rouland

H istorically, there has been an emphasis on Russian camera-work at the roots of cinema in Central Asia. From the influence of the documentary film-makers of the 1920s to the impact created by the evacuations of Russian studios to Central Asia (TsOKS) during the war, scholars have underscored the role of Russians in educating Central Asian film-makers. Even addressing the 1960s, scholars of Soviet cinema have interpreted the role of Andrei Konchalovsky and Larisa Shepitko in Central Asia as an instructive one. The implication was that their 'Russian' wisdom was required for the film 'miracles' of Central Asia. However, a careful examination of the significance and impact of one prominent Central Asian film, the Turkmen director Bulat Mansurov's *The Contest* (1963), serves to re-orient our understanding of cinema in Central Asia during the 1960s and to look beyond paradigms of Russian cultural supremacy.

A New Direction in Turkmen Cinema
In the 1960s Russian films were not the only ones available to aspiring Central Asian film-makers. Studying at Moscow's State Film Institute (VGIK), they witnessed the works of Italian Neorealism in

films by Luchino Visconti, Roberto Rossellini and Vittorio De Sica. Moving beyond the dominant aesthetics of montage to impart political awareness, Neorealism depicted the reality of postwar suffering and the social conditions of the poor through the use of location shooting, intrinsic lighting, non-professional actors, 'slice of life' plots, long takes and handheld camera movements. This is evident in the 'quasi ethnographic veracity of descriptions, with constant attention to the psychology of heroes, generally of simple inhabitants, resorting to black and white', which Jean Radvanyi had identified in Central Asian films of the time.[1] Bulat Mansurov was the first director from Central Asia associated with the embrace of Neorealism, but his influence has been far from straightforward.[2]

Mansurov experienced a rapid ascent to the heart of Turkmen and Central Asian cinema during the 1960s; and his descent into obscurity was similarly abrupt. Mansurov studied music in the late 1950s and eventually served as the musical accompanist and musical head of the Charjou House of Pioneers.[3] His career as a professional musician ended when he enrolled at VGIK in 1961 and studied directing under Sergei Gerasimov and Tamara Makarova. His diploma film, *The Contest*, was shown in Cannes in 1963. Locally, the film was given the jury prize at the Central Asian and Kazakh Festival for Film-makers in 1964. Mansurov recalled in a recent newspaper interview that 'Chingiz Aitmatov praised the film, and Federico Fellini and Giulietta Masina screamed "bravissimo Bulat" at the Moscow Film Festival'.[4] Despite this clear international success, his first film was shelved for two years.

The Contest drew upon the publication in Moscow of Nurmurat Sarykhanov's *Shukur-bakhshi* (1961) and the verses of the thirteenth-century Persian poet Makhtum-Kuli Saadi. The film, scripted by Mansurov, is set in the late nineteenth century and portrays the tale of the khan of Tehran who plundered Turan[5] and took Shukur's brother captive. Threatened with yet another war, the famed musician Shukur goes to the khan for a *dutar* competition to avert war and to rescue his brother. It is the story of the triumph of music over politics and of art over war. Moreover, the film illuminates the universal struggle for peace, prosperity, and happiness that was part of a new cinematic movement in Central Asia.

The political narratives within the film are particularly interesting and can be divided into two groups of commentary. First, the film provides a critique of just rule and the responsibility of the masses to check the power of tyrants. Second, the film includes a commentary on the politics of national identities. While both topics would inspire quite a lot of rancour in the Soviet era, particularly in Central Asia, the film eschewed direct political criticism. Mansurov begins his film with an inscription of Saadi that is repeated later:

> Good and evil are at odds in the world,
> Will Good be preserved in our descendants?
> Or will people again
> Bury the hearts of heroes in the earth.
> The earth has long been sated with their blood.
> Hasn't it choked?[6]

This discussion of the costs and sacrifices of war extends first from the rationale of war to the conversations of khans and masses alike and then to the music and lyrics that triumph in the film. When we first meet Shukur, he is sitting with his *dutar* in the middle of the competition. His brother has just been retrieved from a prison cell, and he thinks to himself: 'Who does Mamedyar khan remind me of? … Chapykh khan.' His Turkmen khan is no different from this Persian (or Kurdish, since there are references to both ethnonyms) khan in his abuse of authority. Much of the film's early dialogue establishes a critique of the rule of Mamedyar khan, and we learn that the contest is a platform for his political-philosophical musings.

Mamedyar muses to his key advisor (Yusup) in the days before the competition, 'There are as many philosophies as people on the earth'. This statement is followed by a retrospective shot of his whipping of captives and another comment, 'For there to be order on earth, it is necessary to rule with a firm hand.' Yusup replies that,

> people are like birds, they rarely disrupt the peace. They are busy creating good on earth. Perhaps, they do not need a ruler at all for that? True, people are accustomed to having one. But it is possible that at first the rulers were just, but various people have come to power… the mistake was making it hereditary. For each family has its fool, my Khan.

While the khan is evidently irritated by Yusup's challenge, Mamedyar khan is not a wholly unsympathetic character. In fact, he recalls the khan in Kamil Yarmatov's *Alisher Navoi* (1947) and Black Abdullah in Vladimir Motyl's *White Sun of the Desert* (1969): powerful, charismatic, yet a relic of another era. This is a stark departure from the model of negative characters in Socialist Realism.

The debate between Mamedyar khan and his advisor provides a framework for the unfolding music competition as well. Their debate is also extended by the competition of Gulam and Shukur. Mamedyar khan provides the aside, 'So we will continue our dispute, Yusup. I arranged this contest to demonstrate the law of life. Life is a contest: the strong win, the weak perishes', to establish that the previous debate was the motivation for the competition. Although the contest begins with instrumental technique on the *dutar*, the political debate enters the music competition when Gulam and Shukur begin to compose their own songs.

The illusion of the khan's influence is similarly challenged in the politics of identity. Faced with the hostile crowd, Shukur asks himself, 'Tell me brother: are only you and I brothers in this country? It cannot be; I don't believe it. For if that is so, life on earth is senseless.' But when his music and his wit begin to command the respect of the crowd later in the film, Shukur suggests a revision, 'No, we're not the only brothers in this country!' The film moralizes that the costs of war, driven by the political antagonisms over borders, are not worth the sacrifice suggested by rulers. The concept of liminal identity would have been particularly important to

Character	Text	Camera
Gulam	The khan is a tree, and his subjects the roots; the stronger the roots, the farther the branches spread. Oh musician! Why do you live in poverty? Talent is good when it feeds the musician – the khan is a tree, and his subjects the root...	
Shukur	You are a moth, Gulam. And your music is like the whir of wings!	Montage: close-up on torch and then Mamedyar khan sipping tea
	And your thought and aspirations are like the flight of the moth around the flame.	Moth flying around flame and Mamedyar khan sipping tea again
	But not with the twang of the strings not fluttering of wings did you or it block off the sun from us.	The moth is caught in the flame and falls.
	You don't know; the sun has a different light, and this is only a torch, which burns...	

Mansurov, given his origins in the desert borderlands of Uzbekistan and Turkmenistan.

In the end, the resolution of the competition and the path that led to it come together. As Shukur convinces the Turks to allow him to use music rather than arms, we hear a woman cry, 'Oh Allah! Don't let there be war! You have already taken away all of my sons. Help Shukur! Let his courage stave off misfortune! May all who kill burn in hell!' And, an *aksakal,* or elder, offers his dying wish that Shukur would be able to use music to mediate the political dispute.

At this moment in the Turkmen desert, the presumptive staging ground for the invasion of Tehran, Shukur exhorts, 'Friends! I brought my *dutar* rather than a sabre. I want to try to save my brother with its help. Only with music... if it doesn't work, then it's your turn.'[7] Chingiz Aitmatov understood this moment as evocative of the entire film: 'The music that beats swords into ploughshares.'[8]

When music enters the film during the daylight scenes, such as this one, however, it is the symphonic music of the State Symphonic Orchestra of Cinematography, directed by David Shtilman. Rather than Turkmen folk music, we have the orientalist fare of ballet orchestration. The competition between Gulam and Shukur, on the other hand, is played entirely on the *dutar.* The film's folk music consultant was Chary Tachmammedov, a key figure in twentieth-century Turkmen *dutar* music. When the crowd turns anxious after Gulam breaks one of his two strings Mamedyar khan exclaims: 'Whatever happens the musicians must keep on playing!' The film at this moment centres entirely on the intensity of the music. In order to appease the increasingly hostile crowd as well as to impress them, Shukur removes one of his own strings as he continues to play. Through this gesture of fairness in competition as well as technical mastery, Shukur wins the crowd and the competition.

There is a Turkic bardic tradition alive in the film in these segments where music is interwoven with a didactic narrative. Shukur achieves his successful performance through both his expert instrumental expressionism and his story-telling ability. Stéphane Dudoignon, a scholar of Central Asian Islam, has observed:

> For the Turkmen Bulat Mansurov (*The Contest*), the power of inspiration found in the Persian words of Saadi and Nizami evokes a colourful world which enriches a language flowered

Figure 6.1 Poster for Bulat Mansurov's *The Contest* (1963).

> by allegory, where one finds all the philosophical depth of
> traditional Persian, in an altogether traditional criticism of
> the despotism and corruption of manners that it generates.[9]

Thus, music extends the political messages of the film that are part
of the long history of social criticism manifest in Central Asia.[10]

While music as political commentary has long been a central part
of traditional Central Asian culture, the use of camera in *The Contest*
is quite innovative. Armed with Bulat Mansurov's cinematic vision,
Khodjakuli Narliev proved to be a virtuoso cinematographer.
Together they would form arguably the most important partnership
in Central Asian cinema. One of the most striking aspects of the film
is the fact that it was shot at night, largely under the natural light of
torches. Still, the film conveys the heat of the Turkmen desert; the
crowd is bathed in sweat and suffers just as the musicians do in this
competition. There are several moments where Narliev demonstrates his masterful use of the handheld camera: a 270-degree
rotating shot of Mamedyar khan in his robes; an impressive overhead
shot of the crowd with torches, followed by flickering light on

Shukur as he plays, and finally the appreciation of the crowd at the climax of the film when Shukur receives their praise; and in the last phase of the contest, the fantastic illumination on Gulam's hands and instrument as he plays.

The camera significantly captures the crowd's emotion. As Shukur criticises the cost of war and explains how he landed in this place, the crowd measures his words with bowed heads. Narliev takes the camera in one smooth movement over the sitting crowd as Shukur reaches his conclusion. When Shukur stops, there is complete silence. Ultimately, the crowd mediates a position that diminishes the authority of the khan; their emotive energy offers a sense of the popular response to the shifting events of the film. Here, the political power of the crowd extends the aesthetic of Socialist Realism, since the crowd is central to the outcome of the music competition.

Facing revolt, Mamedyar khan observes 'Well Shukur, it seems that my people have taken to you.' To which Shukur replies, 'Believe me, khan: I did not come here to pick a fight, but to relay the good wishes of my people. I knew that they would understand.' As Shukur begins his return home, the narrator revises the pessimism of the film's opening inscription:

> The earth is still steeped in blood and ashes. But hope has again returned. Again the sun has come out after so many nights. And the earth has given people a stream. And the stream has turned into a wide river. It sweeps away stones in its way. And they settle on its bottom. The stream became a river, irrigating the crops!

Mansurov transcends the painful memories of collectivization, purges, and war, the combined sacrifices of building socialism in Turkmenistan, to imagine a world of collaboration, productivity and harmony.

In the 1960s, Mansurov provided a model of Central Asian cinematography that was quickly and effectively repeated by his contemporaries to establish a canon of Central Asian cinema, which would become known as the 'golden age' of the region's cinematic history. Local identity, local landscape, local actors and local themes confronted the Soviet tradition of universalism and modernity directed from the 'commanding heights' of Moscow. Mansurov rendered a Central Asian view of humanity that transcended socialist paradigms and created an important precedent in Central Asian culture as it drifted from Moscow's control. While Khodjakuli Narliev would later become recognized as the great director of Turkmen cinema in the 1970s, he underlined the importance of Mansurov and their three films in preparing him for his own directing career:

> I believe that I understood all the responsibilities of a director thanks to the three films which I made with Bulat Mansurov, which gave me an accurate impression of this profession. Mansurov was very young when we met. Gerasimov was still teaching him at VGIK; but he also had a great spiritual, creative maturity. He was born a scriptwriter, born a director.[11]

According to Narliev, Mansurov's success lay in his ability to combine philosophy with the visual richness of realism:

> 1963, the year of the production of the film *The Contest*, is at the same time the year of renaissance for Turkmen cinema. This film was our message to the rest of the Soviet Union as to the rest of the world.

But the transformation was not limited to Turkmenistan: '*The Contest* represented something totally new for the cinema in Central Asia as a whole', Narliev continued.[12] After its initial screening, Chingiz Aitmatov wrote about Mansurov's film:

> I do not know of a similar work in the cinema of Central Asia. This one is on the level of the masterpieces of world art. After such a film, many will have to revise their artistic positions with the cinema, and with this success, one cannot work as before; the criteria have moved to a higher level.[13]

More recently, Davlat Khudonazarov stated: 'Bulat Mansurov's *The Contest* played for us the same part as that of *Rome, Open City* of Rossellini for European cinema.'[14]

Mansurov opened a path to world cinema and a paradigm for Central Asian directors to emulate in their own explorations of local identity, infused with questions about socialism and modernity. 'As the sun circles the earth from sunrise to sunrise, so shall Shukur-bakshi in the history of the people', declares the film's narrator. This remark provides a useful metaphor for Bulat Mansurov's role in cinema in Central Asia. Forgotten for so many years in the canon of

Central Asian cinema, it is time to reconsider the centrality of Bulat Mansurov's *The Contest.*

Notes

1   Jean Radvanyi, 'Naissance et affirmation des cinémas d'Asie centrale soviétique: singularités et parentés', in Radvanyi, ed., *Le Cinéma d'Asie centrale soviétique* (Paris, 1991), p. 49.

2   Radvanyi asserts that 'in Central Asia, the beginning of the sixties consolidated the true revival with Shukhrat Abbasov's *The Whole Neighbourhood is Talking About It* (1960) and especially Bulat Mansurov's *The Contest* (1963)' (p. 57).

3   Charjou, now known as Turkmenabat, is located near the Uzbek border.

4   Galiia Shimyrbaeva, 'Bulat Mansurov: V kino vse zavisit ot politicheskoi kon"iunktury', *Kazakhstanskaia pravda* (7 October 2005), www.kazpravda.kz/print.php?lang=rus&chapter = 1128641618 (accessed 13 March 2011).

5   Turan is the Persian name for Central Asia. In the twentieth century, this term has continued to be used by scholars and geographers to describe Central Asia in a number of European languages.

6   *Ruins of Past Generations* (Shukur-bakhshi, 1871).

7   Here, he offers a reply to Chapyk khan's earlier comments, 'I wonder if a *dutar* can do the same as a horse and sabre?' and 'I wonder if a *dutar* could replace a saber?'

8   Gul'nara Abikeeva, *Kino Tsentral'noi Azii, 1990–2001* (Almaty, 2001), p. 157.

9   Stéphane A. Dudoignon, 'Les cultures de l'Asie centrale dans le miroir du cinéma', in Radvanyi, ed., *Le Cinéma*, p. 101.

10   There is a religious connotation to *bakshi* as well. The word implies musician as well as 'shaman' in Turkic languages. This feature of music and social comment is repeated in Shamshiev's *Manaschi* (1965), a Kyrgyz folk epic that describes their Islamization.

11   Quoted by El'ga Lyndina, 'La poésie unit les hommes', in Radvanyi, ed., *Le Cinéma*, p. 93.

12   Quoted by Lyndina, p. 93.

13   Quoted in Radvanyi, p. 157.

14   Quoted in Radvanyi, p. 57.

7

TAJIK CINEMA AT THE END OF THE SOVIET ERA

Sadullo Rakhimov

> *Flowering Buds called Withering,*
> *Merriment contrived as mourning grief.*
> (Mirzo Abdulkadir Bedil')[1]

I n these lines the philosopher Abdulkadir Bedil' explored the essence and contradictory logic of existence: that in the morning already lay the sunset, at the very birth lies death, and that nothing lasts forever – even societies, political systems, ideologies, and empires are transient. One recurrent source of crisis that drives all human progress is the nature of a certain social stratum, the intelligentsia, which even in a seemingly healthy society was and will stand in opposition to the system, to authority, to society and thus also to itself. The intelligentsia has always been the gravedigger of stagnation and the bearer of progress, but its influence on society at any given historical moment has varied greatly. The philosopher Pulat Shozimov reckons that 'the paradox of the communist system was that, despite the fact that its ideology was formed on the basis of the principles of universalism and internationalism, it was essentially always nationalist'.[2] Thus national elites emerged, which subsequently opposed the Union's power.

In the context of Tajik cinema in the Soviet era, three waves of national identity building can be discerned: the first in the 1930s and 1940s; the second from the late 1950s until the early 1980s; and the third in the late 1980s and early 1990s. According to Shozimov, the first general wave of Tajik identity occurred under the influence of the socio-cultural movement of Jadidism, promulgated by the outstanding Tajik writer Sadriddin Aini.[3] Because Aini was the legitimate, recognized leader of Tajik literature, he had great impact on the literature of the first wave, which was profoundly avant-gardist.

These waves of identity formation were also reflected in Tajik cinema, but differently than in literature and the traditional arts, because in the newly formed Tajik Soviet Socialist Republic cinema was perceived at first as an oddity, an illusion capable only of attracting the masses. The Tajik people were less affected by urbanisation than other new Soviet territories: thus, the population was predominantly illiterate, relying largely on oral traditions for their education and information. Unlike literature, watching films did not require special education or even an elementary knowledge of reading and writing. Films relied largely on the image and were thus accessible to all segments of society, regardless of their level of literacy – a fact that was skilfully used in Soviet ideology, which turned film into a powerful propaganda tool. Although the creation of a national cinema and the expansion of projection facilities were costly, the Soviet system gave priority to cinema over the other arts. However, in Tajikistan film was not the leader of national arts and it did not lend its voice to Tajik identity.

According to Shozimov, the first wave of identity in Tajik cinema of the 1930s and 1940s was a weak reflection of the powerful social transformation of the time. This is explained by the fact that non-Tajik specialists led the development of cinema in the 1930s, and this wave of identity formation was not as conscious or explicit as in literature, theatre, and music. Moreover, the source of this identity was not Jadidism; rather, it was its feeble reflection, expressed for the first time in *The Emigrant* (1934) by Kamil Yarmatov, the first Tajik film-maker, and Gulomirzo Bakhor, the talented Iranian documentary film-maker. These film-makers, however, revealed an early interest in the texture of Tajik life, traditions, folklore, and mentality, so the first documentary film in the Tajik language was made.[4] Tajik identity was also revealed in several other works, such as *The Son of Tajikistan* (1942) and *Tajik Film Concert* (1943), which put on display Tajik song and dance of this time. During this period (consciously or due to a lack of personnel in the Tajik studio, especially in editing – a field which determined the repertoire and the strategy of Tajik cinema) a certain group that presented itself as advocates of Soviet ideology gained a foothold in the studio and – for a variety of reasons – 'filtered' staff, barring local film-makers from the studio. At the initiative of this group, Yarmatov was forced to leave the studio, and Bakhor was removed; scripts by local authors were consigned to oblivion. Lev Kuleshov's project *Dokhunda* (1936), based on Aini's novel of the same title, which could have provided an impetus for further debates about Tajik identity, was shut down.[5] This page of Tajik cinematic history can hardly be called a wave of identity; rather, it was a weak attempt at one.

The second wave of identity in Tajik cinema coincides with a broader wave of identity issues, as outlined by Shozimov.[6] This wave emerged in the late 1950s and early 1960s, following Stalin's death, and is characterized by the growing enrolment in and development of social and educational institutions, demonstrating the republic's strenuous effort in fulfilling its role in the Soviet system. National cadres were formed and joined the political, social, economic, cultural institutions in a drive to legitimize the rights and obligations of Tajikistan as an equal Union republic, including the republic's right to explore its history and spiritual heritage.

This second wave of self-determination and identity promotion in Tajik cinema stretched from the late 1950s until the 1980s. In the process, the so-called 'filtering group' not only retained their positions, but also prepared a worthy group of successors. As a result of these efforts, Tajik films were made with 'touring performances' of writers, directors, cameramen, actors, artists, and composers – specialists who were invited from other parts of the Soviet Union; they often received perks in the form of additional funds or film stock. At best, the national cadres were allowed to serve as backup or assistants to the external specialist. Although the recruitment of non-Tajiks probably had to do with mutual benefits that could be gained by the 'filtering' group, consciously or unwittingly they also obstructed a more consistent preoccupation with identity in Tajik cinema. In the 1970s and 1980s Tajikfilm was a studio that served as production basis for commercial cinema. The primary emphasis was placed on the historical-revolutionary adventure genre, where the

Figure 7.1 Still from Bension Kimiagarov's *The Legend of Rustam* (1970).

heroes were divided into Reds and *basmachi*, one decidedly positive
and the other absolutely bad. Against the backdrop of important
issues of Tajik identity that could have been addressed in cinema,
this dichotomy looked cynical and demeaning. If there was a
breakthrough of truly national art despite the vigil of the 'filtering'
group, it came from the top echelon of the Soviet government to
prove its loyalty to national art, or else it was simply a glitch in the
'filtering' mechanism.

During this period, contrary to (or perhaps because of) the
'filtering' group, the talent of Bension (Boris) Kimiagarov
blossomed. He was a brilliant representative of the second wave of
identity in Tajik cinema. He created entire cycles of feature films and
documentaries on contemporary themes as well as on the distant
past, including *The Fate of the Poet* (1959), which won the Grand Prix
at the Cairo International Film Festival in 1960, *The Banner of the
Blacksmith* (1961), *The Legend of Rustam* (1970), *Rustam and Suhrab*
(1971) and *The Legend of Siyavush* (1976). Without doubt,
Kimiagarov's films were among the first films to address clearly
and consciously the true spiritual origins of a national renaissance.
Although not a Tajik national, Kimiagarov was one of those

film-makers who aroused Tajik national consciousness: he revived the historical memory of the great Rudaki and the spiritual power of poetry and wisdom of Ferdowsi;[7] he adapted the works of Sadriddin Aini and Mirzo Tursunzoda;[8] he created documentaries about Tajikistan and its leading personalities; and he generally restored the moral foundations of the Tajik people, who had inherited a rich, spiritual culture. His works stimulated a re-evaluation of the nation's spiritual roots. Thus, Kimiagarov played a crucial and invaluable role in the history of Tajik cinema. Alongside Kimiagarov other Tajik film-makers emerged: Abdusalom Rakhimov with the films *Zumrad* (1961), *Fire under the Ash* (1967), *Star in the Night* (1972); Tahir Sabirov with the films *Death of the Usurer* (1966), *The Woman from Afar* (1978); Margarita Kasymova with *Djura Sarkor* (1969); and Anvar Turaev with *Third Daughter* (1970), *First Love of Nasreddin* (1977), and even *The Pain of Love* (1989), although the latter already belongs to the third wave in terms of chronology, but it is of interest here because of the visual emphasis on indigenous culture.

One of the most successful Tajik directors of television films was Davlat Khudonazarov, renowned for his *Youth's First Morning* (1979). A talented cameraman, Khudonazarov announced his major theme already in the short documentary *Lullaby* (1966): his admiration for Badakhshan led him to poetically sing about the stark beauty of the mountainous region, its spiritual benevolence, and the inexhaustible talent of its inhabitants. *Youth's First Morning* conveys a touching relationship to the native soil, to customs and traditions and history, in a more sophisticated and conscious manner. With remarkable maturity and professionalism, the young director blended beautiful examples of folklore, customs, and life in Badakhshan into the dramatic fabric of his work. One of his major achievements was his manifestation of civil courage: for the first time Tajik cinema offered a nuanced rather than flat, black-and-white portrayal of the enemy of the Soviet regime – Azizkhan – who comes across as a three-dimensional character, who doubts, thinks, suffers, and loves, thus displaying the full range of qualities attributed to a real hero, while fiercely impeding the establishment of Soviet power in the Pamir. Such a deep and penetrating portrayal also marked his next film, *Murmur of a Brook in Melting Snow* (1982).

Considering the entire second wave of identity in Tajik cinema, however, Tajik films did not become *national* because of the 'filtering' group. Even if the studios developed highly qualified professional crew members among Tajiks, who created a number of feature, documentary and animation films, indicating the emergence of a national cinema, these films did not set a standard for the emergence of a nationally *conscious* Tajik cinema. These films were national through the initiative of their creators rather than through a combination of objective circumstances and the maturity of national cinema as a whole. If they can be regarded as phenomena of national cinema, it is only conditionally, since national art presupposes the existence of a tradition, continuity, innovation and many other things that eventually develop into a coherent school. These films were 'Tajik' only by geographical and external designation, but in essence Soviet. For Soviet cinema the national component was not that important: indeed, there were cases when scripts commissioned by central studios and then rejected would be relegated to Tajikfilm, where the names of the heroes would be 'Tajikified', they would be donned in national costume and endowed with a few ethnically recognizable markers. The national component served as backdrop, while socialist content stood in the foreground. Many of the best films were consigned to oblivion, placed on 'the shelf'. The slogan of the 1930s, 'national in form, socialist in content' remained the main demand of Soviet ideology in relation to national art, and cinema in particular.

Against this background the significance and social context of the third wave of identity formation in the second half of the 1980s and early 1990s becomes clearer. When Mikhail Gorbachev came to power, he radically changed the political climate in the Soviet Union. Even in the provinces, brave men criticized the stagnant social and economic processes and the bureaucratic apparatus. From 13–15 May 1986, the historic Fifth Congress of Cinematographers of the Soviet Union initiated an irreversible process of transformation in Soviet cinema. For the political life of Tajikistan, the Twentieth Congress of the Tajik Communist Party in January 1986 was decisive: Brezhnevian in spirit, it was infused with the new vocabulary of *perestroika*. For the first time film-makers had the right to address the Congress. Davlat Khudonazarov touched on issues associated not only with cinema, but also with the realities significant for film-makers: the formation of moral criteria to address the past; the return of ancestral feasts, rituals and traditions, such as Nowruz, the Iranian New Year, banned by the Party; and the importance of historical memory and consciousness in the formation of a new generation.

The Fifth Congress of the Tajik Film-makers' Union was held under the influence of Gorbachev's ideas, which had not attracted much public attention previously and suddenly were on everybody's lips. For the first time, the Tajik Party leadership (in the face of the Secretary for Ideology, G. Babasadykova) could not impose its own candidates for the post of First Secretary for the Film-makers' Union – and Tajik film-makers felt the taste of a small but sweet victory over the Party bureaucracy. After heated discussions at the plenary session, Khudonazarov was elected First Secretary of the Governing Body of the Union of Cinematographers, despite various intimidations from Babasadykova, who noted the names of all representatives speaking in support of Khudonazarov.

In April 1987, Alexander Yakovlev, Secretary of the Central Committee of the Communist Party (CPSU) and one of Gorbachev's supporters, visited Tajikistan and met with the academic and artistic intelligentsia as well as the mass media. Speaking at the meeting in his new role, Khudonazarov severely reprimanded the Party bureaucracy in the republic. There had recently been a series of incidents of self-immolation of girls and young women to protest against rampant female repression, illiteracy and religious extremism. Khudonazarov noted that the Party apparatus awarded itself state prizes and held celebrations against this tragic background. This statement made a strong impression on the usually silent intellectuals and Khudonazarov became an idol, while the Film-makers' Union of Tajikistan emerged as the unofficial centre of *perestroika* and of the reconstruction of the political and spiritual life of the entire republic.

In September 1988, the House of Cinema arranged the first informal meeting between Tajik film-makers and the First Secretary of the Communist Party of Tajikistan, Kakhar Makhkamov. Although this meeting was a first in history, not all film-makers were present and of those who were there, not all were ready to talk. In control of the situation, Makhkamov – a man with the republic's interest at heart, who had made his contribution with the development of the technical base at the film studio, outdid the film-makers, who had only just gained the reputation of the *avant-garde* of *perestroika*: they voiced merely banal and superficial issues. Only Khudonazarov entertained a conceptualised conversation with Makhkamov on issues of power, culture and spirituality. Yet in February 1990, the events in Dushanbe shocked the world: following repeated mass strikes in the city in 1990 and 1991, the countdown to the Tajik civil war had begun.

In Tajik cinema a number of important changes took place in the late 1980s. A new generation of film-makers emerged, mostly without formal training. With a few exceptions, including Bakhtiyar Khudoinazarov, this generation was largely self-taught: Djamshed Usmonov, Safar Khakdodov, Gulbahor Mirzoeva, Saif Rakhimzodi, and Orzumurod Sharipov. Several of them later studied on the Higher Courses for Scriptwriters and Directors in Moscow. With new themes and a fresh vision they brought new aesthetics to the screen, while also strengthening the author's active role in defending humanitarian principles, an anti-totalitarian ideology, and a genuinely national film language. This generation, which had not been subjected to Stalinist repressions, had no fear of authority, was well educated, embraced the true spirit of the Russian intelligentsia, its traditions of freedom, humanism, and progressive thought, and it opposed all stagnation and bureaucracy.

During this period, the 'filtering' group was identified and neutralized – not in the sense of the Stalinist purges, but rather through severe criticism that had unintended and profound consequences for the development of national cinema. Some people left the studio; others, however, stayed on, but could no longer influence the rapidly changing events at the studio and in Tajik cinema in general. The exposure of the 'filtering' group led to a split within Tajikfilm, following two emerging trends: one represented by Valeri Akhadov; the other by Davlat Khudonazarov – both film-makers from a middle generation.

Akhadov – smart, self-assured and aware of his capabilities – had a clear understanding of the situation in the country. He deliberately left behind the traditionalism of Tajik Soviet cinema and refrained from making films about peripheral, narrow, local topics. He aimed at Union-wide distribution and addressed broad topics that exposed the moral vices of the system. Fortunately, Gorbachev's *perestroika* had arrived and Akhadov assessed the political situation better than many professional politicians and political scientists. For example, anticipating the Tajik civil war of 1992–3 before many others, he moved his 'Peninsula' [*Poluostrov*] Children's Theatre Studio from Dushanbe to Magnitogorsk.

Khudonazarov was the complete opposite to Akhadov. He also foresaw many events, but he had no instinct for self-preservation: his political romanticism prevailed. He also understood the short-comings of the Soviet system, clearly identifying the abstract, dying dogmas of its ideology. However, he believed that the system could be saved if it could be infused with national, social values. Thus, over a relatively short period of time, he produced a cascade of both documentary and feature films, capturing the audience with honesty, depth, artistic maturity and a new, touching sincerity. Meanwhile, Khudonazarov served as the head of the Tajik and Soviet Unions of Cinematographers, and devoted a lot of time to his colleagues, especially the younger ones. As a People's Deputy, he also made many appearances as a politician – talking to his countrymen, who gathered in the squares of Dushanbe for long rallies and travelled to those border regions where the civil war was flaring up.

Many young people supported Akhadov, but the majority followed Khudonazarov's direction. In their work they were independent, searching for their own themes and aesthetics. Some openly criticised the Soviet way of life, others showed the beauty of national traditions and tried to breathe life into a moribund system. The new generation thus represented a stable, well conceived artistic and aesthetic platform and inspired confidence.

After the Fifth Congress of Soviet Cinematographers and its harsh critique of the bureaucratic management of the film industry, Tajik cinema went through a period of significant changes and soul-searching. At the Tajikfilm Studio a new association called 'Non-Feature Cinema' was formed, including the vigorous, talented, fresh-minded young film-makers: Pulat Akhmatov, Mairam Yusupova, Bako Sadykov, Safar Khakdodov, Tolib Khamidov, Djamshed Usmonov, Safarbek Soliev, and later Saif Rakhimzodi and Gulbahor Mirzoeva. As a result of the activity of these film-makers, supported by Khudonazarov, Akhadov, and the studio management, the young creative intelligentsia in Tajikistan made a number of unusual, memorable shorts and documentaries, in which traditional themes were considered from a new ideological point of view and in a new artistic and aesthetic manner.

Akhmatov's *First-Hand* (1987), dealing with themes of religion and Party bureaucracy, sharply criticised the pressure, restrictions of personal freedom, and the bureaucratic games of the state, but it was not released to a wide audience. Gulbahor Mirzoeva's documentary film *Sabbath* [*Shabat*, 1990] sympathetically depicts the lives of Bukhara Jews for the first time in the history of Tajik cinema. Her film debunks many ethnic stereotypes about this group, presenting instead an insider account; the film was also banned. A novel, and most importantly humanistic rethinking of the values of the past, showing contradictions and dehumanizing effects of the Party machine, inspired Mairam Yusupova's *Motive* (1988). This film reached its viewers only with great difficulty. Other short documentatries polemically engaged with the physical and moral health of children.[9] An open challenge to the outmoded aesthetics of official documentaries dominated the tone of a number of innovative documentaries by Tolib and Okil Khamidov, Gulbahor Mirzoeva, Safarbek Soliev, Mairam Yusupova and Saif Rakhimzodi.[10]

The enthusiasm and search for innovation inspired by Gorbachev's *perestroika* had an impact especially on feature films, also those made for television. Bakhtiyar Khudoinazarov's *Bro* (1991) was aired on Soviet Central Television and won nine prestigious awards at international film festivals. *The Time of Yellow Grass* (1991), Yusupova's first feature film, also won several prizes at international film festivals. Rakhimzodi's first feature film, *And the Stars Shine above Tanur* (1991) won at several international film festivals, too. The directors share youthful enthusiasm, audacity, innovative ideas, and a tendency to experiment with means of expression and cinematic language, while bringing a personal touch in the choice of difficult subjects.

Commercial cinema, unfortunately, was less successful. The lovely film by Anvar Turaev, *Pain of Love* (1989), charged with criticism for an ossified system, with a lyrical setting and successful acting, still suffered from a kind of professional sterility, theatricality, and monotony that ultimately did not generate a broad public response. Bako Sadykov's *Blessed Bukhara* (1990) also debunked a dying regime, adopting a more philosophical and allegorical approach, and mainly relying on the techniques used in his previous films. *Little Avenger* (1991), the filmic debut of composer Gennadi Alexandrov, suffered from dramaturgical looseness, directorial timidity, and a lack of integrity. Yunus Yusupov's *The Candidate* (1988) was a comedy, lacking of a sense of scale and taste that stripped the film of social and artistic value. His next film, *The Testament of Nine Prophets* (1992), was too long and undefined in genre terms. Meanwhile, Margarita Kasymova's *A Man and His Two Women* (1991) suffered from a weak screenplay and directing.

In the 1990s, there were two key short debuts: *Day Dream* (1990), directed by Safar Khakdodov and devoted to childhood nostalgia, won the main prize of the Tampere Film Festival in Finland in 1991. A new cinematic language emerged: a multilayered and bold method, an original montage, and organic synthesis of drama, satire, and comedy, an original and persuasive approach to psychology in the depiction of the young heroes – all this made the film a true sensation in Tajik film art. Another highlight was Djamshed Usmonov's *The Well* (1991), which impressed with its transparency, wit, a polyphony of characters, honesty, and the freshness and simplicity of its cinematic language.

The merit of all these works was that they had their fingers on the pulse of Tajik life. This period saw a genuine, unfettered process of Tajik identity building developing on screen, which was dramatic and diverse, particularly in documentary films. The new generation of film-makers was more convincing than the older Soviet generation in depicting society. Despite official efforts to ban some films, in one way or another, local audiences began to show an interest in national cinema.

The early 1990s were marked by the disintegration of the Soviet Union, and cinema was closely linked to social problems, indicating the state of society. When the tragic events of February 1990 occurred, the entire history of the country and its capital split into two halves: before the February events, there was optimism, love and trust; after the events there was confusion, alienation, and a lack of faith in the future. The documentaries of this period reflect this shift,[11] but it is Safar Khakdodov's *Day Dream* that is especially evocative, as one scene shows the February events as a kind of nightmare. Events got out of control and began to spiral into a tragic conflict: Gorbachev's *perestroika* was choked in the smoke and blood of civil wars. Tajikistan did not experience the joy of independence; it was engulfed in a fratricidal war.

In conclusion, we should assess the meaning of Tajik identity in the films of the late 1980s and early 1990s, which differs from previous concepts. Under the influence of Tajik writers, scholars, and respected journalists, issues of identity centred on the development of the Tajik language, with a Farsi orientation and a noticeable trend towards Arabisation, as well as Tajik classical medieval culture and Islam. Questions about the equitable redistribution of territories, i.e. the transfer of the Tajik cities of Bukhara and Samarkand, now in Uzbekistan, were also discussed under the heading 'identity'.

By contrast, Tajik cinema of the time, thanks to the arrival of new figures, advanced ideas of secular and democratic concepts of identity, including language, spirituality, and Islam. In other words, language and Islam were not the only criteria for Tajik identity, but film-makers raised these issues more broadly, rethinking Tajik spiritual heritage in the context of Indo-Iranian culture.[12] Respect for ethnography and folklore, especially in the lives of mountain villagers, was reflected in their short films, along with a cautious, critical attitude rather than one of blind faith towards Islam. In general, the Tajik identity rendered in the era's cinema emerged from the pluralistic ideas of Gorbachev's policy. Such an understanding of identity was a step forward and brought cinema to the vanguard of Tajik art.

Translated by Michael Rouland and Birgit Beumers

Notes

1   Mirzo Abdulkadir Bedil' (1644–1720): thinker and poet, who wrote in the Farsi language and was therefore greatly influential on the Tajik people.

2   Pulat Shozimov, *Tadzhikskaia identichnost' i gosudarstvennoe stroitel'stvo v Tadzhikistane* (Dushanbe, 2003), p. 130.

3   Sadriddin Aini (1878–1954), Tajik intellectual and thinker, national poet. Promulgated Tajik national traditions in literature; author of *Dokhunda* (1927).

4   Ato Akhrorov, *Tadzhikskoe kino* (Dushanbe, 1970), pp. 40–8; Sadullo Rakhimov, *Luch ekrana* (Dushanbe, 2003), pp. 19–20.

5   Akhrorov, pp. 40–56.

6   Shozimov, p. 116.

7   Rudaki (858–941), Persian poet; Ferdowsi (940–1020): Persian poet, author of the Iranian epic *Shahmaneh.*

8   Mirzo Tursunzoda (1911–77), Tajik poet, elevated to the status of a national hero.

9   For example, Margarita Kasymova's *The White Road* [*Belaia doroga*, 1988] and *The Cry* [*Krik*, 1989], or Safarbek Soliev's *Kobus* [1988].

10 For example: *Such is Life* [*I takova zhizn'*, 1989] by Tolib and Okil Khamidov; *Two* [*Dvoe*, 1988] and *Deus Concernat Omnia* [*I bog sokhraniaet vse*, 1989] by Gulbahor Mirzoeva; *In the Name of Ahura Mazda* [*Vo imia Akhuramazdy*, 1989] and *Chiaroscuro* [*Svetoten'*, 1990] by Safarbek Soliev; *Face* [*Litso*, 1989] by Mairam Yusupova; and *Triptych* [*Triptikh*, three shorts: 'Your Name is Autumn' (*Imia tvoe – osen'*), 1989; Pete, 1992; Chore, 1993; doc., Tajikfilm] by Saif Rahimzodi.

11 For example: *Exchanging Dushanbe* [*Meniaiu Dushanbe*, 1990] by Gennadii Artykov or *The Days of the Waning Moon* [*Dni ushcherbnoi luny*, 1991] by Ermukhamed Aralev.

12 For example, in the short documentaries *Ashaglon* [1988] and *In the Name of Ahura Mazda* [1989] by Soliev; in *Triptych* by Saif Rahimzodi; or in *I Believe* [*Veruiu*, 1987] by Mairam Yusupova.

8

A SMALL HISTORY OF KYRGYZ CINEMA

Joël Chapron

I f the reputation of a country's cinematography is measured in relation to that of the producing country, Kyrgyz cinema can obviously not claim to have a broad international following. In its recent history, Kyrgyzstan has hardly been mentioned. Apart from the violent inter-ethnic conflicts of 1990, the brief Tulip Revolution of 2005 (which forced President Askar Akayev to ask for political asylum in Moscow), and the ousting of President Kurmanbek Bakiyev in April 2010, the country remains little known. Principally agrarian, rich in water flowing from the Tien Shan mountains that reach to 7,000 metres (but deprived of oil and gas, unlike its rich neighbours), the young republic is the only one in the region that could truly claim the label 'democratic'– despite corruption and favouritism. This inevitably leads to a particular attitude to film production. Far from the Turkmen or Uzbek censorship issues, and without the heavy burden of the (former, Soviet) 'state command', Kyrgyz cinema is subjected to market laws in a context that is detrimental for the national industry.

The Beginnings

Making its entry onto the Soviet film map quite late (despite Lenin's aim to make cinema a propaganda tool), Kyrgyz cinema only produced the first full-length documentary film in 1946, in a country that was still called Kirghizia, and it took almost another decade, until 1955, for the first full-length fiction film to emerge (in collaboration with Mosfilm). Indeed, the history of Kyrgyz cinema rests primarily on a solid documentary tradition, which saw its hour of glory in the mid-1960s with the films of Tolomush Okeev, Bolotbek Shamshiev and Melis Ubukeev, who would later turn to fiction film. The milestones of Kyrgyz cinema are few and far between, so they quickly transformed the film-makers into key personalities in the country. Moreover, their films were inspired by the work of a local writer, Chingiz Aitmatov,[1] whose works have since been translated into numerous languages. Aitmatov was a legend in his country, which he represented as ambassador to Luxembourg and then Belgium. He furnished the greatest Soviet film directors with stories: Aitmatov's prose inspired Okeev for the film *The Red Apple* (1975); Shamshiev for *The White Ship* (1975), with music by Alfred Schnittke; Gennadi Bazarov for *Mother Earth* (1967); the Ukrainian-born Larissa Shepitko for *Heat* (1962), starring the 22-year-old Bolotbek Shamshiev; and the Russians Sergei Urusevsky (the famous director of photography of Mikhail Kalatozov's Palme d'Or winner *The Cranes are Flying* [*Letiat zhuravli*, 1957]), who adapted *Farewell, Gulsary!* in the film *The Ambler's Race* (1968), and Irina Poplavskaya, who made the film *Djamilia* (1968). This string of good films moved Kyrgyz culture to the cinematic front. Equally worth mentioning is Ubukeev's *The Difficult Passage* (aka *White Mountains*, 1964), which deals with the uprising of the Kyrgyz people during the civil war in 1918.

The Golden Age

Two films marked a turn in the cinematic history of this Soviet republic. Filmed almost at the same time, they placed the country on the map: *The First Teacher* (1965) by Andrei Konchalovsky (then using the name Andrei Mikhalkov-Konchalovsky), based on a novella by Aitmatov; and *The Sky of Our Childhood* (1966) by Tolomush Okeev. Although a Russian film, *The First Teacher* introduced the country, its customs and landscapes to the world and a whole generation admired the beautiful and stunning Natalia Arinbasarova (also the heroine of *Djamilia*), who carried off the Coppa Volpi at the Venice International Film Festival in 1966. However, Soviet propaganda hardly comprehended the

Figure 8.1 Still from *The First Teacher* (1965) by Andrei Konchalovsky.

difficulties which the young teacher encounters when he goes to Central Asia spread the good word about the Revolution. *The Sky of Our Childhood* treated the conflict of generations in the period following the Thaw, when things began to come under more rigid control once again.

In the 1970s and 1980 Okeev and Shamshiev filmed their major works, practically unknown internationally, which were only shown abroad as part of retrospectives: *The Worship of Fire* (1971), *The Fierce One* (1973) and *The Descendant of the Snow Leopard* (winner of Silver Bear in Berlin International Film Festival, 1985) make Okeev the last 'father' of Kyrgyz cinema. Meanwhile Bolotbek Shamshiev made *The Red Poppies of Issyk-Kul* (1971), *The White Ship* (1975) and *The Early Cranes* (1979), without attaining, however, the poetic heights of his compatriot. Finally, in 1989, just before the ancient Soviet Empire collapsed, Okeev's regular director of photography, Kadyrjan Kydyraliev, took the step to film-making with the very poetic *The Valley of the Ancestors* (1989), leaving the post of director of photography to his son Khasan. Whereas Kadyrjan had been actively involved in creating Okeev's reputation, the son would do the same for Aktan Abdykalykov (who later adopted the name Arym Kubat), working on almost all of his feature films. These Soviet years ended, therefore, without a new wave of young film-makers on the horizon.

Figure 8.2 Still from Aktan Arym Kubat's *Beshkempir: The Adopted Son* (1998).

From Kirghizia to Kyrgyzstan

After *perestroika,* Kyrgyz cinema – deprived of financial resources and without any emerging new generation – was considered a goner. However, some film production continued to emerge. First of all, unlike their Kazakh neighbours, Kyrgyz film-makers – rather than forging a new post-colonial identity – turned to a filmed idealization of their cultural traditions, breaking loose from the literary foundations which their precursors had used. From 1991 onwards, Aktan Abdykalykov (Arym Kubat) would spearhead the new generation: he made his first appearance on the international stage with shorts such as the documentary *The Dog Ran Away* (1990) or the medium-length autobiographical film *The Swing*, which won the Golden Leopard for Shorts in Locarno in 1993. These early films reveal already a very strong style, a mixture of poetry, the brutality of everyday life, traditions and superstitions, which would become the trademark in his full-length films: *Beshkempir: The Adopted Son* in 1998 and *The Chimp* in 2001, both distributed in Europe after their respective screenings at Locarno and Cannes International Film Festival. In 1992, Bekjan Aitkuluev made *The Lodger*, marked by Kyrgyz tradition, as the hero is referring continuously to the fabled Manas and to the rituals that ancestral culture has profoundly anchored in the daily life of its citizens. Having made a short animated film in 1989, Marat Sarulu, with whom Abdykalykov wrote *The Adopted Son*, launched into the realization of a feature-length film called *In Spe* (1993), which screened a year later unnoticed at the Festival of Tokyo. In 2001 he made a second feature-length film, *My Brother, Silk Road*, a kind of Kyrgyz 'concise history', where the older boy of a group of children decides to follow a painter wandering along a railway. In 1993, Ernest Abdyjaparov made his first short documentary, followed by several other shorts (e.g. *The Sparrow*, 1995; *Passage*, 2000) that introduced him internationally, before he made with Aktan Abdykalykov the 22-minute short, *The Bus Stop* (1995), shown in Cottbus in the following year. At the same time he continued to work as production manager at Kyrgyzfilm, (performing these duties on *The Chimp*), before moving on to feature-length films with *Village Authorities* (aka *Saratan*) in 2004, co-produced by Germany's Ikon-Film and Fit-Film. Other directors also emerged, such as Bakyt Karagulov, who attracted attention with *Stormy Station* in 1995, based on a script co-written by Chingiz Aitmatov and Marat Sarulu and presented in Berlin in the following year. In 2004, he shot *A Mother's Lament about Mankurt*, an adaptation based on Aitmatov's novel *The Day Lasts More than a Hundred Years* (1980), which the Turkmen director Khodjakuli Narliev had already adapted for cinema in 1990 under the title *Mankurt*. Another new name on the cinematic map was Temir Birnazarov, who debuted with the short documentary *The Devil's Bridge* (1996). The critical lack of finance naturally pushed all these film-makers to look for funding elsewhere. Notably thanks to the ECO Fond (abolished in 1997) and later Fonds Sud of the Ministry of Foreign Affairs, France has been able to support several projects. The funds of Locarno's Montecinemaverità also supported many projects and films, as did the Festivals of Pusan, Rotterdam and Gothenburg through their special funds.

The Turn of the Century

Since the beginning of the 2000s, a new generation of film-makers has begun to break through. *Sanzhira*, the splendid short of the 25-year-old director Nurbek Egen, introduced in Berlin in 2001, paved the path for his first feature film, which gained support from a Russian producer who, in turn, sought a German co-producer, a French actress and a French co-producer to make *The Wedding Chest* (2005). Despite the presence of Natacha Régnier and a Franco-Kyrgyz plot, the film could not attract audiences, neither in France – where it had no theatrical release but went straight on to be broadcast by Arte in 2006, nor in Kyrgyzstan – where it was seen as too cliché-ridden; however, it reinforced production links hitherto only open to Aktan Abdykalykov, thanks to his unfaltering friendship with the French producer Cédomir Kolar, who has backed his feature films.

In 2004, a law on cinema was finally issued, according to which 0.1 per cent of the annual state budget would be assigned to cinema, allowing the production of one feature-length film and some documentaries. Three films were released in that year: *Saratan*, *A Mother's Lament about Mankurt*, and *Oedipus* by Ovliakouli Khodjakuli, which was made on video. Some shorts and documentaries supplement the picture, as well as a television series produced on a local level in quite large numbers. In spite of the promulgation of the law, no feature-length film was produced in 2005.

The year 2006 marked the beginning of a genuine renaissance of cinema with five feature films: *The Wedding Chest*; *Birds of Paradise*, a debut by Talgat Asyrankulov and Gaziz Nasyrov, a Kyrgyz–Kazakh co-production supported by the Soros Foundation, which tells the story of a young reporter whose video camera is stolen in a border town where drug-trafficking and smuggling are at loggerheads; *Love of the Minister's Daughter* by Rustam Atashev, which was such a public success that a first sequel followed in 2007, with a second in production; *Eternal Love* by Adilet Akmatov – a film made with a team of stunt men that also reached large audiences in a country where cinema-goers had for years been deprived of popular national cinema; and finally, Gennadi Bazarov's *Metamorphosis* were made on video.

The year 2007 was, in turn, auspicious with such films as *Pure Coolness*,[2] the second feature film by Ernest Abdyjaparov, relating the story of a girl from the city who follows her fiancé to his village, where she is kidnapped and married off to a young man with whom she eventually falls in love; *The Reading of Petrarch* by Nurlan Abdykadyrov, the second feature film since independence to be entirely produced with public funds, showing life in prison in an almost documentary style; *Adep Akhlak* by Marat Alykulov, made with the help of Hubert Bals Fond and Produire au Sud (a support programme of the Festival of Three Continents in Nantes); *The Arab's Shaitan* by Myrzabek Aidaraliev, a film with popular commercial appeal.

In 2008 three films were at different stages of production. Temir Birnazarov's *The Route of Hope* was being produced by the state studio, Kyrgyzfilm. After *My Brother, Silk Road* (2001), Sarulu made *Song of Southern Seas*, a Kazakh–Russian–German–French co-production (French finance provided by Guillaume de Seille/Arizona Films, with the support of Fonds Sud), which had a good festival life. But it is of course *The Light Thief*, the new project of Aktan Abdykalykov (who now calls himself Arym Kubat, a name composed of the names of his biological father and his adoptive father), which has been a major event for Kyrgyz cinema, reaching wide international distribution with The Match Factory.

Whatever the talent of Aktan Arym Kubat as director, he is much more than that. In effect, his position in Kyrgyz cinema is of key importance today. In 2004 he founded the production company Oy Art, which is headed by Altynai Koichumanova. This young woman has, discreetly and tirelessly, knitted close links with people in the world of international cinema with potential interest in Kyrgyz film. Thanks to Arym Kubat's fame and the professionalism of his production head, Oy Art has produced and co-produced several feature films (notably *Adep Akhlak* and *Pure Coolness*), and the company has been instrumental in launching, in 2005, the programme '10+ ' with several Kyrgyz film-makers, which is designed to move the country's cinematography into an international arena by producing and making shorts and features. In the light of a lack of professional training, the Foundation for the Development of Kyrgyz Cinema was set up in 2006, in collaboration with the private Kyrgyz–Turkish Manas University and Oy Art; it subsequently set up a film school, with every course lasting nine months and financed by the Dutch non-governmental organization Hivos. The majority of students already have a higher education qualification. The best eight from 25 graduates are given the chance of making a short film with the support of Oy Art. In 2008, over a dozen shorts were produced, almost all financed through these mechanisms.

In order to discover Kyrgyz cinema and give a platform to a younger generation, Aktan Arym Kubat invited a small group of foreign professionals in 2007 to the splendid banks of the famous Issyk-Kul Lake to show them, on DVD, the most recent local productions as well as those of the neighbouring countries. Moreover, the first festival of Central Asian art-house cinema, Kinostan, which took place in August 2007, presented the features *Birds of Paradise, Reading of Petrarch* and *Adep Akhlak*, which divided the small number of 30 accredited guests, whilst shorts of the 10+ programme caused a genuine stir. *Everything will be OK* by 24-year-old Akjol Bekbolotov is a pretty film about abandoned children living in the streets. *Running* by 23-year-old Marat Ergeshov tells the story of a young man who accidentally becomes an assassin. The two films of the 24-year-old Nargiza Mamatkulova are especially unforgettable: *I Want to Live* is a documentary in black and white, showing simply a day of a painter who has lost his arms and who, on the steps of a subway passage, draws portraits of one and the same girl by using his foot; and *Toptash* (from the name of a Kyrgyz children's game), a short fiction film, which is autobiographical and tells the story of a sick girl searching for the father she has never known. With these two films – the only ones made by a woman – Nargiza Mamatkulova is undoubtedly going to make a remarkable entrance to the international festival circuit.

However, despite such engaging news from the Kyrgyz cinematic front, we cannot neglect the fact that many cinemas have closed their doors since the collapse of the Soviet Union. Of the 1,217 'cinematic installations' that the Soviet Republic of Kirghizia counted at the beginning of the 1980s, fewer than 10 are left. It appears that only a few cinemas in the capital Bishkek can project films in the 35mm format; the last functioning cinema in Osh closed its doors in the winter of 2007–8. It is, in effect, in Bishkek where a local businessman has decided to re-launch theatrical releases by equipping cinemas in the western style, i.e. with Dolby Digital. After renovating the cinema 'Oktiabr' (two screens) and opening a further two venues with 85 seats each in the Vesa Centre, he inaugurated two further screens in a new and very smart commercial gallery in late 2007. These six screens are today the only cinemas in the country where films can be screened and seen in proper conditions (the House of Cinema, where the local Union of Film-makers is located, and Cine Manas continue, of course, to show 35mm films, but technology and comfort remain rather Soviet-style).

It would be a truism therefore to say that US blockbusters have occupied the screens, as indeed is the statement that French films are few and far between. If the new generation of Kyrgyz film-makers wish to conquer once again their cinematic space, they must conquer mountains that are higher than those that separate this small country – with a huge potential for tourism – from its huge neighbour, China.

Acknowledgements

The author would like to thank Gulnara Abikeyeva, Gulbara Tolomusheva and Charlotte Urbain. This text, which was written in July 2008, appeared in *Culture et Musées*, 12 (January 2009); it is reproduced here with kind permission from the publisher, Actes Sud.

Translated by Birgit Beumers

Notes

1   Aitmatov died on 10 June 2008 during the shooting of a television adaptation of one of his most celebrated novels, *The Day Lasts More than a Hundred Years*. The then president ordered a day of mourning for 20,000 people to attend the funeral.
2   The film was funded by Kyrgyz, Kazakh, Swiss (Southeast Visions), Swedish (fund of the Gothenburg Festival), US (Total Film Initiative) and Dutch (Hubert Bals Fond) sources.

9

RE-VISIONS OF *THE SKY OF OUR CHILDHOOD*

Elena Stishova

We need to be on polite terms with Nature.
With her help we need to search wisely and patiently
for harmony in relationships.

(Tolomush Okeev)

T en years or so ago, when I was selecting films for a retrospective, I watched *The Sky of Our Childhood* (1966) again and was carried away, as I always am, by Okeev's masterpiece. There's a special kick when you know a film shot by shot and savour in advance the emotional impressions that you are ready to experience again and again. That is how it was right up to the last scene when suddenly it was as if I was seeing for the first time these shots that have been described so often: a group of young riders, who have only just taken leave of their parents, charge on horseback into a tunnel, happily rushing towards a helicopter, to the city, to school, to meet their fate. In a parallel montage phrase we see a vertical long shot of mounted elders, slowly receding up a mountain trail. The figures of the children, blinded by the headlights of trucks, are swallowed by the darkness of the tunnel punched through the mountain.

Obviously, you had to amass some experience of life so that, through the familiar text, you could discern the hypertext that had emerged over time and assess the naive metaphor of the final scene, of its spontaneously emerging extra-diegetic meaning, describing a parabola of abundant wisdom. We have grown up with the young heroes of this film and nowadays we understand the price paid for the enticing 'Virgin Lands', towards which these children of the mountains were heading at full tilt.[1]

Now *The Sky of Our Childhood* – with no risk of falling into the rhetoric that is alien to Okeev – may be appropriately described as an ecological parable. In 1967, when the film was released, there was no such genre and the very concept of 'ecology' was not yet current in the Soviet Union. 'In *The Sky of Our Childhood*, when I wanted to deal with the problem of the collision between nature and civilization, I did it primarily because this problem worried me terribly. Incidentally, almost no one mentioned the problem at the time', Okeev confessed in a 1975 interview.[2]

Since Stalin's time society had been brainwashed by the unforgettable slogan: 'We cannot wait for favours from nature. Our task is to take them from her.' It is true that, by the beginning of the 1960s, this slogan had been removed from the agenda. Nevertheless, geologists were at the peak of their popularity, a profession of trailblazers, of romantic vagabonds with theodolites and guitars.

At that time the novice Okeev was 30 years old, but he was one of the few who had all his life soberly assessed the process of civilization and seen its seamy side. You can look for the origins of such early maturity in Tolomush Okeev's childhood. He was born and raised in a small *aul* by Lake Issyk-Kul, ringed by mountains and far from the centres of culture. As a child he was not taken to the theatre, the conservatory or art galleries. Okeev explained:

> Instead I had Issyk-Kul. There were the mountains. I was taught and raised in a way by the majesty and beauty of nature. Then there was folklore – songs, epics, ancient legends. I was lucky: I had already found the greatest of our *manaschi*.[3] Time and again I heard wonderful *komuz*[4] players, folk story-tellers. For me this was the real – the highest! – academy for introducing me to art.[5]

His childhood years gave the future artist an integral and pantheistic sense of the world, the background to the *Weltanschauung* that is already apparent in his first full-length feature film, *The Sky of*

Our Childhood. The young director contemplated the dialectic between the old and the new, brought them into a dialogue that he experienced personally, and the philosophical repository of his artistic thought refashioned the almost autobiographical story of his childhood into an epic drama about the historical fate of his people.

Okeev came into the film process during the short period of the Thaw, renowned for its liberalism – relative, of course, but nonetheless fruitful. Although nobody abolished the 'shelf' on which ideologically unreliable films continued to be left (this happened at the start of *perestroika* in 1986, when the Soviet Union of Film-makers created a Conflict Commission), society was permeated by a romantic faith in the authorities' promise of 'the restoration of Leninist norms of life' – in other words, faith yet again in a communist utopia, but purged of the 'personality cult' and the associated penal institutions.

The Thaw was associated with a boom in national cinema, the so-called 'tidal wave' – the term appeared fleetingly in some official document or other and stuck. The most important cultural, and even political, event in the confines of the whole Soviet Empire occurred at this particular time, not as a result of a decision taken by the authorities, but as a consequence of a long and multi-vectoral process of cultural revolution in the republics of Central Asia and the Caucasus. (There was also an upsurge in the Baltic republics, but it had its own agenda, which was fundamentally different from that of Soviet Asia.)

Figure 9.1 Poster for Tolomush Okeev's *The Sky of Our Childhood* (1966).

At this point it is time to introduce the concept of colonization, which to this day has never entered our critical vocabulary. Unique in all its parameters, the Soviet Empire collapsed overnight. When the Belavezha Accords were signed,[6] the newly independent countries were plunged into the abyss of a systemic crisis, which has still not been overcome, and a revision of the 'brotherhood of nations' under the aegis of Russia has not yet begun on any large scale. This is what Tolomush Okeev said on the subject in 2001:

> When it comes to colonisation, then we should be specific. For us, for Central Asia, Soviet colonialism brought many useful things. Had it not been for the influence of Russian culture, there would have been no Russian-speaking writer Olzhas Suleimenov, no almost Russian-speaking writer Chingiz Aitmatov.[7] There would be no Russian-speaking cinema in Kirghizia. Another question: we moved forward, while the Baltic States stood still, because in their social development and their culture they were closer to Europe and we held them back, slowed them down. They should have been set free long ago... And we hampered the Caucasus, which survived capitalism and stood between Europe and Asia.[8]

Among the 'useful' features mentioned by Okeev were the construction of studios in all the Soviet republics and the determined formation of national creative cadres. Each republic had its quota at VGIK and workshops were set up where film-makers were trained in every film specialism. This happened after the war, but let us not forget the wartime TsOKS in Alma-Ata, where the staff and equipment of Mosfilm and Lenfilm were evacuated. The Studio gave a powerful impetus to the development of creative film culture in Kazakhstan and became a school and opportunity for many.

These are the specific circumstances that preceded the explosion of civilization that established the archipelagos of 'national cinema'. This was no piece-work cinema of the propagandist kind made for the imperial shop-window: planned production was beginning.

The context of the 1960s favoured Okeev, as indeed it favoured the entire generation who went into film-making. *The Sky of Our Childhood,* from the author of the short documentary film poem *These are Horses* (1965), which had astonished people with its raw material, its skill and 'a good attitude towards horses' (Vladimir Mayakovsky),[9] was received favourably and awarded a prize at the

All-Union Film Festival in Leningrad in 1968. The critics were the most complimentary – complimentary, but no more than that. The film was not adequately analysed in aesthetic discourse, or even in the social discourse that prevailed at the time. The battle between the old and the new, presented by Okeev in serene realistic tones, was treated simply as a typical victory for the new; in this vein, the plot was often reduced to the level of: construction of roads through pastureland, levelling of mountains, and replacement of the old – with its strength and weaknesses.

Attempts were made to compare the subject matter of *The Sky of Our Childhood* to 'village prose',[10] which was then a new literary trend, and to identify its main theme as the exodus of young people from the country to the city. Thus, critics paid tribute to the relevance of the film while linking it to the cultural mainstream. Subconsciously, critics tried to find a typological similarity between Okeev's film and the works of his film-making peers in other republics. Evidently, the striking individuality of the young master was obscured in a lyrical fog and in descriptiveness that was the sin of the Zoiluses of the time.[11]

The methodological palette of criticism was firmly set in the Procrustean bed of Socialist Realism. Although it was considered bad taste in the 1960s to use this already compromised concept, the true reason for the critical inadequacy was much more deeply rooted, in the thoroughly ideological concept of the National, which left no room for the image of the Other. We were all obliged, as one, to be national in form and socialist in content. In other words, the skullcap, the sheepskin hat, the quilted robe, the Circassian coat and the Russian tunic and, in extreme cases, the slanted eyes and oval face became part of the widespread representation of national form and of the differences between the peoples. But all our brains, and indeed the other body parts, were deemed to be socialist. Russification was so powerful that the urban population 'from Moscow to the margins',[12] expressed themselves in Russian. (It even got to the point where Ukrainian children were embarrassed to speak in their native tongue – because it was looked down upon.)

As a result, this situation gave rise to the 'skullcap' movie: as the Tajik director Davlat Khudonazarov explained:

> People sit in the frame in their robes and skullcaps, repeating 'amen' or 'asalam aleikum', drinking green tea.... Here everything remains at the level of relishing national colour

and then only those aspects that are visible to tourists [...] My
favourite film, *The Sky of Our Childhood*, grew out of the Kirghiz
land, the prose of Chingiz Aitmatov, who absorbed the unique
Kirghiz national perception of the world, the integrity of
man's consciousness, which has not yet thought up the idea of
colonising his earth and his nature. He is part of it... Okeev's
film is not so much about his childhood but about Kirghizia.[13]

Critical interpretations of the film in the mid-1960s did not focus on
an analysis of its national distinctiveness, but rather on the
description of the plot: the teenager Kalyk's arrival on holiday
home in the mountains, to the summer camp – the *jailoo*, and his
return to the city, to the hostel – contrary to the wishes of his father
Bakay, who wants to keep his youngest son at home and make him
his successor. Kalyk eventually leaves with his classmates, although
his departure is preceded by a furious outburst of his father's wrath.
When he sees the mother Urum bringing the boy to the roadside,
Bakay summons all his strength and whips his wife's back, and she
falls to the ground submissively. Then this son, in an unprecedented
act, rushes to his father: 'Don't beat my mother!' By the law of
patrimonial society, which sanctifies the observance of subordina-
tion, such an act is punishable, and the punishment is severe.
Clearly, the foundation of this society has already cracked, as the hills
and mountains have been attacked by earth-moving machines and
bulldozers. Kalyk is afraid of his father's rage and prefers to leave
without saying goodbye. But the wise Bakay catches his son and gives
him money for textbooks. Bakay understands that the new life takes
its own and resigns himself to the fact that his older children live in
the city, and that his grandchildren do not speak Kyrgyz. But his lot is
that of a herdsman, whose life has been spent is in the mountains, at
the *jailoo*. He accepts it as something immutable, eternal, the legacy
of his ancestors.

It is not Kalyk, the bystander and observer, but Bakay who is the
protagonist and the semantic figure in the film. Kalyk finds his way to
the *jailoo* just at the moment when the surveyors and road builders
have reached the threshold of his family tent. It is time to prepare to
move on, to roll the felts, an almost ritual act depicted in the film in
minute detail, and to drive the herd higher into the mountains in
search of pastures new. The utensils are collected, this is not the first
time Urum has moved, but the ritual of the move clearly signals a
farewell to the old pasture. 'Farewell, old pasture', says Urum,
'Forgive me if I am in some way to blame.' The same words are

spoken by Bakay. The caravan moves on. The *jailoo* looks orphaned, like a ruined dwelling, an extinguished hearth. An old blind golden eagle, which they have left behind, can only shake its wings helplessly.

Nomads block the path of a column of dump trucks. We hear warning shouts: 'You can't go there!' A series of explosions follows. A mixture of rock and soil shoots up high like a tall cloud, covering the sky in a grey haze. The horses go mad. The herd turns sharply in a panic and rushes back with a loud roar. Bakay cannot contain the force of the horses' charge.

The Sky of Our Childhood attracted an audience of four million viewers while it was in distribution. For the time this figure was low. It was estimated that ten million tickets sold compensate for the average film budget. Perhaps this is more apocryphal than factual, but the success of the film lay not at the box-office, but in its artistic power, which has been preserved to this day. Its influence on Soviet cinema cannot be calculated in figures. Or in the fact that Tolomush Okeev's film became a key film of national cinema in the 1960s. As I have tried to show above, it appeared out of nowhere, at the intersection of protracted socio-cultural processes. Time chose the Kyrgyz Tolomush Okeev, who belongs equally to the world of nature in which he was born, to the folklore on which was raised, and to the culture that he mastered. He tied the irrational and the rational into a tight knot and produced an organic work of national art.

Some Western scholars view with great caution the influence of the 'big brother' and its dominant role in the republican studios. Indeed, at virtually every national film studio built, the right to make the first film was given to authorities invited from the capital. They made films on national subject matter – as a rule, properly heroic, ideologically consistent and dictated 'by the centre', but these never actually became national films despite the efforts of the propaganda.

On the one hand, the process was the same everywhere; on the other, each studio developed its own history distinct from the others. For example, nobody remembers that the first Kyrgyz feature film *Saltanat* was made in 1955 by the Russian director Vasili Pronin (who became famous in 1965 for his family drama *Our House*, based on a script by Yevgeni Grigoriev). But everyone remembers that at Kirgizfilm in the first half of the 1960s Larisa Shepitko shot her debut film, *Heat* (based on Aitmatov's novel *The Camel's Eye* [*Verbliuzhii glaz*]), and Andrei Konchalovsky made his first film, *The First Teacher*, again based on Aitmatov's prose. But who said that the débutants harboured any mentoring ambitions towards their schoolmates from VGIK?

Heat was filmed by a team of VGIK students and graduates, who were soon to become masters and create the so-called 'Kirghiz miracle' that is inscribed in the history of Soviet multinational cinema. Behind the panel of the sound truck sat Tolomush Okeev, who had just graduated from the Leningrad Institute of Film Engineers. The assistant directors were Dinara Asanova and Gennadi Bazarov. The leading role was played by Bolot Shamshiev, then still a student at VGIK and now the maître of Central Asian cinema. This is what Tolomush Okeev recalled about this period:

> I have to admit that it was working with Larisa that awakened in me a genuine love for film work. I realised then what a difficult, complex and, at the same time, noble labour it is, requiring you to devote all your moral, spiritual and physical resources and skill, patience and struggle. And how beautiful is the moment of victory.[14]

The First Teacher, where Konchalovsky discovered for Soviet cinema the remarkable actor Bolot Beishenaliev, was completed in 1965, but it nearly landed on the 'shelf'. To Kyrgyz Party ideologues the film's even-handed portrayal of feudal Kirghizia was against the spirit and the Party idea of what Soviet cinema should be. Vladimir Baskakov, then the deputy chairman of the All-Union Committee for Cinematography (Goskino), personally intervened to save the film. He succeeded and the film had an international response. On paper this level of truth was already permitted (the film was based on Aitmatov's prose), but the prohibition on depiction in film remained in force, and remained in force for a long time. I think that the Kyrgyz would not have made the decision to film *The First Teacher* and did not make it in their studio of their own accord. The reasons are much more subtle than rudimentary fear of treading on ideological prohibitions by depicting a Communist as a fanatic on the verge of insanity. The prohibitions here are more internal, related to the national mentality. It is said that a Kyrgyz would never start cutting down a tree, as Duishen does in the film, frenziedly hacking the intractable trunk with an axe merely because the treetop does not allow light into the classroom. I cannot remember where I read or heard about this. Nevertheless it was not the Muscovite Konchalovsky who thought up this action, but the Kyrgyz Aitmatov who wrote it. So perhaps the view put about by Western film scholars that Kyrgyz society was shocked by the crude errors of a director, who had no sense of the national mentality, was apocryphal and derived solely from this fact: a non-Kyrgyz is interpreting Kyrgyz history. In colonial discourse, this really does not appear *comme il faut*, but at the time the entire country lived as if in 'a single human dormitory', and such a reading would not have occurred to anyone. The Communist utopia has not yet outlived its usefulness. There were a few artists who took a sober view, who saw far enough, who did not believe in the bright future, where we were promised a land flowing with milk and honey. By the grace of God, Tolomush Okeev belonged to this artistic circle.

Studying the critical literature on Tolomush Okeev I came across a modest 1989 printed brochure from Soyuzinformkino (an institution that has unfortunately been abolished) in which the film scholar and sensitive analyst Valentin Mikhalkovich provides a profound interpretation of the creative work of the Kyrgyz master. His assessment of *The Sky of Our Childhood* coincides with mine. Mikhalkovich also believes that the artistic and thematic potential of this film was not adequately appreciated at the time of its release, but that its meaning was revealed gradually, as the iron hand of civilization grasped humanity more and more palpably by the throat.[15] Mikhalkovich frequently cites the book *National Images of the World* [*Natsional'nye obrazy mira*, 1988] by the celebrated philosopher and cultural historian Georgi Gachev. Gachev writes wonderfully about *The Sky of Our Childhood*, reacting intensely to those shots and episodes in which the director has captured the damage done to primordial nature. He was also hooked on the ending, where the children on horseback dissolve in the heat haze of the tunnel that has been punched through the mountain. The contrast between the children's cheerful mood and the sombre image cast by the prototype of Hell has nowadays come to the fore. However, even then, when the film was released, the contrast was no accident: 'I always aspire to situate the plot between Heaven and Hell', Okeev said in a 1975 interview.[16]

The optics of the critical view have changed. In the naive 1960s, we identified more with the children, for whom there was certainly a beautiful future ahead. In the bitter 2000s, we have joined Bakay's camp. After all, we have seen Serik Aprymov's film, *The Last Stop* in 1989.

Translated by Richard Taylor

Notes

1   The Virgin Lands Campaign was launched by Khrushchev in 1954 to improve harvests by ploughing and working the Kazakh steppe. Many young people were deployed in the region to complete this task.

2   Tolomush Okeev, 'Nauchis' u zhizni', *Iskusstvo kino* 8 (1975): 99–117 (p. 112).

3   A *manaschi* is someone who can recite the *Manas*, the central epic of Kyrgyz literature.

4   The *komuz* is an ancient fretless stringed instrument.

5   Valerii Fomin, *Peresechenie parallel'nykh* (Moscow, 1976), p. 220.

6   The Belavezha Accords, signed on 8 December 1991 by the leaders of Russia, Ukraine and Belarus, dissolved the USSR and created the much looser Commonwealth of Independent States.

7   Olzhas Suleimenov (b. 1936) is a Kazakh writer, environmentalist and politician. Chingiz Aitmatov (1928–2008) was a Kyrgyz writer, who wrote in both Russian and Kyrgyz.

8   *Informatsionnyi biulleten' Konfederatsii SK 'Sodruzhestvo': spetsial'nyi vypusk* (Moscow, 2001), p. 25.

9   Reference to a poem by Vladimir Mayakovsky entitled 'A Good Attitude Towards Horses' ['Khoroshee otnoshenie k loshadiam'], 1918, dealing with compassion for horses.

10   Village prose (*derevenskaia proza*) was a literary trend that developed during the Thaw, focussing on rural communities.

11   Zoilus or Zoilos (*c.* 400–320 BC) was a Greek grammarian, philosopher and literary critic. His name is here being used as a synonym for critics generally.

12   Reference to 'The Song of the Homeland' from Grigorii Aleksandrov's film *The Circus* [*Tsirk*, 1936].

13   Interview with Tajik director Davlat Khudonazarov, *Iskusstvo kino* 11 (1988), p. 17.

14   Elem Klimov, ed., *Larisa: kniga o Larise Shepit'ko* (Moscow, 1987), p. 113.

15   Valentin Mikhalkovich, *Tolomush Okeev: tvorcheskii portret* (Moscow, 1989).

16   Okeev, 'Nauchis' u zhizni', p. 103.

10

A 'WILD KAZAKH BOY': THE CINEMA OF RASHID NUGMANOV

Vitaly Chernetsky

I n the recent history of Central Asian cinema, the pivotal role
played by Rashid Nugmanov in the late 1980s and early 1990s can
hardly be overestimated. His three major films, *Ya-hha* (1986), *The
Needle* (1988) and *The Wild East* (1993), arguably to a greater degree
than the work of any other film-maker of his generation, were
responsible for bringing the spotlight of both Soviet and global
attention to films from the region. *The Needle* in particular became
one of the most popular films to be released in the Soviet Union
during the Gorbachev era, while also being hailed as 'a manifesto of
[Kazakh] New Wave cinema'.[1] The coining of the term 'Kazakh New
Wave' has also been attributed to Nugmanov.[2] The somewhat
eccentric designation of the 'Wild Kazakh Boys', however, originated
from press materials for the Sundance Film Festival, where
Nugmanov was a guest of honour in 1990.[3] The difference between
the two designations is instructive: while 'New Wave' provides a
distinctly 'high culture' association with innovative French cinema of
the late 1950s and early 1960s, the 'Wild Boys' refers to William
Burroughs's eponymous 1971 novel, an iconic countercultural text.
Both terms suggest a subversive, rebellious streak and exposure to
heterogeneous global influences (openly acknowledged by the

director himself). At the same time, Nugmanov's three major films are also deeply anchored in the experience of the Soviet Union as it underwent transformation and eventual collapse associated with the policies of *glasnost* and *perestroika*. For a number of reasons, however, Nugmanov's name is mentioned relatively infrequently in the more recent discussions of Central Asian cinema. As the shifting geopolitical contexts returned the spotlight to this region in the aftermath of the tragic events of 11 September 2001, critics have been turning to other periods and figures in the region's cinematic history.

One of the reasons for the change of fortunes experienced by Nugmanov's work stems from the director's withdrawal from film-making. In January 1992, while attending a film festival in Tours (France), Nugmanov met a local woman by the name of Catherine Popineau, whom he married a few months later. In early 1993, as the work on *The Wild East* was completed, Nugmanov moved to France where he continues to reside to this day. In his new incarnation, Nugmanov has dedicated his energies primarily to critical writing and human rights activism, and indeed has become one of Kazakhstan's most important political dissidents. His professional career as an active film-maker thus spans only ten years, from his entering VGIK in Moscow in 1984 to the release of *The Wild East* into the international film festival circuit in 1993. I would therefore like to attempt an investigation of the path Nugmanov charted as a film-maker through a reading of his three major films that places them into a broader cultural context.

Nugmanov entered film school at the age of 30, already holding a degree in architecture from the Kazakh Polytechnic Institute; he came from a fairly Russified Alma-Ata intelligentsia family of a mixed ethnic background (Kazakh and Tatar). Like most other film-makers who came to be associated with the Kazakh New Wave, Nugmanov studied directing in the workshop led by Sergei Soloviev; however, his early film school experiences were influenced to an equal extent by interaction with fellow students from other workshops and by an avid interest in the underground rock music scene. Nugmanov's earliest student projects incorporated the music of Akvarium, the leading Leningrad rock band, and depiction of youth subcultures that were gaining increasing visibility (including the Soviet versions of 'hippies' and 'punks'). *Ya-hha*, Nugmanov's first major film was conceived in October 1985 as a term project for the film's cameraman, Alexei Mikhailov, also a student of VGIK. The format approved by the university was a ten-minute 'lighting exercise' in the form of a documentary about the Leningrad rock music scene. The film's enigmatic title refers to the name of one of Leningrad's underground *tusovkas*[4] of that period.

Ya-hha became a remarkable exercise in 'guerrilla film-making' that went to gain considerable acclaim and win the FIPRESCI Prize at the 1987 Moscow International Film Festival. Produced on a shoestring budget of about 1,000 roubles (which would have been $1,500 at the time) on grainy black-and-white film stock, the film follows a group of young people from the Leningrad underground scene, including many iconic rock musicians (among them Boris Grebenshchikov, Konstantin Kinchev, Maik Naumenko and Viktor Tsoi). As Nugmanov himself acknowledged, this was an example of improvisational film-making, without a predetermined final goal. Intellectually, Nugmanov grounded his approach in the theories of Dziga Vertov and their interpretation by the French *cinéma vérité* movement, as well as the cinematic experiments of John Cassavetes (especially his 1959 film *Shadows*) and Andy Warhol. Prior to the actual filming, the intellectual concept and atmosphere of the film were the subject of a spirited debate among the members of the creative team that lasted many months; the filming itself, however, took little more than two weeks, primarily in May 1986.

Similarly to Dziga Vertov's *The Man with a Movie Camera* (1928) and much of the 1960's *cinéma vérité* work, *Ya-hha* is actually a complex hybrid of a spontaneously acted fictional story and documentary filming of 'life caught unawares' both in the sense of the use of a hidden camera and of an openly visible camera confronting the filmed subjects. Thus, the film includes the documentary record of a cancelled rock concert and an actual wedding between two members of the Ya-hha *tusovka*. However, only the original silent filming was conducted in the *cinéma vérité* style; the soundtrack was later added in studio conditions, and it was actually the limited sound studio resources that led to the film's shortening to 40 minutes. The arc of *Ya-hha*'s narrative is likewise a nod to *The Man with a Movie Camera*: both films present a day in the life of a group of people in a big city, focusing on several types of activities and spaces, both public and private.

The film's importance in the history of *perestroika*-era Soviet cinema is hard to overestimate, both in terms of its aesthetic approach and its influence, as one could convincingly argue that

ASSA (1987), the best-known film by Nugmanov's teacher at VGIK, Sergei Soloviev, which likewise features members of the underground music and art scene and was produced and released within months of *Ya-hha*, actually owes its existence to Nugmanov's pioneering experiment and to Nugmanov introducing Soloviev to the underground scene.

Still, for all its innovative boldness, *Ya-hha* can be considered part of Central Asian cinema only in the sense that its director is of Central Asian background. Nevertheless, the film's success at the 15th Moscow International Film Festival in July 1987 paved the way for Nugmanov's active involvement in the film industry of his native Kazakhstan, as already in August 1987 he received an offer from the Kazakhfilm studio to take over a botched project – and make the film that would become his greatest international triumph, *The Needle.*

While the two films have a few elements in common, such as a heavy reliance on the use of non-professional actors, most notably *The Needle*'s main star, Viktor Tsoi, and the avoidance of constructed film sets, overall the aesthetic approaches of the two works could not be more different. In contrast to the heavily improvisational *Ya-hha*, *The Needle* is tightly scripted; its plot is a multilayered post-modern pastiche of multiple Western, generically Soviet, and specifically Kazakh realities.

To speak of the impact of *The Needle* is to follow two essentially diverging narratives: for the wide masses of Soviet and post-Soviet viewers, *The Needle* is a much-loved, indeed a cult film best known for being the only extensive acting performance by Viktor Tsoi, the Russian rock singer of Korean ethnic background and leader of the prominent 1980s band Kino. However, in the aftermath of Tsoi's tragic death in a car accident in August 1990, shortly before he and Nugmanov were due to begin another collaborative film project, his performance in *The Needle* as the coolly composed action hero Moro became the key visual record of a cultural hero comparable in importance in the post-Soviet context to James Dean or Jim Morrison. Tsoi's performance in this film is also a remarkable (and extremely rare in the Soviet and post-Soviet context) instance of a popular musician who 'translated the messages of his songs into action, albeit fictional; he added another dimension to the verbal and acoustic rebellions staged by underground rock groups'.[5] The magnetism's of Tsoi's Moro, however, is of a peculiar kind, as this proud loner of a superhero is himself a pastiche, an assemblage of characteristic traits of lonely outsider heroes from US film noir, French and Hong Kong New Wave cinemas, and numerous other models; the presence of such a character in a film set in the Soviet Union testifies both to the director's bold experimentation and to the shifting fortunes of film-making in the Soviet Union in general and in Central Asia in particular.

The kaleidoscopic, multilayered citational mode visible even in the construction of the film's central hero is what proved particularly fascinating about *The Needle* to Western critics and film festival audiences. Indeed, his film offers arguably the most thoroughgoing and radical appropriation of post-modernist aesthetics in the cinema of the final years of the Soviet Union's existence, a tightly wound combination of genre-specific allusions and seemingly random quotations, topical social commentary, cynicism and parody. As Ludmila Pruner noted in her review essay on the Kazakh New Wave, *The Needle*

> combines western with *bytovoi* film,[7] thriller with tragicomedy, drama with light comedy, social fiction with a musical [...]. Random sounds, words in Russian and foreign languages in the film narrative, as well as the use of phones, television sets and separate soundtracks in the same shot form part of the effect of acute alienation.[6]

For most of the critics and commentators writing shortly after the release of the film, *The Needle* stood out precisely because of its virtuoso combination of cinematic styles and filming techniques, making it 'the most playful and offbeat of the Soviet films of the period'[8] and evoking comparisons to a wide range of acclaimed works of world cinema, from Jean-Luc Godard's *Breathless* [*À bout de souffle*, 1960] to Quentin Tarantino's *Pulp Fiction* (1994). Its aesthetic proved to be remarkably *au courant* for international film festival audiences, bringing Nugmanov unprecedented attention and invitations to the most prestigious film events, from Venice to Sundance and beyond. For these audiences, in the late 1980s and early 1990s, the Soviet Central Asia was for all intents and purposes a *tabula rasa*, and the film's combination of deft use of ambitious but recognizable vocabulary and devices with a presentation of hitherto unknown locales proved irresistible. The film also offered a refreshing counterbalance to the bleak quasi-naturalistic tone of much of the new cinema that was emerging from the Soviet Union at the time. Even though *The Needle* deals with the socially 'hot' topic of drug use, it does not become the logical centre of the film. As Brashinsky notes, 'the film's essence emerges from the director's manipulation of various cultural stereotypes rather than social or psychological problems'.[9] The stereotypes in question are filtered through multiple channels of media representation; in a much-discussed move (and the only aspect of the film that generated censors' objections even during the *perestroika* era), Nugmanov inserted a frame stating that the film is 'dedicated to Soviet television'. While the lines of dialogue spoken by the film's characters are quite sparse, the soundtrack is filled with recycled fragments of film, television and radio programmes, and an ingenious mix of contemporary rock music with 'atmospheric' Soviet pop oldies. The camera frequently pans over multiple television sets operating next to each other, particularly in the apartment of Dina, the film's female protagonist whose late father was a sculptor. The television sets interspersed with Dina's father's works thus acquire qualities of parts of a sculptural conceptualist installation project, inviting a comparison to the iconic works of the famous Korean artist Nam June Paik.

Side by side with this rush of intellectual *jouissance* stemming from this ambitious yet playful pastiche-making, we find in *The Needle* the development of an expressive visual language that creates a stark, powerful impression of both urban and natural spaces. In this endeavour Nugmanov was aided by his brother Murat, an acclaimed cinematographer with whom he also collaborated on several other projects.[10] The film's greatest visual contrast is between the urban spaces of Almaty and the sun-drenched expanse of the former shore of the dried-up Aral Sea. The images of the Aral Sea region in the film have had significant impact as they brought the reality of the surreal landscape of abandoned ships on the dried-up seabed to a wide audience. Yet the striking thing about the Aral Sea section of the film is its visual beauty, vibrant colours, and rich textures of the landscape and the adobe dwelling where Moro and Dina are staying while he tries to get her off drugs. Paradoxically, even the man-made ecological disaster area comes across in the film as a more optimistic space, as here the pressure of Soviet-style urban society is less palpable, even if traces of the technological (in the form of rusted abandoned ships, a railroad track, and airplanes hovering overhead) continuously reappear in the frame.

Figure 10.1 Still from Rashid Nugmanov's *The Needle*. Moro in the desert.

The fascination of Western critics with *The Needle* and other works of the Kazakh New Wave cinema, was often expressed in a combination with the denial of any meaningful regional specificity to its aesthetic approach. Thus, Andrew Horton and Michael Brashinsky categorically stated that:

> the cinema of the 'Wild Kazakh Boys' is not Kazakh except in location [...] *The Needle* is related to anything but Muslim culture. It is a cousin of the stereotypical Hollywood thriller, melodrama, and road movie, seen through the lens of a European film mentality, particularly that of the French new wave.[11]

This argument, however, is fundamentally flawed, indeed prejudiced, as it presupposes that non-Western cinemas are only expected to deal with colourful folkloric themes and ethnographic specificity, and do not bother with entering the global aesthetic dialogue as equals that are as entitled to bold cutting-edge experimentation as their Western or Russian counterparts. It is also highly puzzling why Horton and Brashinsky believe that in the context of Soviet-era secularism, Central Asian cinema is supposed to be somehow essentially 'Muslim', especially in the case of

Kazakhstan where the titular ethnic group constitutes only a slight majority, and where even in the post-Soviet context less than half of the country's population identifies as Muslim.[12]

A welcome counterbalance to this approach to the film can be found in the work of Gulnara Abikeyeva, one of the leading specialists on Central Asian cinema. While noting that initially international commentators on Kazakh New Wave cinema primarily saw 'the qualities of modern Western cinema' in the Kazakh New Wave, she adds:

> The world saw it, was surprised and accepted it. Why did this happen?
>
> Historically, Kazakhs have been living in the region of the intersection of the West and the East, and as nomads, they have been very adaptive to various cultural influences. The Kazakh film-makers used this cultural ability to adapt and enriched it with a thorough knowledge of Western cinema and Western techniques of film-making; this made their films understandable and open to the whole world.
>
> Here, I would like to draw an analogy to Japanese cinema. Akira Kurosawa, the most Western of Japanese film-makers, had to be the first to be critically acclaimed in Europe before the West accepted other Japanese film directors.
>
> The Kazakh New Wave, being the most Western among the Eastern ones, opened the cinema of Central Asia to the world. The westernization of Kazakh cinema came about as the protest of a colonized country against Sovietization.[13]

A similar argument is pursued by Birgit Beumers; she stresses the film's 'Eurasian theme' and asserts that 'the question of national identity stands [...] very clearly as the backdrop of this film'.[14] *The Needle*'s linguistic heterogeneity (Russian and Kazakh spoken by the characters; French, German, and Italian used in the soundtrack) is much more than a playful nod to globalization (especially in the case of German, linked to the presence of a large German minority in Kazakhstan since the Stalin-era deportations). At the same time, Beumers also draws attention to the stylistic continuity between Nugmanov's film and several key works of Russian cinema, including later ones. Intriguingly, she hypothesizes that:

> in a certain sense [Moro] is a predecessor of Danila Bagrov, the killer-hero of [...] Balabanov's *Brat* [...] with the

difference that Danila is not just ready to engage in brawls, but actually does so. And as in the case of Bagrov, we know nothing about Moro: neither who he is nor what he does for a living, nor what debts he is collecting from Spartak [...]. Moro is committed to action rather than words, and this feature made him a cult hero.[15]

Beumers also notes the film's truly prophetic focus on '"dried-up" and derelict spaces', which anticipated the exacerbated crisis of urban infrastructure and industrial spaces all through the former Soviet Union in the first post-Soviet years, reflecting 'the loss of values and the impending collapse of an entire ideological reference system with an extraordinary acuteness'.[16] Post-modernist 'surface' identities of the film's characters thus signify the destruction of traditional identities of the local population (with the possible exception of the Kazakh-speaking old man in the Aral Sea section of the film).

The retrospective glance has allowed Beumers to seize on the ways in which *The Needle* came to register some of the key concerns of the new Central Asian cinema as it was in the process of finding its new voice in the late 1980s and early 1990s. In her opinion, these concerns include a focus on 'the dream world, placing imagination over reality; second, the superiority of Kazakh tradition over Soviet-style city life; third, the corruption of modern life, leading to the destruction of positive values'. Nugmanov, she argues, interrogates the concept of national identity as it was understood in late Soviet Central Asia and 'points to the conflict between Kazakh tradition and "Soviet-style" progress. He anticipates not only the change in the Soviet value system, but more importantly foresees the concepts of a new, national, Kazakh cinema'.[17]

It would not seen to be an exaggeration, then, to assert that *The Needle* offers a particularly powerful example of what Fredric Jameson has termed 'national allegory'. Jameson developed this concept within the study of non-Western literatures and cultures. In his essay 'Third-World Literature in the Era of Multinational Capitalism', he offers what he himself admits to be a 'sweeping hypothesis', namely that all post-colonial texts 'are necessarily [...] allegorical, and in a very specific way: they are to be read as what [Jameson proposes to] call *national allegories*'. While a dominant feature of Western literature, for Jameson, lies in

a radical split between the private and the public, between the
poetic and the political, between what we have come to think
of as the domain of sexuality and the unconscious and that of
the public world, [post-colonial texts] even those which are
seemingly private and invested with a properly libidinal
dynamic – necessarily project a political dimension in the
form of national allegory: *the story of the private individual
destiny is always an allegory of the embattled situation of the public*
[post-colonial] *culture and society.*[18]

I would argue that national allegory constitutes a crucial part of a
constructive artistic/intellectual project confronting the socio-
cultural condition in which Kazakhstan and other Central Asian
nations found themselves as the Soviet Union was collapsing.
Viewing *The Needle* and the rest of Nugmanov's work through this
prism allows us also to uncover the roots of his later impassioned
engagement as a political activist in his earlier, seemingly apolitical,
incarnation as a film director.

A focus on the allegorical dimensions of the plot and imagery of
The Needle also allows us to trace a logical continuity between this and
other films of the director. *Ya-hha*, then, emerges as a document of
disengagement from the social codes and behavioural patterns of
urban Soviet life as a form of political subversion. *The Needle*, in turn,
highlights the critique of Soviet cultural space as a domain of
Baudrillardian simulacra that erase and crumble identities
grounded in historical continuity and national culture. Finally, *The
Wild East* employs its semi-parodic recycling of the plot of Kurosawa's
Seven Samurai (1954) and its US remake, John Sturges's *The
Magnificent Seven* (1960), to construct a parable about the end of
Soviet civilization and of the *Homo Sovieticus* as a cultural
phenomenon.

Essentially, *The Wild East* is a rich hybrid of cultural forces of
globalization and indigenization. As Arjun Appadurai has noted in
his seminal volume *Modernity at Large*, in critiques of globalization,

> most often, the homogenization argument subspeciates into
> either an argument about Americanization or an argument
> about commoditization, and very often the two arguments are
> closely linked. What these arguments fail to consider is that at
> least as rapidly as forces from various metropolises are
> brought into new societies they tend to become *indigenized* in
> one or another way: this is true of science and terrorism,
> spectacles and constitutions.[19]

Nugmanov's film, in my opinion, offers an almost textbook instance of such interplay.

The Wild East, on the surface, is first and foremost an appropriation of a product of US consumer culture, a Hollywood blockbuster, which itself was a repackaging of a non-Western narrative in a Western (in both senses) garb. However, the film blends the borrowed plot with a rich array of references to Soviet and post-Soviet civilization, from scraps of Soviet culture, both high and popular – a marching song of the young pioneers (ironically sung by a character named Marilyn), a canonical quote from the quintessential 1930s Soviet film, *Chapaev* (1934), and even an allusion to Dovzhenko's *Earth* (1930) in the scene of the arrival of the tractor and the preparation to sowing grain – to a parodic referencing of ideological clichés, like the view of youth subcultures associated with rock music as inherently dangerous and criminal, and further to biting social commentary on hyperinflation, the mass return of ordinary post-Soviet citizens to a subsistence economy, and the haunting after-effects of the war in Afghanistan. Most notably, by transforming the villagers from the original plot into a circus troupe of midgets, nicknamed 'Children of the Sun', that has run away from civilization to start a utopian village community, the film comments most mercilessly on legacies of the deceptive dangers of utopian thinking that underlie the Soviet project, especially for the 'little men'. The group's name, of course, is a mocking reference to an eponymous play by Maxim Gorky, the father of Socialist Realism, while the literalization of the metaphoric designation of 'little man', familiar to everyone who has gone through the Soviet secondary school Russian literature curriculum, comments on the instrumentalization of the canon of high culture by the dominating ideological apparatus of the recently collapsed Soviet state.

As Appadurai notes, in the face of the West's, and the US's in particular, 'endless preoccupation' with itself (with either positive or negative value judgments attached), we should seek to maintain an awareness of the fact that 'globalization is itself a deeply historical, uneven, and even *localizing* process. Globalization does not necessarily or even frequently imply homogenization or Americanization', as 'different societies appropriate the materials of modernity differently'.[20] To be able to appreciate that one needs to be aware that 'the United States is no longer the puppeteer of a world system of images but is only one node of a complex transnational construction of imaginary landscapes', and steer clear

Figure 10.2 The settlement of the 'Children of the Sun' in *The Wild East*, constructed for the filming on the south shore of Lake Issyk Kul in Kyrgyzstan (courtesy of www.yahha.com).

of 'a confusion between some ineffable McDonaldization of the world and the much subtler play of indigenous trajectories of desire and fear with global flows of people and things'.[21] In this complex dynamic, the films of Rashid Nugmanov offer a particularly insightful example of productive strategies of engagement with the cultural aspects of globalization, and are strongly deserving of the continuing, indeed increased, attention in the context of Central Asia and of the entire former Soviet empire. From *Ya-hha*, a *glasnost*-era 'guerrilla' film, Nugmanov moved to *The Needle*, a prescient post-modern pastiche of Soviet and Western culture that emerges as a subtle post-colonially-charged national allegory. Finally, it could be argued that in *The Wild East* we see an example of a film-maker moving to explore what Jameson, in his analysis of another film shot in Central Asia, Alexander Sokurov's *Days of Eclipse* (1988), has proposed to term 'international, or geopolitical, allegory'. Jameson then went on to note that:

> it is the national artists and intellectuals who first sense the modifications imposed by the global market on the relative standing of the national artistic production within which they work. Artists (outside the centre or the superstate itself,

certainly) sense the dilemmas of national subalternity and dependency much earlier than most other social groups.[22]

During his short but remarkable career as a film-maker in the late 1980s and early 1990s, Rashid Nugmanov certainly proved that he possessed the kind of artistic insight and sensitivity Jameson noted in his study. More recently, in an interview to the St Petersburg magazine *Free Time*, Nugmanov tantalizingly hinted at a planned returned to film-making.[23] An unusual if fascinating first step in this direction is represented by *Igla Remix* (2010), a film that is a part restoration, making use of contemporary technology, and part meta-commentary on the earlier project. Technically a new film, it re-edits footage from the 1988 version of *The Needle* (and even incorporates some footage from *Ya-hha* featuring Tsoi); there are minor, if significant changes to the plot, a few additional filmed scenes, and even animated sequences introduced for those plot changes that involve the film's deceased star. This return to his earlier landmark film, much more creative than any other remakes of – and sequels to – Soviet-era films that have appeared in recent years, evidences the director's fine professional form. One hopes that Nugmanov's future projects would carry the marks of the insight and ingenuity that characterized his earlier work.

Notes

1   See Ludmila Zebrina Pruner, 'The New Wave in Kazakh Cinema', *Slavic Review*, 51.4 (1992): 791–801 (p. 799).

2   According to Nugmanov's personal website www.yahha.com, he first used this term in the press notes accompanying the screenings of the films by young Kazakh film-makers at the XVI Moscow International Film Festival in July 1989.

3   See Andrew Horton and Michael Brashinsky, *The Zero Hour: Glasnost and Soviet Cinema in Transition* (Princeton, 1992), p. 238.

4   *Tusovka* is a Russian colloquialism, originally referring to spontaneous gatherings of members of bohemian urban artistic circles in the late 1970s and 1980s. The art theorist Viktor Miziano defines *tusovka* in this narrow sense as an original sociocultural phenomenon, a grouping of individuals consolidated not through a particular ideology or institution, but through a prospect of acquiring them, a type of artistic community that sees itself as a 'pure potentiality'. See Miziano, '"Tusovka" kak sotiokul'turnyi fenomen', in *Khudozhestvennaia kul'tura XX veka: Sbornik statei* (Moscow, 2002), pp. 352–63 (p. 353). Available online at: http://ec-dejavu.ru/t-2/Tusovka.html (accessed 13 March 2011).

5   Birgit Beumers, '*Igla/The Needle*', in Beumers, ed., *24 Frames: The Cinema of Russia and the Former Soviet Union* (London & New York, 2007), pp. 213–21 (p. 216).

6   Pruner, 'The New Wave in Kazakh Cinema', 799–800.

7   A genre of Soviet cinema that focuses on the mundane aspects of daily life of its characters; the term derives from the Russian word *byt* that signifies the mundane aspects of daily life. The term was coined in Soviet film criticism during the 1920s to refer to films dealing with contemporary life, and returned to active use in the 1970s. As Anna Lawton notes, the term 'can be approximately translated as 'slice-of-life' film. These are stories about contemporary society, individual lives and relations, current problems, and human values. The *bytovoi* film could be anything from comedy to "problematic melodrama"' (Lawton, 'Towards a New Openness in Soviet Cinema, 1976–1987', in Daniel J. Goulding, ed., *Post New Wave Cinema in the Soviet Union and Eastern Europe* (Bloomington, 1989), pp. 1–50 (p. 6).

8   Michael Brashinsky on filmreference.com, www.filmreference.com/Films-Hi -Ik/Igla.html (accessed 13 March 2011).

9   Ibid.

10   Murat Nugmanov also served as the cinematographer for another seminal film of the Kazakh New Wave, Serik Aprymov's *The Last Stop*.

11   Horton and Brashinsky, pp. 239–40.

12   See the entry on Kazakhstan in the *CIA World Factbook*, www.cia.gov/library/ publications/the-world-factbook/geos/kz.html (accessed 13 March 2011).

13   Gulnara Abikeyeva, 'Ten Years under the Winds of Different Ideologies: The Cinema of Kazakhstan, Kyrgyzstan, Uzbekistan, Turkmenistan and Tajikistan', *KinoKultura: Special Issue on Central Asian Cinema* (2004), www.kinokultura .com/CA/A2tenyears.html (accessed 20 October 2011).

14   Beumers, '*Igla/The Needle*', pp. 215, 217.

15   Beumers, p. 216.

16   Beumers, p. 219.

17   Beumers, p. 221.

18   Jameson, 'Third-World Literature in the Era of Multinational Capitalism', *Social Text* 15 (1986): 65–88 (p.69); emphasis in the original.

19   Arjun Appadurai, *Modernity at Large: Cultural Dimensions of Globalization* (Minneapolis, 1996), p. 32; emphasis in the original.

20   Appadurai, *Modernity at Large*, p. 17; emphasis in the original.

21   Appadurai, pp. 29–30.

22   Fredric Jameson, *The Geopolitical Aesthetic: Cinema and Space in the World System* (Bloomington, 1992), p. 110.

23   Konstantin Fedorov, 'Zhizn' i plany Rashida Nugmanova', interview with Rashid Nugmanov, *Free Taim* 1 (2008), www.freetime-spb.ru/article/43/ 13110/ (accessed 2 October 2011).

PART III

THE ERA OF INDEPENDENCE

11

CINEMATIC NATION-BUILDING IN KAZAKHSTAN

Gulnara Abikeyeva

T he concepts of home and family form the basis of any society. Hence, building a house is often compared to the construction of the state, while the family reflects harmony and prosperity in society; as Walker Conner notes, '[t]he Nation [is] the fully extended family'.[1] The representation of these two concepts in film serves as an indicator of stability and of the level of development of the state. In the Soviet era, many films reflected the nation's consciousness, but the family was often shown as incomplete. The absence of the father figure reflected the dependency and lack of freedom among the people of the 'Soviet east'. What has changed following independence? Has a complete and happy family emerged? In this chapter I shall consider the images of the hero/heroine, the family, and the nation as a whole in Soviet Kazakh cinema and their transformation after independence.

Reverberations of the Thaw: 1964–72

The early history of cinema in the 'Soviet east' reveals how film emerged in the first instance as an instrument of ideology and propaganda. The first films focused on women's liberation in the east, such as Mikhail Doronin's *The Second Wife* (Uzbekistan, 1927),

Yefim Aron's *Botagoz* (Kazakhstan, 1957) or Alexei Ochkin's *The Girl of the Tian-Shan* (Kirghizia, 1960). Other films were devoted to the formation of a new community of the Soviet people, to the great construction projects and to the victory of socialism. Positive male characters tended to be self-sacrificing revolutionaries, as is evident in the protagonists of Andrei Konchalovsky's *The First Teacher* (Kirghizia, 1965), Abdulla Karsakbaev's *Restless Morning* (Kazakhstan, 1966), Ali Khamraev's *Extraordinary Commissar* (Uzbekistan, 1970) and *The Seventh Bullet* (Uzbekistan, 1972). These heroes defended the Revolution, and often went against national traditions.

Only during the Thaw, which arrived in Central Asia with a slight delay and affected culture from 1964 to 1972, did films began to reflect Central Asian national identities as well as the destructive role of Soviet ideology. In Kazakhstan, films such as Abdulla Karsakbaev's *My Name is Kozha* (1963), Mazhit Begalin's *Traces Go Beyond the Horizon* (1964), Shaken Aimanov's *The Beardless Deceiver* (1964) and *The Land of the Fathers* (1966), Sultan Khodjikov's *Kyz-Zhibek* (1969–70) and Kanymbek Kasymbekov's *Shok and Sher* (1972) truly exemplified national cinema and formed the basis of the modern nation-building process that began during the Soviet era. Mira and Antonin Liehm wrote about Soviet cinema that, at the time, 'a true autonomous film culture emerged, so autonomous and natural, so fresh and real that it aroused trepidation',[2] because the representation of national culture introduced alternative ideological values and different outlooks. Despite intense ideological control, the 1960's generation managed to capture their cultural values, because national cadres of directors, screenwriters, actors and artists emerged by that time, who could adequately present the worldview of their people. Aimanov, Begalin, Karsakbaev and Khodjikov represented the traditional Kazakh way of life for the first time in cinema. The films of these years represented the historic and epic heroes of the Kazakh people, unravelled national myths and world views and promoted the concept of national selfhood.

The title of the film *My Name is Kozha* contained an implicit challenge; it could actually be titled *My name is Kazakh*. The name Kozha is unusual, because it refers to the Kazakh word for a person who completes the *Hajj* to Mecca and is respected in society. At the same time, Kozha is the name of one of the aristocratic Kazakh tribes. Interestingly, the action of the film takes place in two completely different spaces. Kozha lives in a village with wooden houses, birch trees, a Soviet school, the Soviet way of life, all of which

Figure 11.1 Poster for Sultan Khodjikov's *Kyz-Zhibek* (1969–70).

were typical for Soviet films of those years. But one day, Kozha's older friend, a shepherd, takes him into the mountains and thus opens up a completely different world to him: the world of the Kazakh *aul*, of nomadic life. If the 'lower' world of the village is artificial and freshly decorated, then the 'upper' world is natural and filmed in a documentary style. This episode shows a celebration on the *jailoo*, as people sit in groups, sing, cook and play the *dombïra*. The director creates a fascinating transition from one world to the other: when the boys go into the mountains and pass by a mountain lake, an older boy offers Kozha a smoke. He begins to feel dizzy after a few puffs, slips from his horse, and seems to be losing consciousness; after that, they enter the 'upper world' of Kazakh life.

Even bolder was the display of Kazakh spiritual values in *The Land of the Fathers*, written by Olzhas Suleimenov and directed by Shaken Aimanov. The film begins with a close-up of a tombstone with an Arabic inscription. For the time this was a bold display, as was the showing of a Muslim burial and an old man's prayers. The first episodes presented the traditional world of the Kazakhs: the steppe, the river, the sounds of the *dombïra*; and then we see that the old man and his grandson leave the newly-constructed tomb in order to fetch the son's ashes from some remote corner of Russia. This small episode points at ethnic codes and at the film's powerful concept:

there is a grave, but there are no ashes. For Kazakhs there is no worse punishment than not to be buried in the native soil.

The remainder of the film takes place along the road, another powerful archetypal code for nomads. Here, on a train passing through the endless Kazakh steppe, the old man and the grandson have meaningful encounters with an archaeologist and his daughter-in-law, an old Chechen man, and a Red Army soldier. However, they fail to bring home the remains of their loved one, but on this journey they lose and find each other, not simply on the level of the action but also in terms of two generations coming closer.

Interestingly, in these two films, and in many other Kazakh films of the Soviet era there is an incomplete family. Typically, the father has died or perished during the war, while the children are raised by the women: mothers and grandmothers, or – as in *The Land of the Fathers* – by grandfathers. The role of the father in Soviet ideology preoccupied the state: first in the image of Stalin, and later in that of the Communist Party. Therefore, there were hardly any films with a strong national hero. This task was fulfilled either by the Russian 'elder brother' or the director of some government agency, such as a chairman of a collective farm or a school director.

Grandmothers and grandfathers – the cinematic heroes of the older generation – became the bearers of national culture in films with a contemporary setting, while young heroes appeared only in historical or mythological contexts, such as *Kyz-Zhibek*. Thus, it is not surprising that films of the Soviet era lacked adult male heroes and strong fathers, but showed the Kazakhs as schoolchildren and adolescents.

The Era of *Perestroika*: 1988–91

A young, handsome, strong, and courageous new hero arrived in Kazakh cinema during *perestroika*. Suffice it to recall Viktor Tsoi from Rashid Nugmanov's *The Needle* (1988), the heroic idol of Soviet youth; and the young people from Serik Aprymov's *The Last Stop* (1989), Amir Karakulov's *A Woman Between Two Brothers* (1991) and Darejan Omirbaev's *Kairat* (1991), those boys from the *aul* and from the city whose faces became emblematic during *perestroika* in Kazakhstan. At last, strong young men emerged on the screen. By definition, they were rebels and revolutionaries, coming from the Soviet underground: the words of Viktor Tsoi's 'We Want Change!' became the mantra for an entire generation. Rashid Nugmanov not only announced a new era in *The Needle*, but he also proclaimed the death of the old age. Thus, the antagonist with the symbolic name Spartak (Spartacus) openly declares, 'I let everybody go, and let myself go' ('*Ia raspuskaiu i sam raspuskaius*'). The name Spartak sounds like a joke; in a climactic scene he climbs on to a pedestal and assumes the pose of Lenin as he shouts: 'Follow me! Forward! And then backward! Freedom for everyone! Existence alone does not mean consciousness!' – which directly parodies Soviet films about Lenin. Spartak embodies the bankrupt Soviet ideology, while Dina – the only female character in the film – depends upon various men. While Moro (played by Tsoi) was away at some distant place, Dina's father (a symbol of the Soviet past) died. Doctor Arthur, a mobster and drug dealer, has assumed the father's role and represents the arrival of a new, semi-criminal rule. Doctor Arthur has made Dina dependent on drugs and used her apartment for storing them. Upon learning of Arthur's background, Moro takes Dina to an abandoned house on the Aral Sea to get her clean – a trip that parodies the romantic journey of two lovers: instead of walking by the sea at sunset, the sea has receded, leaving only salt behind; instead of kisses, there is nausea, pain, and suffering. The greatest amusement is a tin full of scorpions. The image of Dina is a metaphor for modern Kazakh society: subjected to violence from all sides and in need of a period of withdrawal.

If Tsoi's hero was the antithesis of the Soviet system, the hero of Aprymov's *The Last Stop* protested against the foundations of the modern Kazakh village, the *aul*. The heroes of Karakulov's *A Woman Between Two Brothers*, urban kids listening to The Beatles, represented the changing times: this was no longer the Soviet era. The young hero of Omirbaev's *Kairat* had to overcome the disjuncture of epochs and the consequences of the old system. None of these heroes had been seen in Kazakh films before, so that the 'Kazakh New Wave' unleashed a wave of problems previously unheard of.

The male hero changed, and so did the images of women. But the 'liberated women of the east' of the 1930s and the heroines of labour and war of the 1940s were not replaced by strong female characters; in their place appeared drug addicts, prostitutes, the blind and deaf – in short, flawed women. As we have seen in the case of *The Needle*, these female characters were linked to the image of the motherland. One of the story lines of Aprymov's *The Last Stop* concerns the fact that the hero's beloved was forcibly married when

Figure 11.2 Poster for Amir Karakulov's *A Woman Between Two Brothers* (1991).

he served in the army. At the end of the film they meet again in a strange scene: they have sex underneath a lorry, while the girl's mother-in-law holds her foot on the truck's brakes. The hero's beloved woman has been taken away, but there is no other woman waiting for him. In *A Woman Between Two Brothers* Ella is killed; in *Kairat* the ideal image of the beloved collapses when the protagonist sees her having sex with a handsome train conductor. The blind Aimagan in Amanjol Aituarov's *Touch* (1989) is a victim of abuse. The heroic women, beautiful mistresses and caring mothers of the 1960s, have gone; instead women are relegated to roles as prostitutes, exposed to danger and humiliation. The attitude towards women is a barometer of a society's well-being. The more stable a society, the more contented its images of women. If there are no beautiful lovers in a film, there can be no families. Thus, the heroines of the 'New Wave' were single women who wanted to make a revolution, but could not even build a new life.

The First Years of Independence: 1992-7

Perhaps the 1990s were the most difficult years of self-identification under a new way of life. The old system had been destroyed, but the new one was still uncertain. On the one hand, it was a positive sign that there was neither censorship nor ideological constraints; on the other hand, however, values and moral orientations had disappeared. This confusion in the minds of people affected cinema also. It suffices to recall the titles of some Kazakh films of those years: *Journey to Nowhere, Running Target, The Stranger, Wild East, Shanghai, Cardiogram, Tender Heart* and *Killer.*

Cinema was mainly engaged in overcoming various 'complexes': post-Soviet, post-colonial and post-ideological. Therefore, in these years film-makers strove to restore historical truth and tell about important events and figures of a bygone era: the period of collectivization in Kazakhstan in Damir Manabaev's *Surzhekey, The Angel of Death* (1991); the Gulag camps in Gennadi Zemel's *Ravenous* (1991); the tragic events of December 1986[3] in Kalykbek Salykov's *Lovers of December* (1991) and Kaldybai Abenov's *Allazhar* (1993); and simply historical films about legendary figures, such as Ardak Amirkulov's *Death of Otrar* (1991) and *Youth of Abai* (1995), and Kanymbek Kasymbekov's *Zhambyl* (1996). All things Soviet were eliminated and replaced with an heroic, pre-Soviet past when strong *batyrs* were the pillars of the nation. But this chapter is concerned with the transformation of the hero in films with a modern setting.

Tsoi's hero of *The Needle* multiplied and turned into 'The Magnificent Seven' of Rashid Nugmanov's next film *Wild East* (1993). Then, the young heroes of Aituarov's *Journey to Nowhere* (1992) hope to travel to Los Angeles in a stolen airplane, but their journey ended on a military facility, the training area (*poligon*) in the Kazakh steppe. The hero of Aprymov's *The Last Stop* moves to the city, while *Dream within a Dream* (1992) shows urban life also as ridiculous and absurd. The peak of disappointments and frustrations is captured in the image of the protagonist in Ermek Shinarbaev's *The Place on the Gray Triangular Hat* (1993), who transmits the sense of a lost generation, while the Western-oriented characters look empty and lost.

But another hero emerged – a boy openly looking at the world, who is truly rooted in national traditions: the teenager in Darejan Omirbaev's *Cardiogram* (1995); the young musician in Satybaldy Narymbetov's *The Life of a Young Accordion Player* (1994); or the boy who has strange dreams in Timur Suleimenov's *The Stranger* (1993).

In the early years of independence children were once again at the heart of films, symbolizing the birth of a new nation and the formation of the new state. In this context it is clear why Nugmanov turned all the villagers into Lilliputians as they begin to build a new life in *Wild East.*

Unlike the warped heroines of the *perestroika* era, this period sees the emergence of the romantic heroine, sometimes with an ironic touch, as the young pioneer Marilyn (played by Zhanna Isina) in *Wild East*; sometimes in a serious manner, as Dana Kairbekova's character in *Journey to Nowhere*; but there are also purely romantic heroines, as Elmira Makhmutova's character Elya in Amir Karakulov's *The Dove's Bell-Ringer* (1993).

But there is no family yet. The heroine is weak and defenceless in *Journey to Nowhere*; women do not have a place in society in *The Place on the Gray Triangular Hat*; the heroine dies in childbirth in *The Dove's Bell-Ringer*; or the hero dies, as in *The Stranger.* The exception is Omirbaev's *Killer* (1998): this film begins with the main character picking up his wife and newborn son from the hospital. He is then involved in a car accident that triggers a chain of events which ultimately force him to become a killer. Families are not formed, but rather they disintegrate, sometimes as an isolated incident or an absurd tragedy, sometimes echoing the collapse of the large Soviet family.

Thus, in *Shanghai* (1996) Alexander Baranov explains the seemingly simple, everyday story of the residents in a district of Almaty that is to be demolished. First, rumours abound that they can get a better apartment – for a price. After a while it turns out that a crook who takes bribes sold the same new apartment twice, to two friends, a helicopter pilot and a policeman. Having discovered this, the friends quarrel and fight, then suddenly an earthquake hits, a frequent phenomenon in Almaty. The misfortune unites the protagonists, but the cataclysm and the desire to 'disband into individual apartments' is also a metaphor of the time. In fact, the film tells the story of the collapse of the Soviet Union: what kind of family is possible if everyone loafs and the land disappears from under their feet? The film-makers of this period acknowledged the disintegration of the family and the temporary impossibility of its creation.

Nation-Building: 1998–2005

In his famous essay 'On National Culture' (1961),[4] Frantz Fanon describes three stages of post-colonial culture: the first phase is a protest against the colonizers; the second marks a return to the ideal image of traditional culture; the third is the struggle for authentic (genuine, original) culture. According to this division, the first phase coincides with *perestroika* and the first years of independence, while the second phase applies to the cinematic developments after 1998. The process of nation-building begins with the formation of a national idea, which forms the core of the state's ideological concept. Moreover, it is a kind of ideal vision of society and state. But ideals are not a realistic possibility; rather they organize and orientate the minds of people. The creative intelligentsia – artists, writers, film-makers and theatre personalities – are the bearers of such visions and agents of nation-building.

In cinema this process began in 1998 with the appearance of two films: *Aksuat* by Serik Aprymov and *Zamanai* by Bolat Sharipov. Aman, the protagonist of *Aksuat*, declares: 'This is my house, these are my matches', meaning that I'll live here, no matter what – unlike the message to flee the village and old lifestyle in *The Last Stop* ten years earlier. Aprymov's *Aksuat* shows the emergence of a new family. Aman's brother Kanat has a wife and a son; when Kanat goes to the city to sort out his business and his debts, Aman collects his sister-in-law Zhanna and her newborn from the clinic and helps them settle at home. But this is not his family, and this realization causes a crisis for Aman. In the end, he takes Zhanna and the baby back to the city, but he will not leave his native *aul*. The hero is transformed: born and raised in the village, he will not leave it. He is no superman, but he is deeply rooted in his native soil, which gives him strength and makes him fearless.

The heroines also changed, but not as might be expected: mothers were the central characters in films. If in the 1990s the mother almost entirely disappeared from Kazakh cinema, 1998 marks a turning point. In *Zamanai*, Bolat Sharipov creates the character of a strong woman, who fled to China in the 1930s to save her family and not simply returned in the 1990s to her historical homeland – but she does so almost secretly and heroically. Scantily, she steals her infant grandson and takes him with her on the journey. The moment of repatriation, as well as the restoration of their status in their historical homeland is important here, but also the return of the image of the mother and the motherland. Narymbetov's *Leila's Prayer* (2002) goes even further: the heroine of this film is not a grandmother (the past) but a young woman who becomes a mother (the future). As the film's action takes place in a village not far from the Semipalatinsk nuclear test site, the violence of the soldiers against Leila is a metaphor for the violence of the Soviet military system against the Kazakh land. In the film's finale, Leila stands in the window with her infant like the Virgin Mary, thus prompting the viewer to consider Leila as an extension of the Kazakh land, disfigured and worn out by trials and depravations. But she is young and full of strength, as the new independent Kazakh state, so there is hope for salvation.

In this period there is a curious tendency to display an artificial family: people brought together into a family who are not tied by blood. Such a pattern can be found in Karakulov's *Don't Cry!* (2002), Gulshad Omarova's *Schizo* (2004), Aprymov's *The Hunter* (2004), and is a reflection of the real situation in the multinational Kazakhstan. In *Don't Cry!* the old woman is neither the mother nor the grandmother, but she raises the seven-year old girl, while the young woman is neither a daughter nor a mother, but also helps with the girl's education. The desire to share the responsibility and help the child survive matters here more than blood kinship. Sadly, the women do not succeed, but their attempt to support the child is a symbol of the new emerging statehood. Another paradigm operates in Omarova's *Schizo*: He is a young man with mental disabilities, mingling in the criminal world; she is a Russian prostitute who dreams of going to China; but they take a homeless Kazakh boy under their wings. The artificial family is further developed in Aprymov's *The Hunter* in a family composed of a hunter, a prostitute and an adopted boy, Erkin. In the words of Francis Fukuyama,[5] he is a 'non-kin father' and she is a 'non-kin mother'. But she brought him up to the age when the personality is formed: here the hunter appears. He is a strong, single man, a warrior who lives in the mountains, away from the people. When people encounter him they ask for their children to be blessed. His eyes are of an unusual blue; his height is that of a knight. Given the circumstances, the hunter takes Erkin with him to the mountains to teach him everything he knows: to listen to nature, to care for a horse, to love a woman, and even to breathe correctly. The film explains how a non-kin father raises a boy, that is a human father raises a wolf-cub child. Erkin was born to a she-wolf who died when giving birth, while a five-toed wolf from the Altai for some reason all the time is in the same place as the hunter and the boy. It turns out that it is not the hunter who tracks down the five-toed wolf, but the wolf-father who wants his son back. Then the story takes on an entirely different meaning: the origin of the first Turkic man. Aprymov was the first film-maker in Central Asia – and perhaps the entire post-Soviet space – to create a myth about the birth of a new man, a new nation, based on ethnic roots, making a first attempt at building a story on a blank sheet of paper without post-Soviet reflections. Maybe this is the approach required for the third Fanonian phase which marks the struggle for authentic culture.

Considering the diverse family models in the film, the father emerges as the hero and the mother as the heroine. Films from 1998 to the present day can essentially be divided into three categories: first, films without fathers: Aprymov's *Three Brothers* (2000), Karakulov's *Don't Cry!* and Narymbetov's *Leila's Prayer*; second, films where the function of the father is taken on by stepfathers or strangers: Aprymov's *Aksuat*, Omarova's *Schizo*, Aprymov's *The Hunter* and even Sergei Bodrov, Talgat Temenov and Ivan Passer's *The Nomad* (2005) and Rustem Abdrashev's *Patchwork Quilt* (2007); third, films that attempt to build a strong father-image: Abdrashev's *Renaissance Island* (2004), Aituarov's *Steppe Express* (2005) and Zhanabek Zhetiruov's *Notes of a Railwayman* (2006). The first category of films addresses primarily the Soviet era; the second reflects upon the process of independence; and the third reveals the present day as the state gains stability.

Renaissance Island tells a retro-story of the 1960s set on a remote fishing island; the central teenage character not only has a father, but is a man with self-respect and confidence. He is able to resist the local authorities and raise his sons. He even has two wives, *baibishe* and *tokal*, senior and junior. The appearance of such a father in Kazakh cinema – a self-sufficient, and freethinking man – marks a turning point in the process of nation-building. In this film the father is no hero or sacrificial character, which was a prerequisite of Soviet ideology (when he would certainly have been reproached for bigamy). He is just a father, a strong man, who is respectfully remembered by his son, a poet.

Another important film in this context is Zhetiruov's *Notes of a Railwayman*, which is set along the railway, underlining once again underlines the archetypal topos of the road for Kazakhs. The protagonist, an old man who has turned blind in old age and determines faults in the tracks by the sound of the wheels: he represents the Soviet past. His son, the new foreman of repairmen, symbolizes the present. The grandson, a pupil at the school, embodies the country's future. For the first time in independent

Kazakh cinema a family appears with an apparent continuity of generations in the male line: grandfather, father, and son. There is a quiet harmony in their relationships: the son listens to the advice of his father, the father protects his son, and the grandfather engages with his grandson. Of course, there are family problems and scandals, but these are quite normal.

The manner in which fathers appear in Kazakh cinema indicates that society, 15 years after independence, is finally beginning to gain a sense of well-established life, where there is room for everybody: fathers, sons and grandfathers. The heroes are masters of their land again. Obviously, the next step in Kazakh cinema should be a picture of a complete and harmonious family with a mother, father, child or, even better, a few children. Given the Asian mentality, one should see not only the nuclear family, but also the family over several generations, which has been and remains a major social capital of Central Asian societies. As soon as cinema reflects the complete family in our society, we can talk about stability and state development again.

Translated by Michael Rouland and Birgit Beumers

Notes

1   Walker Connor, 'A Few Cautionary Notes on the History and Future of Ethnonational Conflicts', in Andreas Wimmer et al., eds, *Facing Ethnic Conflicts: Towards a New Realism* (Oxford, 2004), p. 23.

2   Mira Liehm and Antonin Liehm, *The Most Important Art: Soviet and East European Film after 1945* (Berkeley, 1977), p. 325.

3   The riots from 16 to 19 December 1986 in Alma-Ata, known as *Jeltoqsan*, were a protest against Mikhail Gorbachev's dismissal of the ethnic Kazakh Dinmukhamed Konaev as First Secretary of the Communist Party of Kazakhstan and replacing him with the Russian Gennadii Kolbin. The initially peaceful riots ended in violence after the intervention of Special Forces.

4   Frantz Fanon, *The Wretched of the Earth* (New York, 1963).

5   Francis Fukuyama, *The End of History* (New York, 1992).

12

AESTHETIC INFLUENCES IN YOUNG KAZAKH CINEMA

Eugénie Zvonkine

T he films of young Kazakh film-makers in the 2000s strike local and international audiences with their abrupt aesthetic changes: 'Even at first sight the changes in their cinematographic language and in the choice of characters and subjects are obvious.'[1] Of course, the mere desire to stand apart from the previous generations can be observed in every successive generation and does not account for the way in which directors' styles and the entire cinematography evolve. Among possible explanations are not only the complete transformation of modes of film production and of political and social context within the country, but also a real disruption in the way of discovering cinema in the 1990s and 2000s. The observation of these numerous, disorderly and eclectic aesthetic influences are instrumental in the analysis of these transformations.

Speaking of the emerging film culture in this way does not, however, suggest its reduction to a sum of heterogeneous influences. Each subject, character or aesthetic tendency is specifically and personally transformed by the young film directors and finds its proper place in their universe. But tracing the source of these influences will allow us a better understanding of the internal evolution of their personal styles.

This necessitates a brief excursion into the work of the previous generation. The 1990s were a crucial epoch for all the Central Asian republics, not only politically but also culturally. During this period the cinematographic landscape underwent drastic changes. But among all the republics Kazakhstan seems to have gone further than the rest at this historical moment, since it has seen a true cinematographic renaissance.[2]

Most Kazakh film-makers of the 'New Wave' studied at the Film Institute VGIK in the 1980s: Serik Aprymov, Darejan Omirbaev, Amir Karakulov, Rashid Nugmanov, Abai Karpykov and Ardak Amirkulov were selected for a course run by Sergei Soloviev,[3] who equipped them with a set of aesthetic references ranging from Italian Neorealism to the French New Wave.[4]

The film-makers of this period are well aware of their common tastes and educational background: '"The New Wave" are people born ten to fifteen years after the war. They were brought up on certain models of Soviet and foreign cinema. This can be felt in their culture, in their approach, in their aesthetics',[5] states Abai Karpykov. Years later, when asked to name the most important sources of his aesthetic inspiration, Darejan Omirbaev spoke above all of a sequence in Jean-Luc Godard's *My Life to Live* [*Vivre sa vie*, 1962], using a high angle shot when the heroine returns home and tries to escape from her landlady.[6] The name of their movement chosen at the Moscow Film Festival was also justified by another resemblance with the French New Wave: as the French film-makers shared a desire to make a new cinema different from the one that had existed rather than a particular style.

The first films of the 'Kazakh New Wave' adopt an idiosyncratic way of dealing with the formal constraints of the epoch. Suffice it to recall the anecdote of what happened to Serik Aprymov, when he was asked to add something to his film to reach the 80 minutes imposed by the state standard: he inserted in the beginning frontal portraits of his heroes in a documentary manner, thus disrupting the narrative of the film. Thus, when making an inventory of the present situation in the young Kazakh cinema of the 2000s, i.e. the generation that follows, we should keep in mind their relationship to a movement of world renown as well as an awareness of a completely transformed film production and distribution system.

The first characteristic of these young film-makers shooting their first short or feature-length films in the 2000s is that they did not go through VGIK.[7] Many young film-makers went to the Zhurgenov

National Academy of Arts in Almaty.[8] Others, like Rustem Abdrashev or Sabit Kurmanbekov, began to work in the cinema as production designers before starting to shoot films in the 2000s.

In order to understand the various aesthetic influences of these young film-makers, the kind of teaching provided in the Academy of Art is central. The film-making department is organized in the same way as in VGIK, that is by workshops. Here, a film-maker selects his own students and teaches them. Obviously, like at VGIK, the instructor has a clear influence in their aesthetic evolution, which shows in three ways.

First, a student can be directly affected by the films of one of his teachers, the more so that the latter are Kazakh film-makers of renown. For instance, after systematic use of non-professional actors by the film-makers of the Kazakh New Wave,[9] it seems absolutely natural for the young cinematographers of the 2000s to draw exclusively on non-professionals. In several short films certain parts are even performed by the members of the film crew: in *The Touch* (2005) by Abai Kulbai, the principal part is played by Alexei Shindin, his production designer, and in *The Lip* (2004) by Erzhan Rustembekov the part of the boy who gets his lip bitten off is played by his assistant; in the same way Sabit Kurmanbekov, production designer to Serik Aprymov, performs the leading parts in *The Last Stop* (1989) and *Aksuat* (1998). In the short *Bakhytzhamal* (2007) by Adilkhan Erzhanov, the main part is performed by another young director, Serik Abishev, just as Djamshed Usmonov plays the main part in Darejan Omirbaev's *The Road* (2001).

Moreover, some of the films are on the border between fiction and documentary: this concerns *The Potter* (2000) by Abai Kulbai, a film that observes life in a small village whose inhabitants are played by real local people, but also *Asel, through the Eyes of Men,* a film-encounter in the form of a conversation with a girl met by the film-maker where a few exaggerated fictional elements only emphasize the ambiguity and ambivalence of the real person and the fascination she exercises on the film-maker.[10] Emir Baigazin's *Zhan's Diary* (2009), as its title suggests, displays a style close to the tradition of a cinematographic diary.

But within this influence we are able to discern another, indirect one. The teacher and well-known film-maker shows his students those films that shaped him during his apprenticeship. His own preferences leave traces in his teaching. In the case of the Kazakh New Wave the heritage is at least twofold. The most obvious example is that of Nariman Turebaev, who attended Darejan Omirbaev's courses in the Academy of Arts. Much has been written on the aesthetic resemblance of Omirbaev's cinema to that of Robert Bresson. Even Turebaev's first short films are clearly influenced by the aesthetic choices of his teacher: frontal staging, minimal dialogues, distant and impenetrable play of actors. The recurrent device of putting characters out of frame also resembles that of Omirbaev: the young couple of Turebaev's *Antiromantika* (2001) that disappears by the lower side of the frame when making love is reminiscent of Omirbaev's method of systematically leaving scenes of sex or violence out of frame. At the Academy of Arts students are also acquainted with the classics of Soviet cinema. As former VGIK students, the masters initiate their students to the Soviet heritage. In certain films we discover framing or editing that resemble that of great Soviet film-makers.

Last but not least, the teachers select the students, who enter the professional world. Thus, Darejan Omirbaev, convinced of the bonds between his own work and that of his student Nariman Turebaev, took him under his wings after his graduation from the Academy.

Turebaev's first full-length film *Little Men* (2003) was produced by Limara Zheksembaeva, Darejan Omirbaev's wife and producer. In the same way, Ardak Amirkulov, who led a workshop and taught numerous students, later helped them to enter the professional world. Two of his students, Erlan Nurmukhambetov and Erzhan Rustembekov, have been credited as co-scriptwriters of his film *Farewell, Gulsary* (2008) but according to certain accounts they also worked as co-directors during the film making.[11]

In this connection, the Grand Prix to Abai Kulbai at the Eurasia International Film Festival for his first full-length *Swift* (2007) is extremely important: the young film-maker insisted on offering this prize to his teacher, Ardak Amirkulov, whom he called to the stage.

Yet another source of influence concerns those who become film directors after having worked in a different function in film-making. It is only natural that they should feel the influence of their previous experience. Thus, Rustem Abdrashev has worked, among others, with Satybaldy Narymbetov for *The Life of a Young Accordion Player* (1994). In his first film, *Renaissance Island* (2004), the influence of Narymbetov is clear. The interplay of black-and-white and colour, the choice of the plot (in Narymbetov's film the action takes place in the postwar, Stalinist Kazakhstan), and the main character (the village is seen through the eyes of a young boy) are the same in both films.

Figure 12.1 Still from the film *Swift* (2007) by Abai Kulbai.

Another source of inspiration for Abdrashev is the Kyrgyz film, *The Adopted Son* (1998) by Aktan Abdykalykov (Arym Kubat) who made similar aesthetic and narrative choices. Otherwise, while Abdykalykov has chosen autobiography, Abdrashev has openly preferred his father's biography.

Besides the changes in the educational system in the last decade, the aesthetic views of the young directors of the 2000s have also been affected by another element. Political changes accompanied the upheaval of the film distribution system, which had collapsed in the republics of Central Asia, with the majority of cinemas closed. When Omirbaev explains how he became a cinephile, we can see the importance of his education:

> In Almaty there was no film library and there is none today. On the other hand, at that time cinemas were the only distraction accessible to everybody, therefore much frequented. In general, we went to see Soviet films but from time to time we could also see foreign films. Later, in Moscow, I discovered many films, particularly French cinema.[12]

For the new generation, their knowledge of cinema comes through videos (often pirated) accessible on the market, mostly with rudimentary translations. Their cinematographic education is self-made, eclectic, erratic and often dependent on chance encounters before they enter the Academy. Abai Kulbai stated in an interview:

> As a child, I often stayed alone at home. The only thing that saved me was television and films. Later I started collecting films on videotapes. I was 13 or 14 when I came up to a video stall and asked the salesman for *Scent of a Woman* with Al Pacino. The guy was really proud I had asked for this film. Or *Blue Velvet...* Imagine a little brat in a baseball cap asking the salesman for *Blue Velvet...*[13]

In another interview he explained that, seeing his interest, the video salesmen started to propose certain films from their collections.[14]

The influence of films varies from one film-maker to another, yet clearly the video markets, as well as the few films released in the cinemas, are heavily dominated by commercial US films. Unsurprisingly, the characteristics of 'commercial cinema' manifest themselves in certain films and certain aesthetic choices. This could explain the abrupt and surprising reversal of the young film-maker Serikbol Utepbergenov who, with his short *Mute Coolness* (2004), clearly positioned himself in the camp of *auteur* cinema; then he made his first feature film, *The Jackal: Umarasa* (2007), which awkwardly links the typical features of commercial and genre cinema: fight scenes, mafia, gypsies, a bar singer who is the mistress of a fat and cruel mafia boss, and who falls in love with a nonchalant young thief.

Among these encounters of the young Kazakh film-makers and foreign cinema, one example is Rustem Abdrashev, drawing his inspiration for *Patchwork Quilt* (2007) from the universe of Emir Kusturica and his gallery of colourful characters animated by jovial, everyday craziness.

Moreover, there are nods to *Hate* [*La Haine*, 1995] by Mathieu Kassovitz. Certain film-makers willingly speak of the importance of this film.[15] Its influence is especially evident in the short film by Erzhan Rustembekov, *The Stains* (2001). It tells the story of bored, young people wandering in the maze of concrete buildings and amusing themselves with petty crimes and short-lived attempts of seduction. Everything in this short film, from the plot to the somewhat loose narrative structure and the film-maker's way to observe the actors' charisma and their way of filling space, points to the influence of *Hate*.

On the other hand, Rustembekov's script for *Push* (2010) is a compilation of borrowings from US cinema and contemporary Russian commercial films. It is the story of a young athlete who has to get back to basketball after a serious injury, while winning back the love of his life. Everything – from swift camera movements, clip-like editing, a Russian star cast for the role of the miracle-making coach to the voice-over – makes the film look like a typical teenager film. However, it has a complicated timeline with numerous flash-backs that makes the plot less easily understandable and reminds of an *auteur* approach to cinema.

Another source of inspiration for these young film-makers is television. In our days it exercises an important influence on all contemporary young directors, but its impact in Kazakhstan is increased by the almost complete absence of theatrical distribution in the 1990s. Thus, Abai Kulbai does not hide the fact that he discovered the majority of Kazakh films of the 1960s as well as latest Kazakh 'easterns' through television.

The Kazakh film shown on television that seems to have exercised the greatest impact on these young directors is Kalykbek Salykov's *The Balcony* (1988), the film-precursor of the 'Kazakh New Wave'. Its influence goes back to many recent films either in the choice of the plot or in certain episodes. *Balcony* tells the story of two opposing gangs of teenagers in the 1950s, who fight in Alma-Ata's streets. The theme of fights between two teenage clans often appears in the films of young Kazakh film-makers. *The Lip* by Erzhan Rustembekov begins in this way: two rows of teenagers face each other to await the signal to start a scuffle. A similar scene opens the film in one of the intermediate script versions of Kulbai's *Swift*.

However, the heterogeneous influences visible in these films do not in any way cast a doubt on the individuality of the artists or their artistic universe. Maybe it is precisely their method to appropriate and blend influences, no matter how eclectic, that allows them to make films that are truly innovative for Kazakh cinema.

Thus, Nariman Turebaev draws on the aesthetics of Darejan Omirbaev. Abai Kulbai in *Swift*, as well as in his script *Mushel Zhas* (2009), takes up one of the typical elements of Kazakh cinema: the incessant motion of the main character, who seems unable to stop.

Feature films, such as *Little Men, Swift, Zhosha* (2005) and *Together with Father* (2008) by Daniyar Salamat, *Schizo* (2004) and *Native*

Dancer (2008) by Gulshad (Guka) Omarova, as well as *Karoy* by Zhanna Issabaeva (2007), give credit to the classic narration in the *oeuvre* of the elder generation. Some of their tributes, however, are openly ironic: *Little Men* starts by a close-up on what looks like the traditional ornament on a Kazakh carpet or quilt. This kind of shot sends us back to a whole school of Central Asian cinema focusing on local traditions. But a few seconds later, the bemused and amused spectator discovers that it was a close-up on the hero's underpants.

In the same way the short *Mute Coolness* by Serikbol Utepbergenov, which tells the story of a young drug-addict put in a cell with a dumb old man who has a cricket for a pet, is indebted to Soviet cinema in its choice of sepia, its framing and perfectly mastered narration, as well as its sound track inspired by Andrei Tarkovsky. *Mute Coolness* is also indebted to silent cinema – the dumbness of the old man is a pretext to make a film without a single word – and to Central Asian cinematographers who explored the links between sound and silent cinema, like Aktan Abdykalykov in *The Swing* and *The Bus Stop*, co-directed with Ernest Abdyjaparov. Last but not least, in *Mute Coolness*, the director investigates the disturbing aspect of close-ups. This is evident in the cut-ins of close-ups of the cricket in the matchbox. This approach is very reminiscent of American genre cinema. In *The Wanderer* (2010), director Talgat Bektursunov inserts references to other young directors by using a very similar sequence (at the hairdresser's) to the one that opens *Swift*. He also mixes two different quotations from the same cinematographic period: we see a group of young men running through the streets of Almaty to the soundtrack of a song by Viktor Tsoi.[16] The image of the group running is borrowed from *Balcony*, while the music quotes Nugmanov's cult film *The Needle*, where Tsoi played the main part and composed the soundtrack.[17] But the director also chooses to make this reference in a more international manner, using the song 'Blood Group' ('Gruppa krovi') performed in English.

Maybe the younger generation feels freer when it comes to playing with references, influences and narrative rules. Their cinema highlights the disappearance of a hierarchy of influences. In this way we can analyse three recent short films that were shot with little financial support and rudimentary audiovisual equipment. In his short film *Bakhytzhamal*, Adilkhan Erzhanov shocks viewers with his eccentric filming style. Anton Sidorenko describes it as 'careless cinematography, which occasionally looks like home-made video' with 'jerky editing that gives the action a peculiar disjointedness';[18] he adds that 'many accuse the twenty-five year old director of filming as if cinema had not existed before him'. But the director is perfectly aware of the existing aesthetic rules. His motto is not simply to be different, but to disobey. The beginning of the film with the frontal shot of the hero addressing the camera recalls the first shots of Aprymov's *The Last Stop*, but this time the hero is not in a police station: he performs for mobile telephone ad.

Disobedience is reflected in the characters: Kuybych in *Bakhytzhamal* has escaped from a psychiatric hospital; the hero of *113th* (2007) is imprisoned in a place that resembles a psychiatric hospital and escapes only at the end of the film. But being crazy, being *out of order* is a way to be free – and a path to creativity. The heroes are demiurgic figures: Kuybych's craziness sets the film in motion, and his buddy Serik, even though he pretends to be reluctant, is happy to play along in his phantasmagorical search for a girl who has long gone abroad; the hero of *113th* puts on a show that fascinates the doctor-observer. At one crucial point, even though the camera observing the patient works only one way, the patient starts imitating the gestures of the doctor. This omniscient capacity discloses him as the *metteur en scène*, and therefore the character is quite logically performed by the film director himself. These two films are also striking in their new level of reflexivity: Sidorenko accurately remarks that the director holding the camera becomes a third, main character in *Bakhytzhamal*. The whole of *113th* is a meditation on the cinematographic process. Both films valorise the pleasure of the gratuitous gesture, of the mere pleasure of performing in front of a camera.

Emir Baigazin moves in the same direction in his *The Steppe* (2007) a two-minute film showing a couple. It is a black-and-white silent film, storyboarded and lit as if it were shot in a studio, and edited in a spectacular way to resemble the grand masters of the Soviet epoch. It also explores the agony and extreme tension conveyed by close-ups on the characters' skin, accompanied by the sound of a knife being sharpened. No blood-soaked catharsis follows (the knife is used to cut bread), but the violence of human relationship is evoked to perfection. This is quite a surprising first film inspired both by US and Soviet cinema.

Everyone wishes Kazakh cinema well and hopes that a new cinematographic movement will emerge. But can we really speak of a movement here? Most of them refuse the name of 'New New

Figure 12.2 Still from the short film *113th* (2007) by Talgat Bektursunov.

Wave', even though several young directors claim common aesthetic positions and interests.[19] It is not useful to force them into a group that they themselves do not feel exists. The mere emergence of radically diverse directors in this challenging epoch is a sign of the potential 'good health' of the national cinematography, even though few of these young directors have yet managed properly to enter the world of film production by making films on a regular basis. The first words of their motto are worthwhile remembering: 'Nobody sees us, nobody hears us, but we do exist.'[20] Today, these films *are* 'seen' and 'heard': Turebaev's *Little Men* and Kulbai's *Swift* have travelled the world from festival to festival; most of Nurmukhambetov's short films were shown in Oberhausen; Utepbergenov's *Mute Coolness* was shown in France and in Italy; Bektursunov's *113th* was screened in Locarno; and Issabaeva's *Karoy* was selected for the Horizons competition in Venice. Their contributions to Kazakh cinema are nourished by eclectic and erratic aesthetic influences specific to their epoch and rather than a cinematographic movement, it is a cinematographic phenomenon.

Notes

1   This is how the young cinema critic Inna Smailova describes the new films in the 2000s: 'Typical for the production of these films are complete absence of the budget, outdoor shooting, natural light, colour and sound. As to the plot, it addresses [...] the private side of life of the contemporary youth', in Gul'nara Abikeeva, *Kino Tsentral'noi Azii, 1990–2001* (Almaty, 2001), p. 326.

2   The young Kazakh film-makers, hardly out of VGIK, inventively and courageously called themselves 'the Kazakh New Wave'. At the International Film Festival in Moscow in 1989. According to Rashid Nugmanov: 'It was at the Moscow Festival where we brought a programme of Kazakh cinema: short and full-length films. And we had to think of something, to make an announcement... They gave me a large sheet of paper 60 × 90 of golden colour and black Indian ink [...] How would I call all that stuff – I had no idea. Certainly not the "Gagarin generation"! Nothing new under the moon. Let it be a "New Wave"... but from Kazakhstan', in Abikeeva, *Kino Tsentral'noi Azii*, 260.

3   Others, even those who did not study in Soloviev's famous workshop, still graduated from VGIK at almost the same time: Ermek Shinarbaev graduated from Sergei Gerasimov's workshop in 1985 and Amanjol Aituarov from that of Yuri Ozerov in 1986.

4   'I made the students [...] watch as much as possible of Italian Neorealism and the French 'New Wave', Godard, Kurosawa, FEKS and contemporary US films' Sergei Soloviev in Abikeeva, *Kino Tsentral'noi Azii*, 300.

5   Abai Karpykov in Abikeeva, *Kino Tsentral'noi Azii*, 264. In the same vein Serik Aprymov tells the following anecdote: 'Once they showed on TV the film *A Woman Between Two Brothers* (1991) by Amir [Karakulov] and a person who had nothing to do with cinema told me: "I can hear by the sound that this is one of your guys". That's true, there are things that have become inherent: in VGIK we started all together to watch films, discuss them, speak of composition, staging, sound', *Kino Tsentral'noi Azii*, 322. In turn, Marilyne Fellous states that *The Needle* 'swarms with sound citations from the European cinema' and more precisely from Antonioni's universe, 'Nouvelle vague au Kazakhstan', in Jean Radvanyi, ed., *Le Cinéma d'Asie centrale soviétique* (Paris, 1991), p. 66.

6   Interview with the film-maker by Jean-Michel Frodon in November 2001, at the Festival of Three Continents in Nantes.

7   Even if there was a group of young Kazakh sent to VGIK in 2006 we cannot yet assess whether and how those years will affect young Kazakh cinema.

8   The Academy of Arts has existed since 1955, but its cinema department was established only in 1991. This was one of the landmarks of decentralization in the film education of the post-Soviet epoch.

9   'It's possible that I like to work with non-professional because of my scientific background. It's in science that the discoveries are made. I am not interested in familiar faces or well-known actors, since they have already been discovered. I am attracted by freshness', Darejan Omirbaev, interview by Thierry Jousse, Almaty, 7 October 1998, translated from Russian by Olga Garifoullina, 'Alexandre Sokourov, Alexeï Guerman, Darezhan Omirbayev et la Nouvelle Vague Kazakh', Supplément *Cahiers du Cinéma* – Festival d'Automne à Paris (Paris, 1998), p. 10.

10   In the same way, the lack of political engagement, typical of the films of the New Wave ('The main character of *Last Stop* comes home after military training and not after Afghan war which would have uselessly politicized the discourse',

Marilyne Fellous, 'Nouvelle vague au Kazakhstan', p. 66) can be found in recent films, as was pointed out by Gul'nara Abikeeva: 'ideological or political motives are totally absent', *Kino Tsentral'noi Azii*, 326.

11 Erlan Nurmukhambetov, Abai Kulbai, personal communications, September 2007.

12 Darejan Omirbaev, interview by Thierry Jousse, Almaty, 7 October 1998, in 'Alexandre Sokourov...', p. 10.

13 Abai Kulbai in Baubek Nogerbek, '"Vse v poriadke!" Ispoved' intelligentnogo khuligana', *Kinoman* 2 (2007): 9.

14 An interview by Audrey Pernis, 30 November 2007.

15 Abai Kulbai, Erzhan Rustembekov, personal communications, May 2005.

16 Viktor Tsoi was an extremely popular singer and considered the representative of a whole generation in the 1990s.

17 The film also reminds of *ASSA* (1987) by Sergei Solov'ev, where Tsoi also played an episodic role and performed a song.

18 Anton Sidorenko, 'Bakhytzhamal', *KinoKultura* 23 (2009), www.kinokultura. com/2009/23r-bakhytzhamal.shtml (accessed 12 December 2010).

19 See Jane Knox-Voina, 'Young Kazakh Film-makers: The Kazakh New "New Wave" on the Road', *KinoKultura* 27 (2009), www.kinokultura.com/2010/27-knoxvoina.shtml (accessed 12 December 2010).

20 Abikeeva, *Kino Tsentral'noi Azii*, p. 326.

13

GROWING UP IN CENTRAL ASIAN CINEMA

Birgit Beumers

T he child is a universal symbol of the future: its presence or absence indicates the health of a society and its future. The significance of the concept of the family in Central Asian cinema has been discussed by Gulnara Abikeyeva, who argues that the family was absent in Central Asian cinema during the stagnation (broadly speaking the 1960s and 1970s), until a new model of the family emerged on the screen, forming the basis for a new process of nation-building in post-Soviet Central Asia.[1] Abikeyeva contends that the shift towards family suggests hope for a new nation. She differentiates between Central Asian cinematographies, claiming that Uzbek children are shown as happy, Kazakh children as dying and Kyrgyz children as supportive of their family; moreover, children are primarily adopted or unwanted.[2]

While it is certainly a fruitful approach to relate the image of family and child to the process of nation-building, I have chosen to adopt a different approach here and look at the stages of childhood, from infant to child and teenager, across Central Asian films. I focus on children and teenagers as shown in films set in the present, not in historical epics. I argue that the infant is largely absent in cinema, while teenagers play a central role in films across Central Asia, both during the 1990s and in the new millennium. The teenager's shift in attitudes towards his own roots and cultural origin is connected to the world in which children grew up: the Soviet or post-Soviet world, an urban or rural background.

The Roots

Teenagers have played a major role in Central Asian cinema's new wave, as for example in *ASSA* (1987) and *The Needle* (1988), where teenagers conquered the screen with their own culture, offering a new vision of life: optimistic, but detached from reality. They escaped into rock music in *ASSA* and through a dream sequence of the hero's resurrection in *The Needle*.[3]

In the late 1980s Sergei Soloviev had selected a course at the Film Institute VGIK, from which the Kazakh New Wave emerged.[4] *ASSA* represents a change in the perception of underground culture in general, and rock music in particular, for the first time shown as a positive force.[5] Bananan (played by the Leningrad artist Sergei Bugaev, known as Afrika) is a non-violent and innately good character, who stands apart from the others because of his behaviour and his appearance (he wears one earring). He is juxtaposed to the 'Soviet' official Krymov, played by the documentary film-maker Stanislav Govorukhin – a representative of the establishment – who holds power over his mistress Alika (Tatiana Drubich). He may have the power to have Bananan killed, but Alika becomes aware of the plot and kills Krymov. Bananan is a romantic hero, who triumphs – even if in death. In the finale a concert by the rock idol Viktor Tsoi takes place against all rules and regulations, and the song 'I want change' ['*Ia khochu peremen*'] expresses the dissatisfaction with a world where happiness is possible only through escapism into a dream world. *ASSA* marked a watershed in the representation of rock music, but it also diagnosed Soviet oppression of youth culture in general.

ASSA influenced heavily Rashid Nugmanov's *The Needle*, the first Soviet film to openly address the issue of drugs. Moro (played by Viktor Tsoi) returns to his native Alma-Ata to collect debts from Spartak (Alexander Bashirov), visits his former girlfriend Dina and finds she is on drugs. He tries to get her clean, taking her to a deserted place by the dried-up Aral Sea. When Moro discloses the dealer's identity (a freaky doctor who is played by the rock star Petr Mamonov) just before leaving with Dina, he is stabbed to death on a winter road. However, heroes never die: Moro lives on, walking down the snow-covered road with his blood leaving red dots on the white surface to the tune 'Blood Type'. The positive moral values are perpetuated as he continues to live, but only in a world of dream and escape, while the drug-dealer triumphs in reality. Nugmanov's film not only showed the meaninglessness of life, but also the barrenness of the land as a symbol for the absence of a future: the future is only possible on the snow-covered road that leads to the land of illusions and dreams.

Soloviev and Nugmanov addressed the dislocation of teenagers: salvation from the empty and stale Soviet value system was offered through rock music which, for Nugmanov, facilitated a return to simple life beyond all (Soviet) civilization. If Soviet teenagers faced a crisis of identity, then this would be brought out even more in the films of the post-Soviet era, where children and teenagers were the products of one value system and in search for another, for a new national identity beyond the Soviet Empire.

An important feature of Central Asian films of the 1990s is the clash between Soviet past and non-Soviet present, between progress and tradition, between city and countryside. As adults are torn between these binaries, children are often forgotten: they play a secondary or no role.

The Infants

The infant is strikingly absent from films, with very few exceptions. One is Serik Aprymov's *Aksuat* (1998), which shows two brothers leading opposite lifestyles: Kanat lives in the city, Aman in his *aul*. When Kanat is bankrupt, he returns to his village for help, bringing along his pregnant wife, Zhanna, whose presence drives a rift between the brothers. Aman is held responsible for his brother's breach of traditions – Kanat offends the local policeman by intruding into his yard to take a car and drive to the maternity clinic where his wife has given birth – and his engagement to the village elder's daughter is broken off. The birth of Kanat's son brings about catastrophe: children are not innocent, but have a detrimental effect on their fathers, leading them to ruin and death. Finally, Aman sends Zhanna away. The village life is doomed by the force of entropy, reflected in the rejection of the child as representing a future.[6]

Another example is Darejan Omirbaev's *Killer* (1998). Marat is a chauffeur who, one day, collecting his wife from hospital with their newborn son, turns round to look at the child – and hits a Mercedes.

Marat has to pick up the bill for the accident, yet neither family nor friends can help and Marat loses his job. He falls victim to a credit shark who urges him to kill a journalist in order to have his debts annulled. Marat shoots the journalist as the latter is fishing a ball from the river for a playing child. Without words Omirbaev shows how Marat effectively kills himself: he shoots the journalist in the presence of a child, inferring the presence of Marat's own child. At night, Marat is shot while taking out the rubbish. Omirbaev draws a fine portrayal of Marat's deadlock. In a situation of utter despair, and for good reasons – intending to provide for his family – Marat gets caught up in a circle of crime, which offers no way out. When Marat contemplates suicide, standing on a tower block of flats, his attempts are marred by the presence of children in the yard, reminding him

Figure 13.1 Poster for Serik Aprymov's *Aksuat* (1998).

of his own offspring. Marat's child grows up not only without a father, but is also the cause of the disaster: it is because of the child that Marat had the accident.

In the cinema of the 1990s infants play a very negative, destructive role: they have no place in the new Kazakhstan. In other cinematographies of Central Asia they are plainly absent.

The Children

Children have a presence in films, although they are not always pointers towards a future. In the early 1990s children are often portrayed as caught up between tradition and progress, between the old, ethnic way of life associated with the countryside and the Sovietized (and therefore negative) way of life on the city. The process of the child's maturation parallels the respective country's independence from the Soviet Union seen as a political process of growing up.

Growing up as a transformation from one world to another is the theme of Aktan Abdykalykov's (Arym Kubat) *The Swing* (1993). The black-and-white film explores the life of a nine-year-old boy (played by the director's son Mirlan) as he adores a teenage girl, who falls in love with a sailor. The secure and secluded world of the child is threatened by an intruder: 'with the appearance of the sailor the surrounding space which was everything suddenly becomes a mere part of something larger [...], of the big incomprehensible world'.[7] The sailor gives the boy a shell, capturing the sound of this other, adult world for the boy. The boy goes into the mountains to smash the 'other world', but he reconsiders his decision and instead leaves the shell on a mountain slope. Abdykalykov investigates the problem of childhood and the recognition of the world. The theme of a secluded world from which children are suddenly removed reflects on the one hand the process of breaking away from an accustomed environment (the republics breaking away from the Soviet Union), and on the other hand the process of (sexual) awakening and initiation to the world.

Similarly, in Omirbaev's *Cardiogram* (1995) growing up means exposure to a world where the child is not protected. Because of a cardiac condition Josulan is sent to a sanatorium, where all the children, the doctor and the nurse speak only Russian. Only one boy knows Kazakh, as he has been taught by his grandmother. Josulan is isolated, but he differs in no way from the other children: he loves television, he has an innate sense of curiosity about the other sex, observing in an innocent and naïve manner a girl on the bus or the nurse, or looking at the painting of a nude in an art magazine. An outsider, he is teased by a gang of teenagers and Josulan eventually runs away, back home: the child – the small Kazakh man – is not yet ready for the big world. Both films echo the political state of transition through children.

The film poeticizes and praises the secluded life in the *aul*, although Omirbaev refrains from showing moral corruption as an inherent feature of city life. Josulan lives in the steppe, portrayed in warm golden colours. At the sanatorium that accommodates children from the city, which is a medical institution, the landscape is again covered in sterile white snow, and likewise the doctors in their white gowns are part of a hostile world that knows no love. The steppe is an open space, while the hospital with its commodities of modern civilization lies in a mountain gorge. The child has no chance of integration or survival in the city.

A more pessimistic view permeates Serik Aprymov's films, where children are deprived of a future. In *Three Brothers* (2000), Aprymov explores the friendship between three boys in a village. The children are a perfect team and act already as a collective; together they steal melons together, or rob a van and enter a military base, trying to become part of the world of adults as they know it from the tales told by the old ex-prison-camp victim Klein. They dream of travelling to the lake, where they will be able to realize their adolescent reveries about looking at naked women. In order to realize their dream, the boys – leaving only the narrator, the little boy Chibut behind – hijack a locomotive and venture into the military zone (the world of grown-ups) in order to reach the legendary lake. At this moment, the Soviet military test new missiles directed at moving targets: the two locomotives, one with the boys and the other with Klein who follows them to come to their rescue. Aprymov tells a parable of the collapse of a system: the Soviet air power still rules Kazakhstan, ultimately destroying the dreams of the boys and their lives by launching an attack on what was once the pride of Soviet transport and means of conquering unknown territories: the train with its red star on the front of the engine. Aprymov embodies in the children's death the annihilation of Kazakhstan's future.

In the new millennium children on screen appear as unwanted and adopted, struggling to find their place in society. In Amir Karakulov's *Don't Cry!* (2002), the little girl Bibinur lives alone with her grandmother until the singer Maira Mukhamed kyzy joins them, trying to recover from the loss of her voice. Bibinur develops an illness and can only be saved by medication, which the women cannot afford: Bibinur dies. In Abikeyeva's reading, the film is a parable for the orphaned child who cannot be saved: the parents are ominously absent (the past is blurred), the present is voiceless and helpless, while the future dies.[8]

Numerous films centre on children who find alternative homes and parents: in Guka Omarova's *Schizo* (2004) Zina adopts a five-year old boy with a learning disability; in Gulyandom Mukhabbatova and Daler Rakhmatov's *Rover* (2005) the boy Abdullo lives with grandparents and waits for his father to return; in Rustem Abdrashev's *Patchwork Quilt* (2007), little Kenje has no mother and lives with his grandparents.

In Satybaldy Narymbetov's *Leila's Prayer* (2002) the past is bleak, but there is a glimpse of hope at the end – yet the film is set in the 1960s and echoes the atmosphere of a different period. The film is set in Delegen, a village in the atomic testing ground of the 'polygon' in north-east Kazakhstan. The teenager Leila fails to leave the village during an evacuation, is caught and evacuated, and raped by a Soviet soldier. Her rape is symbolic of the Soviet abuse of the Kazakh land where dangerous experiments are conducted. Along with the condemnation of Soviet rule there is the legacy of that domination: the unwanted child held by the beautiful Leila in a pose reminiscent of the Madonna with the infant. The child is a legacy of the past, but a pointer to the future that is, in this instance, inseparable from the past.

The Teenagers

Teenagers are most prominent in Central Asian cinema: they behold the clash of past and present in their characters, since they were born when the republics still belonged to the Soviet Union, while they were raised in a country that tried to find its own national identity. This parallel of political and personal transition remains valid for the teenage generation until the present, when the first teenagers born and raised in the independent country begin to appear on the silver screen. Central Asian teenagers have been exposed to a series of binaries that they 'embody': Soviet and ethnic, urban and rural, past and present.

In the 1990s teenagers were shown as young adults faced with existential problems as the transition from childhood to adulthood coincided with the collapse of a social and political world around them.

Such an existential crisis is the theme of Omirbaev's black-and-white film *Kairat* (1991), the story of an adolescent boy, who is a university student living in hall. A normal teenager, he takes a girl to the movies, but when she takes up a job as train hostess, she starts dating a colleague. Disappointed, Kairat takes a ride on a Ferris wheel, which stops when he reaches the top – visually capturing the sense of stasis. Abruptly, an alarm clock rings: Kairat wakes up from the dreams of a teenager afraid of the adult world. Omirbaev captures in this film the fears of a teenager of making his first social and sexual experiences. In a world that is crumbling around him (the malfunctioning Ferris wheel, the dilapidated building site, the wacky repertoire of the cinema) Kairat has no indication of a path to take. Instead, he is distraught by the process of growing up. *Kairat* addresses the issue of a lack of a meaning in life and of the inability of the young Kairat to find his place in a modern, urban society.

Kazakh film-makers continued to explore the existential issues of growing up. Ermek Shinarbaev's *Place on a Grey Triangular Hat* (1993) shows student life, where the lack of meaning and stability leads a sensitive student to a suicide attempt. Amir Karakulov's *The Last Holidays* (1996) follows a group of students in their summer vacation, when they get involved in all sorts of forbidden things: they smoke, steal and get involved in crime. They return to school after the holidays, continuing with their Soviet-style parades and a school curriculum that hardly prepares them for life. The holiday has turned into a nightmare by forcing an encounter with reality. Kazakh film-makers show teenagers without a future, suspended between two worlds: past and present. Kairat's stop on the Ferris wheel captures this suspended status (as would the cable car in *Kosh-ba-Kosh*).

The Tajik director Bakhtiyar Khudoinazarov offers alternatives to family life: he addresses the issue of family relationships, notably the lack of a strong father-figure. *Bro* (1991) follows the teenager Farukh travelling on a train with his seven-year old brother Azamat, whom he intends to leave with their father in a small village. However, Azamat wants to stay with his elder brother instead, thus replacing the father–son axis with a new brotherhood and breaking with the old way of life in a society where family ties have collapsed (there is no mother). In the much-acclaimed *Kosh-ba-kosh* (1993) Khudoina-zarov portrays another broken family: Mira's father gambles and loses everything – including his daughter (played by the Chilean-born Spanish actress Paulina Galvez). Mira is rescued and taken to a hiding place by the teenager Daler, and together they 'nest' in a cable car, suspended between the city and the mountain, between present and tradition. Their love unfolds against the backdrop of an historical and spatial rift, and of an ongoing civil war. Khudoinazarov places hope at the film's end when love remains the only powerful force capable of a future.

In the new millennium film-makers focus less on the problems of growing up: the complex transition from childhood to adulthood overlapping with the country's transition from Soviet to independent has subsided to teenagers who spent most of their childhood within one political system and one historical era. Teenagers begin to accept and appreciate traditions as a part of life: they display a more mature attitude to old, and new, values.

The opening sequence of Abdykalykov's *Beshkempir: The Adopted Son* (1998) shows in colour the ritual of adoption of a baby placed into a cradle performed by five old women (translated as *besh kempir*). The film then turns to black and white for the life of the 15-year-old boy Beshkempir, who makes bricks with his play-mates. The teenagers poke a stick in a beehive, or jump into a mud-bath together, only to be embarrassed when a local girl walks past; they break into a chicken farm to steal eggs, or look at the woman who is putting leeches on her back; or they play 'love-making' with a female figure they draw in the sand. When Beshkempir is teased by one of the boys as a foundling, Beshkempir's world falls apart: he leaves his home, but returns when his beloved grandmother is dying: she has designated Beshkempir as heir to her debts and belongings, effectively giving him a heritage and a tradition that re-establish the balance of his small world. *The Adopted Son* is a film of maturation, or growing up, but also of finding a place in life: through the grandmother's legacy Beshkempir knows where he belongs, echoing the newly found sense of belonging of the new Central-Asian nation-states in their traditions – inherited by birth or through adoption.

In *The Chimp* (2001) the protagonist is an 18-year-old teenager about to be drafted into the army: at the beginning of the film he undergoes the medical fitness check. At home, Chimp has a lot of responsibilities, but he also enjoys the company of his friends, discussing sex and smoking, listening to Western music and dancing, and playing games that bring them physically closer to the girls (kissing when blindfolded, looking under girls' skirts with a mirror tied to the shoe, etc). Chimp's world is overturned when his mother and sister leave home, the prostitute Zina sexually overpowers him on his motorbike, and Zina's house burns down. His world collapses and Chimp's departure for the army is the final step in the process of growing up and leaving home.

In Abdykalykov's films children are firmly embedded in Kyrgyz traditions and protected by them. As they grow up, they realize the existence of other worlds, and ultimately the seclusion from those worlds is no longer natural: the boys depart into the world. The world out there never threatens the indigenous land, whose values are colourful and poetic.

The Uzbek film-maker Yusup Razykov set the process of maturation against the backdrop of tradition. *The Shepherd* (2005) shows the young Djamshed look after his brother's bride Yanga in a mature and responsible manner: 'he will grow up and become a support for the family, for his *kishlak*, for his people'.[9] Traditional upbringing makes boys more mature, as *The Chimp* also demonstrated. Ernest Abdyjaparov's *Pure Coolness* (2007) goes even further and shows the initial rejection of rural, traditional life followed by an

Figure 13.2 Still from Aktan Arym Kubat's *The Chimp* (2001).

appreciation, as the teenage Asem visits her boyfriend's *aul* on Issyk-Kul. Due to a mix-up she is kidnapped and married to the shepherd Sagyn, a good-hearted young man whom she does not know – and yet she finds happiness and harmony with herself. The superficial urban teenager becomes a grown-up, mature woman in the *aul.*

But maturity can also be achieved in the city: Abai Kulbai's *Swift* (2007)[10] addresses the problem of growing-up as parallel to a changed perception of the urban environment, the cityscape of Almaty. The 15-year-old Ainura is confronted with the breakdown of her personal, familial and social relationships, and bravely steers her path through the adult world. She is the first teenager to suffer not from the clash between past and present, or new and old, but 'just' faces the transition from childhood to adulthood. The film leaves open whether she manages that transition or not.

Having paralleled the transition from childhood to adulthood with the transition from Soviet to independent, past to present, tradition to civilization, in the new millennium film-makers have begun to appreciate teenagers as role models: they understand, are capable of compromise, they honour tradition and manage where their predecessors of the 1990s and children failed. In the new world order, urban and rural, new and old can coexist; indeed there is an increased interests in the old way of life, no longer seen as reactionary but as connecting back to a national heritage that people share. However, the absence of infants on the screen – except for a few, unwanted and fatherless children in *Killer* and *Aksuat* would not seem to suggest, as Abikeyeva argues, that the family as a social and nation-building institution has been reinstated. The fact that teenagers straddle borders does, however, give hope that such children might appear on the screens.

Notes

1   Gul'nara Abikeeva, *Natsiostroitel'stvo v Kazakhstane i drugikh stranakh tsentral'noi Azii i kak etot protsess otrazhaetsia v kinematografe* (Almaty, 2006), pp. 296–7.
2   Abikeeva, pp. 267–9; 244.
3   Birgit Beumers, 'Igla/The Needle', in Beumers, ed., *24 Frames: The Cinema of Russia and the Former Soviet Union* (London, 2007), pp. 213–21.
4   The course graduated in 1988 and included Rashid Nugmanov, Darejan Omirbaev, Serik Aprymov, Ardak Amirkulov, Abai Karpykov and Amir Karakulov.
5   For example, Valerii Ogorodnikov's *Burglar* [*Vzlomshchik*, 1986] had underscored the negative influence of a rock musician, inciting his younger brother to steal a synthesizer for him. In Vasilii Pichul's *Little Vera* [*Malen'kaia*

Vera, 1988] and the Jūris Podnieks' documentary *Is it Easy to be Young?* [*Legko li byt' molodym?*, 1985], rock concerts are crushed by the police.

6   Natal'ia Sirivlia, 'Aksuat. 10 let spustia', *Iskusstvo kino* 9 (1999): 33–6.

7   Natal'ia Sirivlia, 'Detskii mir', *Iskusstvo kino* 5 (2002): 55–63 (p. 57).

8   Abikeeva, p. 211.

9   Abikeeva, p. 280.

10   Ainura's nickname is Strizh, which is derived from the phrase *strizhennaia suka* [a bitch with her hair cut] that her class mates scribble on her cap after she had her hair cut very short, like a boy. Ainura effaces all but the letters Strizh.

14

KYRGYZ CINEMA: AN ATTEMPT AT ETERNAL BREAKTHROUGH

Gulbara Tolomushova

A symbolic frame of the cinema of Soviet Kirghizia is probably a scene from Tolomush Okeev's *Sky of Our Childhood* (1966), which shows boys running across the screen. Their enthusiastic race highlights the perpetual attempt to break through. In this regard, post-Soviet Kyrgyz cinema is characterized by several attempts to break into a new era, starting with *The Swing* (1993) by Aktan Abdykalykov (later known as Arym Kubat), which initiated a strong emotional charge among young Kyrgyz film-makers, who were inspired by the amazing story of the inner crisis of a 12-year old boy and its powerful expression. The young hero mastered his everyday circumstances and turned to creativity; thus he talked about his personal drama through the language of art. Marat Sarulu worked in a more aesthetic vein, more reserved and more complex, when he captured the epoch of a collapsed world with the powerful film *My Brother, Silk Road* (2001). Then Ernest Abdyjaparov came into the spotlight, giving us hope when we were naive enough to believe that our problems would evaporate, before President Askar Akayev fled the country, a year after the release of *Village Authorities* (*Saratan*, 2004). Finally came the visionary Talgat Asyrankulov, who started shooting *Birds of Paradise* under Akayev and was able to anticipate many of the political, social and social changes in our lives. With lightness and grace he showed that our country is controlled by semi-criminal powers, murderous drug barons who have become commonplace in everyday life, 'noble' killers who behaved like Robin Hood. Today, Kyrgyz film-makers are trying to break through again by means of a strategic development, the '10+' cinema programme, which values the importance of cinema for Kyrgyz culture.

The First Breakthrough: Aesthetics

Aktan Arym Kubat created a reputation for himself in 1990 with a 17-minute short film, *The Dog Ran Away*, a parable about good and evil in the life of a dog. In 1992 he released his first full-length feature, *Where is Your House, Snail?*. His next work, the short feature *The Swing*, was an autobiographical story discovering the world of adult emotions, as an 11-year old boy falls in love with an older girl. His film won the Leopard of Tomorrow at the Locarno International Film Festival in 1993, and attracted the attention of the French company Noé Productions. *Beshkempir: The Adopted Son* (1998), his most famous film, was a joint creation of Noé Productions and Kyrgyzfilm. It was filmed in Bar-Bulak, 300 miles from the capital Bishkek, with non-professional actors and almost entirely in black and white, with colour highlights to reflect the shift to memory:

> My film is put together like patchwork [...]. Each piece of cloth contains information about a person who has passed away. According to custom, during the funeral such patches of material are distributed to all those who have come to remember the deceased. Then, a quilt is made from the collected scraps of fabric, which tells a story about each person who departs to the other world. My film is an attempt to create a collective memory of the Kyrgyz people.[1]

The Chimp (2001), which completed the autobiographical triptych, was shown in the 'Un Certain Regard' programme at the Cannes International Film Festival.

The Swing is made in the aesthetics of pure cinema: the film uses expressive visual imagery rather than dialogue. Words are used sparingly. Arym Kubat gives his young hero Mirlan, a 'Kierkegaardian man', a phrase that he cries out from the rooftop of an abandoned rural club, when he wants to capture the imagination of his beloved, beautiful Ainur, as he jumps down with a parachute-handkerchief: 'Ainura! I'm Gagarin! You're Titov!' He makes a gesture to the early 1960s when boys all over the world dreamed of flying into space. *The Swing* portrays a man with a creative impulse, as he embarks on an existential journey. The film was not based on literature, as the original screenplay was written by the director; it abandoned theatrical staging, as the action is set in nature; and it did not draw on professional actors, since all the roles were performed by amateurs. After *The Swing*, other films in Kyrgyzstan also preached the aesthetics of pure cinema where predetermined silence implied superior visual quality. But *The Swing* is unique and in a class by itself, because it gave an impetus to many young people to test their artistic power.

The Swing is an existentialist picture about the difficult path of personal development, from 'genuine existence' to the 'original and authentic' in the Kierkegaardian sense. The story is about,

> a little boy who falls in love with a girl; they spend a lot of time together, sitting on the swings. Then a sailor appears, who begins a romance with the girl, but for the boy this is a disaster, the first moment of maturation.[2]

The little boy is the same Kierkegaardian 'existential man' who gradually makes the transition from a contemplative and sensual way of being, determined by external environmental factors, to his identity, singular and unique.

Kierkegaard identified three stages of upward movement to achieve 'authentic' existence: the aesthetic, ethical and spiritual. The principle of the aesthetic stage is the determination of the external, the orientation towards pleasure. Here, the choice is made in the most primitive form, because only an object is selected, while the attraction is already there in the sensory elements of human life. Thus, the boy admiringly looks at the girl he likes, and their fun games and simple relationship are united by a common inner state of serenity, as long as they have no worries. This state is characteristic of all residents of the village. A young man's return from military service to this remote village disturbs this atmosphere. The sailor interests the girl, and the boy enters a new stage of life that Kierkegaard calls 'ethical'. The boy is no longer just a naive, simple-hearted lad: forced to change his habits, he unwittingly begins to reflect. The boy feels that the sailor was able to interest the girl by some secret attraction that the boy does not command. He is constantly thinking about this, and finally finds the 'culprit' of his grief, an unusual shell brought by the sailor. The shell, in turn, helps the hero overcome certain habits, gradually bringing him to the final stage on the path to existence, the spiritual. Indeed, through an incredible effort of will, the boy renounces his past experiences and accepts suffering as a life-asserting principle. This in turn opens the path to creativity: the boy begins to feel the overwhelming need to express his feelings in primitive art.

The shell, which awakened the boy's creative ability through 'contemplative acoustic worship', functions as a communicative link in the film. The shell is unusual in shape and size; it resembles the sun, whose image is a favourite ornamental motif of the Kyrgyz people.[3] The shell has suddenly found its way into the hands of the people of a forlorn village, bringing much needed warmth and joy to their souls. The shell-sun unites the inhabitants of the village for some time, exposing them to another world and another life through the sound of waves emanating from within it, even if the residents just experience enough of the atmosphere of that distant life before they lose interest in the giant shell.

Yet the shell opens the fleeting moments of first love for the charming young heroine of the film; it touched her and excited her world of sensual love. The association between the sailor, the girl and the shell harbours a strong erotic tension that vicariously affects the development of the heroine. Aktan Arym Kubat explains: 'Through the image of the shell, another life, unknown and inaccessible, becomes a declaration of love, a kiss. The shell, too, carries an erotic principle like the swing. In Kyrgyz poetry they are both symbols of love.'[4]

The naive world view collapses three times in the film before the sailor arrives: first, when the girl leaves; second, when the boy ruthlessly thrashes the madman; and third, when the madman dies. Prior to the sailor's arrival, the boy and girl were inseparable; it was the madman who fuelled the immediacy of this friendship, giving it a lightness and simplicity that underline the narrow limitations of an 'inauthentic existence'. The shell, which so strongly influenced the spiritual transformation of the boy and girl, did not affect the madman. Despite the fact that he had his own share of suffering, his agony does not elevate him in the eyes of others. He cannot remain alone; his former friends are already far away; so he can only leave the world which has no more room for him.

The film immediately occupied a special place in Kyrgyz cinema, primarily because of its ability to expose the inner world of the people. *The Swing* showed the inner condition of the Kyrgyz as simple, naive and unsophisticated on the one hand, and mobile, curious and inquisitive on the other. *Beshkempir* develops the same theme in a different light: there is a deepening existential conflict of the hero, both with himself and with the outside world. Eventually he escapes all the circles of inner emotions and finds a clear and conscious path. Finally, in *The Chimp* the hero leaves Kyrgyzstan to find his place on the earth.

The Second Breakthrough: Critical Success

At the beginning of the 2000s, Marat Sarulu completed his feature film, *My Brother, Silk Road* that drew a line under Kyrgyz cinema. His images in the prologue repeat Arym Kubat's *The Swing*: the frame shows some space outside time, where children try to comprehend the mysteries of creation. But Sarulu's film develops like Quentin Tarantino's *Pulp Fiction* (1994), which explored separate stories linked by episodic characters.

My Brother, Silk Road is important for Kyrgyz cinema also for its entertainment value, achieved largely through virtuoso acting. While Arym Kubat uses only non-professional actors, Sarulu engaged here the great masters of the Kyrgyz drama theatre: Busurman Odurakaev, Choro Dumanaev, Tynara Abdrazaeva and Mukambet Toktobaev, alongside non-professionals, children and adults. More-over, Sarulu returned dialogue to Kyrgyz cinema: his characters talk a lot in an animated manner, exposing their pain and joy. This went against a long-running trend, as Talgat Asyrankulov, the artist and set designer, famously declared:[5] 'In our films people do not speak!' Kyrgyz cinema tends to divide into two categories: on the one hand, popular audience favourites, particularly from the Soviet era; and on the other, *auteur* films exploring the aesthetics of pure cinema with visual and semantic associations. Sarulu's creative path once again confirmed the feasibility of filmic exploration and experimentation for the mainstream.

Sarulu's first full-length film, *In Spe* (1993), was replete with signs and symbols, understandable only to a small circle of devotees. His medium-length film, *Mandala* (1999) was simple yet wise and deep. Sarulu's *My Brother, Silk Road* brought together his knowledge of a century of cinema, and almost 20 years of service in Kyrgyz cinema (Sarulu started as an animator, directing the exquisite animated feature *Prayer for the Chaste Bird* (1989), which used folk parables and myths to reconstruct the path of the Elder Helmsman with his sons to the Great Goddess Umai-Ene for their initiation to spiritual heritage). In the 1990s Sarulu had worked as a screenwriter on Aitmatov adaptations for Bakyt Karagulov, including scripts for *Lament of the Migratory Birds, A Day Lasts Longer Than a Hundred Years,* and *Milky Way.* Then, Arym Kubat invited him to the script group for *Beshkempir.* Hence the transition from the conceptual form of *In Spe* to the wise simplicity of *Mandala* came about without losses. *My Brother, Silk Road* combines elements of both films: a clear theme and a non-linear composition.

In Spe tells the story of three brothers, where each represents a facet of national character: the eldest carries the experience of the ancestors, preserving national traditions; the middle represents the intellectual stratum of the nation; and the youngest is a trickster, troublemaker, and revolutionary:

> This is a story of the collapse of a single family, the collapse of mentality, of a certain primitive integrity, [...] and with hindsight I realized that indeed there was a breakdown of primitive cohesiveness in 1993. But our integrity has not been destroyed in the absolute sense; now we should achieve unity on a higher level.[6]

Once Marat Sarulu came upon a friend in the street who suddenly put on his dark glasses. This paradoxical situation stunned the

Figure 14.1 Still from Marat Sarulu's *Song of Southern Seas* (2008).

director and for a long time he thought about it and inserted this episode in his film. Sarulu believes that the image of a man in dark glasses is the image of the nation after the collapse of the Soviet Union: 'We all walked around in dark glasses and our current understanding of the world is marked by a clash with darkness. We wallowed in the dark corners of consciousness, struggling to get out of it.'[7] Referring to the style of his films, Sarulu clarified: 'This sort of quasi-seriousness is no longer relevant for me. I would have preferred to introduce an ironic layer, some sort of suspense, but nothing can be done once the film is complete.'[8] Sarulu is a fan of the work the cinema pioneer of Georges Méliès. Thus the inventiveness and authorial imagination in Sarulu's *In Spe* introduced the style of Méliès to Kyrgyz cinema, moving away from the documentary realism of the Lumière Brothers. Even though his ideas have not caught on in Kyrgyz cinema, for Sarulu this is not so much his own failure, but a symbolic defeat in the overall direction of the national film industry:

> Attempts to create such films have been made on video, and maybe in the new millennium a younger generation will develop just such a cinema, if we suppose that there is a resonant, cultural atmosphere, where the understanding of symbols and images is granted.[9]

The film *Mandala* is very straightforward: a mother brings her son, a drug addict, from the city to the village to have him in the care of his grandmother for a possible cure. Before leaving, the mother holds a modest farewell, dressing her beloved son in a new, white shirt bought with money from the sale of hand-made felt. The problem remains the darkness: the teenager returns to the city where he has nothing to do. He has no purpose and no future. His inner voice tells him that he needs to 'kill time' in the disco, but there, someone will likely offer him the needle or to smoke grass. So the circle closes: once again the young man is brought to his grandmother, who loyally and steadfast looks after her offspring. The film is divided into two unequal parts: the first, 'Mother' (Ene), occupies two-thirds of the screen time and is shot in colour; the second, 'Grandson' (Nebere), is black and white and given only one-third of the time. Under the surface of a mundane story, Sarulu is concerned with one of the most urgent contemporary problems, and the author sides with the older generation:

> Basically we are all pulled in various directions, fragmented,
> divided into some pieces, and the Mandala can bring us
> together. I tried to show the inner meaning of each step of the
> heroine, allowing her to bring order into the lives of those
> who enter her life.[10]

My Brother, Silk Road shows disorder, uncertainty, and other
contemporary realities, though it is filmed in the tradition of
Sarulu's beloved classic European black-and-white films of the late
1950s and early 1960s. He especially draws on Jerzy Kawalerowicz's
Night Train [*Pociag,* 1959] for the sense of lived-through tragedy,
psychological trauma and uncertainty about the future. The action
of *My Brother, Silk Road* unfolds in two directions: on the speeding
train, carrying unfortunate, impoverished and wretched people; and
in the wide steppe that the train passes in a flash. Only children (and
an old patriarch herding sheep) live in the steppe, while adults ride
on the train. The only exception is a poor girl who poses the
romantic artist for a painting, before disappearing forever, unable to
remain among the 'ugly, dirty, evil, and abhorrent'. But these people
throw the artist off the train, not knowing that they thus save him
from imminent death, because the train is on a one-way track. In the
steppe, a Kyrgyz Hamlet (played by Busurman Odurakaev who also
played this part on the stage of the Kyrgyz theatre) meets the
children and serves as a Sancho Panza on their journey. They make
an interesting pair: eternal travellers of the 'true nomadic spirit'.
The strange characters on the train, not knowing why and where,
earn the director's sympathy as they forge their course into the
unknown future while 'the others move in known life trajectories
and offer nothing new'.[11]

The Third Breakthrough: Hopefulness
On 6 September 2001 the Kyrgyz Parliament adopted a law about
state support for Kyrgyz cinema. This was a truly historic moment
because, after 10 years of independence, the state returned to the
business of sustaining national cinematography. The law was passed
following a great effort by the Union of Film-makers of Kyrgyzstan,
and the 'Magnificent Seven', which included many famous directors
of the middle generation, art managers and representatives of the
state's film management department. The parliamentary deputy and
former director, Dooronbek Sadyrbaev, played an invaluable role in
returning cinema to Kyrgyz politics. Soon afterwards, in November

2001, officials solemnly celebrated the 60th anniversary of Kyrgyz cinema. By the end of 2002, Kyrgyzfilm had launched three new films: Erkin Saliev's *The Cloud* (2004); Ernest Abdyjaparov's *Village Authorities* (2004); and Bakyt Karagulov's *A Mother's Lament about Mankurt* (2004).

Introducing his film to local journalists in May 2004, Abdyjaparov said that 'he wants to return viewers to the cinemas'. A week later, the film was shown in Moscow in the programme of the Eighth Forum of National Cinematography of the Commonwealth of Independent States and the Baltics, where the audience enjoyed the film. Abdyjaparov offered a virtuoso dramatic structure, weaving together the nuanced portrayal of different social strata and the eternal interdependence of the people and the authorities. Abdyjaparov embraced folk favourites, *kuuduldar* (variety comedians), as well as the most popular theatrical actors, so the film appealed both at home and abroad. He had two specific objectives: to make a simple and affordable mass-market film and position himself as a director for mainstream cinema.

After the collapse of the Soviet Union, Kyrgyz cinema had only one celebrated film-maker: Arym Kubat. Before *Village Authorities*, Abdyjaparov had shot several short films, addressing creative problems by purely cinematic means. His shorts participated in international film festivals and received awards, but did not bring prestige at home. Abdyjaparov's idea to make a film about the life of the people and for the people came from nowhere. He often recalls Lenin's mantra that man cannot be free from society, and the fate of common man, whose lot was disrupted by the collapse of the Soviet Union, mattered to Abdyjaparov. Many villagers still cannot get out of their stupor; they loiter about on dusty roads, or sit on mounds of dirt, selling cheap household items, and taking the pitiful proceeds to drink away the bitterness. Only when casting a chance glance at the strikingly beautiful native land do they think about eternity and ask about their own worthiness in the light of this natural splendour. The lower classes do not want to live in the past; the upper classes cannot improve their lives. The village head, Kabylbek, goes to work everyday as if it were a holiday. And why not? He has a job, while many are forced to languish without work. The retired wait for their pensions for months, if not years; the farmers plough the land, but all the same Kabylbek seems to ignore the difficulties of transition. Only after an encounter with the female tractor-driver, Boke, does the dashing chairman of Ayil-Okmotu understand that he must not only listen to the requests and suggestions of the villagers, but that he must change his style of work, be active and lead the people. The passive Kabylbek suddenly begins to manipulate the situation, and between these two states of passive and active comes the song 'Saratan'. A few couples in love sing the song on a warm summer evening: it brings a breath of life, and they can sense that it is time for a change in the village administration. Then Kabylbek passes along: he just concluded a one-sided deal with the richest man in the area to supply fuel for the diesel tractors. For two years the land rested, and Kabylbek only cared about his reputation: taking no bribes and not getting involved in any dubious deals. But Boke laments: 'It is already summer and no one has sewn anything, the people have no fuel.' She begins to teach Kabylbek new agricultural techniques. Then, Kabylbek negotiates his agreement with the wealthy Kyrgyz, and he is pleased to see that the world is not so grey and dull as it seemed a few hours earlier.

Village Authorities is a film full of hope for Kyrgyz cinema. The late Kyrgyz documentary film-maker Yevgeni Kotlov once lamented: 'Bishkek is difficult to film.'[12] But the remarkable cinematographer Manasbek Musaev, in Sarulu's exquisite film *Rough River, Placid Sea* (2004), proved otherwise. Erkin Saliev's *Cloud* stylishly captured the same places in the Kyrgyz capital that were made famous in Sarulu's first full-length film. Together, these three films gave an idea of the overall situation in Kyrgyz cinema: the collapse of eternal values in *Rough River, Placid Sea*; the pessimism of *Cloud*, and the importance of society coming together in *Village Authorities*.

The Final Breakthrough: Independence

Talgat Asyrankulov and Gaziz Nasyrov's *Birds of Paradise* (2006) was filmed at the Kyrgyz-Uzbek border in the Fergana Valley. The directors managed to convey the southerners' spirit of optimism in situations which seem to offer no way out. Kyrgyz southerners are special people: they differ from the law-abiding northerners and they are afraid of nothing and no one. They like to say the phrase: 'no problem' (*beimaral*) and they overcome barriers easily, with a smile. This is a film about risky, brave adventurers fighting for their place under the sun: they want to live for the pleasure of the here-and-now. In general, the characters are positive, young people seeking a better life. At the most critical moment, their leader Shima makes the right choice and accomplishes a feat. In the role of the long-awaited hero Kyrgyz viewers saw the young charismatic actor

Aziz Beishenaliev. Asyrankulov explained that he wanted to make a film that explored the continuous overcoming of obstacles:

> One time, my friend, the artist Baiysh Ismanov, visited me from Jalalabad. On a long winter evening, he told me about the situation in our hometown. In particular, he told me about how people survived by trafficking contraband: what they take to the Uzbek side, and what they bring back from there. Usually people take bread and Chinese consumer goods there; and they bring back mainly fuel and lubricants as we had problems with petrol. Then we discussed the nature of smuggling. Almost every house in the Uzbek-Kyrgyz village of Begavad had an underground capacity for fuel canisters. I was fascinated by the situation there. On the one hand, it was a violation of the law and the border. On the other hand, it was dangerous. And at the same time it was so touching. The border follows the river where we swam as children, bathing on one side and enjoying the fresh air on the other. I was so touched that I imagined these men who had three, four, or five canisters in their sheds and who cross the river under the cover of the night (and faced by gunshots). So I thought to develop a basic plot around the issue of gasoline.[13]

Birds of Paradise made two breakthroughs. The first was the idea of the film: the heroes face a choice, and each must make a choice

Figure 14.2 Still from Talgat Asyrankulov and Gaziz Nasyrov's *Birds of Paradise* (2006).

because there is no retreat; the second was technological – the film was funded with the film-maker's own money, which was only enough for the video format. Only later did Asyrankulov find an opportunity to transfer to 35 mm.

Birds of Paradise was shown at many international festivals, but did not receive any awards or prizes. Nevertheless, it attracted the interest of critics and viewers. Daria Borisova wrote: 'This film is brilliant, bursting with talent, and is certainly worthy of attention. It touches upon such relevant topics, "shouting" from all of Central Asia about drug trafficking and cross-border smuggling. Even if the film-makers do not exploit the theme, they talk about it as a bitter part of everyday life.'[14]

In Kyrgyzstan many people want to make films, but the state has been unable to provide the requested budgets, even at a minimum level. The history of *Birds of Paradise* preceded a transformation in the film industry in Kyrgyzstan, with the emergence of the production company Oy Art and its strategy of '10+' begun in May 2004. The Beshkempir Studio declared a 'Manifesto of New Central Asian Cinema', where the central idea advocates making videos and then converting them into 35 mm. This process is supposed to unleash creativity, as it is not restrained by complicated technological requirements and a budget.

Translated by Michael Rouland and Birgit Beumers

Notes

1   Aktan Arym Kubat in a conversation with the author in December 1998 for the television programme 'Komponuem kinokadr', Kyrgyzteleradio, Bishkek.
2   A. Abdykalykov, 'Interv'iu,' *Aziia-kino* 3 (1993).
3   See K. Urmatava, 'Natsional'naia mozaichnaia tekhnika "Kurak"' in *Nekotoroe aspekty izucheniia kirgizskogo iskusstva* (Bishkek, 1993).
4   Abdykalykov, 'Interv'iu'.
5   Asyrankulov made this remark in November 1998 during a visit of the INPUT selector Sergio Borelli to Bishkek.
6   Marat Sarulu in a conversation with the author in autumn 2001 for the television programme 'Komponuem kinokadr', Kyrgyzteleradio, Bishkek.
7   Ibid.
8   Ibid.
9   Ibid.
10   Ibid.
11   Ibid.
12   Evgenii Kotlov in July 1998 on the television programme 'Komponuem kinokadr', Kyrgyzteleradio, Bishkek.
13   Asyrankulov in conversation with the author on 16 November 2006 on the programme 'Kinostan', Manas Radio, Bishkek.
14   Dar'ia Borisova, 'Predchuvstvie geroia', *Kinoforum* 1 (2007): 11–13 (p. 12).

15

A VIEW FROM MOSCOW: MYTHS AND REALITIES OF THE UZBEK FILM BOOM

Daria Borisova

A fter 2000, we started to hear about the 'Uzbek film boom'. Anyone even remotely familiar with the cinema of the former Soviet republics knows that Uzbekistan holds a unique position in Central Asia: the country produces a large number of films that are extremely popular with local audiences. Year after year we hear enthusiastic reports from the Uzbek envoys at regional festivals that more and more films are being made, and more and more people are watching them. Television series from Uzbek directors with Uzbek movie stars have achieved amazingly popular ratings on television. People struggle to get to see the premieres of new Uzbek films in Tashkent, and numerous films remain in distribution for six to nine months. Video pirates have not been asleep either, hurrying to release the new instalments of national hits. This Uzbek phenomenon has evoked the admiration and envy of colleagues from other neighbouring countries, because the problem for cinema in the post-Soviet era has been the same: the percentage of domestic films at the box office is negligible. But in Uzbekistan – what joy!

A few years ago a similar process started in Kazakhstan, Kyrgyzstan and even Tajikistan (where the pulse of cinema can hardly be felt): small, private studios emerged, which made films focused entirely on maximum success with local mass audiences and on fast recoupment of outlay; in most cases the profit from distribution and DVD sales of such films significantly exceeds the production budget. But Uzbekistan has been the 'trailblazer'; it even had a special word for such cinema: 'chopping board' films, from the word *khon-takhta* – the chopping board for vegetables. This term renders accurately the nature of this phenomenon: we see something that is made quickly, mechanically, on a conveyor belt. The 'chopping board' is, however, the output of private, non-state studios, which practically have no reach beyond the region (such Uzbek films are in high demand in the southern areas of Kazakhstan, in Kyrgyzstan and Tajikistan, but no further). In the beginning such films were made by amateurs, and gradually professional scriptwriters and directors got involved in the process. The owners of these private studios began to understand that without professional help the quality of their films would soon fail to satisfy even the most undemanding audience, and professionals discovered for themselves in such 'commercial' cinema (as the 'chopping board' industry is called in Uzbekistan) almost the only source of a secure income, because the state budget only pays for a few films every year that are made at Uzbekkino, the National Agency of Cinema, and no film-maker can make a film there more often than once in two years.

The cheap and fast production of 'commercial' films is possible because the creators manage without many components of classical film-making. They shoot not on film but on digital media; they do not waste time on location search and original objects, but frequently work even without a production designer. The film-makers' energy is concentrated on the plot, the adherence to the laws of the genre (mainly melodrama or crime) and on the soundtrack. The music is a major component of *khon-takhta*, and often not actors, but singers, stars of the national music scene, perform the main parts. During the film's action the characters sing, and sometimes dance, which brings the contemporary commercial cinema of Uzbekistan in line with Indian cinema that is traditionally popular in the region.

An example of such 'commercial' cinema is Said Mukhtarov's *Marjona* (2004), which was shown at the Kinoshock Film Festival in Anapa (Russia) in 2005. The film was shown in the competition of popular hits from the region, which took place away from the main festival location largely for local audiences, where critics would not normally venture. The film was a musical film based on the patterns of Indian cinema. The plot served as a web that strung together a range of concert numbers – song and dance. The difference to films such as Yusup Razykov's *The Shepherd* (2005) or Yolkin Tuichiev's *The Teenager* (2005), which screened in the main competition, could not be greater. But equally dumbfounding was the reaction of the local audience: no one moved, but all stared at the screen with bated breath. They empathized with the heroes: the men shook their heads and clicked their tongues to express agreement or disagreement, while the women wept. After the screening, the film's producer was surrounded by a dense ring of well-wishers who had missed such 'emotional' films. The Uzbek guests at the festival confirmed that *Marjona* was very popular indeed in Uzbekistan.

In January 2007 I finally went to Tashkent. Within the first few days I noticed the abundance of film posters in the city, largely for screenings of Indian films and the notorious 'commercial' Uzbek ones. I only once went into a cinema. At the height of the working day at the House of Cinema (one would think the centre of cinematic life in the country) there was an Indian film with Uzbek translation. The large auditorium was full, and the audience watched the film in the same manner as the locals in Anapa had fixed their gaze on the screen when watching *Marjona*, holding their breath.

The director and screenwriter of 'commercial cinema', Rustam Sagdiev, underlined during a conversation that the ratings of his films were incomparably higher than any others, even the films by Zulfikar Musakov, *Boys in the Sky* (2002) and *Boys in the Sky 2* (2004), which were held by many observers from Moscow to be the most popular with audiences. Sagdiev's film *The Unexpected Bride* (2006) won the main audience prize of MTV-Uzbekistan, reflecting the trust and love of audiences. When talking about the unprecedented success of Uzbek cinema locally, the protagonists are not Yusup Razykov, Zulfikar Musakov or Yolkin Tuichiev; Uzbek audiences watch the movies of Rustam Sagdiev and his ilk. There is a clear division between 'festival' films and films 'for internal use'. The first is the flag-bearer of the national film school, and these films garner prestigious awards and maintain the world's image of Uzbek cinema as modern art. They are known abroad, but little in demand at home. The second group does not go beyond Uzbekistan at all, but holds a monopoly on the domestic market.

Figure 15.1 Still from Rustam Sagdiev's film *The Unexpected Bride* (2006).

Films such as *Marjona* and *The Unexpected Bride* make up the 'film boom', but what kinds of films are they? The films are quite uneven in quality, but they are made on the principles of audience demand. They are constructed along simple lines that cannot misfire, similar to the simplicity of the Russian *lubok*: they duplicate ready-made plots, exploit popular prejudice and reject original heroes in favour of proven types. One might say that the production of such films is a conveyor belt and that the authors of 'commercial cinema' are faceless artisans, but this is not true. The popularity of Sagdiev is no accident, as his talent lies in his subtle and fine understanding of his audience: Sagdiev 'knows the soul of the people'.

In *The Unexpected Bride* the heroes are clearly divided into 'positive' and 'negative'. The characters are caricatures. The plot and ideological underpinning hanker to please the good, proper citizens of today's Uzbekistan. Two young men live in a dormitory room of the Tashkent Institute: Elbek is serious, diligent and hardworking; Sotimhon is frivolous and a man about town. They have both come from the village to study. Elbek intends to return to his *kishlak* after graduation, while Sotimhon only thinks about how to cling to something in the capital. According to the laws of the genre, the good guy is good in everything – handsome, with rosy cheeks and curly hair, while the bad guy has the appropriate characteristics as well: he is small-minded, restless and absurdly pretentious in his appearance. But the key indicators to determine the quality of the heroes are their relationships to older people and women. Sotimhon mechanically shows signs of respect for teachers and the parents of his roommates, occasionally even argues with them. Elbek indiscriminately respects elders, where his manners border on worship. In conversations with them, he hardly removes his hand from his heart and does not dare lift his eyes. Sotimhon imagines himself a heartthrob, prowling for a rich Tashkent bride, hoping to get all the good things of life overnight: a residence in the capital, prosperity, well-being. Elbek does not look at women at all. After all, he will soon return home, where his loving and caring mother will choose the 'right bride'. For him, nothing can happen without his mother and without a wedding.

As often happens, fate gives one man what the other wants. A rich beauty, Charoz, a typical girl from the capital, spoiled and capricious, falls for Elbek. She prefers to speak in Russian, and Elbek frowns with disapproval: 'Why does she not speak our native language?' Elbek indignantly asks Sotimhon. 'What's the matter? She grew up without her mother and was raised by a Russian nanny', his friend answers with pity. The girl, who is used to getting everything she wants first time round, decisively chooses Elbek. He politely but firmly declines her approaches and affection; her vigour, lack of inhibitions and independence are entirely foreign to him. But Charoz will not let go. Upon learning that Elbek has received his diploma and gone home immediately to his *kishlak*, she packs a suitcase and jumps on a train straight to his home.

As she travels, we see our 'positive' hero in his natural surroundings. Despite the fact that he returns home a certified specialist and finds a prestigious job as an engineer, Elbek continues to be completely subjugated to his mother (his father is long dead and the elder sister is married). She is an overbearing and proud woman, who commands respect in the village. Her love for her only son has translated into a desire to shield him from any initiative, in order to arrange his life literally step by step. The neighbours admire her son for his wisdom, modesty and good looks, and they are vying with each other to offer brides. But she does not fall for the first good offer. Indeed, by choosing a bride for her son, an Uzbek mother chooses a daughter-in-law for herself, who will do all the housework, take care of her son, of the grandchildren and of herself. The ideal option is a woman like the daughter-in-law of the nearest neighbour, a quiet young woman with forever downcast eyes. She dresses only in

Uzbek national dress and, although once again pregnant, does her everyday chores: she fetches water, bakes bread, sweeps the courtyard, shakes out patchwork mattresses, washes and cleans. The mother-in-law sits on the bed with her tea and controls the process. This is the ideal that Elbek's mother wants. But, while she hesitates, an unexpected bride lands on her head.

Charoz, in tight jeans and a frivolous tube top, in high-heeled sandals and with make-up, appears in Elbek's yard and introduces herself as his fiancée. Of course, not only is the mother shocked, so is Elbek. The young man sincerely tries to distance himself from this 'gift'. Then the young predator sets heavy artillery in motion: she says that she is expecting a child from her 'fiancé'. His mother almost faints. On the one hand, she wants to drive off the young impudent girl, and on the other, this is the mother of her future grandson. Reluctantly, she takes Charoz into her home.

Then begins the story of transformation. Charoz is now compelled to rise before daybreak, to help her future mother-in-law with the burdens of the household, to withstand the nagging at home and the venomous attacks by neighbours. At night she sleeps next to Elbek's mother, tied to her with a rope. Happiness does not come. Yet she tries hard: she washes the cattle (as best as she can), she takes lunch to Elbek at work, and cares for her new family. Change comes very slowly, and it happens within her. In a patriarchal environment, her transformation is visible: she ceases to chatter incessantly, to dress provocatively, and to be capricious. Finally, she performs an heroic deed. When the ambulance does not arrive in time to take the neighbour to the hospital to deliver her baby, Charoz recalls her introductory medical skills from the institute, where she studied – paid for by her dad's money. Now the villagers begin to respect her and consult her as a doctor. Along the way she treats her 'mother-in-law', whose heart has weakened from the recent events. In short, the ice melts, and the renegade becomes a heroine.

The trouble is that her beloved does not show any feelings and keeps in his mother's shadow. So it seems Charoz has not achieved her goal. Waiting for the right moment, she slips out of the house and goes to the train station to return to Tashkent. Discovering her departure, Elbek's mother suddenly realizes that she appreciates Charoz and has become attached to her (no doubt helped by Charoz's popularity with the neighbours). So she accepts Charoz as her son's bride and sends him after her. Soon enough, there is a happy ending: Charoz is prevented from leaving, while Elbek gets the approval of the parents and confesses his love. In the end, people are more tolerant towards each other, everyone finds harmony and happiness.

It is a story of re-education, of rebirth. Elbek is a static figure, who is good from the start: an obedient son, a diligent student, a patriot. The heroine undergoes a great transformation: she was not good, but careless, indiscreet, frivolous, and not accustomed to housework, but she is modest, domestic and bashful in the end. All these miraculous transformations occur under the influence of Elbek's mother: she is a simple woman from an ordinary Uzbek village, who is the bearer of true values. Two different cultures are juxtaposed: the old, patriarchal life and the new, urban culture with its alien influences (such as her secular pastimes, excessive independence of women, Russian language). The comparison does not favour the latter. Thus, the plot, the characters and their presentation in Sagdiev's film reflect the mood of current Uzbek society, which emphasizes the return to the roots. Indeed, a lack of education and willingness to do household chores are the main assets for marriageable girls nowadays. The unquestioning implementation of elders' demands is the norm for any young person, male or female.

A common thread that runs through the film is the theme of public opinion as a decisive factor in the formation of reputation, assessment and decision-making. The *mahalla,* or the walled neighbourhood – this unique form of Uzbek coexistence – remains at the heart of Uzbeks' life today as a traditional and correct model of the world order. The film's atmosphere implicitly reveals another feature of modern Uzbek society, perhaps unconsciously: the tendency to closure, to safeguard their identity from external influences. Perhaps that is why now, more than ever, such a naive propaganda cinema that identifies what is good and what is bad is in such demand. For the simple spectator this instruction manual to life is also entertaining.

Another facet in the success of this 'commercial cinema' is the fulfilment of the audience's need for passions and beauty: to provide what ordinary people do not have in their daily lives. Mukhtarov's *Marjona* (2004) serves as an example, where story and plot are quite irrelevant. A young man from a good family (performed by the same actor who played Elbek in *Unexpected Bride* (2006)) falls in love – with a gypsy. This cunning girl called Marjona whirls everybody around.

She sings and dances, rustles with her skirt like the characters in Indian cinema. However, the intensity of the passions, the crudely constructed dialogue and the carelessly conventional staging evoke the worst examples of Latin American soap operas. This fulminating mixture is cheered in Uzbekistan, because it is a fairy tale, which unfolds in the present: it gives the viewer a sweet pill of miracles of what can happen when you meet a beautiful, wild gypsy girl who lures you in a mad cycle of passion. Then you too begin to sing and dance in the middle of the streets of Tashkent, and everybody will join in.

The ingredients for audience success have not changed in centuries. What has changed is the ratio of people able to perceive high art and those who prefer light entertainment to burdensome innovative visual forms. As civilization developed, it offered the opportunity for education and for the cultivation of taste to increasingly larger sections of mankind. During the 1960s and 1970s Uzbek audiences watched the pioneering films of Shukhrat Abbasov's *The Whole Neighbourhood is Talking About It* (1960) and *You are Not an Orphan* (1963); Elyor Ishmukhamedov's *Tenderness* (1966) and *Lovers* (1969); Ali Khamraev's *The Seventh Bullet* (1972) and *Without Fear* (1972). Ishmukhamedov and Khamraev left the country long ago, while Abbasov stayed to oversee the production of *The Unexpected Bride,* in which he even appeared in a cameo role. The masters of Uzbek cinema either leave, or transform, while commercial cinema booms. The young Uzbek generation considers films such as *Marjona* and *The Unexpected Bride* are the whole of national cinema.

The commercial cinema of Uzbekistan continues to develop, and a number of national hits have followed the films discussed above. In 2008 Ayub Shahobiddinov's film *The Other,* made in the genre of melodrama, had a deafening success in Uzbekistan and participated in the main competition of the International Film Festival Eurasia in Astana. The lead part was played by Dilnoza Kubaeva, the same actress who starred as Charoz in *The Unexpected Bride.* Uzbek films made with state funding appear rarely in international festival programmes. It is obvious that the sectors of state and commercial cinema are quite separate and need to come closer, so both sides can learn from each other. Commercial cinema can gain professionalism and genre variety, while state-funded cinema can learn about the mechanisms of creating popular films to audience demand. A similar process is under way in Kazakhstan, where even directors of the Kazakh New Wave and veterans of art-house cinema have condescended to the creation of genre cinema. However, in Kazakhstan there are still people at those peaks who can step 'down' and condescend to teach the emerging young professionals. The Uzbek masters of cinema have practically all left the country.

Translated by Michael Rouland and Birgit Beumers

16

CONTEMPORARY TAJIK CINEMA IN CONTEXT: ON DJAMSHED USMONOV

Seth Graham

A s other chapters in this volume attest, film-making in three of the five former Soviet republics in Central Asia – Kazakhstan, Kyrgyzstan, and Uzbekistan – has been more or less steady, if modest, for much of the post-Soviet period.[1] In the other two countries in the region, however – Turkmenistan and Tajikistan – that is far from the case. Turkmenistan's paucity of film output, of course, has been almost entirely due to its repressive 'Dear Leader' government, which has effectively made feature film-making impossible there since 1996, even after the death in December 2006 of 'President for Life' Saparmurat Niyazov and the emergence of a less psychotic government.[2] Tajik cinema's dormancy has been a lasting consequence of the civil war (1992–7) and the subsequent instability and lack of resources in (not to mention the exodus of film personnel from) the country. This period of 'cinemalessness' came after Tajikistan's long history of film production as a Soviet republic, beginning with documentary footage in the 1920s, and well-regarded features since the establishment of Tajikfilm Studio in 1930.

As Sadullo Rakhimov has pointed out, from 1992 to the present Tajik cinema has 'existed in two states', one inside the borders, the other in emigration. Moreover, the films that are being produced inside the country are almost exclusively shot on video and for television broadcast. Rakhimov detects in such films the influence of Indian genre films, which are widely shown in Tajikistan, both on television and in cinemas.[3] Yet Tajik directors have in recent years produced a handful of films (with a growing number of them, including the three films I will discuss below, shot on film stock rather than video) that have attracted attention at festivals in the former Soviet Union and abroad, most notably Djamshed Usmonov's *Angel on the Right* (2002) and *To Get to Heaven First You Have to Die* (2006), both of which were screened at the Cannes Film Festival (in the latter case, as part of the official programme), Safarbek Soliev's *Calendar of Expectations* (2005), Gulyandom Mukhabbatova and Daler Rakhmatov's *Rover* (2005),[4] which were shown at the 2006 Eurasia Film Festival in Almaty, Kazakhstan, and Nosir Saidov's *True Noon* (2009), the first film shot on 35 mm stock inside the country and financed primarily with domestic funding since the end of the civil war (it screened at the Pusan International Film Festival). Bakhtiyar Khudoinazarov has made several features since 1992 (including *Bro* (1991) and the only feature film shot inside the country during the civil war, *Kosh-ba-kosh* (1993), as well as his well-known film *Luna Papa* (1999)). Both Usmonov and Khudoinazarov, however, have lived outside the country (in France and Germany/Russia, respectively) for most of their careers, exemplifying the artistic brain-drain that followed independence and civil war. The emigration of the creative intelligentsia intersected with the political instability in Tajikistan soon after the collapse of the USSR; the best-known Tajik director of the late Soviet period, Davlat Khudonazarov, who was briefly head of the Soviet Film-makers' Union, and before the civil war was an unsuccessful candidate for president of Tajikistan, abandoned film-making entirely and has recently worked full-time in defence of the rights of migrant Tajik labourers in Moscow, symbolizing the simple fact that Tajiks have been occupied with more urgent concerns than attempting to represent life in their country in 90-minute fiction films shot on 35mm stock.[5] Still, a few people are doing just that, and here I want to examine one such Tajik artist, Djamshed Usmonov, in the context of post-Soviet Central Asian culture(s) more generally.

The Geo-Political Context: Central Asia as a Cultural Region

The Western analyst of post-Soviet Central Asian cinema is productively guided by questions first posed by a discipline that only relatively recently has given any attention to the former Second World: post-colonial studies.[6] Such questions include: What has been the role of cinema in the new nations' efforts to define themselves as cultural entities? Can we detect in Central Asian cinema something analogous to what Ashish Rjadhyaksha calls the 'nationalist reconstruction agendas' that informed the development of the New Cinema movements in former colonies in Africa, Latin America and Asia beginning in the 1950s?[7] The condition of 'sudden sovereignty', as evidenced across Asia and Africa in the wake of de-colonization, tends to elevate the category of nation to the top layer of cultural consciousness, and scholarship and criticism on post-Soviet Central Asian film (and indeed in all the former Soviet republics) has reflected this tendency, especially the work of Gulnara Abikeyeva.[8] The novelty of independence has intersected with the novelty of access to world cinema; film-making in all 15 of the former Soviet republics has been significantly marked by negotiation between the tropes of emerging nationhood and the multiple filmic languages now at the disposal of film-makers; in the case of Central Asia, film artists have had free rein to adopt, adapt and/or ignore an entire range of global influences, including Hollywood, European cinema, Bollywood, East Asian cinema and Iranian cinema. An equally prominent 'artistic interlocutor', it is essential to keep in mind, is Soviet film, the legacy of which can be traced on multiple fronts. The influence of the Soviet genre of the 'film about children' (*detskii fil'm*), for example, has informed quite a large number of films from the newly independent republics of Central Asia, especially the work of the Kyrgyz director Aktan Arym Kubat (formerly known as Abdykalykov), but also such films as Usman Saparov's *Little Angel, Make Me Happy* (1992), Darejan Omirbaev's *Cardiogram* (1995), Murat Aliev's *Night of the Yellow Bull* (1997), Serik Aprymov's *Three Brothers* (2000) and *The Hunter* (2004), Satybaldy Narymbetov's *Ompa* (1998) and *Leila's Prayer* (2002), Rustem Abdrashev's *Renaissance Island* (2004) and Yusup Razykov's *The Shepherd* (2005).[9] On a different level, the legacy in a nascent market environment of the Soviet film industry, which often overvalued *auteur* and other non-commercial film-making, is an area of continuity to be explored, and has clear implications for the most prominent characteristic shared by the five Central Asian national cinemas: financial anemia, though the various ways that problem is addressed get more various every year. Finally, the influence of *perestroika*-era and post-Soviet film, with its (re-)discovery of the gangster film and other crime genres, among other popular forms, is traceable in many works from Central Asia since the late-1980s, especially those associated with the 'Kazakh New Wave', but also Usmonov's films *Angel on the Right* and *To Get to Heaven First You Have to Die*.

The rarefied atmosphere of international film festivals, where a significant percentage of the most celebrated Central Asian (especially Kazakh and Kyrgyz) films have been consumed since the mid-1990s, is scarcely conducive to the development of popular domestic cinemas. Festival standouts such as Omirbaev's *Killer* (1998), Abdykalykov's *The Swing* (1993) and *The Adopted Son* (1998), Razykov's *The Orator* (1998), Khudoinazarov's *Luna Papa* (1999) and others have quite literally represented 'the national beyond the nation', to use Dudley Andrew's phrase.[10] If Central Asian cinema has a 'soul', it has spent a great deal of time being astrally projected abroad for well over a decade now. Again, while these circumstances afford the peripatetic film critic and scholar access to Central Asian films as exotic aesthetic specimens from a relatively newly discovered region (Dmitri Karavaev has called them 'moon rocks': exotic and isolated from native audiences),[11] they are hardly an engine for domestic popular cinema. The situation in Tajikistan, where many of the best-known and most experienced film professionals are absent, compounds the problem and has contributed to the scarcity of artistically sophisticated cinematic representations of Tajik reality, past and present. The films from the region have (fairly or unfairly) earned the reputation as being 'ethnoscapes' made with an eye to appealing to foreign festival audiences, who are attracted to them not only because of the exotic content, but by the heroic efforts of film-makers from such places to make cinema under 'third-world' conditions. Sergei Anashkin relates a telling anecdote about Usmonov in this regard:

> 'Did you scratch the film on purpose?' the Iranian director Mohsen Makhmalbaf asked the directors of *Flight of a Bee* (1998, co-directed by Usmonov and Min Boung Hun). They admitted that the scene in question had been damaged when the film was being developed, and that there had been no money to reshoot it. 'Don't tell anyone that. Make up

something about "the aesthetics of poverty", and those scratches will only help underscore the film's verisimilitude', advised the master.[12]

Without characterizing any of the so-called 'stans' as third-world countries, or even as post-colonial in the same way that many African and other Asian nations are, there are useful parallels to be drawn between post-Soviet Central Asian cinema and the cinema of other emergent nations that have the potential to guide observers from outside. One avenue of inquiry is one that post-colonial film studies might pursue: to detect and describe a dialogue between Soviet cinema's representations of Central Asian 'ethnoscapes' and the representation of the same in recent, autochthonous films. The political emphases of post-colonial studies are perhaps not so applicable to the Central Asian case; the multiplicity of influences on cultural production under conditions of post-Sovietness makes concepts like complicity versus resistance, not to mention the concept of 'revolutionary' cinema, problematic. The expanded reservoir of influences and allusions is analogous to the expanded range of stimuli – icons, discourses, images, belief systems, tropes, and so on – to which the post-Soviet consciousness is exposed, and from which post-Soviet subjectivity must be constructed. There is a two-way metaphorical link to be drawn between cinematic subjectivity and individual consciousness, a link made explicitly by Deleuze himself, who considered cinema 'an exploration of consciousness'.[13] This suggests an approach that yields insight into the *auteur*-esque films of the subject of this chapter: Djamshed Usmonov. Contemporary Central Asia is a place where, as Gulnara Abikeyeva argues, the subject is defined (in variable proportions) by four different identities or mentalities: ethnic (that is Kyrgyz, Tajik, Uzbek, etc); Muslim; Soviet; and Western.[14] This useful schema can be applied not only to the consciousness of characters in the films, but to the film-makers and their 'aesthetic consciousness', as well.

This discussion of Central Asia as a cultural region (linked by geography and shared history in the imperial and Soviet periods of Russian history), of course, does not do justice to the significant differences among the countries. Tajikistan stands out among the other four former Soviet Central Asian republics not only because of its particularly violent transition to independence, but also by virtue of its Persian (rather than Turkic) linguistic and cultural heritage, which has caused a re-orientation of Tajik cultural producers towards

Iran and away from the other four former Soviet republics, both on a stylistic level and in terms of self-identification. At the 2004 Didor Film Festival in the Tajik capital Dushanbe, for example, the jury was chaired by Iranian director Mohsen Makhmalbaf (whose 1997 film *Silence* and 2005 film *Sex and Philosophy* were shot and set in Dushanbe, where the director and his family have in fact lived for many years). At one point during the festival some participants complained that the Persophone discussions among the Iranian, Tajik and Afghani participants were not being translated into Russian or English.[15] At the forefront of not only Tajik cinema, but the pan-Persian cinema represented at Didor, is Djamshed Usmonov (b. 1965), who studied directing at Tajikfilm Studio and later at the Higher Courses for Directors and Scriptwriters in Moscow. His feature films to date comprise not only a sustained artistic representation of contemporary Tajik society, but also an instructive example of film-making in the cultural atmosphere I have described above as characteristic of post-Soviet Central Asia since the fall of the Soviet Union.

Flight of the Bee

Usmonov co-directed *Flight of the Bee* (1998) with the South Korean cinematographer (and graduate of VGIK) Min Boung Hun, and they begin their film with a dedication to the memory of Indian film-maker and composer Satyajit Ray, whose music also forms the basis for the film's soundtrack. These two Asian associations, as well as the film's particularly lyrical treatment of a theme common in Japanese, Indian and other cinema traditions – revenge for an insult to one's (and one's wife's) honour – link it to Eastern aesthetic and narrative traditions in a way that Soviet Central Asian cinema, for all its vivid local colour ('national in form, socialist in content') could not. There are also westward nods, however: an implicit assertion of Central Asia's geopolitical role as a crossroads among cultures, as well as the influence of globalization on the aesthetic sensibilities of Central Asian directors. The title of the film, for instance, refers to a legend, recounted by the schoolteacher protagonist to his pupils, about a soldier in Alexander the Great's army who hides his aged father in a trunk and carries him on his back to save him from being killed (at that time, the legend goes, people were routinely killed once they reached a certain age). The army ends up lost in the desert, and the old man saves them by telling his son to find a bumblebee, tie a white thread to it, and follow it to water. The moral, says the teacher, is that elders must be respected and valued. The oral lesson becomes an object lesson for the teacher's own family when an old man moves into their house after the teacher buys the old man's house as part of his revenge project. The man's quiet traditional (Muslim and Tajik) values begin to have a positive effect on the teacher's son, who begins to answer the call to prayer, and his wife, who starts to buy her flour directly from the mill, rather than the shop. The old man also tends to the family's orchard, ensuring both a lasting connection to the earth and a (literally) fruitful future. The scene with the fruit trees also represents an implicit reversal of the metaphorical use of the tree in some Soviet Central Asian cinema, for example in Andrei Konchalovsky's film *The First Teacher* (1965), in which a Kyrgyz village's sole surviving tree is doubly coded as a symbolic vestige of the traditional allegiances that Soviet peoples were expected to sever, and as the personal fetish and stubbornness of a backward-thinking village resident, who – in a graphic gesture of severing – takes an axe to the tree in the climactic scene.

The plot of Usmonov's film has been characterized as a 'parable', and one that offers an instructive and happy ending to a story that for most of the film seems destined to end badly for the protagonist. The schoolteacher is angered by his rich, powerful neighbour's decision to build an outhouse directly next to the schoolteacher's house, and thus befoul the air. The teacher is also angry because the neighbour makes a habit of brazenly staring at the teacher's wife as he uses the outhouse. In response, the teacher sells his livestock, purchases the house and land on the other side of his neighbour's house, and begins single-handedly digging a pit, to be used as a public toilet, directly under the man's bedroom window. The powerful neighbour retaliates with threats, attempted bribery (one morning the teacher arrives to find the pit filled in and a gold ring atop the pile of dirt), and even arranges for the unjustified arrest of the teacher's young son. The teacher becomes more and more obsessed and determined to complete his project, and less and less attentive to his family, and the pit gets deeper and deeper until he unexpectedly taps into an underground water source, thus ensuring that the village will have a badly needed well, not to mention referring neatly back to the legend of the bee told at the beginning of the film.

As Anashkin has pointed out, the film combines the traditions of Asian and European Neorealism with the realia of Soviet (or

post-Soviet) life:[16] a portrait of Lenin on an office wall, and the fact
that the schoolteacher is also an unpublished novelist and – initially,
anyway – trusting in the system, which he expects will respond
promptly to his entirely justifiable complaint about his neighbour.[17]
The man's idealism (and/or *naiveté*) is contrasted to the practicality
of his wife, who, for instance, advises their son to fight back against a
bully tormenting him at school (his father told him to do the exact
opposite), and especially her response to the neighbour's
imprisonment of her son. She goes into the neighbour's house
and (by means – sexual? – and/or words to which the viewer is not
privy) convinces him to let her son go. The film ends on a note of
nationalism: the children in the teacher's class sing the Tajik
national anthem.

Angel on the Right

In Usmonov's next feature, *Angel on the Right*, the elements of
realism – both the mundane reality of everyday life and the
conventions of contemporary drama – are even more present. The
dialogue-free pre-credit opening shots show an elderly woman
preparing for the day in 'ethnographic' detail that recall Usmonov's
earlier film, as well as other films from the region. Still, the influence
of traditional oral culture and legend remains central. At two key
points in the narrative, a character tells a potentially instructive story
of religious belief.[18] In the first scene after the credits we see three
men in a taxi, one of them carrying a live sheep. As they drive along
the bleak Tajik road he explains that he plans to sacrifice the sheep
to give thanks to a Tajik saint, whose intercession he credits for
saving him from a long prison term in Russia for heroin trafficking.
The Russian border guards strip-searched him thoroughly, but
forgot to ask him to remove his hat, where the drugs were stashed.
The second oral testimony to faith (and the source of the film's title)
is the elderly woman's explanation to her grandson of how each
person is sent to Heaven or Hell. We all have an angel on our right
shoulder and on our left shoulder. The angel on the right keeps
track of our good deeds, the one on the left records our bad deeds,
and after we die the two books are weighed to determine where we
are to spend eternity. The theme of moral redemption comes to the
fore in a mildly surprising way after the taxi scene. Perhaps contrary
to viewer expectations, the man with the sheep is not the
protagonist, and indeed is not seen again. The other passenger in
the car becomes the focus of the narrative. Hamro is a career

criminal returning to his small Tajik village after 10 years in Moscow, in the criminal underworld and in prison. He is not consciously a returned prodigal son, however; he is lured home by his mother (the elderly woman from the pre-credit sequence), who is apparently terminally ill, but is actually part of a plot hatched by the mayor and others to whom Hamro owes money to make him return to Asht to make retribution. Once home, he discovers he has a 10-year-old son he did not know about (whose mother has since died), and takes (literally, by force) a lover. There is also a meta-cinematic element in the film: Hamro is a projectionist at the town's only cinema, which (of course) shows only Indian genre films. Significantly, the proprietor of the cinema cut down a small orchard to make room for the new venture, and the implicitly less noble use of the land is confirmed when Hamro uses the job as an alibi for burglary – he has time to break and enter before having to change reels.[19] Realizing that her son is just getting further into trouble since his return, the mother appeals to the mayor to help hasten her actual death, which will allow Hamro to sell her house and belongings and pay off his debts. In a scene that combines a touch of magical realism with a light satire of the Soviet/Eastern theme of the vast power of local bosses, the mayor consults a thick tome in which the future date of everyone in the village's death is listed. After some negotiation, and a phone call to a higher official for approval, he agrees to allow her to swap her death date – scheduled for seven years hence – with that of his own mother, who is due to die the next day. She prepares her things and herself for her passage to the next world, and peacefully dies.

The ending of the film is somewhat ambiguous, and much more so than the conclusion of *Flight of the Bee*. Hamro pays off his debts and even makes a bit of profit on the sale of his late mother's house. He leaves the village together with his son, although he leaves his devastated lover behind without even saying goodbye. Before her death, Hamro's mother secretly gave a piece of the family jewellery to the boy, telling him to hide it and give it to Hamro only when Hamro has become a good man. One of the last shots is of the boy looking at the jewellery in his hand and then at Hamro, a symbolic nod to the theme of children as the future, but also as the moral judges of adult behaviour. In this way, as in Usmonov's first work, the conclusion neatly returns to and gives new, contemporary meaning to the titular legend of the film.

Figure 16.1 Still from Djamshed Usmonov's *To Get to Heaven First You Have to Die* (2006).

To Get to Heaven First You Have to Die

The protagonist of this film is younger than Hamro, who was in turn younger than the teacher in *Flight of the Bee*. 19-year-old Kamal lies naked in a doctor's office. On the wall is a portrait of Avicenna, the eleventh-century Persian physician and philosopher, as if establishing the doctor's credentials. Kamal is there because he has not been able to consummate his three-month-old marriage. The doctor asks him some questions about his mood and reading habits, but does not really prescribe a remedy for his impotence, which implies a kind of impotence on his part, as well, or on the part of his generation; the middle-aged 'fathers' are perhaps short on wisdom to pass on to the younger, first post-Soviet generation. We next see Kamal on a train bound for Dushanbe, where he is going to visit his cousin, Said. Kamal is apparently looking for an opportunity to cure himself of impotence by sleeping with another woman, and begins a series of rather pathetic attempts to pick one up.

The ensuing first act of the film is characteristic of the profoundly subtle comedy Usmonov had already used in his two previous works. Kamal clumsily makes a pass at an older woman sharing his train compartment, who tells him he is too young and strange. She gets off at the next stop and he sees her reunion with her husband and children. He then sees a woman on a bus and slyly moves his hand closer to hers as they hold the overhead bar. She moves hers away, but he persists and follows her off the bus into the factory where she works, only to be shooed away by the security guard. The pattern continues: a pretty girl he follows from the library turns out to be a Tae Kwan Do instructor; a woman whose groceries he carries several flights up to her apartment turns out to have a large, grumpy-looking husband. Kamal's symbolic impotence at meeting women, we are reminded, is symptomatic of his literal impotence; when his cousin Said arranges for them to sleep with two prostitutes, Kamal is unable to perform, further confirming his harmlessness. The film then takes a sharp turn towards the serious when Kamal reconnects with Lena, the girl from the bus, and is surprised in her bed the next morning by her ex-husband, who – rather than killing or otherwise harming Kamal – enlists him as his accomplice to burglary. The two are successful at first, but during their next heist, they surprise the owners of the house, and the ex-husband reveals himself to be a psychopath, killing the husband and raping the wife. Kamal at first leaves in disgust, but decides to return to the house, where he shoots his partner dead. He returns to Lena's apartment, where he finally is able to have sex before leaving the capital for good to return to his village, and to his young wife (whom we never see). For a film so thematically concerned with sex and violence, *To Get to Heaven* is a sometimes painfully slow-paced work, a quality that, in this and other films from the region, is tempting to interpret as aesthetically 'Eastern'. The contemplatory camera, for instance, lingers on Kamal in what feels almost like real time as he waits at a bus stop hoping to run into Lena, who had earlier caught his eye on a bus at the same spot.

Soviet film in its most institutional form operated on the principle of double metaphor: both the protagonist's biographical arc (*fabula*) and the filmic narrative (*siuzhet*) were instructive, symbolic rehearsals of an established (one might say rooted) master narrative. In Usmonov's last film, however, the ontogeny on the screen does not recapitulate any particular phylogeny. Such cinema attends to material that is, as Deleuze said, 'essentially laden with singularities'. The individual and the collective on the screen, like the screenwriter at the keyboard and the director behind the camera and at the editing table, are free to draw on, reject, or ignore the extant vestiges of representational systems, and to adapt them to individual motivations and aspirations. Kamal kills his partner-in-crime/love rival not out of his fealty to a system of religious belief, but out of personal disgust, anger, and moral outrage at the man's gratuitous violence. Kamal's concerns are biological, psychological and ultimately individualistic.

Taking in Usmonov's three films together, we can trace a trajectory from the village (his home village of Asht) to the city, and from the recognizable and symbolically national (recall the Tajik national anthem in *Flight of the Bee*) to the global/universal. In *Flight of the Bee* we never leave Asht, and the concerns of the villagers are not outwardly affected by any external influences. In *Angel on the Right*, Hamro's return to Asht after 10 years in Moscow brings elements of the urban underworld to the village, including thugs from 'the city' (i.e. Dushanbe) who come to collect a debt from the prodigal son. In *To Get to Heaven* the hero is from Asht, but we do not see the village at all; it is a variant on the 'man takes a journey' narrative, with the character arc of the man of more significance than the destination of his journey. The move towards the urban is also a move towards a cinema less rooted in a time or a place, which is a trajectory we might expect as Tajikistan's chaotic leap to independence recedes into the past, and the globalization of the consciousness of its film-makers continues apace: Usmonov's *Le roman de ma femme* (2011) was shot in France, in French, with a French cast.

Notes

1   By far the most comprehensive study of recent film-making across the region is Gul'nara Abikeeva's *Kino Tsentral'noi Azii: 1990–2001* (Almaty, 2001). An updated and translated version of the book was published as *The Heart of the World: Films from Central Asia* (Dana Zhamanbalina-Mazur, trans., Jonathan Mazur, ed.) (Almaty, 2003). Several chapters from the English version have also been published on the web journal *KinoKultura*, Special Issue 1, 2004, www.kinokultura.com/CA/index.html (accessed 18 March 2012).

2   On recent film-making in Turkmenistan (or rather its non-existence), see Gul'nara Abikeeva and Birgit Beumers, 'In Lieu of a Gap: The Absent Cinema of Turkmenistan', *Studies in Russian and Soviet Cinema* 4.2 (2010): 240–3.

3   Sadullo Rakhimov, 'The Contemporary State of Tajik Cinema', *Studies in Russian and Soviet Cinema* 4.2 (2010): 234–40. On the 'double life' of post-Soviet Tajik cinema see also Gul'nara Abikeeva, 'Tadzhikistan: Dve ipostasi odnogo kinematografa', in her *Natsiostroitel'stvo v Kazakhstane i drugikh stranakh tsentral'noi Azii, i kak etot protsess otrazhaetsia v kinematografe* (Almaty, 2006), pp. 263–71.

4   See Seth Graham, 'Ovora' *KinoKultura* 16 (2007), www.kinokultura.com/2007/16r-ovora.shtml (last accessed 18 March 2012).

5   There have, however, been several noteworthy Tajik documentaries produced since the 1990s. See Abikeeva, 'Tadzhikistan' and Rakhimov for lists and

descriptions of film by such documentary film-makers as Mairam Yusupova and others.

6   Prominent exceptions include David Chioni Moore, 'Is the Post- in Postcolonial the Post- in Post-Soviet? Towards a Global Postcolonial Critique', *PMLA* 116.1 (2001): 111–28, Jonathan Brooks Platt, ed., *Empire, Union, Center, Satellite: The Place of Post-Colonial Theory in Slavic/Central and Eastern European/(Post-)Soviet Studies. Ulbandus* 7 (New York, 2003), and an issue of the journal *Kritika* 1.4 (2000) devoted to the question of Russian orientalism.

7   Ashish Rjadhyaksha, 'Realism, Modernism, and Post-colonial Theory', in John Hill and Pamela Church Gibson, eds, *The Oxford Guide to Film Studies* (Oxford, 1998), pp. 413–25 (p. 415).

8   The title of Abikeeva's most recent book clearly indicates this emphasis in her work: Nation-building in Kazakhstan and other Central Asian countries, and how this process is reflected in cinema.

9   See Abikeeva, *Natsiostroitel'stva*, pp. 209–15 for an analysis of the image of children in recent Central Asian cinema, which she attributes in part to the metaphorical 'childhood' of the newly independent states.

10 Dudley Andrew, 'The Roots of the Nomadic: Gilles Deleuze and the Cinema of West Africa', in Gregory Flaxman, ed., *The Brain is the Screen: Deleuze and the Philosophy of Cinema*, (Minneapolis, 2000), pp. 215–49 (p. 226).

11 Dmitrii Karavaev, 'Amneziia ili anemiia?', *Kinoforum* 3 (2002): 35.

12 Sergei Anashkin, 'Blagodat' ritual', *Iskusstvo kino* 9 (1999): 29–32 (p. 32).

13 Laura U. Marks, 'A Deleuzian Politics of Hybrid Cinema', *Screen* 35.3 (1994): 244–64.

14 Abikeeva, *Natsiostroitel'stvo*, p. 25.

15 Gulnara Abikeeva, personal communication, November 2004.

16 Anashkin, pp. 29 and 32.

17 Abikeeva calls the character 'a typical Soviet intellectual' (*Natsiostroitel'stvo*, p. 204).

18 Abikeeva points out that all of Usmonov's films contain a scene of a character relating a legend or a story, usually connected in some way to the title of the film (*Natsiostroitel'stvo*, p. 202).

19 Other post-independence Central Asian films in which cinema-going is represented as an element of everyday life include the aforementioned *The Adopted Son* (1998), *Night of the Yellow Bull* (1997) and Omirbaev's *The Road* (2001), which, incidentally, featured Usmonov in the main role.

PART IV

REFERENCE SECTION

FILM-MAKERS' BIOGRAPHIES

Gulnara Abikeyeva

ABBASOV, Shukhrat
Kokand (Uzbek SSR), 1931

Director, founder of Uzbek cinema. People's Artist of the Soviet Union (1980). Graduated from the directing department of the Tashkent Theatre and Arts Institute in 1954, and from Advanced Directing Courses at Mosfilm in 1958. His first film, *The Whole Neighbourhood is Talking About It* (1960), remains one of the most popular and beloved films of the Uzbeks. The plot of the film is simple: a mother is looking for a bride for her son, and in the end a brilliant comedy with a poignant image of Uzbek life emerges, with plenty of songs and national colour. *You are Not an Orphan* (1963) focuses on the 14 different nationalities of children orphaned during World War II who learned to live as one family. His most famous film is *Tashkent – City of Bread* (1967) based on Andrei Konchalovsky's script. The film describes a Russian boy, Misha Dodonov, who in the early 1920s was sent to buy bread in Tashkent to save his mother and brothers from starvation. In *Abu Raihan Beruni* (1974) Abbasov explores the life of one the world's great teachers; and, in the later film *Land of Our Fathers* [*Zemlia nashikh ottsov*, 1998], he illustrates the lives of three generations in the post-Soviet era. There are two central themes for Abbasov: World War II and Uzbek history.

ABDRASHEV, Rustem
Alma-Ata (Kazakh SSR), 1970

Director and production designer. In 1988 graduated from Alma-Ata Art School, specializing as a theatre designer. In 1993 he completed an art degree at VGIK, as well as a degree in intellectual property law from the Kazakh University of Law. He began his career in film as production designer, working on such complex films as Rashid Nugmanov's *The Wild East* (1993), and Satybaldy Narymbetov's *The Life of a Young Accordion Player* (1994). Then he distinguished himself as a director of social and fashion commercials, as well as music videos, becoming one of the best video directors in independent Kazakhstan. As a director, he debuted in 2004 with *Renaissance Island*, loosely based on the poetry of his father, Zharaskan Abdrashev. This work immediately attracted attention because of the high artistic quality of the images. The film is set in the postwar era on the island of Barsa-Kelmes, from where people do not return. The story relates the life of a boy-poet who lives in a totalitarian atmosphere. His second film, *Patchwork Quilt*, is a comedy, describing modern life in the city and countryside. However, the film – comprising a mosaic of many different stories – lacked coherence and was less successful than his debut film. His next film, *Gift to Stalin* (2008) addresses the orders of Stalin to deport Chechens, Koreans, Germans and Jews to Kazakhstan. The film explores how Kazakhs adopted the immigrants, saved lives and shared their houses and their food. *Gift to Stalin* screened at the opening ceremony of the 2008 Busan International Film Festival.

ABDYJAPAROV, Ernest
Frunze (Kirghiz SSR), 1961

Director. In 1983 he graduated from the Pedagogical Institute in Frunze, specializing in Russian language and literature. In film, he began working as an editor and then as director of documentary films. In the 1990s he made a series of shorts, which were remarkable for their ethos and sense of the moment. His documentary *Alhambra* (2001) describes in 10 minutes, through images and music rather than words, a talented guitarist who can only find work selling vodka in a kiosk. Through the sound of music, we understand that there is a world of illusion and hope and that there is a harsh reality. Yet the human soul can live in both worlds. In 2004, Abdyjaparov shot his first feature film *Village Authorities* (*Saratan*), which enjoyed great popularity because the picture reveals the comic side of the Kyrgyz village. The film centres on tough local businessmen, grieving alcoholics, thieves and prophets, who awake to the morning prayer of a poor mullah. Yet the picture is uplifting and full of humour. His comedy *Pure Coolness* (2007) describes a young couple who are married by mistake. During the traditional ritual of bride theft, the groom's family stole the wrong bride; but in the end, there is harmony and happiness.

ABDYKALYKOV, Aktan. *See* ARYM KUBAT, Aktan

AGISHEV, Odelsha
Tashkent (Uzbek SSR), 1939

Scriptwriter. State Prize of the Uzbek SSR (1971) and the USSR (1984). Graduated from the Tashkent Suvorov School in 1956, then the scriptwriting faculty at VGIK in 1962. His first screenplay *White, White Storks* (1966), directed by Ali Khamraev, was revolutionary for Uzbek cinema. He sought to tell the truth about life in the *mahalla*, about the fate of women, and about Uzbek national traditions. However, much of the footage had to be cut due to censorship pressures. The brilliant creative tandem of Agishev and director Elyor Ishmukhamedov continued to create the Uzbek classics, *Tenderness* (1966) and *Lovers* (1969). These films were not only important in Uzbekistan but also for the entire Soviet Union, as the films convey the romantic spirit and freedom of the 1960s. Uzbek and Russian actors featured in both films, and both films expanded the boundaries of traditional Uzbek culture, bringing allusions of modern cinema from Federico Fellini and Marlen Khutsiev while reflecting Uzbek life. Since 1990 Agishev has lived and worked in Moscow, where he teaches at VGIK.

AIMANOV, Shaken
Bayan-Aul (Russian Empire), 1914 – Moscow, 1970

Actor, director, founder of Kazakh cinema. Kazakhfilm Studio is named in his honour. He graduated from the acting studio at the Kazakh Drama Theatre where he worked from 1933. He played over 100 roles and directed several productions for the theatre. His first notable role in cinema was in Moisei Levin's *Raihan* (1940), but Yefim Dzigan's *Dzhambul* (1952) was his breakthrough, with the truly national character of the great singer-bard. His directorial debut, alongside Karl Gakkel, was *Poem about Love* (1954), a filmic interpretation of the beloved opera *Kozy Korpesh and Baian-Sulu*. Then he co-directed with Gakkel *Daughter of the Steppe* (1954), which evoked the ethos of Soviet propaganda on land redistribution.

Subsequently Aimanov was a prolific director and his films defined the golden age of Kazakh cinema: his films communicated a deep sense of national pride. *The Beardless Deceiver* (or *Aldar-Kose*, 1964) brought humour to national folklore. *Land of the Fathers* (1966) occupies a special place in Kazakh cinema: it is a filmic journey of an old man and his grandson on a train through Kazakhstan and Russia. As they travel, they meet Russian archaeologists and the film turns into a dialogue of civilizations, where they debate the values of different cultures. Throughout his career Aimanov demonstrated his ability to work with different genres: comedies, such as *Our Dear Doctor* (1957) and adventure films, such as *The End of the Ataman* (1970), which was awarded the State Prize of the Kazakh SSR in 1972.

AIMEDOVA, Maya-Gozel
Ashkhabad (Turkmen SSR), 1941

Actress and darling of cinema for the Turkmen people. Winner of the State Prize of the Soviet Union (1973); People's Artist of the Turkmen SSR (1982); and People's Artist of the USSR (1987). From 1990 to 1992 she was a deputy of the Supreme Council of Turkmenistan. Graduated from the Russian Academy of Theatre Arts in 1964 and immediately began working in Ashkhabad. She played her first film role, Jahan, in Mered Atakhanov's *Incident in Dash-Kala* [*Sluchai v Dash-Kale*, 1963]. After a long break, she was internationally recognized for her role in Khodjakuli Narliev's *Daughter-in-Law* (1972). Almost without words, she played the daughter-in-law, Ogulkeik, who hopelessly waited for her husband to return from the war front. But there is so much love and vitality that it seems like a ghostly fantasy. Henceforth she formed a creative partnership with and married Khodjakuli Narliev. She co-wrote their next two films, *When a Woman Saddles a Horse* (1974) and *Jamal's Tree* (1980); the latter earned her huge success and the Best Actress award at the Moscow IFF in 1981. She often plays strong women as well as representing the epitome of Central Asian womanhood and motherhood. In this sense, her role of the mother in *Mankurt* (1990) is iconic as an image of the motherland.

AITMATOV, Chingiz
Seker (Kirghiz ASSR), 1928 – Nuremberg (Germany), 2008

Novelist, screenwriter and public figure. He is the spiritual leader of Kyrgyz and Central Asian cinema. Three-time winner of the USSR State Prize (1968, 1977, 1983) for his literary achievements. His novels, stories and scripts contributed to more than 20 films. In 1953 he graduated from the Kirghiz Agricultural Institute; in 1958 he completed the Higher Courses in Literature. From 1964 to 1986 he led the Kirghiz Union of Film-makers, and from 1991 to 2008 he was Kyrgyz Ambassador to Benelux and France. He created many important female characters for Kirghiz/Kyrgyz cinema: Altynai in *The First Teacher* (1965); Tolgonai in *Mother Earth* (1967); and several women in *Djamilia* (1968). His key male characters were developed in *Heat* (1962), *The Red Apple* (1975), and *Stormy Station* (1995). He had a special skill in developing themes of man's relationship with nature. *The White Ship* (1975), directed Bolotbek Shamshiev, centres on the folk legend of the mother-deer; the audience understands that the modern heroes of the film are not only connected with nature, but also share her destiny. Metaphorical prose and philosophical abstractions are the main characteristics of Aitmatov's creativity. He manages to create images that are symbols of epochs, and his image of a mankurt from his novel *The Day Lasts Longer than a Hundred Years* (1980) is the subject of two film adaptations: *Mankurt* (1990) and *A Mother's Lament about Mankurt* (2004). In 1996 he was awarded the Golden Camera of the Berlinale for his contribution to world cinema.

ALIEV, Murat
Ashkhabad (Turkmen SSR), 1951

Director. Alongside Jūris Podnieks and Vladimir Tiulkin, he belongs to the generation of documentary film-makers of the late 1980s who embraced the era of *glasnost* and *perestroika*. In 1977 he graduated from the scriptwriting department of VGIK. From 1975 to 1990 he worked as a newsreel director at Turkmenfilm Studio. He directed over 30 documentaries, many of which have received prestigious awards. His greatest success was the film *The Story of a Race* [*Istoriia odnogo probega*, 1986] about the meaninglessness of a famous horse race and the trials that befell its participants. A year later, he made another scandalous film, *Aura* (1987), which explores the problem of drug addiction in Turkmenistan. Following independence, he became the first artistic director of the Nusai Turkmen Centre of Film and Television for Children (1990–2), then deputy chairman of the state film video company of Turkmenistan (1993–9). He was expelled from this position in 1999 and persecuted for his feature film *Night of the Yellow Bull* (1997): President Niyazov did not appreciate that the plot did not celebrate his person, but was devoted to the entire generation that survived the massive earthquake of October 1948. Since 2001 he has lived and worked in Moscow.

ANNANOV, Baba
Ashkhabad (Turkmen SSR), 1934 – Ashgabat, 1991

Actor and director. People's Artist of the Soviet Union (1985). He played over 30 roles in Turkmen and Central Asian cinema from the 1960s to the 1980s. In 1959 he graduated from the Tashkent Art Institute and worked at the Chardjou Theatre in Turkmenistan. His first major role in cinema, in Alty Karliev's *The Decisive Step* (1965), earned him the Magtymguly State Prize of the Turkmen SSR. He played the role of a poor farmer, Artyk, who could not marry his beloved girlfriend because of the bride price, but the lovers decide to elope and find happiness. He was most in demand after the mid-1970s and played several lead roles: the conqueror of the virgin lands in Munid Zakirov's *It was in Mezhgore* [*Eto bylo v Mezhgor'e*, 1975], the builder of a dam in Kimiagarov's *A Man Sheds his Skin* [*Chelovek meniaet kozhu*, 1978], and a man returning from the war in *Jamal's Tree* (1980). In the last film he reveals a deep psychology: he has lost his faith in life and even suspects his wife of treason. During the 1980s he made several films as a director, wrote novels, short stories and film scripts. After his death, his son Kerim Annanov completed his last film, *Zohre and Tahir* (1993).

ANNANOV, Kerim
Ashkhabad (Turkmen SSR), 1958

Actor, director, screenwriter. In 1980 graduated from the department of philology of Turkmen State University. In 1987 graduated from the directing department of VGIK. He is the son of actor/director Baba Annanov. He began acting at the age of 19 in Khalmamed Kakabaev's *Kidnapping a Quarter Horse* [*Pokhishchenie skakuna*, 1978], about a young man who wants to protect his horse from those who want to take purebred Akhal-Teke horses abroad. In 1991 he opened a private film studio, Turan-Film. Together with his father he made the film *Zohre and Tahir* (1993), based on the popular Turkic epic poem and tragic tale. Thus, father and son forged a professional relationship in addition to their familial bond. They acted in films together; they worked together on scripts. After the death of his father, he made *The Legend*, based on elements of his father's biography. The film teaches a lesson: the father gathers his seven sons and one daughter and begins to create order, distributing functions to his children, as a farmer, shepherd, hunter, etc. As their lives begin to form, a fierce khan (played by the director himself) appears and chases their tribe in search of the world mountain, from where you can go straight to Heaven. *The Legend* was filmed at his private studio, and it was the last film on 35 mm film before film production in Turkmenistan came to a virtual halt.

APRYMOV, Serik
Aksuat (Semipalatinsk region, Kazakh SSR), 1960

Director of the Kazakh New Wave. He graduated from the directing department of VGIK in 1989. His diploma film, *The Last Stop* (1989), became a milestone for Kazakh cinema and was screened during the Critics' Week at Cannes. On the other hand, it was banned from the screen in Kazakhstan because of its harsh view of life in a Kazakh village. Alongside Rashid Nugmanov's *The Needle* (1988), *The Last Stop* launched the Kazakh New Wave. The films destroyed the myth of prosperity in Soviet society both in urban spaces and in the village. In contrast to *The Last Stop*, where the hero is forced to leave his village, Aprymov's subsequent film *Aksuat* (1998) presents a protagonist, Aman, who continues to live in his native village despite corruption and oppression. Rather than a social critique, he echoes a process of growing national consciousness; humour and irony remain. Aprymov returns to a critique of the Soviet past in *Three Brothers* (2000), which is a metaphor for the Soviet system of militarism and deception that ultimately kills the three central characters. Perhaps his most interesting film is *The Hunter* (2004), in which Aprymov creates a new myth about the origin of the Turks. The father-hunter teaches his adopted son the principles of life: how to breathe, how to hunt and how to love women. Although the son has faced poignant social problems in the here-and-now, he strives to become timeless hunter.

ARINBASAROVA, Natalia
Frunze (Kirghiz SSR), 1946

Actress. She graduated from the Bolshoi Ballet School in 1964 and VGIK in 1971. She worked as a stage actress in Moscow and starred in over 30 films. She made an important contribution to cinema in her first screen role of Altynai in Andrei Konchalovsky's *The First Teacher* (1965), where she created the image of a young girl who runs away from her wealthy husband. She simultaneously communicates a child's fear as well as the determination of a woman raised in the steppe, simple naiveté, and sage beauty. She was awarded the Coppa Volpi for Best Actress at the Venice Film Festival in 1966. She then appeared in films across Central Asia, playing the role of Saule in Shukhrat Abbasov's *Tashkent – City of Bread* (1967). In 1970 she received accolades for her role in Mazhit Begalin's *Song about Manshuk* (1969) and further international acclaim for her role in Ermek Shinarbaev's *Tender Heart* (1994).

ARYM KUBAT, Aktan (formerly ABDYKALYKOV)
Kuntuu Sokuluk (Chui region, Kirghiz SSR), 1957

Director. He graduated from the Kirghiz State Art College in 1980. Then he worked first as a designer and later as art director of four full-length feature films at Kirghizfilm. In 1990 he made his first documentary film, *The Dog Ran Away* (1990). The film was revolutionary in telling a story of vagrant dogs through their eyes and experiences. At the same time the film addresses various social strata of society during *perestroika*. His second path-breaking short film, *The Swing* (1993), was shot in black and white and has almost no words, whilst presenting vivid images of the Kyrgyz nation. The film won the Golden Leopard in Locarno in the category of short films, and prizes in Italy and Germany. International renown came in 1998 with his full-length feature *Beshkempir: The Adopted Son*. The film won prizes at over 20 international film festivals, including Locarno, Tokyo, Angers, Vienna, Cottbus and Singapore. But more importantly, the director became a national hero: he mirrored the Kyrgyz spirit and mentality through cinema. The story of Beshkempir, a foster child, follows the stages of his maturation and adaptation to his family as well as the Kyrgyz community. His next feature film, *The Chimp* (2001), is a sort of sequel to *Beshkempir*. Parallel to his work in feature films, he is actively involved in public life, making documentaries and helping young directors. In 2006 he launched the programme 10+ at the Kyrgyz Union of Cinematographers, which reformed the system of education, production and distribution in Kyrgyzstan. His film *The Light Thief* (2010) was selected for the Directors' Fortnight at Cannes.

ASHIMOV, Asanali
Baikadam (Zhambyl region, Kazakh SSR), 1937

Actor, director. The most popular actor of Kazakh cinema, with over 30 roles. People's Artist of the Soviet Union (1980). Graduated from the acting department of the Kazakh State Conservatory. While a student played in the film *Botagoz* (1957). After graduation worked at Kazakhfilm, and from 1964 at the Kazakh Academic Theatre, where he created over 50 roles. His recognition in cinema began in the early 1970s, after he starred in Shaken Aimanov's *End of the Ataman* (1970) and Sultan Khodjikov's *Kyz-Zhibek* (1970). In the former, he created the unforgettable image of a young and idealistic Bolshevik sent to spy on Ataman Dutov; in the latter, he had the epic role of the Kazakh Batyr Bekezhan, who separated the star-crossed lovers Zhibek and Tulegen. For each of these roles he was awarded the State Prize of the Kazakh SSR. He directed several historical films.

ASYRANKULOV, Talgat
Jalal-Abad (Kirghiz SSR), 1962

Production designer, director. In 1982 graduated from the Frunze College of Art, and in 1989 from the art department of VGIK. In the early 1990s he collaborated with Aktan Arym Kubat on two films: *Where is Your House, Snail?* (1992) and *The Swing* (1993). From 1994 to 1996 he worked as the art director of the Ordo State Television Channel; and from 1996 to 2001 he was the director of the Independent Bishkek Television Channel. The Kazakh film-maker Gulshad Omarova invited him as production designer for *Schizo* (2004), which allowed him to reveal his talent in cinema. The film is visually stunning, with magnificent exteriors and interiors; and the overall graphic style of the film conveys the spirit of survival and a certain kind of insanity typical of the first years of independence. From 2004 to 2006 he worked with Kazakh director Gaziz Nasyrov to make his full-length feature debut, *Birds of Paradise*. The film describes a student-journalist, who arrives in a frontier town in order to make a three-minute report about the border region. Suddenly, a teenager steals her video camera; she wanders aimlessly through the town, until she meets three friends, who reveal to her the truth about the city: drug trafficking, illegal transport of gasoline, and the trade with stolen cars. The film occupies a special place because it was made as a Central Asian co-production and illuminates the border problems in the region. Without a unified regional system of film distribution, the film did not reach audiences at large, but screened successfully at film festivals. Asyrankulov worked with Arym Kubat again as art director on the film *The Light Thief* (2010).

BAZAROV, Gennadi
At-Bashi (Tian-Shan, Kirghiz SSR), 1942

Director. People's Artist of the Kirghiz SSR (1974). He graduated from the directing department of VGIK in 1967. While still a student he made two shorts, *Prayer* [*Molitva*, 1964] and *Pause* [*Pauza*, 1965], after which Chingiz Aitmatov offered him the screenplay of his novel *Mother Earth* for his diploma film. He was only 26 years old when he made the film (1968), which brought him recognition and fame. The film tells the story of an heroic mother, Tolgonai, who loses three sons and her husband during the war, but still finds the strength and courage to survive. One of the artistic strengths of the film is the conversation between Tolgonai and Mother Nature, the field where she arrives alone to share her troubles. Baken Kydykeeva, who played the role of Tolgonai, was awarded a special award for Best Actress at the Central Asian and Kazakh Festival for Film-makers in 1968. Although he never repeated his initial success, Bazarov experimented with genres, such as the adventure film *Ambush* [*Zasada*, 1970] and the intellectual drama *Apple of My Eye* (1976). He also made socially engaged and critical films, such as *Metamorphosis* (2006).

BEGALIN, Mazhit
Village No. 13 (Semipalatinsk, Kirghiz ASSR), 1922 – Moscow, 1978

Director, founder of Kazakh cinema. Honoured Artist of Kazakh SSR (1966). In 1942 he was badly wounded in the war and demobilized. In 1943 he joined the directing department of VGIK, which had been evacuated to Alma-Ata during the war years. His filmic signature first appeared in *His Time will Come* (1958), devoted to the life and work of the Kazakh intellectual Chokan Valikhanov. The film covers the most dramatic periods in the life of the scholar and ethnographer: his journey to Kashgar under the guise of a merchant and his conflicts with Tsarist policy in the Kazakh steppe. *Traces Go Beyond the Horizon* (1964) was even more successful: the film poetically interweaves the story of the harsh life of shepherds with a love story. Since the action takes place in a remote location, Begalin also managed to convey the nomadic life of the Kazakhs. His full skill as director is evident in two films devoted to military topics: *Moscow, For Luck* [*Za nami Moskva*, 1967] and *Song about Manshuk* (1969). The first is based on a book by Bauyrzhan Momysh-Uly, which describes the heroism of the Panfilov division that was formed in Alma-Ata and succeeded in stopping the German army advancing on to Moscow in December 1941. The second film depicts the life of the Hero of the Soviet Union, Manshuk (Mansiya) Mametova. Both films raise the status of Kazakh heroes during World War II. His last film, *Steppe Sounds* [*Stepnye raskaty,* 1975], about events in Uralsk on the border between Russia and Kazakhstan in the early twentieth century, was shelved for ideological reasons. This injustice undermined his health.

BEISHENALIEV, Bolot
Toktogul (Kirghiz SSR), 1937 – Bishkek, 2002
Actor. People's Artist of Kyrgyzstan. The representative face of Kyrgyz and Central Asian cinema, he played over 100 roles. He graduated from the actors' studio of the Kirghiz Opera and Ballet Theatre in 1957 and from the Tashkent Theatre and Art Institute in 1963. His powerful and lucid performance in Andrei Konchalovsky's *The First Teacher* (1965) secured his place in the history of Kyrgyz cinema. His hero, a true revolutionary, believes that the time will come when children will understand him. He worked with many important Central Asian directors, including Gennadi Bazarov on *Mother Earth* (1968) and *Apple of My Eye* (1976), Melis Ubukeev on *Ak Meer* (1969), Tolomush Okeev on *Fire Worship* (1971) and Ali Khamraev on *White, White Storks* (1966) and *The Seventh Bullet* (1972). Since he spent most of his life in Moscow, he also filmed with many Russian directors. A notable success was the role of the Tatar Khan in Andrei Tarkovsky's *Andrei Rublev.* Despite his exotic appearance, he played stately heroes with an imperious gaze and strong character.

BIRNAZAROV, Temir
Naryn (Kirghiz SSR), 1967
Director. Author of many award-winning short fiction films and documentaries. In 1994 he graduated from the directing department of the Kazakh State Institute of Theatre and Cinema. He began working in cinema in the early 1990s when film production in Kyrgyzstan had practically ceased to exist due to lack of state funding. From his first film onwards he has won awards: the short film *Don't Cry Rhinoceros!* [*Ne plach', nosorog,* 1994] received awards at Montecatini, Vila do Conde and Clermont-Ferrand. His real breakthrough came with the television documentary *The Devil's Bridge* (1996), which described life in a Kyrgyz mountain village where people are connected to the rest of the world by a rope bridge.

His vivid portrait sketches and lyrical montage are unforgettable. At this point, he decided to work in feature films. He shot several short features with a distinct existential style. The most interesting film, the short *The Duty of a Son* [*Paryz*, 2007], depicts a young man who had escaped from prison in order to return home and provide the ritual meal to his entire village in honour of his recently deceased father. His feature debut, *The Route of Hope* (2008), is set on a bus where each character represents a distinct social class and the bus stands as microcosm for Kyrgyz society.

CHOKMOROV, Suimenkul
Chon-Tash (Chui region, Kirghiz SSR), 1939 – Bishkek, 1992

Actor, artist. Winner of State Prize of the Kirghiz SSR (1980). People's Artist of the Soviet Union (1981). He graduated from the Academy of Fine Arts in Leningrad in 1967. The Kyrgyz people have three songs: the song of the warrior, the song of horses and the song of the motherland. He was the embodiment of the warrior. His image became a symbol of the Thaw in Central Asian cinema. His very first role, Bakhtygyl in Bolotbek Shamshiev's *Gunshot at the Mountain Pass* (1968), became his flagship. He played a solitary hero who tries to undermine the land agreements between the Kirghiz elite and the Russian merchants. He appears as a fearless *batyr* from the pages of the *Manas*. But he was versatile as well: he was the epitome of a warrior in *Gunshot at the Mountain Pass* (1968) and *The Red Poppies of Issyk-Kul* (1971); an embittered and persecuted man in *The Fierce One* (1973); and a reflective and alcoholic city dweller in *Ulan* (1977). For the mass Soviet audience, he was most remembered as the hero of the Red Westerns by Ali Khamraev: *Extraordinary Commissar* (1970) and *The Seventh Bullet* (1972). However, he managed to perform a few romantic roles, such as the artist Temir in *Red Apple* (1975). He was attractive, and created a deep psychological image filled with passion and temperament.

DJALLYEV, Artyk
Turkmen SSR, 1933

Actor. Outstanding personality of Turkmen cinema, who featured in many Central Asian films. He began immediately with leading roles in *Ten Steps to the East* (1960) and *The Contest* (1963). As an actor with a distinct charismatic appearance, he often played strong, positive heroes. His most memorable roles are historical, such as the great Turkmen poet and thinker of the thirteenth century, Magtymguly, in the film *Fragi, Deprived of Happiness* (1984). He worked with virtually every Turkmen director and played over 60 roles. He also starred in Uzbek and Kazakh films. His creative collaboration and friendship with Bulat Mansurov continued in the film *Sultan Beibars* (1989), where he played a major role. Although he was no longer young, he remained in demand and performed throughout the 1990s.

FAIZIEV, Latif
Tashkent (Uzbek SSR), 1929

Director. One of the founders of Uzbek cinema. People's Artist and Winner of the State Prize of the Uzbek SSR (1979, 1982). He made numerous features and documentaries and played small roles in the theatre. He graduated from the directing department of VGIK in 1951. His first film, *Chief and Labourer* [*Bai i batrak*, 1954], was drawn from the famous play of the Hamza Theatre. He was in many ways a pioneer by bringing the play to life. He also made the first Uzbek colour film, *Downfall of the Emirate* (1955). One of his most important works was *The Stars of Ulugh Beg* [*Ulugbek yulduzy*, 1964], about the grandson of Timur, ruler of Samarkand. This Ulugh Beg was an outstanding mathematician and astronomer, who made one of the first important maps of the sky. He continued his innovation as director with the first Uzbek film-ballets and participated in the first major Uzbek-Indian co-production, *Adventures of Ali Baba and the Forty Thieves* [*Prikliucheniia Ali-Baby i soroka razboinikov*, 1980], which was a huge box-office success both in the Soviet Union and in India.

GANIEV, Nabi
Tashkent (Russian Empire), 1904 – Tashkent, 1952

Director, actor, and a founder of Uzbek cinema. Honoured Artist of the Uzbek SSR (1944). In 1924 he entered the Higher Art Technical Workshop in Moscow. In 1925 he returned to Tashkent and began work at the newly created studio, Stars of the East. First, he acted in some of the very first Uzbek films: *The Second Wife* (1927), *Jackals of Ravat* (1927), *Covered Wagon* (1927) and *The Leper* (1928). Then he worked as assistant director, and in the early 1930s he started his directorial career with *The Rise* (1931) and other titles on various themes of industrialization and Soviet policies. In 1943 he was the second director for Yakov Protazanov's classic comedy *Nasreddin in Bukhara*. It was permeated by the subtle humour of the beloved hero of Central Asians and remains a popular success. His greatest film was *Tahir and Zuhra* (1945), based on national folklore. All of its components – the visual, musical, and dramatic – evoke folk traditions. The peak of his creativity came with *The Adventures of Nasreddin* (1946) that captured Uzbek speech and manners. There is a rich and precise image of a bazaar that remains iconic. The actors in his films were often drawn from folk traditions, such as *kyzykchi* (narrators) and *maskorobozov* (buskers). From 1949 to 1952 he made several documentary films.

ISHMUKHAMEDOV, Elyor
Tashkent (Uzbek SSR), 1942

Director. One of the most brilliant Uzbek film-makers of the 1960s. Winner of the State Prize of the Uzbek SSR in 1967 and 1986, and the State Prize of the Soviet Union in 1984. From 1959 he worked as production assistant and assistant director. He graduated from the directing department of VGIK in 1967. His directorial debut, *Tenderness* (1966), surprised everyone with its freshness and romance. His images of boys floating down the river on automobile tyres become a signature in Soviet cinema of the 1960s. His next film, *Lovers* (1969), elaborated the same style: a strangely modern Central Asian city, bleached in summer heat, becomes the unusual setting for the love story between two Russian characters, played by Rodion Nakhapetov and Anastasia Vertinskaya. Again, his new aesthetics have more in common with Michelangelo Antonioni, albeit with a more romantic tone. The film's title characterizes the global culture of the 1960s, the spirit of love for friends, work, and women. *Youth of a Genius* (1982) portrayed the youth of Avicenna. Since the mid-1990s he has lived in Moscow.

IVANOV-BARKOV, Yevgeni
Kostroma (Russian Empire), 1892 – Ashkhabad, 1965

Director, artistic director, scriptwriter. People's Artist of the Turkmen SSR (1953). In 1915 he graduated from the Stroganov Artistic and Industrial College. His most significant silent film work is *Judas* (1929). He was an energetic organizer of film production and founded, along with Vladimir Gardin, the State Film School. He arrived at the Ashkhabad Studio in 1938 when they were already beginning production. There, he made the first Turkmen film *Dursun* (1940). In pursuit of truth and steadfastness of the environment and of the hero's nature he spent two years preparing for the shooting of the film, learning about the traditions and life of the Turkmen people. The film's plot was typical of that era: the emancipation of women and the Turkmen struggle against Islam. The role of Dursun was played by Russian actress Nina Alisova, but almost every other role was played by Turkmen actors. Still, *Dursun* is considered a truly national film and the pride of Turkmen cinema. In 1941 the film was awarded the Stalin Prize. *Dursun* was also a launch pad for the young actor Alty Karliev, who later worked with Ivanov-Barkov on *Extraordinary Mission* (1957). Despite the fact that he made typically Soviet films, some of them were quite popular. The first postwar film made in Turkmenistan, *The Distant Bride* (1948), was a musical comedy about the Don Cossack Zahar who arrives in Turkmenistan in the hope of finding his bride Gusel, whom he met during the war. This film also won a Stalin Prize in 1949.

KARAKULOV, Amir
Alma-Ata (Kazakh SSR), 1965

Director, significant figure of the Kazakh New Wave. Graduated from the directing department of VGIK. His feature debut, *A Woman Between Two Brothers* (1991), is marked by its simultaneous elegance and minimalism. It was also successful in its depth of emotions; on the one hand, the characters are modern city dwellers who love The Beatles; on the other hand, their behaviour is rooted in Turkic mentality. The film is formed like a sculpture and uses cinematic language over dialogue to convey meaning. *The Dove's Bell-Ringer* (1993) is more lyrical: this is the elegiac love story of a boy and girl, who leave their apartment for a place in the provinces but cannot build a family. *The Last Holidays* (1996) is a reflection on the Soviet way of life: it tells of three young guys, whose fate has already been ruined at school. Karakulov's heroes are always contemporaries, and he examines the psychology of their relationships. This film won the Grand Prix at Tokyo and the Tiger Award at Rotterdam. He is also not afraid to experiment: *Don't Cry* (2002) is Kazakhstan's first film on digital video. The film relates the story of three women who are not related by blood but help each other to survive. The social aspects of the film are inextricably linked with complex images of time. Each of the three women corresponds to an entire era: the grandmother represents the Soviet era; the opera singer, who has lost her voice, reflects a country in the difficult stages of independence; and the young girl projects the future.

KARLIEV, Alty
Babadaikan (Russian Empire), 1909 – Ashkhabad, 1973

Director, actor, founder of Turkmen cinema. During the Soviet era the Turkmenfilm Studio was named after him. People's Artist of the Soviet Union (1955). In 1928 he graduated from the Turkmen Drama Studio in Ashkhabad, and from the directing department of Baku Theatre College in 1931. From 1931 to 1953 he worked as actor, director, and then director of the Magtymguly Turkmen Academic Drama Theatre. He starred in the films *I'll Be Back* (1935), directed by Alexander Ledashchev, and *Soviet Patriots* (1939) by Grigori Lomidze. His roles in *Dursun* (1940) and *The Distant Bride* (1948), both directed by Yevgeni Ivanov-Barkov, twice earned him the Stalin Prize. He played over 20 roles, marked by his cheerfulness and national consciousness. From 1956 to 1960 he stood at the head of Turkmenfilm. He co-directed his debut film *Extraordinary Mission* (1957) and took an active role in the new national cinema of Turkmenistan. His most significant film was *The Decisive Step* (1965), based on Berdy Kerbabaev's novel about the establishment of Soviet power in Turkmenistan. The film relates the tale of lovers, whose fate is closely intertwined with the fate of the country. The famed composer Nury Khalmamedov wrote the score for the film, which also sparked the careers of illustrious actors, such as Baba Annanov and Artyk Djallyev. The film won the State Prize of the Turkmen SSR in 1965. He continued to make films based on national themes: *Magtymguly* (1968), about the life of the great national poet-philosopher; and *The Secrets of Maqam* (1974), depicting the plight of female musicians and the pre-Revolutionary singer Karkara. Posthumously, he was awarded the State Prize of the Turkmen SSR.

KARSAKBAEV, Abdulla
Zhambyl region (Kazakh ASSR), 1926 – Alma-Ata (Kazakh SSR), 1983

Director. One of the founders of Kazakh cinema. Honoured Artist of Kazakh SSR (1979). He graduated from the directing department of VGIK in 1957. His first film, *My Name is Kozha* (1963), was not only a great directorial success, but the film was also a template for Kazakh cinema. Karsakbaev demonstrated two distinct spaces: a typical Soviet town in the valley, and an authentic Kazakh village in the mountains. He highlighted the differences between these two cultures, one superficial and the other genuine. His next feature film, *Restless Morning* (1966), also conceptualized the 1920s in Kazakh history, when almost one million Kazakhs crossed the border to China. He presented the finale in a manner that could be interpreted in two ways: on the one hand, the protagonist Tokhtar (based the historical prototype of Tokash Bokin) returns to 'his' Red Army; on the other hand, we know that treason and death lay ahead of him. The film was not banned, but limited in distribution. In a kind of censorship, Karsakbaev was then forced to make the children's films: *Journey to Childhood* [*Puteshestvie v detstvo*, 1968], *Yoo Hoo Cowboy!* [*Ei, vy, kovboi!*, 1974] and *Alpamys Goes to School* (1976). But even here he managed to convey the spirit of Kazakh national culture.

KHAKDODOV (HAQDADOV), Safar
Tajik SSR, 1961

Documentary film-maker, actor, producer, and director of the Didor International Film Festival. In 1983 he graduated from the department of philology at Tajik State University. Since 1986 he has worked as film editor and screenwriter for feature films, then as a director of documentary films, such as *Mumijo* (1990). His acting in Mairam Yusupova's short film *Window* [*Okno*, 1989] and *Time of the Yellow Grass* (1991) and Saif Rakhimzod's *And the Stars Shine above Tanur* [*I zvezdy blestiat nad tanurom*, 1991] was expressive and earned him respect. In 1989 he also made a short feature debut, *Day Dream* (1990), about a young man in the city and his recollections of childhood. His film received the Grand Prix at the International Film Festival in Tampere, and his prospects seemed bright at the time. But with the collapse of the Soviet Union and the beginning of the Tajik civil war the local film industry was destroyed. During the most difficult years after independence he remained in cinema, shooting documentaries such as *Dushanbe – City of Bread* [*Dushanbe, gorod khlebnyi*, 1995]. He worked as editor on Bakhtiyor Khudoinazarov's *Bro* (1991) and *Kosh-ba-kosh* (1993). From 1996 to 1998 he served as deputy director of Tajikfilm, where he helped develop film production in video format. In 1999, together with Sadullo Rakhimov, he created the independent studio Kinoservis, and a small film school for the new generation of young film-makers in Tajikistan. In six years the studio has made over 30 shorts and documentaries, the animated film *Cheya-cheya* (2002), and a number of commercials. In 2004, supported by the Iranian director Mohsen

Makhmalbaf, he established (and now directs) the Didor International Film Festival, which is held bi-annually.

KHAMRAEV, Ali
Tashkent (Uzbek SSR), 1937

Director, key figure of Uzbek cinema of the Soviet period. Honoured Artist and Winner of State Prize of the Uzbek SSR (1969, 1970). In 1961 he graduated from the directing department of VGIK. His filmic signature was established in *White, White Storks* (1966), vividly detailing life in an Uzbek village. The parents of young Malika want her to marry a man she does not love, but she rebels against her family when she falls in love someone else. Khamraev helped establish the genre of the Soviet 'Eastern' (or 'Red' Western): *Extraordinary Commissar* (1970), *The Seventh Bullet* (1972), *Without Fear* (1972) and *Bodyguard* [*Telokhranitel'*, 1980] depicted the establishment of Soviet power in Central Asia and the fight against the *basmachi*. Khamraev's last Soviet film was *Garden of Desires* [*Sad zhelanii*, 1987], after which he went to Italy to work on a project on Tamerlane. In 1998, with Italian support, he made the parable *Bo Ba Bu* about the relationship between two Asian men and a European woman in a post-apocalyptic desert. Along with his contemporaries, Andrei Tarkovsky, Sergei Paradjanov and Otar Ioseliani, he made intelligent and worthwhile films in Central Asia; he lives and works in Moscow.

KHODJIKOV, Sultan-Akhmet
Jambyl (Kirghiz ASSR), 1923 – 1988

Director. Honoured Artist and winner of the State Prize Winner of the Kazakh SSR (1971, 1972). In 1953 he graduated from the directing department of VGIK. His first films in the 1950s faithfully rendered Soviet ideology with stories about the Virgin Land campaign and the establishment of Soviet power in Kazakhstan. Beginning with *Aisulu* (1965) he appeals to popular folklore, integrating modernity and the legend of the beautiful Aisulu. His truly national recognition and popularity came with *Kyz-Zhibek* (*The Silk Maiden*, 1970), based on the folk legend and scripted by Gabit Musrepov. Against the backdrop of the Kazakh land, torn by internecine strife during the sixteenth and seventeenth centuries, the legend unravels a Romeo and Juliet love story in the steppe. The plot is less important than his recreation of the image of the Kazakh nomad. The steppe landscapes, national costumes, rituals, folk songs and melodies written by the composer Nurgis Tlendiev, all made this film a true Kazakh classic.

KHUDOINAZAROV, Bakhtiyar
Dushanbe (Tajik SSR), 1965

Director, representative of independent Tajik cinema. In 1988 he graduated from VGIK's directing department. He made a brilliant debut with *Bro* (1991), which won the Grand Prix at the Mannheim-Heidelberg International Film Festival as well as other prizes. The film tells a simple story about an older brother, who takes his younger brother to their father. Their path is filled with a lively sense of the moment as well as national colour. *Kosh-ba-kosh* (1993) had even greater resonance, winning the Silver Lion at Venice in 1993. It tells a love story against the backdrop of Dushanbe during the civil war, with nightly curfews, tanks in the streets, shootings and corpses floating in the city's canal. But life continued, people met and fell in love with each other, and this film is also light and cheerful. In the mid-1990s Khudoinazarov moved to Germany and his films since then have been international co-productions. In *Luna Papa* (1999) he created a unified image of post-Soviet Central Asia: the heroine's name Mamlakat, means 'motherland' in Tajik. After Mamlakat becomes mysteriously pregnant, her father and brother search for the possible father of the child, who turns out to be a Russian pilot. Khudoinazarov has also worked in Russia and on Russian themes, as in the films *Chic* (2003).

KHUDONAZAROV, Davlat
Khorugh (Tajik SSR), 1944

Cameraman and director, documentary film-maker. Khudonazarov came to Tajikfilm studio at the age of 14 as assistant cameraman. He graduated from the cinematography faculty of VGIK in 1965. His first independent work was *Lullaby* [*Kolybel'naia*, 1966], which became a landmark for Tajik documentary cinema. He provides more than the glance of a casual observer in this vision of his land and the rites and customs of the people of the Pamir. Khudonazarov shot over 20 documentaries, but *Birth* [*Rozhdenie*, 1985] must be singled out as fundamental for offering an historical chronicle of the 1930s. He debuted as director of photography in Kasymova's *Djura Sarkor* (1969). Later he made with Kimiagarov *The Legend of Rustam* (1970) and *Rustam and Suhrab* (1971), for which he received the State Prize of the Tajik SSR. In the late 1970s Khudonazarov experimented as director of feature films with *Youth's First Morning* (1979) and *Murmur of a*

Brook in Melting Snow (1982), demonstrating a profound sense of patriotism. From 1987 to 1993 Khudonazarov was enmeshed in the tumultuous politics of Tajikistan's civil war and did a lot to prevent conflict and in 1991 stood for the presidential elections in Tajikistan. From 1990 to 1991 he was chairman of the Film-makers' Union of the USSR. He now lives and works in Moscow.

KIMIAGAROV, Boris
Samarkand (Turkestan ASSR), 1920 – Dushanbe, 1979

Director. People's Artist of the Tajik SSR (1960). The Tajikfilm Studio is named in his honour. He studied at the Pedagogical Institute of Stalinabad (now Dushanbe), and in 1944 graduated from VGIK. From 1944 to 1956, no feature films were made in Tajikistan; during these years Kimiagarov made documentaries: *Tajikistan* (1945) was awarded the Bronze Medal at Venice in 1946, and *Soviet Tajikistan* (1951) won the State Prize of the USSR. In 1956 Kimiagarov made his first feature film, *Dokhunda*, which was followed by *Fate of the Poet* (1959), both dedicated to the life of the great poet Rudaki. Kimiagarov also made films about his time: *Hasan Arbakesh* (1965) deployed Aesopian language to criticize the arrival of Soviet civilization, which destroyed Tajik culture. When this film was unsuccessful, he turned to the genre of historical films. His tetralogy, based on the *Shahnama* – *The Banner of the Blacksmith, The Legend of Rustam, Rustam and Suhrab* and *The Legend of Siyavush* – revealed an extraordinary talent at a truly Hollywood level. The films received numerous prizes and Kimiagarov was awarded the State Prize of the Tajik SSR (1973) for raising national consciousness.

KYDYRALIEV, Kadyrzhan
Kirghiz SSR, 1936

Cinematographer and documentary film-maker. Winner of the State Prize in 1972. People's Artist of the Kirghiz SSR (1982). In 1961 he graduated as cameraman from VGIK. As cinematographer, he shot almost all of the films of Tolomush Okeev, beginning with the documentary *These are Horses* (1965), where he conveyed the natural beauty of Kirghizia alongside unforgettable portraits of people. He offered remarkably accurate compositions and filled the frames with breathtaking images. His work with Marat Sarulu on *My Brother, Silk Road* (2001) has been recognized at the Festival des Trois Continents.

KYDYRALIEV, Khasan
Frunze (Kirghiz SSR), 1960

Cinematographer. In 1988 he graduated as cameraman from VGIK. His most successful cooperation has been with Aktan Arym Kubat (Abdykalykov), with whom he has created wonderful images of Kyrgyz life and culture. The short *The Swing* (1993) recreated the atmosphere of a Kyrgyz village from the 1960s. The monochrome aesthetic effect gave an almost documentary feel to the film's characters. Kydyraliev forged an important bond with Kazakh film-makers through his work with Satybaldy Narymbetov on *The Life of a Young Accordion Player* (1994), Serik Aprymov on *The Hunter* (2004), Gulshad Omarova on *Schizo* (2004), Rustem Abdrashev on *Renaissance Island* (2004) and Amanjol Aituarov on *Steppe Express* (2005). He is particularly popular thanks to his ability to convey the special beauty of the mountains and the breath of the steppe. Yet his greatest achievements are his unforgettable portraits of people and brilliant folk images in the films of Arym Kubat: *Beshkempir: The Adopted Son* (1998) is a perfect model for this. His success as a cameraman continued in Abdrashev's *Gift to Stalin* (2008), which recounts the salvation of a Jewish boy during Stalin's repressions. In addition to his memorable landscapes, he created a distinct colour palette, exposing the steppe in dust and sand and at the same time revealing the warmth in the human relationships on a visual level.

MANSUROV, Bulat
Chardjou (Turkmen SSR), 1937

Director, screenwriter. People's Artist of Russia (2004). Mansurov initiated a regional trend of poetic cinema in Central Asia. In 1954 he enrolled at Chardjou Pedagogical Institute and in 1963 he graduated from the directing faculty of VGIK. His debut film, *The Contest* (1963), centres on a music competition and characterized by expressive film language and clear national idiom. This film defined the path for Turkmen cinema for many years ahead and remains popular today. *Quenching the Thirst* (1966) describes the construction of the Karakum Canal in the 1950s. Mansurov's films reached across Central Asia, and in 1972 he made *Kulager*, about the Kazakh poet and composer Akhan-sere. At the horse races Akhan-sere put his deaf-and-dumb son on his favourite horse, Kulager. Although victory seemed certain, a treacherous shot strikes Kulager. The story was based on a repressed poem by Ilyas Zhansugurov, and the film was 'put on the shelf' as anti-Soviet sedition for 15 years. Another landmark was *Sultan Beibars* (1989) about the Kazakh historical figure of the thirteenth century, who led his people from humiliating slavery to sovereignty. Mansurov lives and works in Moscow.

MUSAKOV (MUSAQOV), Zulfikar (Zulfiqor)
Ak-Kurgan (Uzbek SSR), 1958

Director, screenwriter. He graduated from the directing department of the Tashkent Art Institute and completed the Higher Courses of Scriptwriters and Directors in Moscow in 1989. His directorial debut, *Judgment Day* [*Sudnyi den'*, 1983], received wide recognition. Musakov oscillates between commercial and art-house cinema and his films often reflect an element of ordinary life. In *The Bomb* [*Bomba*, 1994], a resident finds an unexploded bomb in a village square, and nobody knows what to do. The hero reveals the unusual gift of anticipating the desires of others in *I Want!* [*Ia khochu!*, 1997], and often fairy-tale elements make his films light-hearted and effervescent, but deeper moral issues always lie below the surface. His films *Boys in the Sky* (2002) and *Boys in the Sky 2* (2004), about the friendship of four boys living in the modern Tashkent, enjoyed great popularity in Uzbekistan. Musakov moved away from comedy to serious psychological drama in *Motherland* (2006), which tells the story of Uzbekistan over the past 70 years through the hero, who was arrested and spent time in the camps, before fleeing and emigrating to America.

NARLIEV, Khodjakuli
Junction 30, Ashkhabad Railway (Turkmen SSR), 1937

Director, cinematographer, screenwriter, actor. His films brought international recognition to Turkmen cinema. Winner of USSR State Prize (1973), People's Artist of the Turkmen SSR (1986). In 1960 he graduated as cameraman from VGIK. In 1972 he made his first feature film, *Daughter-in-Law*, which brought him international fame. The two central characters, an old man and his daughter-in-law, live in the desert, raise Karakul sheep, and manage the household; yet this routine of traditional Turkmen life represented major ethno-cultural codes of the nation. The absent heroes in the film are the old man's son, her husband who went to the front, and the unborn child of which she dreams. Another landmark was the film *Jamal's Tree* (1980), which explores the fate of strong women who struggle with their husbands. In 1990, Narliev made *Mankurt*, based on Aitmatov's novel *The Day Lasts Longer than a Hundred Years* (1980). Narliev scripted all his films. From 1976 to 1999 he was chairman of the Cinematographers' Union of Turkmenistan and made a great contribution to the development of Turkmen cinema. Since the late 1990s Narliev has lived in Moscow.

NARYMBETOV, Satybaldy
Achisai, Shymkent Region (Kazakh SSR), 1946
Director and screenwriter. Winner of State Prize of Kazakhstan (1996). He graduated from the scriptwriting faculty of VGIK in 1969, and the Higher Courses for Scriptwriters and Directors in Moscow in 1984. His first success in cinema came as a playwright for *Shok and Sher* (1972), directed by Kanymbek Kasymbekov. He has written scripts, experimented with documentary film and made film comedies. His success as director came with *The Life of a Young Accordion Player* (1994), a series of autobiographical recollections of his postwar childhood. Despite the hardships of the era, Stalin's repression and the presence of prisoners, he revealed the romanticism of his childhood and demonstrated the coexistence of different languages and peoples in Kazakhstan. In *Leila's Prayer* (2002), he raised the issue of nuclear testing in Kazakhstan during the 1950s when the residents of villages near Semipalatinsk were taken away during the day of the explosions and returned to the contaminated zones. No less important for independent Kazakh cinema is *Mustafa Shokai* (2008), which describes the leader of the Kazakh national liberation movement of the early twentieth century, whose name was banned from Soviet history books.

NUGMANOV, Rashid
Alma-Ata (Kazakh SSR), 1954
Director, founder of the Kazakh New Wave. He graduated from the faculty of architecture of the Kazakh State Polytechnic University in 1977, and the directing faculty of VGIK in 1989. As a student, he made the medium-length film *Ya-hha* (1986), which announced his commitment to youth culture, exploring the underground music scene in Leningrad. The film was awarded the FIPRESCI prize at Moscow in 1987. In 1988 he made *The Needle*, based on the script by the young writers Bakhyt Kilibaev and Alexander Baranov. *The Needle* was not only a starting point

for the Kazakh New Wave, but also a symbol of Soviet cinema of *perestroika*, which legalized the artistic culture of the Soviet underground. The popular rock musician Viktor Tsoi performed the main role in the film: he was a cult figure in those years. His lyrics 'Change: we want change!' became a slogan for the late Soviet era. Rashid Nugmanov briefly headed the creative unit Alem at Kazakhfilm studio, and from 1989 to 1992 he served as chairman of the Kazakh Union of Cinematographers. In 1993 he made the post-modern drama *The Wild East*, a kind of remake of Akira Kurosawa's *Seven Samurai* and an ironic critique of the Soviet era. In 1994 Nugmanov moved to France, where he focused on production.

OKEEV, Tolomush
Bokonbaevo (Issyk-Kul, Kirghiz SSR), 1935 – Ankara (Turkey), 2001

Director, screenwriter. Winner of Toktogul State Prize (1972) and People's Artist of the Soviet Union (1985). In 1958 he graduated from the Leningrad Institute of Film Engineers. He worked for Kirghizfilm first as sound engineer, on Larissa Shepitko's *Heat* (1963) among others. In 1966 he graduated from the directing department of the Higher Courses for Scriptwriters and Directors in Moscow. His *Sky of Our Childhood* (1966) is inscribed in the history of Kyrgyz cinema. The film is about a shepherd, Bakai, and his family who must leave their familiar pastures now that a construction crew has arrived to build a mountain road. Two words are synonymous with the new Soviet government: destroy and build. The arrival of the Soviet crew represents the rejection not only of people but also all living things. If it were not for the Thaw, this film would certainly have landed on the shelf. In all his films he created outstanding characters who were spiritual bearers of the nation. His strong female protagonist, Urkuya (played by Tattybiubiu Tursunbaev) in *Fire Worship* (1971) won the Kirghiz State award in 1972. His old patriarch (played by Muratbek Ryskulov) in *Fire Worship* and *Sky of Our Childhood* was iconic. His rebel Akhangul (played by Suimenkul Chokmorov) in *The Fierce One* (1973) won numerous awards. Finally, his young warrior (played by Dokhdurbek Kydyraliev) in *The Descendant of the Snow Leopard* (1984) won the Silver Bear in Berlin. In the 1990s Okeev was Ambassador of the Republic of Kyrgyzstan to Turkey.

OMIRBAEV, Darejan
Zhambyl region (Kazakh SSR), 1958

Director. He graduated from the Mathematics Department of the Kazakh State University in 1980. In 1984 he enrolled in the directing department of VGIK, but graduated as film scholar in 1987. His short film *July* [*Shil'de*, 1988] immediately showed his extraordinary directorial talent. It is the story of a little boy from a village, who watches the passing trains. His first feature film *Kairat* (1991) was awarded the Silver Leopard at Locarno. The film is about a village boy, who comes to the city to study, which is told in a Kafkaesque style, set in an urban environment that is hostile and alien. The film reflects not only the personal story of a young man, but also the general mood of uncertainty and discomfort in Kazakhstan in the early 1990s. Omirbaev continued his subtle artistry in *Cardiogram* (1995), where he explores the challenges of parallel lives as led by Kazakh speakers from the villages and Russian speakers from the city. The protagonist is a boy from the village who is forced to adapt to his new environment in a health clinic. His greatest recognition as director came with the film *Killer* (1998), which was awarded the main prize in the section 'Un Certain Regard' at Cannes in 1998. The film is a continuation of the history of Kairat, who did not go to college, but started working as a driver for the director of a research institute. After a random accident, he falls into a debt trap and turns a killer in order to pay his debts. It is a pointed story, told in a clear cinematic language, striking in its simplicity and brevity. Omirbaev's subsequent films have been distributed internationally: *The Road* [*Jol*, 2001], followed by *Shuga* (2007) and *Student* (2012), both transferring the plots of *Anna Karenina* and *Crime and Punishment* respectively onto a modern Kazakh context.

RAZYKOV, Yusup
Tashkent (Uzbek SSR), 1957

Director, screenwriter. Honoured Artist of Uzbekistan (2000). In 1986 he graduated from the scriptwriting faculty of VGIK. After proving to be a brilliant writer, fighting for limited positions in Moscow and writing scripts for seven feature-length films in 10 years, he arrived in Uzbekistan in 1997 and began to shoot television series and films. He immediately received international recognition for *The Orator* (1998), which premiered at the Berlinale. It is an ironic film about a poor cabman, who becomes a representative for the

Soviets only because he speaks Russian. The protagonist has three wives, two of whom he inherited after his elder brother's death. Since the new Soviet government does not allow polygamy, he must choose. This may be the first Central Asian film with biting irony and sarcasm about the Soviet period. In 1999 Razykov was appointed as head of Uzbekfilm studio, and he actively promoted a new generation of young film-makers: Jahongir Kasymov, Zulfikar Musakov and Yolkin Tuichiev started to modernize Uzbek cinema. At the same time, he continued to direct films with national character and fine artistic questions, such as *Women's Kingdom* [*Ayollar Saltanati*, 1999] and *Men's Dance* [*Dilhiroj*, 2002]. *Comrade Boykenzhaev* [*Ortok Boykenjaev*, 2002] explores the fate of a middle-aged Uzbek man who depicted Lenin in official parades during the Soviet era. Razykov's compassion for Uzbekistan is also felt in *Healer* [*Dard*, 2005], which alludes to an ailing society in need of emergency treatment. All of these films have been shown at numerous international film festivals and received awards. However, after completing *The Shepherd* in 2005, Razykov moved to Moscow and now produces Russian television serials and soap operas.

SABITOV, Alim
Kamensk-Uralsky (RSFSR), 1956

Production designer. In 1980 he graduated from the Architecture Faculty of the Alma-Ata Architecture and Construction Institute. In 1987 he graduated from the Central Research and Design Institute of Model and Experimental Houses in Moscow. He is the author of several monographs and holds a doctorate in architecture. He was production designer for the Kazakh New Wave, working with the young film-makers Alexander Baranov, Bakhyt Kilibaev and Abai Karpykov. He introduced a new sense of time and space, creating an image of Almaty that reflects both the post-Soviet and the cosmopolitan sides. From 1990 to 1994 he worked in Moscow, where he was production designer for Sergei Livnev's *Kiks* (1991) and Bakhyt Kilibaev's *Gongofer* (1992). In these films he experimented with colour symbolism. His landmark work was the film *Killer* (1998) by Darejan Omirbaev, an ascetic picture designed to reveal the psychologically unsettling transition in the post-Soviet era. For the past 20 years, he has taught at the Kazakh Architecture and Construction Academy, training a new generation of designers, production and set designers and contemporary artists.

SADYKOV, Bako
Bukhara (Uzbek SSR), 1941

Director. Honoured Artist of the Tajik SSR (1988). Winner of Rudaki State Prize (1992) for *Blessed Bukhara*. In 1967 he graduated from the directing department of the Tashkent Theatre and Arts Institute. In 1971 he began work at Tajikfilm as director of documentary films. His films reflect the work of challenging professions: road builders, electricians, and the flight crew who disperse clouds. In 1978 he completed the Higher Courses for Scriptwriters and Directors in Moscow. He continued to make vivid and colourful films such as the shorts *The Clay Birds* [*Glinianye ptitsy*, 1979] and *Whirlwind* [*Smerch*, 1983]. His international success came with the short documentary *Adonis XIV* (1985), the story of an agent-provocateur who led his kinsmen to their slaughter, which served as a metaphor for the Soviet system. The film received the Grand Prix at the Berlin International Film Festival, and a FIPRESCI prize in Moscow. *Blessed Bukhara*, a poetic phantasmagoria of people who lived during the 1950s, was shown at Cannes in the Certain Regard section. Since the mid-1990s Sadykov lives and works in Tashkent.

SAPAROV, Usman (also Usmaan)
Pechan-Ali (Turkmen SSR), 1938

Director, cameraman. USSR State Prize (1984) and People's Artist of Turkmenistan (1994). In 1963 he graduated as cameraman from VGIK. In 1978 he completed the Higher Courses for Scriptwriters and Directors in Moscow. As director of photography he shot 11 feature films and directed and filmed over 60 documentaries. *Masculine Upbringing* [*Muzhskoe vospitanie*, 1982] brought him initial success with the simple story of a nine-year-old boy who visits his grandfather on vacation. His grandfather herds camels alone in the desert, and this harsh solitude quickly makes the capricious boy mature when he realizes the importance of his help. The film not only reflects the Turkmen national space, but also shows the difficult, yet harmonious life of a desert nomad; it evoked the beauty of the desert and the warmth of human experience. A decade later, a new wave of international recognition came for *Little Angel, Make Me Happy* (1992), which garnered numerous awards at international film festivals. The film depicts an episode when Germans were deported from Turkmenistan to Siberia during World War II. The film begins with the tragedy when the parents are separated from their children, who are taken to orphanages. The film's hero, six-year-old Georg, manages to hide from the Bolsheviks but he has to face life without parents, food, or caring neighbours. The tragedy of war, multiplied by the national question, serves as a warning for the future. Saparov has lived and worked in Moscow since 1994.

SARULU, Marat
Talas (Kirghiz SSR), 1957

Director, screenwriter. In 1984 he graduated from the animation department of the Higher Courses of Scriptwriters and Directors in Moscow with his diploma film *Prayer for the Chaste Bird*. His directorial debut *In Spe* (1993) reveals images of three brothers as archetypes of post-Soviet heroes: the elder brother is the heir and successor of the Soviet past; the middle brother chooses flight into nothingness; and youngest brother is an anarchist who denies reality. At the same time, each of the brothers represents Soviet, Eastern or Western mentalities. From 1993 to 2001 there were few funds available for film production, and Sarulu turned to scriptwriting: he wrote the screenplay for Arym Kubat's *Beshkempir: The Adopted Son* (1998) and made several short films, notably *Mandala* (1999) and *Fly-Up* [*Ergu*, 2001]. *Mandala* explores two places and two cultures, village and city; *Fly Up* reflects the transition from the Soviet era to independence. International recognition was awarded to *My Brother, Silk Road*, which shows a group of teenagers along the railway track, who travel to the Soviet past and back. In 2008 he made *Song of the Southern Seas* with support from Kazakhstan, Russia, Germany and France. It is a story of family relations between the two neighbours, Russian and Kazakh, and how a Russian family bore a boy of Asian appearance. This is not a story about adultery, but rather historical blood bonds.

SHAHOBIDDINOV, Ayub
Tashkent (Uzbek SSR), 1977

Director, screenwriter. In 1999 he graduated from the Tashkent State Institute of Arts, department of cinema and television. In 2002 he graduated from the Higher Courses of Scriptwriters and Directors in Moscow. Shahobiddinov came into film-making with his friend Yolkin Tuichiev. They studied together in Moscow and together made their feature-length debut *Tulip in the Snow* [*Tiul'pan v snegu*, 2003]. The two film-makers represent a new generation of Uzbek directors in the 2000s. Their films were successful creatively and professionally, as well as internationally. Shahobiddinov's film *The Yurt* (2007), scripted by Tuichiev, describes a middle-aged man who lives in solitude in the wilderness in a yurt with his 11-year-old son. After Stalin's repression took his grandfather and parents away, he decided that he must stay away from other people. But his young son cannot stand the father's tyranny and runs away. Alone, the father suddenly begins to understand and support a deaf-and-dumb girl he meets. Thus, two social outcasts begin to build their lives anew. His next film, *The Other* (2008), boldly showed the social rupture between the rich and the poor in Uzbekistan. The heroine, from a wealthy family, falls in love with the guy who takes care of their dogs. Her parents are against the marriage, but she decides to leave her family and be with him. His film *Heaven, My Abode* [*Parizod*, 2012] took the Grand Prix at Kinoshok in Anapa. Both directors of art-house cinema work on commercial productions, thus significantly raising the bar of popular cinema in Uzbekistan, which now constitutes 90 per cent of the Uzbek market.

SHAMSHIEV, Bolotbek
Frunze (Kirghiz SSR), 1941

Director, screenwriter. People's Artist of the Kirghiz SSR (1975). People's Artist of the Soviet Union (1991). In 1964 he graduated from the directing department of VGIK. He made a powerful debut with the documentary film *Manaschi* (1965), which revealed the spiritual culture of the Kyrgyz people. The film not only explains the national epic *Manas* with its narrator Sayakbai Karalaev, but also shows major Kyrgyz milestones in the twentieth century. He made a similarly brilliant debut in feature film with *Gunshot at the Mountain Pass* (1968). The film refers to the pre-Soviet era, when the Kyrgyz elite confronted Russian merchants as a last attempt to oppose the arrival of the colonizers. His *White Ship* (1975), based on the novel by Chingiz Aitmatov, brought international recognition: it is a story of the deep societal crisis in the 1970s, when a boy without parents has a good but powerless grandfather and a rude and brutal uncle as role models. National landmarks are desecrated and ruined; the natural world is no longer governed by just gods, since their place was taken by leaders who trampled the people and forced them to live by the laws of the crowd. Despite the conspicuous criticism, the film participated in the Berlinale competition in 1976 and was awarded the USSR State Prize in 1977.

TUICHIEV, Yolkin
Tashkent (Uzbek SSR), 1977

Director, screenwriter. In 2000 he graduated from the Tashkent State Institute of Arts, and from the screenwriting department of the Higher Courses of Scriptwriters and Directors in Moscow in 2002. His feature-length debut was with his friend Ayub Shahobiddinov: *Tulip in the Snow* (2003). His next film, *Teenager* (2005), is a subtle psychological drama that tells the story of a young boy growing up in a family consisting entirely of women. At first he feels their care to be excessive, but gradually he realizes that their attention and support are not for him, but have to do with the fact that he is the man of the house. The film effectively conveys Uzbek mentalities and the relationships between men and women. His film *Source* [*Chashma*, 2006] is the story of a bride going to her wedding. She visits her aunt, who lives behind the mountain pass, takes part in various festivities, and washes in a mountain spring. During her journey, she meets fellow villagers and understands the outward calm and intense passions in each of them. Tuichiev also writes plays for the world-famous Ilkhom Theatre. He makes music videos for MTV in Uzbekistan. His recent film *Silence* [*Sukunat*, 2008] explores the life of an actress who is rapidly going deaf.

TURAEV, Anvar
Samarkand (Uzbek SSR), 1934

Director, actor of the Tajik Academic Drama Theatre. In 1958 he graduated from the Shchepkin Theatre School in Moscow, and in 1970 from the directing department of VGIK. In his youth he played several roles in Tajik cinema. His first directorial work, *Third Daughter* (1970), revealed his talent in identifying national traits in the protagonists. In the film, a father had hoped to transfer his pottery craft to a son, but he has only daughters. When he returns from the war, he finds his third daughter to have inherited his artistic talent. Fame came with *The First Love of Nasreddin* (1977), based on Timur Zulfikarov's screenplay, which offers an unusual interpretation of Nasreddin, the witty hero of many Tajik fairy tales. Although he is shown in his youth, as a poetic and romantic young man, Nasreddin reveals his character as a defender of justice and protector of ordinary people. The film appealed to Tajik poetic traditions by mixing scenes from everyday life with fantasy. Although the film did not receive any international acclaim, it enjoyed great popularity in

Central Asia. Turaev's international recognition came with *Pain of Love* (1989), about the life behind the lines in Tajikistan during the Second World War. Turaev lives and works in Dushanbe, passing on his cinematic experiences to a younger generation.

TURSUNOV, Ermek
Alma-Ata (Kazakh SSR), 1961

Screenwriter, director. His film *Kelin* (2009) was the first Central Asian film to make the short list for an Academy Award nomination in the category Best Foreign Film. He graduated from the journalism department of Kazakh State University in 1984. He completed the Higher Courses for Scriptwriters and Directors in Moscow in 1990 and between 1993 and 2008 worked in television and journalism. Since 2007 he has turned to scriptwriting, and scripted Rustem Abdrashev's lyrical comedy *Patchwork Quilt* (2007) as well as Satybaldy Narymbetov's historical drama *Mustafa Shokai* (2008), demonstrating a high level of professionalism and ability to work in various genres. In 2009 he debuted as film director with *Kelin*, or *Daughter-in-Law*. Although a scriptwriter, he decided to make this film without words. The film explores how people survived in ancient times, how men competed for women, and how closely everyone was connected with the natural and the divine. His second feature, *The Old Man* [*Shal*, 2012] also received a lot of critical praise.

UBUKEEV, Melis
Frunze (Kirghiz SSR), 1935 – Bishkek, 1996

Director. His debut film, *The Difficult Passage* (1964), which is also known as *White Mountains*, was his best work and effectively began Kyrgyz cinema. The film describes the tragic consequences of the popular uprisings in 1916. He first expressed the spirit of the nation, its wisdom and inflexibility, during a difficult era. The symbolic image of the blind mother, played by Baken Kydykeeva, was a symbol of an impoverished homeland as she mourned her dead husband and son. In Kyrgyz cinema of the 1960s the leading directors played an important role in the formation of national consciousness. In this vein, Ubukeev made the documentary *I Serve the Soviet Union* [*Sluzhu sovetskomu soiuzu*, 1966], which – despite its seeming Soviet patriotism – was a film about two Kyrgyz sailors in the Soviet Navy who face a difficult test. In a dream they see poetic images of their native village, contrasted with the sharp cry: 'Get up!', that calls them to their military service. For over 30 years Ubukeev studied the

Kyrgyz epic *Manas* and he devoted several documentaries to the subject. He often stressed that *Manas* was 'a family nest for all kinds of art, a variety of religious meanings, and floors which evolved from the wisdom of the past'. His last film, *The World of Manas* [*Vselennaia Manasa*, 1995], remains unfinished.

USMONOV, Djamshed
Asht (Tajik SSR), 1965

Director. He graduated from the Higher Courses for Scriptwriters and Directors in Moscow in 1990. His debut film, *The Well* (1991, completed 2000), largely determined his future themes and style. He unfolds a local story, usually within a single family, creating an internal or external conflict, and then employs a substantive solution rooted in folk culture. *The Well* seems to contain a purely internal conflict: the father digs a pit in the courtyard so that the family can live entirely independently, while his son spends all day by the stream, dreaming to go to the mythical place of Sangaron. In fact, the film reflects conflicts at the turn of an epoch. His next film, *Flight of the Bee* (1998), begins in the form of a joke: a rich neighbour places a toilet right by the entrance to the house of a village teacher. To avenge this, the teacher buys land on the other side of the rich man's house for a pittance and begins to dig a pit right under his windows. But the director builds up the drama of the household and turns the story into a philosophical parable. Even more successful was his film *Angel on the Right* (2002), where a family dispute unfolds between mother and son. Upon hearing that his mother is mortally ill, the son returns to his native village. At the same time a little boy arrives at the house as well, allegedly his son. So the three of them live together, but the mother does not die. It turns out that the protagonist did not come to bury his mother but to take his son with him. *To Get to Heaven You Have to Die First* (2006) was shown in 'Un Certain Regard' at Cannes.

YARMATOV, Kamil
Kanibadam (Russian Empire), 1903 – Tashkent, 1978

Director, screenwriter, actor. People's Artist of the Soviet Union (1959). In 1923 he went to Moscow to study at the Workers' Faculty, where he met with Vladimir Gardin, who invited him to attend film school. But he did not complete either school, returning to Kanibadam to become the local police chief. During one of his visits to Tashkent he met Nabi Ganiev, who invited him to the Stars of the

East Studio. He acted in Kazimir Gertel's *Behind the Vaults of the Mosque* (1928) and *Jackals of Ravat* (1927). From 1928 and 1931 he returned to Moscow, studying first in the acting, then directing department of VGIK. After graduation he went to Tajikistan to shoot his first propaganda films. His first feature film, *The Emigrant* (1934) explores the changing psychology of the Tajik peasants at a time of socialist transformation. His next film at Tajikkino was *Friends Meet Again* (1939). The following year he transferred to the Tashkent Film Studio, where he made film concerts during the war years. After the war he began to shoot the historical and biographical film *Alisher Navoi* (1947), which was a real success and was shown in many countries around the world. The film received the State Prize of the Soviet Union. His next achievement as director was the film *Avicenna* (1956), about the great doctor, philosopher, and scientist Abu Ali Ibn Sina. His historical-revolutionary trilogy *Storm over Asia* (1965), *Horsemen of Revolution* (1968) and *Death of the Black Consul* (1970) was also awarded state prizes. From 1957 until his death he was the artistic director of Uzbekfilm, which now bears his name.

YUSUPOVA, Mairam
Dushanbe (Tajik SSR), 1949

Director. Her work is distinguished by her personal approach. She graduated from the directing department of VGIK in 1976. From 1978 to 1991 she made over 30 documentaries at Tajikfilm. Many of her films rediscover Tajik traditions and culture, but her documentaries on contemporary social life are no less interesting. Typically, she uses a minimum of words, but evokes eloquent portraits with detailed observation. A particularly striking film is *Face* [*Litso*, 1990], which reveals a peaceful moment in Dushanbe just before the onset of the civil war. During the civil war Yusupova went to Moscow, but remained active as a film-maker. Her film *Field Trip* [*Komandirovka*, 1998] was shot in Dushanbe from a personal viewpoint, full of pain and compassion. Her feature film *The Time of the Yellow Grass* (1991) described how the inhabitants of a mountain village find the corpse of a young man: a sign of impending war. She continues to shoot documentary films related to the Tajiks, like the film *Mardikeri* (2001) on labour migration of Tajiks to Russia.

Translated by Michael Rouland and Birgit Beumers

APPENDIX

FILMOGRAPHY

The filmography contains all the films mentioned in the volume, except some shorts and documentaries that are mentioned only once in passing, which are annotated in the text or in the endnotes.

D stands for director; S stands for scriptwriter; and, where important, DoP is listed (Director of Photography). The film title is followed by the Russian title, and/or – where appropriate – the title in the original language, the film studio and year of production.

Transliteration is the same as in the text, except for Russian names and titles, which follow Library of Congress transliteration. In the names of the studio, we have omitted the soft sign (i.e. Mosfilm instead of Mosfil'm).

For co-productions with the independent republics of Central Asia, we have listed only the countries, not the studios or producers/production companies.

113th [*113yi*, short, Kazakhstan, 2007], D: Talgat Bektursunov
Abu Raihan Beruni [Uzbekfilm, 1974], D: Shukhrat Abbasov; S: Shukhrat Abbasov, Pavel Bulgakov; Cast: Pulat Saidkasymov, Razzak Khamraev, Bimbolat Vataev
Accursed Trails [*Vrazhdy tropy*, Mosfilm 1935], D: Ivan Pravov and Ol'ga Preobrazhenskaia; S: Ivan Shukhov, Ivan Pravov; Cast: Andrei Abrikosov, Marina Ladynina, Ivan Liubeznov
Adep Akhlak [Kyrgyzstan: Oy Art, 2008], D&S: Marat Alykulov, Cast: Marat Kozukeev, Ermek Ibraimov, Nikita Salimbaev

Adopted Son, The [*Beshkempir,* Kyrgyzstan/France, 1998], D: Aktan Abdykalykov, S: Aktan Abdykalykov, Avtandil Adykulov, Marat Sarulu; DoP: Khasanbek Kydyraliev, Cast: Mirlan Abdykalykov, Adir Abilkassimov

Adventures of Nasreddin, The [*Khoja Nasriddinning sarguzashtlari,* Tashkent Film Studio, 1946], D: Nabi Ganiev; S: Viktor Vitkovich; Cast: Razzak Khamraev, Rahim Pirmuhamedov, Yulduz Rizaeva

Ayna [Turkmenfilm, 1960], D: Viktor Ivanov, Alty Karliev; S: Lev Cherentsov; Cast: Antonina Rustamova, Alty Karliev, Artyk Djallyev

Aksuat [Kazakhstan, Japan: Kazakhfilm, 1998], D&S: Serik Aprymov, Cast: Sabit Kurmanbekov, Erzhan Ashim, Makangali Abdullaev

Aldar-Kose see *Beardless Deceiver,* 1964. D: Shaken Aimanov

Alisher Navoi [Tashkent Film Studio, 1947], D: Kamil Yarmatov; S: Aleksei Speshnev, Izzat Sultanov, Viktor Shklovskii; Cast: Razzak Khamraev, Asad Ismatov, Tamara Nazarova, Rahim Pirmuhamedov

Allazhar [Kazakhstan: BARS, 1993], D: Kaldybai Abenov; S: Aleksandr Lapshin, Nurlan Segizbaev, Kaldybai Abenov; Cast: Akhan Sataev, Zhazira Kojabergenova, Nazira Balaeva

Alone among the People [*Odna sredi liudei,* Uzbekfilm, 1973], D: Kamil Yarmatov; S: Mikhail Melkumov; Cast: Sairam Isaeva, Baba Annanov, Anvara Alimova

Alpamys Goes to School [*Alpamys idet v shkolu,* Kazakhfilm, 1976], D: Abdulla Karsakbaev; S: Roza Khusnutdinova; Cast: Ermek Tolepbaev, Uran Sarbasso, Baken Kydykeeva

Amangeldy [*Amangel'dy,* Lenfilm, 1938], D: Moisei Levin; S: Vsevolod Ivanov, Beimbet Mailin, Gabit Musrepov; Cast: Yelubai Umurzakov, Serke Kozhamkulov, Kurmanbek Dzhandarbekov

Ambler's Race, The [*Beg inokhodtsa,* Mosfilm, 1968], D: Sergei Urusevskii; S: Chingiz Aitmatov; Cast: Nurmukhan Zhanturin, Baken Kydykeeva, Farida Sharipova

And the Stars Shine above Tanur [*I zvezdy svetiat nad Tanurom,* Tajikfilm, 1991], D&S: Saif Rakhimzodi; Cast: N. Samadi, M. Abdullaeva, P. Rakhimov

Angel on the Right [*Farishtai kifti rost,* Tajikistan, Italy, Switzerland, France, 2002], D&S: Djamshed Usmonov; Cast: Uktamoi Miyasarova, Maruf Pulodzoda, Malohat Maksumova

Antiromantika [Kazakhfilm, 2001], D&S: Nariman Turebaev; Cast: Liazat Dautova, Talgat Sultanov

Apple of My Eye [*Zenitsa oka,* Kirghizfilm, 1976], D: Gennadi Bazarov; S: Ashim Djakypbekov, Leonid Diadiuchenko; Cast: Bolot Beishenaliev, Baken Kydykeeva, Suimenkul Chokmorov

Arab's Shaitan, The [*Shaitan Araba (Chertovo kolymaga),* Kyrgyzstan: M&B Studio, 2007], D&S: Myrzabek Aidaraliev

Asal [*Asal',* Tashkent Studio, 1940], D: Mikhail Yegorov and Boris Kazachkov

Asel, through the Eyes of Men [*Asel, glazami mushchin,* short, 2005], D: Abai Kulbai

ASSA [Mosfilm: Studio Krug, 1987], D: Sergei Solov'ev; S: Sergei Livnev, Sergei Solov'ev, Natan Eidel'man; Cast: Tat'iana Drubich, Stanislav Govorukhin, Sergei Bugaev (Afrika)

Avicenna [Tashkent Studio 1956], D: Kamil Yarmatov; S: Viktor Vitkovich, Satym Ulug-zade; Cast: Marat Aripov, Tulkun Tadjiev, Abbas Bakirov

Azamat [aka *Obeshchanie Azamata,* Tashkent Studio, 1939], D: Arnol'd Kordium, S. Iskanderov, S: Kuz'ma Gorbunov, Arnol'd Kordium; Cast: Abbas Bakirov, Bori Khaidarov

Bakhytzhamal [short, Kazakhstan, 2007], D: Adilkhan Erzhanov

Balcony, The [*Balkon,* Kazakhfilm, 1988], D: Kalykbek Salykov; S: Shakhimarden Khusainov; Cast: Ismail Igil'manov, Iurii Goroshevskii, Karina Zibagul'

Ballad of a Soldier [*Ballada o soldate,* Mosfilm 1959], D: Grigorii Chukhrai; S: Valentin Ezhov, Grigorii Chukhrai; Cast: Vladimir Ivashov, Zhanna Prokhorenko, Antonina Maksimova

Banner of the Blacksmith, The [*Znamia kuznetsa*, Tajikfilm, 1961], D: Bension Kimiagarov; S: Evgenii Pomeshchikov, Nikolai Rozhkov (based on Ferdowsi); Cast: Mukhametdjan Kasymov, Makhmut Tahiri

Beardless Deceiver, The [*Besborodyi obmanshchik*, aka *Aldar-Kose*, Kazakhfilm, 1964], D: Shaken Aimanov; S: Shaken Aimanov, Lev Varshavskii; Cast: Shaken Aimanov, Yelubai Umurzakov

Before Dawn [*Pered rassvetom*, Uzbekgoskino, 1933], D&S: Suleiman Khodjaev

Before Dawn [*Pered rassvetom (Do rassveta)*, Uzbekistan: Novda, 1994], D: Yusuf Azimov; S: Yusuf Azimov, Sergei Zorin, Ramil' Yamalaev; Cast: Pulat Saidkasymov, Azamjon Shakirjanov, Saida Rametova

Behind the Vaults of the Mosque [*Iz-pod svodov mecheti*, Uzbekgoskino, 1928], D: Kazimir Gertel'; Cast: Ol'ga Spirova, Kamil Yarmatov

Beloved's Scarf, The [*Sharf liubimoi*, Odessa Film Studio, 1956], D: Evgenii Ivanov-Barkov; S: Zinoviia Markina, Evgenii Ivanov-Barkov; Cast: Nodar Shashik-ogly, Tamara Kokova, Khusein Tovkuev

Birds of Paradise [*Raiskie ptitsy/Zymak kystary*, Kyrgyzstan/Kazakhstan, 2006], D&S: Talgat Asyrankulov and Gaziz Nasyrov, Cast: Assol' Abdullina, Aziz Beishenaliev, Ulanbek Omuraliev

Blessed Bukhara [*Blagoslovennaia Bukhara*, Kazakhstan: Studio Katarsis, 1990], D: Bako Sadykov; S: Bako Sadykov, Ulugbek Sadykov; Cast: Ato Muhamedjanov, Umed Sadykov, Bakhtiyar Zakirov

Botagoz [Alma-Ata Studio, 1957], D: Efim Aron; S: A. Filippov, Madi Khasenov; Cast: Gul'fairus Ismailova, Asanali Ashimov, Nina Grebeshkova

Boys in the Sky [*Osmondagi bolalar*, Uzbekfilm, 2002], D: Zulfikar Musakov; S: Rikhsivai Muhammedjanov, Zulfikar Musakov; Cast: Timur Musakov, Nazim Tuliakhodjaev, Radjab Adashev

Boys in the Sky 2 [*Osmondagi bolalar 2*, Uzbekfilm, 2004], D: Zulfikar Musakov; S: Rikhsivai Muhammedjanov, Zulfikar Musakov; Cast: Marika Alimova, Davron Guliamov, Timur Musakov, Muzaffar Sagdullaev

Bro [*Bratan*, Tajikfilm, 1991], D: Bakhtiyar Khudoinazarov; S: Leonid Makhkamov Jr, Bakhtiyar Khudoinazarov; Cast: Firus Sasaliev, Timur Tursunov

Bus Stop, The [*Beket*, short, Kyrgyzfilm, 1995], D&S: Ernest Abdyjaparov, Aktan Abdykalykov; Cast: Mirlan Abdykalykov, Ernest Abdyjaparov

Calendar of Expectations [*Taqvimi intizori*, Tajikistan: Kahkashon, 2005], D&S: Safarbek Soliev; Cast: Nurullo Abdulloev, Shoddi Soliev, Aleksandr Rubtsov

Candidate, The [*Kandidat*, Tajikfilm/Tajiktelefilm, 1988], D: Yunus Yusupov; S: Valentin Maksimenkov; Cast: U. Radjabov, Yunus Yusupov

Cardiogram [*Kardiogramma*, Kazakhfilm, 1995], D&S: Darejan Omirbaev; Cast: Jasulan Asauov, Saule Toktybaeva, Altynai Tattybekova

Carpets [*Kovry*, doc., Vostokkino, 1930], D: Mikhail Verner

Chapaev [Lenfilm, 1934], D & S: Georgii and Sergei Vasil'ev; Cast: Boris Babochkin, Boris Blinov, Varvara Miasnikova

Children of the Pamir [*Deti Pamira*, Tajikfilm, 1962], D: Vladimir Motyl'; S: Zinaida Filimonova; Cast: Mansur Gurmindjaev, Valerii Lebedev, Bodurbek Mirzobekov

Chimp, The [*Maimyl*, Kyrgyzstan, France, Japan, 2001], D: Aktan Abdykalykov (Arym Kubat), S: Aktan Abdykalykov, Tonino Guerra, Avtandil Adykulov; DoP: Khasanbek Kydyraliev; Cast: Mirlan Abdykalykov, Aleksandra Mitrokhina

Cloud, The [*Oblako*, Kyrgyzfilm, 2004], D: Erkin Saliev; S: Temir Birnazarov, Emil' Dzhumabaev, Erkin Saliev, Aktan Arym Kubat; Cast: Adil' Chekilov, Nariste Alieva

Contest, The [*Sostiazanie*, Turkmenfilm, 1963], D&S: Bulat Mansurov; DoP: Khodjakuli Narliev; Cast: Aman Khandurdyev, Artyk Djallyev

Covered Wagon, The [*Krytyi furgon*, Uzbekkino, 1928], D: Oleg Frelikh; S: Valentina Sobborei, K. Gertel', Lolakhan Seifullina; Cast: Aisha Tiumenbeva, Rustam Tura-Khodzhaev

Cunning of Old Ashir, The [*Khitrost' starogo Ashira*, Turkmenfilm, 1955], D: Rafail Perel'shtein, Khangel'dy Agakhanov; S: Valentin Morozov; Cast: Sarry Karryev, Antonina Rustamova, Murad Kurbanklychev

Daughter of a Saint, The [*Doch' sviatogo*, Uzbekgoskino 1931], D: Oleg Frelikh; S: Mikhail Ruderman; Cast: Rustam Tura-Khodzhaev, I. Mir-Iusupov, Z. Shakirova

Daughter of Fergana [*Fergana kizi*, Tashkent Studio, 1948], D: Nabi Ganiev; S: Nabi Ganiev, Mikhail Melkumov; Cast: Yulduz Rizaeva. Asad Ismatov, Rahim Pirmuhamedov

Daughter of the Koran see *Muslim Woman*

Daughter of the Steppe, The [*Doch' stepei*, Alma-Ata Studio, 1954], D: Shaken Aimanov, Karl Gakkel'; S: Roman Fatuev; Cast: Zamzagul' Sharipova, Svetlana Nazarova

Daughter-in-Law [*Nevestka (Ogul'keiik)*, Turkmenfilm, 1972], D: Khodjakuli Narliev; S: Khodjakuli Narliev, Khodjadurdy Narliev; Cast: Maya-Gozel Aimedova, Khodjan Ovezgelenov, Khodjaberdy Narliev

Day Dream [*Son naiavu*, short, Tajikfilm, 1990], D&S: Safar Khakdodov; Cast: Shahzod Radjabov, G. Safaralieva, Tolib Khamidov

Days of Eclipse [*Dni zatmeniia*, Lenfilm, 1988], D: Aleksandr Sokurov; S: Iurii Arabov, Boris Strugatskii, Arkadii Strugatskii; Cast: Aleksei Ananishnov, Eskender Umarov, Vladimir Zamanskii

Death of Otrar [*Gibel' Otrara (Otrardyn kuyreyi)*, Kazakhfilm, 1991], D: Ardak Amirkulov; S: Aleksei German, Svetlana Karmalita; Cast: Dokhdurbek Kydyraliev, Tungyshbai Jamankulov, Bolot Beishenaliev

Death of the Black Consul [*Gibel' chernogo konsula*, Uzbekfilm, 1970], D: Kamil Yarmatov; S: Mikhail Melkumov, Kamil Yarmatov, Cast: Shukur Burkhanov, Shukhrat Irgashev, Roman Khomiatov

Death of the Usurer [*Smert' rostovshchika*, Tajikfilm, 1966], D: Tahir Sabirov; S: Igor' Lukovskii; Cast: Zahir Dustmatov, Khabibullo Adburazakov, Ato Mukhamedja-nov

Decisive Step, The [*Reshaiushchii shag*, Turkmenfilm, 1965], D: Alty Karliev; S: Igor' Lukovskii, Cast: Baba Annanov, Alty Karliev, Sarry Karryev

Descendant of the Snow Leopard, The [*Potomok belog barsa*, Kirghizfilm, 1984], D: Tolomush Okeev; S: Mar Baidjiev, Tolomush Okeev; Cast: Dokhdurbek Kydyraliev, Ashir Chukubaev, Marat Zhanteliev

Devil's Bridge, The [*Chertov most*, TV doc., Kyrgyzstan, 1996], D: Temir Birnazarov

Difficult Passage, The (aka *White Mountains*) [*Belye gory*, aka *Trudnaia pereprava*, Kirghizfilm, 1964], D: Melis Ubukeev; S: Nikolai Roshkov, Melis Ubikeev; Cast: Baken Kydykeeva, Muratbek Ryskulov, Bolat Beishenaliev

Distant Bride, The [*Dalekaia nevesta*, Ashkhabad Film Studio, 1948], D: Evgenii Ivanov-Barkov; S: Evgenii Pomeshchikov, Nikolai Rozhkov, Viktor Shklovskii; Cast: Alty Karliev, Vasilii Neshchiplenko, Aman Kul'mamedov

Djamilia [Mosfilm, 1968]. D: Irina Poplavskaia; S: Chingiz Aitmatov; DoP: Kadyrjan Kydyraliev; Cast: Natal'ia Arinbasarova, Suimenkul Chokmorov, Bolot Beishe-naliev

Djigit [*Dzhigit*, Uzbekgoskino, 1935], D: Nabi Ganiev; S: Ergash Khamraev

Djigit Girl, The [*Devushka-dzhigit*, Alma-Ata Studio, 1954], D: Pavel Bogoliubov; S: Vladimir Abyzov, Shakhmet Khusainov; Cast: Lola Abdukarimova, Kenenbai Kozhabekov

Djura Sarkor [Tajikfilm, 1969], D: Margarita Kasymova; S: Leonid Rutitskii (based on A. Sidki); DoP: Davlatnazar Khudonazarov, Cast: Khikmat Latypov, Makhmud-jan Vakhidov

Dog Ran Away, The [*Bezhala sobaka*, short, Kirghizfilm, 1990], D: Aktan Abdykalykov (Arym Kubat); S: Erkin Ryspaev

Dokhunda [Stalinabad Studio, 1956], D: Bension Kimiagarov; S: Viktor Shklovskii; Cast: Tahir Sabirov, Asli Burkhanov, Muhametdjan Kasymov

Dokhunda, [Tajikfilm, 1936], D: Lev Kuleshov; S: Osip Brik, based on Sadriddin Aini; Cast: Sergei Komarov, Kamil Yarmatov

Don't Cry! [*Jylama!*, Kazakhfilm and MCR Agency, 2002], D: Amir Karakulov; S: Elena Gordeeva, Amir Karakulov, Raushan Baiguzhaeva; Cast: Maira Mukhamed kyzy, Bibinur Aldabergenova, Bakira Shakhinbaeva

Dove's Bell-Ringer, The [*Golubinyi zvonar'*, Kazakhfilm, 1993], D: Amir Karakulov; S: Amir Karakulov, Elena Gordeeva; Cast: Chingiz Nogaibaev, El'mira Makhmutova, Elena Gordeeva

Downfall of the Emirate [*Krushenie emirata*, Mosfilm and Tashkent Studio, 1955], D: Vladimir Basov and Latif Faiziev; S: Vladimir Kreps; Cast: Evgenii Samoilov, Vladimir Krasnopol'skii, Sanat Divanov

Dream within a Dream [*Son vo sne*, Miras and Kazakhfilm, 1992], D&S: Serik Aprymov; Cast: Baurjan Ibragimov, Bakhytjan Alpeisov, Gul'nara Dusmatova

Dursun [Ashkhabad Film Studio, 1940], D: Evgenii Ivanov-Barkov; S: Mikhail Vitukhnovskii, Zinoviia Markina; Cast: Nina Alisova, Alty Karliev, Aman Kul'mamedov

Dzhambul [Alma-Ata Studio, 1952], D: Efim Dzigan; S: Nikolai Pogodin, Abdil'da Tazhibaev; Cast: Shaken Aimanov, Nurmukhan Zhanturin, Kurmanbek Dzhandarbekov

Early Cranes, The [*Rannie zhuravli*, Kirghizfilm/Lenfilm, 1979], D: Bolotbek Shamshiev; S: Chingiz Aitmatov, Bolotbek Shamshiev; Cast: Emil' Boronchiev, Suimenkul Chokmorov, Gul'sara Azhibekova

Earth [*Zemlia*, VUKFU, 1930], D&S: Aleksandr Dovzhenko; Cast: Semen Svashenko, Stepan Shkurat, Iuliia Solntseva

Earth Thirsts, The [*Zemlia zhazhdet*, Vostokkino, 1930], D: Iulii Raizman; S: Sergei Ermolinskii; Cast: Dmitrii Konsovskii, Nikolai Sanishvili, Kira Andronikashvili

Emigrant, The [*Emigrant*, Tajikfilm, 1934], D: Kamil Yarmatov; S: N. Iskritskii, Gabriel Ureklian, Cast: Kamil Yarmatov, Sofiia Tuibaeva

End of the Ataman, The [*Konets atamana*, Kazakhfilm, 1970], D: Shaken Aimanov; S: Andrei Konchalovskii, Eduard Tropinin; Cast: Asanali Ashimov, Viktor Avdiushko, Gennadii Iudin

Eternal Love [*Vechnaia liubov'*/ *Ochpos suiuu*, Kyrgyzstan: Yug-Stunts, Set'Servis, 2007], D&S: Adilet Akmatov

Everything will be OK [*Vse budet khorosho*, short, Kyrgyzstan, 2007], D&S: Akjol Bekbolotov; Cast: Balkhash uulu Renat, Turat uulu Kuban

Extraordinary Commissar [*Chrezvychainyi komissar*/*Favqulodda komissar*, Uzbekfilm, 1970], D: Ali Khamraev; S: Odel'sha Agishev, Ali Khamraev; Cast: Suimenkul Chokmorov, Armen Dzhigarkhanian, Sergei Iakovlev

Extraordinary Mission [*Osoboe poruchenie*, Turkmenfilm, 1957], D: Alty Karliev, Evgenii Ivanov-Barkov; S: Kurbandurdy Kurbansakhatov, Iakov Aizenberg; Cast: Alty Karliev, Pavel Volkov, Valentina Kutsenko

Faraway in Asia [*Daleko v Azii*, doc., Vostokkino, 1931], D: Vladimir Erofeev; DoP: Roman Karmen

Farewell, Gulsary! [*Proshchai, Gul'sary!*/ *Kosh bol, Gul'sary*, Kazakhfilm, 2008], D: Ardak Amirkulov; S: Erlan Nurmukhambetov and Erzhan Rustembekov; Cast: Dogdurbek Kydyraliev, Nurlan Sanzhar, Raikhan Aitkozhanova

Fate of a Poet, The [*Sud'ba poeta*, Tajikfilm, 1959], D: Bension Kimiagarov; S: Satym Ulug-zade; Cast: Marat Aripov, Nozukmo Shomansurova, Dil'bar Kasymova

Fierce One, The [*Liutyi*/*Kok-serek*, Kirghizfilm, 1973], D: Tolomush Okeev; S: Andrei Konchalovskii, Eduard Tropinin (based on Mukhtar Auezov); DoP: Kadyrjan Kydyraliev; Cast: Kambar Valiev, Suimenkul Chokmorov

Fire under the Ash [*Pod peplom – ogon'*, Tajikfilm, 1967], D: Abdusalom Rakhimov; Cast: Ul'mas Alikhodjaev, Maksud Imatshoev, Tamara Kokova

Fire Worship [*Poklonis' ogniu*, Kirghizfilm, 1971], D&S: Tolomush Okeev; Cast: Tattybiubiu Tursunbaeva, Bolot Beishenaliev, Suimenkul Chokmorov

First Love of Nasreddin [*Pervaia liubov' Nasreddina*, Tajikfilm, 1977], D: Anvar Turaev; S: Timur Zul'fikarov; Cast: Nino Dolidze, Hoshim Gadoev, Ato Mukhamedjanov

First Teacher, The [*Pervyi uchitel'*, Mosfilm, Kirghizfilm, 1965], D: Andrei Konchalovskii; S: Chingiz Aitmatov, Boris Dobrodeev, Andrei Konchalovskii; DoP: Georgii Rerberg; Cast: Bolot Beishenaliev, Natal'ia Arinbasarova, Darkul' Kuiukova

First-Hand [*Iz pervykh ruk*, doc., Tajikfilm, 1987], D: Pulat Akhmatov; S: Pulat Akhmatov, M. Mirrakhimov

Flight of a Bee [*Parvoz-e zanbur*, Tajikistan, South Korea, 1998], D&S: Djamshed Usmonov, with Boung-Hun Min; Cast: Beknazar Kabirov, Vladislav Savinov, Gairat Azamatov, Zafar Madchonov

Fragi, Deprived of Happiness [*Fragi – razluchennyi so schast'em*, Turkmenfilm, 1984], D: Khodjakuli Narliev; S; Bulat Mansurov, Khodjakuli Narliev, Moris Simashko; DoP: Ovez Vel'muradov, Usman Saparov; Cast: Annaseid Annamuradov, Maya-Gozel Aimedova, Baba Annanov

Freeze, The [*Dzhut*, Vostokkino-Yalta, 1931], D: Mikhail Karostin; S: Sergei Ermolinskii and Mikhail Karostin

Friends Meet Again [*Druz'ia vstrechaiutsia vnov'*, Stalinabad Studio, 1939], D: Kamil Yarmatov; S: Aleksei Speshnev, Aleksandr Filimonov; Cast: Oleg Zhakov, Konstantin Muhutdinov, Nikolai Sanishvili

Furkat [Uzbekfilm, 1959], D: Yuldash Agzamov; S: Mikhail Melkumov, T. Tula; Cast: Iakub Akhmedov, Petr Sobolevskii, Razzak Khamraev

Gift to Stalin [*Podarok Stalinu*, Kazakhstan: ALD, 2008], D: Rustem Abdrashev; S: Pavel Finn, Rustam Ibragimbekov, Viktor Markin; Cast: Nurmzuman Ikhtymbaev, Dalen Shantemirov, Ekaterina Rednikova

Girl of the Tian-Shan, The [*Devushka T'ian-Shania*, Frunze Studio, 1960], D: Aleksei Ochkin; S: Mikhail Aksakov, Kasymaly Djantoshev; Cast: Baky Omuraliev, Jamal Seidakmatova, Muratbek Ryskulov

Golden Horn [*Zolotoi rog*, Kazakhfilm, 1948], D: Efim Aron; S: S. Shatrova; Cast: Shaken Aimanov, Petr Aleinikov, Rakhiia Koichubaeva

Golden Shores [*Zolotye berega*, doc., Vostokkino, 1930], D: Aleksandr Lemberg

Gunshot at the Mountain Pass [*Vystrel na perevale Karash/Karash-Karash okuiasy*, Kazakhfilm/ Kirghizfilm, 1968], D: Bolotbek Shamshiev; S: Asanali Ashimov, Akim Tarazi, Bolotbek Shamshiev; Cast: Suimenkul Chokmorov, Viktor Ural'skii, Baken Kydykeeva

Hasan Arbakesh [Tajikfilm, 1965], D: Bension Kimiagarov; Cast: Bimbolat Vateev, Miassara Aminova, Gurmindj Zavkibekov

Heat [*Znoi*, Kirghizfilm, 1962], D: Larisa Shepit'ko; S: Iosif Ol'shanskii, Larisa Shepit'ko, Irina Povolotskaia; Cast: Bolotbek Shamshiev, Nurmukhan Zhan-turin, Klara Iusupzhanova

His Time will Come [*Ego vremia pridet*, Lenfilm, Alma-Ata Studio, 1958], D: Mazhit Begalin; S: Mikhail Bleiman, Sergei Ermolinskii; Cast: Nurmukhan Zhanturin, Kalibek Kuanyshpaev, Kurmanbek Dzhandarbekov

Horsemen of the Revolution [*Vsadniki revoliutsii*, Uzbekfilm, 1968], D: Kamil Yarmatov; S: Mikhail Melkumov, Kamil Yarmatov; Cast: Mukhtar Aga-Mirzaev, Shukur Burkhanov, Abbas Bakirov

Hunter, The [*Okhotnik*, France, Japan, Switzerland, Kazakhstan, 2004], D&S: Serik Aprymov, Cast: Dogdurbek Kydyraliev, Gulnazid Omarova, Alibek Juasbaev

I'll Be Back [*Ia vernus'*, aka *Batrak*, Turkmenfilm, 1935], D: Aleksandr Ledashchev; S: Evgenii Shatunivskii, Aleksandr Ledashchev; Cast: Nina Ol'shevskaia, Alekper Melikov, Aleksandr Ledashchev

In Spe [*V nadezhde*, Kazakhstan/Kyrgyzstan, 1993], D&S: Marat Sarulu; Cast: Rustem Turkenbaev, Adil' Turkenbaeva

It's Called Life [*Eto nazyvaetsia zhizn'*, Turkmenfilm, 2008], D: Basim Agaev

Jackal, The [*Umarasa*, Kazakhfilm, 2007], D: Serikbol Utepbergenov; S: Bekbolat Shekerov; Cast: Erlan Kokeev, Dinara Koskeldieva, Farkhad Abdraimov

Jackals of Ravat [*Shakaly ravata*, Uzbekgoskino, 1927], D: Kazimir Gertel', S: Valentina Sobborei

Jamal's Tree [*Derevo Dzhamal*, Turkmenfilm, 1980], D: Khodjakuli Narliev; S: Maya Aimedova, Khodjakuli Narliev; Cast: Maya Aimedova, Baba Annanov, Nikolai Smorchkov

Journey to Nowhere [*Puteshestvie v nikuda*, Kazakhstan: KADAM, 1992], D: Amanjol Aituarov; S: Amanjol Aituarov, Nurlan Segizbaev; Cast: Aidos Djanseitov, Sattar Dikambaev, Dana Karibekova

Judas [*Iuda*, aka *Antikhrist*, Sovkino, 1929], D: Evgenii Ivanov-Barkov; S: Pavel Bliakhin; Cast: Boris Ferdinandov, Emma Tsesarskaia, Vasilii Kovrigin

Kairat [Kazakhfilm, 1991], D&S: Darejan Omirbaev; Cast: Kairat Makhmedov, Indira Zheksembaeva

Kara-bugaz [Vostokfilm, 1935], D: Aleksandr Razumnyi; S: Konstantin Paustovskii and Ivan Popov

Karoy [Kazakhstan: Sun Production, 2007], D&S: Zhanna Issabaeva; Cast: Erzhan Tusupov, Rymkesh Omarkhanova, Aiman Aimagambetova

Kelin [*Nevestka*, Kazakhfilm, 2009], D&S: Ermek Tursunov; Cast: Gulsharat Zhubaeva, Turakhan Sadykov, Erzhan Nurymbet

Killer [Kazakhstan, France, 1998], D: Darejan Omirbaev; Cast: Roksana Abuova, Talgat Asetov

Kosh-ba-kosh [Tajikistan, Switzerland, Russia, Japan, 1993], D: Bakhtiyar Khudoinazarov; S: Leonid Makhkamov Jr, Bakhtiyar Khudoinazarov; Cast: Daler Madjidov, Aibarchin Bakirova, Alisher Kasimov

Kyz-Zhibek [*The Silk Maiden*, Kazakhfilm, 1969–70], D: Sultan Khodjikov; S: Gabit Musrepov; Cast: Meruert Utekesheva, Kuman Tastanbekov, Asanali Ashimov

Land of the Fathers [*Zemlia ottsov*, Kazakhfilm, 1966], D: Shaken Aimanov; S: Olzhas Suleimenov; DoP: Murat Aimanov; Cast: Yelubei Umirzakov, Murat Akhmadiev, Iurii Pomerantsev

Last Bey, The [*Poslednii bei*, Uzbekgoskino, 1930], D: Cheslav Sabinskii; S: Mikhail Ruderman; Cast: Kamil Yarmatov, Rahim Pirmuhamedov, Saib Hodjaev

Last Holidays, The [*Poslednie kanikuly*, Kazakhstan: Studio D, 1996], D: Amir Karakulov; S: Amir Karakulov, Elena Gordeeva; Cast: Sanzhar Iskakov, Shalva Gololadze, Anatolii Gapchuk

Last Stop, The [*Konechnaia ostanovka*, Kazakhfilm, 1989], D&S: Serik Aprymov; DoP: Murat Nugmanov; Cast: Sabit Kurmanbekov, Bakhytzhan Alpeisov, Murat Akhmetov

Legend, The [*Legenda/Rovaiat*, Turkmenfilm/Turan-Film, 1999], D: Kerim Annanov; S: Baba Annanov; Cast: Kerim Annanov, Khodjadurdy Narliev

Legend of Rustam, The [*Skazanie o Rustame*, Tajikfilm, 1970], D: Bension Kimiagarov; S: Grigorii Koltunov; DoP: Davlatnazar Khudonazarov, Cast: Bimbolat Vataev, Otar Koberidze, Makhmudjan Vakhidov

Legend of Siyavush, The [*Skazanie o Siiavushe*, Tajikfilm, 1976], D: Bension Kimiagarov; S: Grigorii Koltunov; DoP: Davlatnazar Khudonazarov; Cast: Farhad Yusufov, Svetlana Orlova, Bimbolat Vataev

Leila's Prayer [*Molitva Leily/Kyz jylagan*, Kazakhfilm, 2002], D: Satybaldy Narymbetov; S: Roza Mukanova; Cast: Azhanat Esmagambetova, Baadur Tsuladze, Iurii Kapustin

Leper, The [*Prokazhennaia*, Uzbekgoskino, 1928], D: Oleg Frelikh; S: Lolakhan Seifulina; Cast: Rakhil' Messerer, Grigol Chechelashvili, Rahim Pirmuhamedov

Life of a Young Accordion Player, The [*Zhizneopisanie iunogo akkordeonista*, Kazakhfilm: MIRAS, 1994], D: Satybaldy Narymbetov; S: Iztule Izmaganbetova, Satybaldy Narymbetov; Cast: Raikhan Aitkozhanova, Daulet Kaniev, Bakhytzhan Al'peisov

Light Thief, The [*Svet ake*, Kyrgyzstan/Germany, 2010], D: Aktan Arym Kubat; S: Aktan Arym Kubat, Talip Ibragimov; Cast: Aktan Arym Kubat, Taalaikan Abazova, Askat Sulaimanov

Lip, The [*Guba*, short, Kazakhstan, 2004], D: Erzhan Rustembekov

Little Angel, Make Me Happy [*Angelochek, sdelai radost'*, Turkmenistan/Russia, 1992], D: Usman Saparov; S: Usman Saparov, Larissa Papilova; Cast: Lidiia Brestel', Ata Dovletov, Volodia Frank

Little Avenger [*Malen'kii mstitel'*, Tajikfilm, 1991], D: Gennadii Aleksandrov; S: Leonid Makhkamov; Cast: Hoshim Rakhimov, Zalina Revazova, Hasan Ibragimov

Little Men [*Malen'kie liudi*, Kazakhstan/France: Kazakhfilm, 2003], D&S: Nariman Turebaev; Cast: Erzhan Bekmuratov, Oleg Kerimov, Liazat Dautova

Living God [*Zhivoi bog*, Tajikkino, 1934], D: Mikhail Verner, Dmitrii Vasil'ev; S: Sergei Ermolinskii; Cast: Maksim Straukh, Aleksandr Chargonin, Lev Fenin

Lodger, The [*Kvartirant*, Kyrgyzfilm, 1992], D: Bekjan Aitkuluev; S: E. Shalabaev, Bekjan Aitkuluev; Cast: M. Mambetov, Zhamal Seidakmatova, G. Abdykadyrova

Love of the Minister's Daughter [*Liubov' docheri ministra/Ministrdin kyzynyn makhabaty*, Kyrgyzstan: Studio Zhan, 2006], D: Rustam Atashev

Lovers [*Vliublennye*, Uzbekfilm, 1969], D: Elyor Ishmukhamedov; S: Odel'sha Agishev; Cast: Rodion Nakhapetov, Anastasiia Vertinskaia, Rustam Sagdullaev

Lovers of December [*Liubovniki dekabria*, Kazakhstan: SKIF, 1991], D: Kalykbek Salykov; S: Kalykbek Salykov, Marina Drozdova, Aleksandr Kiselev; Cast: Viacheslav Baranov, Iuliia Tarkhova, Vitalii Petrov

Lullaby [*Kolybel'naia*, doc., Tajikfilm, 1966], D: Davlat Khudonazarov

Luna Papa [*Lunnyi papa*, Tajikistan, Russia, Germany, Austria, Switzerland, 1999], D: Bakhtiyar Khudoinazarov; S: Iraklii Kvirikadze, Bakhtiyar Khudoinazarov; Cast: Chulpan Khamatova, Moritz Bleibtreu, Ato Muhamedjanov, Merab Ninidze, Nikolai Fomenko

Magic Crystal, The [*Volshebnyi kristall*, Ashkhabad Film Studio, 1945], D: Mered Atakhanov, Abram Naroditskii; S: Abram Naroditskii; Cast: Alty Karliev, Bazar Amanov, Maiia Kulieva

Magtymguly [*Makhtumkuly*, Turkmenfilm, 1968], D: Alty Karliev; S: Alty Karliev, Khaiyt Yakubov; Cast: Khommat Mullyk, Mukhammed Cherkezov

Man and his Two Women, A [*Muzhchina i dve ego zhenshchiny*, Tajikfilm, 1991], D: Margarita [Marvorit] Kasymova; S: Abdurafi Rabiev; Cast: Margarita Kasymova, L. Mirzoradjabov

Man Overboard [*Chelovek za bortom*, Turkmenfilm, 1969], D: Khodjakuli Narliev; S: Ivan Repin, Iakov Aizenberg, Kurbandurdy Kurbansakhatov; Cast: Khodjadurdy Narliev, Baba Annanov, Khodjan Ovezgelenov

Man with a Movie Camera, The [*Chelovek s kinoapparatom*, VUKFU, 1928], D: Dziga Vertov, DoP: Mikhail Kaufman

Man Sheds his Skin, A [*Chelovek meniaet kozhu*, Tajikfilm, 1959], D: Rafail Perel'shtein; S: Dmitrii Vasiliu, Leonid Rutitskii; Cast: Gurmindj Zavikibekov, Sergei Stoliarov, Vladimir Emel'ianov

Manaschi [doc., Kirghizfilm, 1965], D: Bolotbek Shamshiev

Mandala [*Oium*, short; Kyrgyzstan: Kumai, 1999], D&S: Marat Sarulu; Cast: Kalia Omorova, Stalbek Kaparov, Soken Asanbekova

Mankurt [Turkmenfilm, 1990], D: Khodjakuli Narliev; S: Mariia Urmatova; Cast: Tarik Tardjan, Maya Aimedova, Khodjakuli Narliev

Marjona [Uzbekistan: Muzaffar Film/Sheikhantaur Film, 2004], D: Said Mukhtarov; Cast: Dilshoda Ganieva, Farruh Saipov

Melody of the Soul [*Melodiia dushi*, Turkmenfilm, 2007], D: Oraz Orazov; S: Ya. Shadurdyev, N. Alimov; Cast: L. Giulisenova, M. Yaagshimuradov, O. Khaniyeva

Metamorphosis [*Metamorfoza*, Kyrgyztelefilm, 2006], D: Gennadii Bazarov; Cast: Marat Alyshbaev, Gul'sina Chotonova

Minaret of Death, The [*Minaret smerti*, Sevzapkino and Bukhkino, 1925], D: Viacheslav Viskovskii; S: Aleksandr Balagin and V. Viskovskii

Mongol [Russia, Kazakhstan, Germany: CTB, Kinofabrika, 2007], D: Sergei Bodrov; S: Arif Aliev, Sergei Bodrov; Cast: Tadanobu Asano, Hulan Chuluun

Mother Earth [*Materinskoe pole*, Kirghizfilm, 1967], D: Gennadii Bazarov; S: Chingiz Aitmatov, Boris Dobrodeev, Igor' Talankin; Cast: Baken Kydykeeva, Raushan Sarmuzina, Bolot Beishenaliev

Mother's Lament about Mankurt, A [*Naiman-enenin koshogu/Plach materi o mankurte*, Kyrgyzfilm, 2004], D: Bakyt Karagulov; S: Chingiz Aitmatov, Marat Sarulu; Cast: Gul'sara Azhibekova, Sayat Isembaev, Asel' Sagatova

Motherland [*Rodina*, Uzbekfilm, 2006], D&S: Zulfikar Musakov; Cast: Timur Musakov, Mannon Ubaydullayev

Murmur of a Brook in Melting Snow [*V talom snege – zvon ruch'ia*, Tajikfilm, 1982], D: Davlat Khudonazarov; S: G. Surmanoz, Valerii Tal'vik; Cast: Mukhutdin Salokhov, Shodi Davronov, Sherali Abdulkaisov

Muslim Woman, The [*Musul'manka*, aka *The Daughter of the Koran* [*Doch' Korana*], Proletkino and Bukhkino, 1925], D: Dmitrii Bassalygo; S: A. Maier and D. Bassalygo; Cast: Ol'ga Tret'iakova, V. Massino, G. Levkoev

Mute Coolness [*Nemaia prokhlada*, short, Kazakhstan, 2004], D: Serikbol Utepbergenov

Mutiny [*Miatezh*, Sovkino Leningrad, 1928], D: Semen Timoshenko; S: Mikhail Bleiman, Semen Timoshenko

My Brother, Silk Road [*Zhibek zholu ademi*; aka *Zolotoi fazan (Altyn kyrghol)*, Kazakhstan/Kyrgyzstan, 2001], D&S: Marat Sarulu; Cast: Busurman Odurakaev, Tynara Abdrazaeva, Mukanbek Toktobaev

My Name is Kozha [*Menia zovut Kozha/Menin atym Kozha*, Kazakhfilm, 1963], D: Abdulla Karsakbaev; S: Nisson Zeleranskii; Cast: Nurlan Segizbaev, Kekenbai Kozhabekov, Raisa Mukhamed'iarova

Nasreddin in Bukhara [*Nasreddin v Bukhare*, Tashkent Studio, 1943], D: Iakov Protazanov, Nabi Ganiev, Roman Tikhomirov; S: Viktor Vitkovich, Leonid Solov'ev; Cast: Lev Sverdlin, Emmanuil Geller, Vasilii Zaichikov

Native Dancer [*Baksy*, Kazakhfilm/CTB, 2008], D: Guka Omarova; S: Sergei Bodrov, Guka Omarova; Cast: Nesipkul Omarbekova, Farkhad Amankulov, Tolepbergen Baisakalov

Naughty Brothers, The [*Djapbaki*, aka *Ozornye brat'ia*, Turkmenfilm, 1972], D: Kakov Orazsiakhedov, Haijit Yakubov; S: Semen Listov; Cast: Enver Annakuliev, Muratgel'dy Rakhimov

Needle, The [*Igla*, Kazakhfilm, 1988], D: Rashid Nugmanov; S: Bakhyt Kilibaev; Cast: Viktor Tsoi, Marina Smirnova, Petr Mamonov

Night of the Yellow Bull [*Noch' zheltogo byka (Deti zemletriaseniia)*, Turkmen Centre for Film and Television for Children Nusai/Mosfilm, 1997], D: Murat Aliev; S: Bulat Mansurov, Ashimurad Mameliev; Cast: Maksat Pulatov, Artyk Djallyev, Rolan Bykov

Nomad, The [*Kochevnik/Köshpendiler*, Russia/USA/Kazakhstan, 2005], D: Sergei Bodrov, Talgat Temenov, Ivan Passer; S: Rustam Ibragimbekov; Cast: Kuno Becker, Jason Scott Lee, Jay Hermandez, Doskhan Zholzhaksynov

Notes of a Railwayman [*Zapiski putevogo obkhodchika*, Kazakhfilm, 2006], D: Zhanabek Zhetiruov; Cast: Nurjuman Ikhtymbaev, Aldabek Shalbaev, Aigerim Zhanylbaeva

Oath, The [*Kliatva*, aka *Ia ne predatel'*, Uzbekfilm, 1937], D: Aleksandr Usol'tsev-Garf

Oedipus [*Edip*, Kyrgyzstan/Turkmenistan/Uzbekistan, 2004], D&S: Ovliakuli Khodjakuli, Cast: Anna Mele, Djamilia Sydykbaeva

Ompa [Gala TV Kazakhstan, 1998], D&S: Satybaldy Narymbetov; Cast: Doskhan Zholzhaksynov, Aleksandr Pankratov-Chernyi, Meruert Tusupbaeva

Orator, The [*Voiz*, Uzbekfilm, 1998], D&S: Yusup Razykov; Cast: Bahodyr Adylov, Lola Eltoeva, Javahir Zakirov

Other, The [*Telba*, aka *The Idiot*, Uzbekfilm, 2008], D: Ayub Shahobiddinov; S: Yolkin Tuichiev; Cast: Dilnoza Kubaeva, Ulugbek Kadyrov, Alisher Uzakov

Our Dear Doctor [*Nash milyi doktor*, Alma-Ata Studio, 1957], D: Shaken Aimanov; S: Iakov Ziskind; Cast: Iurii Pomerantsev, Roza Ismailova, Evgenii Diordiev

Our House [*Nash dom*, Mosfilm, 1965], D: Vasilii Pronin; S: Evgenii Grigor'ev, Cast: Anatolii Papanov, Nina Sazonova, Ivan Lapikov

Pain of Love, The [*Bol' liubvi*, Tajikfilm, 1989], D: Anvar Turaev; S: Iurii Kharlamov; Cast: Tago Razykov, Madina Makhmudova, Dil'bar Umarova

Passage [*Bosogo*, short, Kyrgyzfilm, 2000], D&S: Ernest Abdyjaparov; Cast: Taalaikan Abazova, Ernest Abdyjaparov

Patchwork Quilt [*Kurak korpe*, Kazakhfilm, 2007], D: Rustem Abdrashev; S: Ermek Tursunov; Cast: Valentina Durumbetova, Nurzhuman Ikhtymbaev, Tamara Kosubaeva

Path of the Burning Wagon [*Doroga goriashchego furgona*, Turkmenfilm, 1967], D: Mered Atakhanov; S: Gusein Mukhtarov, Mered Atakhanov; Cast: Tanrykuli Seitkuliev, Baba Annanov, Artyk Djallyev

Pedestal of Death [*Podnozhie smerti*, doc., Vostokfilm, 1928], D: Vladimir Shneiderov

Place on the Grey Triangular Hat, The [*Mesto na seroi treugolke*, Kazakhfilm: ALEM, 1993], D: Ermek Shinarbaev; S: Nikita Djalkibaev; Cast: Adil'khan Esenbulatov, Saule Sleimenova, Iuliia Sukhova

Poem about Love [*Poema o liubvi*, Alma-Ata Studio, 1954], D: Shaken Aimanov, Karl Gakkel'; S: Gabit Musrepov; Cast: Sholpan Dzhandarbekova, Serke Kozhamkulov

Potter, The [*Goncharka*, short, Kazakhstan, 2000], D: Abai Kulbai

Prayer for the Chaste Bird [*Plach pereletnoi ptitsy*, animation; Kirghizfilm, 1989], D: Marat Sarulu

Procurator, The [*Prokuror*, Ashkhabad Film Studio, 1941], D: Evgenii Ivanov-Barkov, Boris Kazachkov; S: Nikita Shumilo; Cast: Natal'ia Efron, Nina Alisova, Alty Karliev

Pure Coolness [*Boz Salkyn/Svetlaia prokhlada*, Kyrgyzstan, 2007], D&S: Ernest Abdyjaparov; Cast: Asem Toktobekova, S"ezdbek Iskenaliev

Push [*Ryvok*, Kazakhfilm, 2010], D: Kanagat Mustafin; S: Erzhan Rustembekov, Erlan Nurmukhambetov, Kanagat Mustafin; Cast: Arystan Myrzagereev, Ol'ga Shishigina, Gosha Kutsenko

Quenching the Thirst [*Utolenie zhazhdy*, Turkmenfilm, 1966, rel. 1968], D: Bulat Mansurov; S: Bulat Mansurov, Iurii Trifonov; DoP: Khodjakuli Narliev; Cast: Khodjakuli Narliev, Artyk Djallyev, Anatolii Romashin

Raihan [*Raikhan*, Lenfilm, 1940], D: Moisei Levin; S: Mukhtar Auezov; Cast: Yelubai Umurzakov, Serke Kozhamkulov, Shaken Aimanov

Ramazan [Uzbekgoskino, 1933], D&S: Nabi Ganiev; Cast: Ergash Khamraev, Yunis Narimanov

Ravenous [*Liudoed*, Kazakhstan: Katarsis, 1991], D: Gennadii Zemel'; Cast: Oleg Gushchin, Vladimir Talashko, Petr Derbenev

Reading of Petrarch, The [*Chtenie Petrarka*, Kyrgyzfilm, 2007], D: Nurlan Abdykadyrov; S: Nurlan Abdykadyrov, Sapar Koichumanov; Cast: Gul'nara Kadyralieva, Bolot Tentimyshev

Red Apple, The [*Krasnoe iabloko/Kyzyl alma*, Kirghizfilm, 1975], D: Tolomush Okeev; S: Chingiz Aitmatov, El'ga Lyndina, Tolomush Okeev; Cast: Suimenkul Chokmorov, Gul'sara Azhibekova, Tattybiubiu Tursunbaeva

Red Poppies of Issyk-Kul, The [*Alye maki Issyk-kulia*, Kirghizfilm, 1971], D: Bolotbek Shamshiev; S: Ashim Djakypbekov, Iurii Sokol; Cast: Suimenkul Chokmorov, Boris Khimichev, Sovetbek Djumadylov

Renaissance Island [*Ostrov vozrozhdeniia*, Kazakhfilm: Khan-Tengri, 2004], D: Rustem Abdrashev; S: Rustem Abdrashev, Galiia Eltai, Gaziz Nasyrov; Cast: Temirzhan Daniarov, Zhanel Makazhanova, Sayat Merekenov

Repentance [*Pokaianie*, Turkmenfilm, 2008], D: Durdy Niyazov; S: M. Orazov; Cast: Ya. Gurbanazov, B. Khodjamamedova, E. Khamraev

Restless Morning [*Trevozhnoe utro*, Kazakhfilm, 1966], D: Abdulla Karsakbaev; S: Zein Shashkin; Cast: Idris Nogaibaev, Asanali Ashimov, Anuarbek Moldabekov

Return to A. [*Vozvrashchenie v A. (Nastoiashchii polkovnik)*, Kazakhfilm, 2011], D: Egor Konchalovskii; S: Vladimir Moiseenko, Aleksandr Novototskii-Vlasov; Cast: Arman Asenov, Seidulla Moldakhanov, Gul'nara Dusmatova

Rich Guy [*Boyvachcha*, Uzbekfilm, 2008], D: Jahongir Poziljonov, Edgor Nosirov; S: Jahongir Poziljonov, Sherzod Ulmasov; Cast: Jahongir Poziljonov, Mumin Oripov, Nigora Ismailova

Rise, The [*Pod''em*, Uzbekfilm, 1931], D: Nabi Ganiev; S: Nikolai Klado

Road, The [*Jol*, Kazakhstan/France/Japan, 2001], D&S: Darejan Omirbaev; Cast: Djamshed Usmonov, Serik Aprymov

Rough River, Placid Sea [*Burnaia reka, bezmiatezhnoe more*, Kazakhstan, Kyrgyzstan, 2004], D&S: Marat Sarulu; Cast: Rustem Turkenbaev, Adil' Turkbenbaev, Ainur Kabatai kyzy

Route of Hope, The [*Neizvestnyi marshrut (Beglisiz marshrut)*, Kyrgyzfilm, 2008], D&S: Temir Birnazarov; Cast: Diuishen Baitobetov, Mukanbek Toktobaev

Rover [*Sergelden (Ovora)*, Tajikfilm, 2005], D&S: Gulyandom Mukhabbatova and Daler Rakhmatov; Cast: Alidjon Shokirov, Fotima Guliamova, Abduholik Sufiev, Bakhtiyer Rahimov

Running [*Beg/Zhuguruu*, short, Kyrgyzstan, 2008], D: Marat Ergeshov

Running Target [*Begushchaia mishen'*, Kazakhfilm, 1991], D: Talgat Temenov; S: Oleg Mandzhiev, Talgat Temenov; Cast: Kanat Akhanov, Nonna Mordiukova, Gul'nara Dusmatova

Rustam and Suhrab [Tajikfilm, 1971], D: Bension Kimiagarov; S: Grigorii Koltunov; Cast: Bimbolat Vataev, Hoshim Gadoev, Sairam Isaeva

Salt for Svanetia [*Sol' Svanetii*, Gruziafilm, 1929], D: Mikhail Kalatozov

Saltanat [Mosfilm and Kirghizfilm, 1955], D: Vasilii Pronin; S: Roza Budantseva; Cast: Baken Kydykeeva, Nurmukhan Zhanturin, Alty Karliev

Sanzhira [*Sanzhyra*, short, Kyrgyzstan/Russia, 2001], D: Nurbek Egen; S: Serik Beiseu, Ekaterina Tirdatova, Nurbek Egen; Cast: Nursultan Sayakbaev, Jypara Kalygulova

Schizo [*Shiza*, Kazakhstan/Russia: Kazakhfilm/CTB, 2004], D: Gul'shad (Guka) Omarova; S: Sergei Bodrov, Gul'shad Omarova; Cast: Eduard Tabishev, Viktor Sukhorukov, Ol'ga Landina

Second Wife, The [*Vtoraia zhena*, Uzbekgoskino 1927], D: Mikhail Doronin; S: Valentina Sobborei, Lolakhan Seifullina; Cast: Rakhil' Messerer, Nabi Ganiev

Secret of Karatau, The [*Taina Kara-Tau*, Vostokkino, 1932], D: Aleksandr Dubrovskii; S: A. Dubrovskii, Vera Inber, El'-Registan; Cast: Vladimir Gardin, Nikolai Kutuzov

Secrets of Maqam, The [*Tainy Mukama*, Turkmenfilm, 1974], D: Alty Karliev; Cast: Elizaveta Karaeva, Alty Karliev, Khommat Mullyk

Seven Hearts [*Sem' serdets*, Turkmenfilm, 1935], D&S: Nikolai Tikhonov; Cast: A. Miliaev, V. Zanoni, Viktor Kulakov

Seventh Bullet, The [*Sed'maia pulia*, Uzbekfilm, 1972], D: Ali Khamraev; S: Andrei Konchalovskii, Fridrikh Gorenshtein; Cast: Suimenkul Chokmorov, Dilorom Kambarova, Bolot Beishenaliev, Talgat Nigmatulin

Sex and Philosophy [*Sex o phalsapheh*, Tajikfilm, 2005], D&S: Mohsen Makhmalbaf; Cast: Daler Nazarov, Mariam Gaibova, Farzona Beknazarova, Tahmineh Ebrahimova

Shanghai [*Shankhai*, Kazakhfilm, 1996], D&S: Aleksandr Baranov; Cast: Vladimir Tolokonnikov, Zhanas Iskakov, Dimash Akhimov

She Defends the Motherland [*Ona zashchishchaet rodinu*, TsOKS, 1943], D: Fridrikh Ermler; S: Aleksei Kapler; Cast: Vera Maretskaia, Nikolai Bogoliubov

Shepherd, The [*Erkek*, Uzbekfilm, 2005], D: Yusup Razykov; S: Erkin Agzamov, Yusup Razykov; Cast: Elnur Abraev, Lola Eltoeva, Zebo Navruzova

Shepherd's Son, The [*Syn pastukha*, Turkmenfilm, 1954], D: Rafail Perel'shtein; S: G. Mukhtarov, K. Seitliev; Cast: Alty Karliev, Sona Muradova, Aman Kul'mamedov

Shok and Sher [*Shok i Sher*, Kazakhfilm, 1972], D: Kanymbek Kasymbekov; S: Satybaldy Narymbetov; Cast: Talgat Ukmiev, Kambar Valiev, Tamara Kosubaeva

Shuga [Kazakhstan, France, 2007], D: Darejan Omirbaev; Cast: Aidos Sagatov, Ainur Turgambaeva

Silence, The [*Sokout*, Tajikistan: Makhmalbaf Productions, 1998], D&S: Mohsen Makhmalbaf; Cast: Tahmineh Normatova, Nadereh Abdelahyeva, Goibibi Ziadolahyeva

Silk Maiden, The see *Kyz-Zhibek*

Sixth Part of the World, A [*Shestaia chast' mira*, doc., Goskino, 1926], D: Dziga Vertov; DoP: Iakov Tolchan

Sky of Our Childhood, The [*Nebo nashego detstva*, Kirghizfilm, 1966], D: Tolomush Okeev; S: Kadyrkul Omurkulov, Tolomosh Okeev; DoP: Kadyrjan Kydyraliev; Cast: Muratbek Ryskulov, Aliman Dzhangorozova, Sovetbek Dzhumadylov

Slave Girl, The [*Rabynia*, Turkmenfilm, 1968], D&S: Bulat Mansurov; DoP: Khodjakuli Narliev; Cast: Aman Odaev, Gevkher Nurdjanova

Son of Tajikistan, The [*Syn Tadzhikistana*, Stalinabad Studio/ Soiuzdetfilm, 1942], D: Vasilii Pronin; S: Evgenii Pomeshchikov, Nikolai Rozhkov, Mikyail Rafili; Cast: Vera Altaiskaia, Boris Andreev, Mukhamedzhan Kasymov

Son, Time to Get Married [*Synu pora zhenit'sia*, Tajikfilm, 1959], D: Tahir Sabirov; S: Shamsi Kiiamov; Cast: Marat Aripov, Dil'bar Kasymova, Sofiia Tuibaeva

Song about Manshuk [*Pesn' o Manshuk*, Kazakhfilm, 1969], D: Mazhit Begalin; S: Andrei Konchalovskii; Cast: Natal'ia Arinbasarova, Leonid Reutov, Nikita Mikhalkov

Song of Happiness [*Pesnia o schast'i*, Vostokfilm, 1934], D: Mark Donskoi, Vladimir Legoshin; S: Georgii Kholmskii; Cast: Ianina Zheimo, Mikhail Viktorov, Vladimir Gardin

Song of Southern Seas [*Pesn' iuzhnykh morei*, Germany, Kazakhstan, Russia, France, 2008], D&S: Marat Sarulu; Cast: Mikhail Zhigalov, Irina Ageikina, Vadim Andreev

Song of the Steppes, The [*Pesn' stepei*, Vostokkino, 1930], S: Efim Aron; D and DoP: Aleksandr Lemberg; Cast: Serke Kozhamkulov

Songs of Abai [*Pesni Abaia*, Alma-Ata Studio, 1945], D: Efim Aron, Grigorii Roshal'; S: Mukhtar Auezov; Cast: Kalybek Kuanyshpaev, Serke Kozhamkulov, Shaken Aimanov

Soviet Patriots [*Sovetskie patrioty*, Ashkhabad Film Studio, 1939], D: Grigorii Lomidze; S: Nikolai Rozhkov; Cast: Stepan Krylov, Alty Karliev

Sparrow, The [*Taranchy*, short, Kyrgyzfilm, 1995], D&S: Ernest Abdyjaparov; Cast: Taalaikan Abazova, Kanybek Bekbatyrov

Stains, The [*Kliaksy*, short, Kazakhstan, 2001], D: Erzhan Rustembekov

Star in the Night [*Zvezda v nochi*, Tajikfilm, 1972], D: Abdusalom Rakhimov, Igor' Usov; S: Valentin Maksimenkov, Rasul Khadi-zade; Cast: Makhmudzhan Vakhidov, Khurram Kasymov

Steppe Express [*Stepnoi ekspress*, Kazakhfilm, 2005], D: Amanjol Aituarov; S: Odel'sha Agishev, Khuat Akhmetov; Cast: Aizhan Aitenova, François Labbé, Arman Asenov

Steppe, The [*Step'*, short, Kazakhstan, 2007], D: Emir Baigazin

Storm over Asia [*Buria nad Aziei*, Uzbekfilm, 1965], D: Kamil Yarmatov; S: Vladimir Alekseev, Odel'sha Agishev, Mikhail Melkumov, Nazir Safarov, Kamil Yarmatov; Cast: Shukur Burkhanov, Ruslan Akhmetov, Abbas Bakirov

Stormy Station [*Burannyi polustanok*, Kazakhfilm, 1995], D: Bakyt Karagulov; S: Chingiz Aitmatov, Marat Sarulu, Bakyt Karagulov; Cast: Gul'sara Azhibekova, Gul'nizat Omarova, Kauken Kenzhetaev

Stranger, The [*Streindzher*, Kazakhstan: KADAM, 1993], D&S: Timur Suleimenov; Cast: Kanat Esentaev, John Goldstein, Gabit Mukhamed'ianov

Surzhekey, The Angel of Death [*Surzhekei – Angel smerti*, Kazakhstan: Katarsis, 1991], D: Damir Manabaev; S: Smagul Elubaev, Damir Manabaev; Cast: Nurmukhan Zhanturin, Meirman Nurekeev, Zhanas Iskakov

Swift [*Strizh*, Kazakhfilm, 2007], D: Abai Kulbai; S: Abai Kulbai, Eugénie Zvonkine; Cast: Inessa Kislova, Anar Kakenova

Swing, The [*Selkinchek/Kacheli*, short, Kyrgyzstan/France, 1993], D: Aktan Abdykalykov; S: Ernest Abdyjaparov, Talgat Asyrnakulov, Aktan Abdykalykov; DoP: Khasanbek Kydyraliev; Cast: Mirlan Abdykalykov, Bakyt Toktokojaev

Tahir and Zuhra [*Tohir va Zuhra*, Tashkent Studio, 1945], D: Nabi Ganiev; S: Aleksei Speshnev, Sabir Abdulla; Cast: Guliam Aglaev, Yulduz Rizaeva, Asad Ismatov

Tajik Film Concert [*Tadzhikskii kinokontsert*, Tajikfilm/Soiuzdetfilm, 1943], D&S: Klimentii Mints, Cast: Sh. Mullodjanova, A. Nosyrova, A. Azimov

Tashkent – City of Bread [*Tashkent – gorod khlebnyi/Toshkent – non shaqri*, Uzbekfilm, 1967], D: Shukhrat Abbasov; S: Andrei Konchalovskii; Cast: Vladimir Vorobei, Vova Kudenkov, Bakhtiyar Nabiev, Natal'ia Arinbasarova

Teenager [*Orzu ortida*, Uzbekfilm, 2005], D&S: Yolkin Tuichiev, Cast: Nigara Karimbaeva, Zulhumor Muminova, Roustam Muradov, Umida Narbaeva

Ten Steps to the East [*Desiat' shagov k Vostoku*, Turkmenfilm, 1960], D: Khangel'dy Agakhanov; S: Aleksandr Abramov, Mikhail Pismannik; Cast: Artyk Djallyev, Aman Kul'mamedov, Evgenii Markov

Ten Years of Kazakhstan [*10 let Kazakhstana*, doc., Vostokkino, 1929–30], D: Kaium Pozdniakov

Tender Heart [*Slaboe serdtse/Älsiz jürek*, Kazakhfilm, 1994], D: Ermek Shinarbaev; S: Leila Akhinzhanova; Cast: Natal'ia Arinbasarova, Adil'khan Esenbulatov, Saule Suleimenova

Tenderness [*Nezhnost'/Sevgi*, Uzbekfilm, 1966], D: Elyor Ishmukhamedov; S: Odel'sha Agishev; Cast: Mariia Sternikova, Rodion Nakhapetov, Madina Makhmudova

Testament of Nine Prophets, The [*Zavet deviati prorokov*, aka *Mest' deviati prorokov, Taina deviati prorokov*, Tajikfilm/Genemfilm (Syria), 1993], D: Yunus Yusupov; S: Odel'sha Agishev; Cast: Bakhrom Akramov, Anatolii Romashin, Boris Khmel'nitskii

These are Horses [*Eto – loshadi*, doc., 1965], D: Tolomush Okeev; DoP: Kadyrzhan Kydyraliev

Third Daughter [*Tret'ia doch'*, Tajikfilm 1970], D: Anvar Turaev; S: Fateh Niyazi; Cast: Ato Mukhamedjanov, Tamara Kokova, Khabibullo Abdurazakov

Thirteen [*Trinadtsat'*, Mosfilm, 1937], D: Mikhail Romm; S: Iosif Prut, Mikhail Romm; Cast: Ivan Novosel'tsev, Elena Kuz'mina, Aleksandr Chistiakov

Three Brothers [*Tri brata*, East Cinema, National Producers' Centre, Kazakh Film Factory, 2000], D: Serik Aprymov' S: Meirin Larbozov, Serik Aprymov; Cast: Aibar Temenov, Zhakir Viliamov, Iura Dankov, Baurjan Seitbaev

Three Songs for Lenin [*Tri pesni o Lenine*, Mezhrabpomfilm, 1934], D: Dziga Vertov

Time of Yellow Grass, The [*Vremia zheltoi travy/Mavsimi Alafchai Sard*, Tajikfilm, Soiuztelefilm, 1991], D: Mairam Yusupova; S: Aleksei Katunin, Saif Rakhimov, David Chubinishvili; Cast: Roland Ter-Makarov, Sherali Abdulkaisov, Bobodjon Khasanov

To Get to Heaven First You Have to Die [*Bihisht faqat baroi murdagon*, Tajikistan, France, 2006], D&S: Djamshed Usmonov; Cast: Dinara Drukarova, Hurshed Golibekov, Maruf Pulodzoda

To the Sounds of the Dombïra [*Pod zvuki dombr*, film concert, Lenfilm, 1943], D: Adol'f Minkin and Semen Timoshenko

Today or Tomorrow [*Segodnia ili zavtra*, Vostokkino, 1930–1], D: Muguev and Kazangapov

Together with Father [*Vdvoem s otsom/ Akem ekeumiz*, Kazakhfilm, 2008], D&S: Daniyar Salamat; Cast: Bakhytzhan Al'peisov, Nurmakhanbet Aitenov, Gul'shat Tutova

Toptash [short, Kyrgyzstan: Oy Art, 2008], D&S: Nargiza Mamatkulova

Touch, The [*Prikosnovenie*, Kazakhstan: MIRAS, 1989], D: Amanjol Aituarov; S: Amanjol Aituarov, Bayan Sarygulov; Cast: Nurzhuman Ikhtymbaev, Bakhyt Sabirzhanov

Touch, The [*Prikosnovenie*, short, Kazakhstan, 2005], D: Abai Kulbai

Traces Go Beyond the Horizon [*Sledy ukhodiat za gorizont*, Kazakhfilm, 1964], D: Mazhit Begalin; S: Akim Tarazi; Cast: Farida Sharipova, Asanali Ashimov, Kuatbai Abdreimov

True Noon [*Qiyami roz*, Tajikfilm, 2009], D: Nosir Saidov; S: Safar Khakdokov; Cast: Iurii Nazarov, Nasiba Sharipova, Alovuddin Abdullaev

Tulpan [Russia, Germany, Switzerland, Kazakhstan: Pandora and CTB, 2008], D: Sergei Dvortsevoi; S: Sergei Dvortsevoi, Gennadii Ostrovskii; Cast: Askhat Kuchinchirekov, Samal Esliamova, Tolepbergen Baisakalov

Turksib [doc., Vostokkino, 1929], D: Viktor Turin

Turksib is Open [*Turksib otkryt*, doc., Vostokkino 1930], D: Gaiana Room; DoP: Leonid Kosmatov

Ulan [Kirghizfilm, 1977], D: Tolomush Okeev; S: Tolomush Okeev, Eduard Tropinin; Cast: Suimenkul Chokmorov, Natal'ia Arinbasarova

Umbar [Turkmenfilm, 1937], D: Aleksandr Makovskii; S: Aleksei Ian; Cast: Barri Khaidarov, Irina Alimova

Unexpected Bride, The [*Kelgindi kelin*, Uzbekistan, 2006], D: Rustam Sagdiev; Cast: Faruh Soipov, Dilnoza Kubaeva, Jahongir Poziljonov

Valley of Tears [*Dolina slez*, Goskino, 1924], D: Aleksandr Razumnyi; S: Valentin Turkin

Valley of the Ancestors, The [*Dolina predkov*, Kirghizfilm, 1989], D: Kadyrjan Kydyraliev; S: Murza Gaparov; DoP: Khasanbek Kydyraliev; Cast: Darkul' Kuiukova, Rusul Ukachin

Veil, The [*Chadra*, Uzbekkino, 1927], D: Mikhail Averbakh; S: M. Insarov, P. Korotokov, V. Bulakh, M. Averbakh; Cast: Safiyat Askarova, Grigorii Chechelashvili, Saib Khodjaev

Village Authorities [*Saratan/Sel'skaia uprava*, Kyrgyzstan/Germany, 2004], D&S: Ernest Abdyjaparov; Cast: Kumendor Adylov, Askat Sulaimanov, Taalaikan Abazova

Wanderer, The [*Strannik*, Kazakhstan, 2010], D&S: Talgat Bektursunov; Cast: Cast: N. Orazalin, G. Ibraimova, S. Bakaev

Wedding Chest, The [*Sunduk predkov*, France, Germany, Russia, Kyrgyzstan, 2005], D: Nurbek Egen; S: Ekaterina Tirdatova; Cast: Bolat Tentimyshov, Natacha Regnier

Well, The [*Kolodets*, Tajikfilm, 1991, completed 2000], D&S: Djamshed Usmonov; Cast: T. Rozikov, H. Naimova

When a Woman Saddles a Horse [*Kogda zhenshchina osedlaet konia*, Turkmenfilm, 1974], D: Khodjakuli Narliev; S: Maya Aimedova, Khodjakuli Narliev; Cast: Maya Aimedova, Khodjaberdy Narliev, Baba Annanov

When Emirs Die [*Kogda umiraiut emiry*, Tajikfilm, 1932], D: Liudmila Pechorina; S: Gabriel Ureklian; Cast: D. Saidov, H. Orbitov

Where are You, My Zulfia? [*Gde ty, moia Zul'fiia?* aka *Yor-Yor*, Uzbekfilm, 1964], D: Ali Khamraev; S: Rakhmat Faizi; Cast: Saib Khodjaev, Bakhtiyor Ikhtiyarov, Shukur Bukhanov

Where is Your House, Snail? [*Gde tvoi dom, ulitka?/Kelechek*, short, Kyrgyzstan, 1992], D: Aktan Abdykalykov (Arym Kubat); S: Larisa Evgen'eva; Cast: Lola Soboleva, Tursun Omurkanov, Akylbek Abdykalykov

White Gold [*Beloe zoloto*, doc., Turkmenfilm, 1929], D: Aleksandr Vladychuk; DoP: A. Gel'gar

White Mountains [*Belye gori*, aka *Difficult Passage, The*, Kirghizfilm, 1964], D: Melis Ubukeev; S: Nikolai Rozhkov, Melis Ubukeev; Cast: Baken Kydykeeva, Muratbek Ryskulov, Bolot Beishenaliev

White Ship, The [*Belyi parokhod/Aq keme*, Kirghizfilm, 1975], D: Bolot Shamshiev; S: Bolot Shamshiev, Chingiz Aitmatov; Cast: Nyrgazy Sydygaliev, Sabira Kumush-alieva, Orozbek Kutmanaliev

White Sun of the Desert [*Beloe solntse pustiny*, Mosfilm/Lenfilm, 1969], D: Vladimir Motyl'; S: Rustam Ibragimbekov, Valentin Ezhov, Mark Zakharov; Cast: Anatolii Kuznetsov, Pavel Luspekaev, Spartak Mishulin

White, White Storks [*Belye belye aisty/Lailak keldi, ez buldi*, Uzbekfilm, 1966], D: Ali Khamraev; S: Odel'sha Agishev, Alim Khamraev; Cast: Bolot Beishenaliev, Rahim Pirmuhamedov, Saib Khodjaev

Who is This? [*Siz kim siz?*, Uzbekfilm, 1989], D: Djanik Faiziev; S: Djanik Faiziev, Iurii Dashevskii; Cast: Bakhtiyar Zakirov, Elyor Nasyrov, Tulkun Tadjiev

Whole Neighbourhood is Talking About It, The [*Maqallada duv-duv gap/Ob etom govorit vsia makhallia*, Uzbekfilm, 1960], D: Shukhrat Abbasov; S: O. Ramazanov, B. Rest, Cast: Khalida Iskhakova, Khamza Umarov, Tulkun Tadjiev

Wild East, The [*Dikii vostok*, Kino (Kazakhstan) 1993], D&S: Rashid Nugmanov; Cast: Konstantin Fedorov, Zhanna Isina, Gennadii Shatunov

Without Fear [*Bez strakha*, Uzbekfilm, 1972], D: Ali Khamraev; S: Kamil' Iashen, Ali Khamraev, Dilshad Fathulin; Cast: Rustam Sagdullaev, Tamara Shakirova, Bolot Beishenaliev

Woman Between Two Brothers, A [*Razluchnitsa*, Kazakhfilm and Soiuztelefilm, 1991], D&S: Amir Karakulov; Cast: Adil' Turkenbaev, Rustem Turkenbaev, Dana Kairbekova

Woman from Afar, The [*Zhenshchina izdaleka*, Tajikfilm, 1978], D: Tahir Sabirov; S: Nikolai Figurovskii; Cast: Irina Kalinovskaia, Hoshim Gadoev, Iurii Dedovich

Worship of Fire, The [*Poklonis' ogniu*, Kirghizfilm, 1971], D&S: Tolomush Okeev; DoP: Kadyrjan Kydyraliev; Cast: Tattybiubiu Tursunbaeva, Isken Ryskulov, Suimenkul Chokmorov, Bolot Beishenaliev

Ya-hha [*Ia-khkha*, short, VGIK, 1986], D&S: Rashid Nugmanov; Cast: Boris Grebenshchikov, Maik Naumenko, Viktor Tsoi, Konstantin Kinchev

You are Not an Orphan [*Ty − ne sirota*, Uzbekfilm, 1963], D: Shukhrat Abbasov; S: Rakmat Faizi; DoP: Khatam Faiziev; Cast: Liufti Sarymsakova, Obid Dzhalilov, Gena Tkachenko

You're My Delight [*Maftuningman/Ocharovan toboi*, Uzbekfilm, 1958], D: Yuldash Agzamov (Akzamov); S: T. Tula; Cast: Klara Dzhalilova, Gani Agzamov, Turgun Azizov

Youth of a Genius [*Iunost' geniia*, Uzbekfilm and Tajikfilm, 1982], D: Elyor Ishmukhamedov; S: Odel'sha Agishev, Elyor Ishmukhamedov; Cast: Bakhtiyar Zakirov, Ato Mukhamedjanov, Rano Kubaeva

Youth of Abai [*Abai*, Kazakhfilm/ASS, 1995], D: Ardak Amirkulov; S: Serik Aprymov, Leila Akhinzhanova, Aleksandr Baranov; Cast: Gabiden Turykbaev, Bolot Beishenaliev, Farida Zhantelova

Youth's First Morning [*Iunosti pervoe utro*, Tajikfilm, 1979], D: Davlat Khudonazarov; S: Vera Luknitskaia, Aleksandr Mar'iamov; Cast: Sherali Abdulkaisov, Shamsi Khaidarov, Maksud Imatshoev

Zamanai [*Zaman-Y*, 1998], D: Bolot Sharip(ov); S: Saken Junusov, Bolat Sharip; Cast: Zamzagul' Sharipova, Gul'nara Setimbetova, Erik Zholzhaksynov

Zelim-Khan [Vostokkino 1929], D: Oleg Frelikh; S: Dzakho Gatuev, Khalid Oshaev; Cast: Lado Bestaev, Kira Andronikachvili, Lidiia Iskritskaia-Gardina

Zhambyl [aka *Iunost' Dzhambula*, Kazakhfilm, 1996], D: Kanymbek Kasymbekov; S: Myrzatai Zoldasbekov; Cast: Mukhamedzhan Tazabekov, Gul'mira Imangalieva, Nurzhuman Ikhtymbaev

Zhan's Diary [*Dnevnik Zhana*, short, Kazakhstan, 2009], D: Emir Baigazin

Zhosha [Kazakhstan, 2005], D&S: Daniyar Salamat; Cast: Kenzhebek Shaikakov, Almat Yesimov, Aigerim Agyltaeva

Zumrad [Tajikfilm, 1961], D: Abdusalom Rakhimov, Aleksandr Davidson; Cast: Tamara Kokova, Stalina Azamatova

INDEX

Bold page numbers indicate images of the relevant film. References in notes are marked with 'n'.

113th 183, **184**

Abbasov, Shukhrat 15, 18, 19, 75–8, 86, 218
Abdrashev, Rustem 27, 173, 177–80, 223
Abdyjaparov, Ernest 28, 131–32, 196, 199, 207
Abdykadyrov, Nurlan 133
Abdykalykov, Aktan *see* Arym Kubat
Abenov, Kaldybai 169
Abishev, Serik 177
Abu Raihan Beruni 19
Accursed Trails 9, 38, 41, 61, 63
Adep Akhlak 133, 134
Adopted Son, The see *Beshkempir*
Adventures of Nasreddin, The 13
Agaev, Basim 28
Agakhanov, Khangeldy 14
agitfilm 39
Agzamov, Yuldash 15
Aidaraliev, Myrzabek 133
Aimanov, Shaken 12, 14, 16–18, 64, 66–68, 75, 78–81, 164–65
Aimedova, Maya-Gozel 24, 96, 97, 101
Aini, Sadriddin 14, 116, 117, 119, 126n
Aitkulov, Bekjol 131

Aitmatov, Chingiz 95, 100–2, 112, 128, 131, 135n, 140, 142–44, 146n
Aituarov, Amanjol 21, 168, 169, 173
Akayev, Askar 127, 199
Akhadov, Valeri 122, 123
Akhmatov, Pulat 123
Akmatov, Adilet 132
Aksuat 25, 171, 173, 177, 189, **190**, 197
Akvarium 148
Aldar-Kose (ballet) 12; (film) 16
Alexandrov, Grigori 11–12
Aliev, Murat 24, 223
Alisher Navoi 13, **54**, 55, 107
Alisova, Nina 90
Allazhar 169
Alone among the People 19
Alpamys Goes to School 20
Alykulov, Marat 133
Amangeldy 10, 58–59, **60**, 62–67
Amanshaev, Ermek 27
Ambler's Race, The 128
Amirkulov, Ardak 21, 67, 169, 176, 178
And the Stars Shine above Tanur 124
Angel on the Right 222, 224, 228–30, 232

Anna Karenina (Tolstoy) 27
Annaev, Shadurdy 90
Annanov, Baba 93, 103
Annanov, Kerim 103
Antiromantika 178
Appadurai, Arjun 156, 157
Apple of My Eye 20
Aprymov, Serik 21, 22, 27, 67, 145,
    166–7, 169, 171–73, 176–77,
    183, 189, 190, 192, 223
Arab's Shaitan, The 133
Arinbasarova, Natalia 28, 128
ARK (Association of Revolutionary
    Cinema) 50
Aron, Yefim 12, 13, 39, 64, 164
Arym Kubat, Aktan (Abdykalykov)
    24, 28, 129–33, 179, 182, 190, 195,
    196, 199, 200, 203–4, 207, 223–4
Asal 10, 54
Asanova, Dinara 144
Asel, through the Eyes of Men 177
ASSA 150, 188
Asyrankulov, Talgat 132, 199,
    208, 209
Atakhanov, Mered 12, 18
Atashev, Rustam 132
Auezov, Mukhtar 12, 20, 68
Averbakh, Mikhail 6, 8, 36, 49
Avicenna 15
Ayna 92
Azamat 53
Azimov, Yusuf 25

Babochkin, Boris 68
Bahbudov, Rashid 15
Baigazin, Emir 177, 183
Bakhor, Gulomirzo 116
Bakhytzhamal 177, 182, 183
Bakiyev, Kurmanbek 127
Balcony, The 181, 182
Ballad of a Soldier 78
Banner of the Blacksmith, The 118
Baranov, Alexander 170
Barnet, Boris 12
Barsky, Vladimir 3
Bashem, Boris 4, 7, 89

Bashirov, Alexander 188
Baskakov, Vladimir 144
basmachi 7, 9, 10, 18, 20, 65, 118
Basov, Vladimir 15
Bassalygo, Dmitri 6, 36, 47
Battleship Potemkin, The 5, 47
Bauer, Yevgeni 3
Bazarov, Gennadi 20, 128, 132, 144
Beardless Deceiver, The 164
Bedil' Abdulkadir 115, 126n
Before Dawn (1933) 51, 53
Before Dawn (1994) 25
Begalin, Mazhit 14, 19, 67, 164
Behind the Vaults of the Mosque 6,
    47, **48**
Beishenaliev, Aziz 209
Beishenaliev, Bolot 20, 144
Bekbolotov, Akjol 134
Bekmambetov, Timur 28
Bek-Nazarov, Amo 3
Bektursunov, Talgat 182–84
Belavezha Accords 140, 146n
Beloved's Scarf, The 91
Berdymukhammedov, Gurbanguly
    103
Bergenova, Yazgul 11
Berlin IFF 129, 131, 132
Beshkempir 24, **130**, 131, 179, 195,
    200, 203, 204, 224
Birds of Paradise 132, 134, 199, 208,
    209, 210
Birnazarov, Temir 131, 133
Bleiman, Mikhail 68
Blessed Bukhara 124
Bodrov, Sergei (Sr) 27, 173
Bogoliubov, Pavel 64
Bollywood 25, 223
Bolshevism, Bolshevik 4, 5, 25, 26,
    29n, 33, 35, 36, 37, 46, 53, 56n,
    58, 59
Boris Babochkin 67
Botagoz 164
Boys in the Sky 27, 213
Boys in the Sky 2 27, 213
Bresson, Robert 178
Brezhnev, Leonid 17, 19, 120

Bro 21, 22, 23, 124, 194
Bugaev, Sergei (Afrika) 188
Bukhara, Bukharan 4, 5, 6, 12, 15,
    19, 35, 45, 46, 55n, 123, 125
Bukhkino 35, 46, 55n
Bus Stop, The 131, 182
Bystrytsky, Mikhail 8

Calendar of Expectations 222
Candidate, The 124
Cannes IFF 25, 106, 131, 200, 222
Cardiogram 25, 169, 191–92, 223
Carpets 41
Cassavetes, John 149
Chapaev 51, 58, 59, 65, 157
Chardynin, Petr 3
Cherkasov, Nikolai 67
Cherkezov, Mukhammed 100
Cherviakov, Yevgeni 8
Children of the Pamir 16
Chimp, The 24, 131, 195, **196**, 200, 203
Chirkov, Boris 67–68
Chokmorov, Suimenkul 20
Chukhrai, Grigori 78
cinefication (*kinefikatsiia*) 34, 44n
cinéma colonial 48
cinéma vérité 149
Cloud, The 207–8
collectivisation 7, 9, 13, 41, 53, 61,
    63, 68n, 90, 92, 111, 169
colonialism, colonial 7, 9, 42, 51, 58,
    130, 140, 145, 155, 156, 158, 169,
    170, 223, 225
Contest, The 2, 16, 94–96, 105–113,
    110
Covered Wagon, The 6, 44n
Cranes are Flying, The 128
Cunning of Old Ashir, The 15, 92

Daughter-in-Law 19, **97**, 99, 100
Daughter of a Saint, The 9, 36
Daughter of Fergana 13
Daughter of the Steppe, The 64, 67
Davidson, Alexander 16
Davletbekov, Khakim 39
Day Dream 124, 125

*Day Lasts More than a Hundred Years,
    A* 101, 131
Day Watch 28
Days of Eclipse 158
De Sica, Vittorio 106
Dean, James 150
Death of Otrar 169
Death of the Black Consul 18
Death of the Usurer 119
Decisive Step, The 92, **93**
Descendant of the Snow Leopard, The
    129
Devil's Bridge, The 131
Didor IFF (Dushanbe) 226
Difficult Passage, The 128
Distant Bride, The 13, 91
Divanov, Kudoibergan 3
Djallyev, Artyk 93
Djamilia 128
Djangildin, Alibi 3
Djigit 51
Djigit Girl, The 10, 64
Djura Sarkor 119
Dog Ran Away, The 130, 200
Dokhunda (1936) 117
Dokhunda (1956) 14
Don't Cry! 27, 172, 173, 192–93
Donskoi, Mark 8, 41
Doronin, Mikhail 6, 35, 36, 47, 163
Dove's Bell-Ringer, The 170
Dovzhenko, Alexander 157
Downfall of the Emirate 15
Dream within a Dream 169
Drubich, Tatiana 188
Dubrovsky, Alexander 41
Dursun 90–92
Dvortsevoi, Sergei 27
Dzhambul 13, 63, 67
Dzhandarbekova, Sholpan 65
Dzhansugurov, Ilyas 38, 63
Dzigan, Yefim 13, 64

Early Cranes, The 20, 129
Earth 157
Earth Thirsts, The 9, 41, 42, 90
Egen, Nurbek 132

Eisenstein, Sergei 5, 11, 47, 67, 68, 74
El-Registan, Gabriel 41
Emigrant, The 9, 116
End of the Ataman, The 18
Erdman, Nikolai 68
Ergeshov, Marat 134
Ermler, Fridrikh 12, 68, 74
Erzhanov, Adilkhan 177, 182
Eternal Love 132
Eurasia IFF 178, 218, 222
Everything will be OK 134
Extraordinary Commissar 20
Extraordinary Mission 15, 91, 92

Fairbanks, Douglas 47
Faiziev, Latif 15, 22
Faraway in Asia 41
Farewell, Gulsary! 178
Fate of a Poet, The 14, 118
Fellini, Federico 17, 100
Ferdowsi 19, 55, 119, 126n
Fierce One, The 20, 129
film famine (*malokartin'e*) 12, 13, 63
film noir 151
FIPRESCI 149
Fire under the Ash 119
Fire Worship 19
First Love of Nasreddin 19, 119
First Teacher, The 128, **129**, 143, 144, 164, 227
First-Hand 123
Five-Year Plan 7, 11, 34
Flaherty, Robert 7
Flight of a Bee 23, 226–28, 229, 230, 232
Fragi, Deprived of Happiness 100
Freeze, The 9, 38, 39, 41, 61, 63, 64
Frelikh, Oleg 5, 6, 9, 36, 41, 44n, 47
Friends Meet Again 10
Frunze, Mikhail 15
Furkat 15

Gakkel, Karl 14, 65
Galperin, Alexander 67
Ganiev, Nabi 6, 9, 10, 11, 12, 13, 46, 50, 53

Gerasimov, Sergei 106
Gertel, Kazimir 6, 35, 47–49
Gift to Stalin 27
Girl of the Tian-Shan, The 164
Glavrepertkom (censorship committee) 49
Glière, Reinhard 9
Godard, Jean-Luc 151, 176
Golden Horn 13, 63, 67
Golden Shores 41
Golovnia, Anatoli 67
Gorbachev, Boris 67
Gorbachev, Mikhail 120, 122, 124, 125, 126, 147, 174n
Gorky, Maxim 157
Govorukhin, Sergei 188
Grebenshchikov, Boris 149
Grossman, Vasili 84
Gunshot at the Mountain Pass 18

Hafez 55
Hasan Arbakesh 16
Heat 128, 143, 144
His Time will Come 14
Hollywood 6, 20, 26, 27, 153, 157, 223
Horsemen of the Revolution 18
Hunter, The 27, 172, 173, 223

I'll Be Back 10, 90
Igla Remix 159
Imanov, Amandelgy 59
imperialism 2, 36, 43
In Spe 131, 203, 205
indigenization (*korenizatsiia*) 34, 38
Ishmukhamedov, Elyor 17, 18, 19, 218
Issabaeva, Zhanna 182, 184
It's Called Life 28
Ivanov, Viktor 92
Ivanov-Barkov, Yevgeni 8, 10, 13, 15, 39, 90–2

Jackal, The (Umarasa) 180
Jackals of Ravat 6, 49, 54
Jadidism 116
Jagdfeld, Grigori 8

Jamal's Tree 20, 98, 100
Jameson, Fredric 155
Journey to Nowhere 169, 170
Judas 90

Kadochnikov, Pavel 67
Kairat 21, 22, 25, 166–68, 194
Kalatozov, Mikhail 8, 128
Kapler, Alexei 68
Kara-Bugaz 41, **42**
Karagulov, Bakyt 204, 207
Karakulov, Amir 27, 67, 166–8, 170, 172–73, 176, 192–94
Karimov, Islom 86
Karliev, Alty 91–93, 100
Karmen, Roman 41
Karostin, Mikhail 9, 41
Karoy 182, 184
Karpykov, Abai 67, 176
Karsakbaev, Abdulla 164
Kassovitz, Mathieu 180
Kasymbekov, Kanymbek 164, 169
Kasymova, Margarita 119, 124
Kawalerowicz, Jerzy 206
Kazachkov, Boris 10, 54
Kazakhfilm, aka Alma-Ata Studio 27, 28, 38, 57, 62, 64, 65, 69n, 150
Kelin 28
Kerbabaev, Berdy 92
Khakdodov, Safar 122–25
Khalmukhamedov, Zakirdjan 15
Khamidov, Tolib 123
Khamidov, Tolib & Okil 124
Khamraev, Ali 16, 18, 20, 164, 218
Khodjaev, Suleiman (Saib) 6, 46, 50, 51, 52, 53
Khodjakuli, Ovliakouli 132
Khodjikov, Sultan 19, 67, 164, 165
Khorezm 3, 19
Khrushchev, Nikita 74, 75
Khudoinazarov, Bakhtiyar 21–23, 122, 124, 194, 222, 224
Khudonazarov, Davlat 112, 119–23, 141, 222
Killer 25, 169, 170, 189–91, 197, 224

Kimiagarov, Bension (Boris) 13, 14, 16, 19, 118, 119
Kinchev, Konstantin 149
Kirgizfilm/Kyrgyzfilm 14, 131, 133, 143, 200, 207
Kirov, Sergei 53
Kjalmamedov, Nury 93, 95
Klado, Nikolai 8
Koichumanova, Altynai 133
Kolar, Cédomir 132
Komsomol 9, 18, 91, 92
Konchalovsky, Andrei 28, 105, 128, 129, 143, 144, 164, 227
Konchalovsky, Yegor 28
Kopysov, Nikolai M. 90
Kordium, Arnold 54
Kosh-ba-kosh 194, 222
Kosmatov, Leonid 67
Kovarsky, Nikolai 68
Kozhamkulov, Serke 65
Kozintsev, Grigori 12, 67, 68
Kozlovsky, Alexander 12
Kozy Korpesh and Baian-Sulu (opera) 14; (film) 65
Kriuchkov, Nikolai 67
Krupskaya, Nadezhda 44n
Kuban Cossacks, The 14
Kuibyshev, Valerian 15
kulak 41, 61
Kulbai, Abai 177–81, 184, 197
Kuleshov, Lev 8, 117
Kulieva, Aina 19
Kulmamedov, Aman 91
kulturfilm 8, 29n, 39, 40, 44n
Kurbanklychev, Murad 94
Kurmanbekov, Sabit 177
Kurosawa, Akira 156
Kusturica, Emir 180
Kydyraliev, Kadyrjan 129
Kyz-Zhibek (Silk Maiden) (opera) 12; (film) 19, 164, **165**, 166

Ladynina, Marina 67
Land of the Fathers 17, 75, 78–81, **80**, 86, 164, 165, 166
Last Bey, The 5

Last Holidays, The 194
Last Stop, The 21, 22, 25, 145, 166, 167, 169, 171, 177, 183
Lavrov, Vladimir A. 90
Lebedev, Sergei 4, 7, 89
Ledashchev, Alexander 10, 90
Legend, The 103
Legend of Rustam, The 19, **118**
Legend of Siyavush, The 19, 118
Legoshin, Vladimir 39
Leila's Prayer 171, 173, 193, 223
Lemberg, Alexander 41
Lenfilm 11, 14, 57, 59, 62, 64, 68, 140
Lenin, Vladimir 4, 16, 35, 44n, 46, 55n, 127, 139, 167, 207, 228
Leontev, Yuri 39
Leper, The 5, 44n, 47, 48
Levin, Mikhail 64
Levin, Moisei 60
Leyda, Jay 39
Life of a Young Accordion Player, The 169, 178
Light Thief, The 133
Lip, The 177, 181
Little Angel, Make Me Happy 24, 75, 81–83, 84, 86, 223
Little Avenger 124
Little Men 178, 181, 182, 184
Living God 9
Locarno IFF 131, 184, 200
Lodger, The 131
Love of the Minister's Daughter 132
Lovers 18, 218
Lovers of December 169
Lullaby 119
Lumière Brothers 205
Luna Papa 23, 222, 224
Lunacharsky, Anatoli 37

Magic Crystal, The 12, 92
Magtymguly 93, 100
Magtymkuly, Fragi (Pyragy) 93
mahalla 15, 78, 79, 86, 218
Mailin, Beimbet 61, 65
Makhkamov, Kamar 121

Makhmalbaf, Mohsen 26, 224, 226
Makovsky, Alexander 10
Mamatkulova, Nargiza 134
Mamedov, Djavanshir 90
Mamonov, Petr 188
Man and his Two Women, A 124
Man Overboard 96
Man Sheds his Skin, A 15
Man with a Movie Camera, The 149
Manabaev, Damir 169
Mandala 203–5
Mankurt 101, 103, 131
Mansurov, Bulat 2, 16, 18, 24, 94, 96, 105–13
Maretskaya, Vera 67
Marjona 212, 213, 217–18
Mayakovsky, Vladimir 140
Melford, George 47
Méliès, Georges 205
Melody of the Soul 28
Memedova, Manshuk 19
Messerer, Rakhil 35, 36, 44n
Metamorphosis 132
Mezhrabpomfilm 34, 43n
Min, Boung-Hun 23, 224, 226
Minaret of Death, The 5, 6, 35, 36, 45, 47, 54
Minkin, Adolf 12
Mints, Klimenti 8, 12
Mirzoeva, Gulbahor 122, 123, 124
Moana 7
Mongol 27
Morrison, Jim 150
Moscow IFF 149, 150, 159n, 176, 185n
Mosfilm 11, 14, 15, 38, 57, 61, 62, 68, 74, 78, 128, 140
Moskvin, Andrei 67
Mother Earth 128
Mother's Lament about Mankurt, A 131, 132, 207
Motherland 75, 83–85
Motyl, Vladimir 16, 20, 107
Mukanov, Sabit 38, 61
Mukhabbatova, Gulyandom 222
Mukhtarov, Said 212, 217–18
Mullyk, Khommat 100

Murmur of a Brook in Melting Snow 119

Musakov, Zulfikar 27, 75, 83–6, 213

Muslim 9, 35, 36, 46, 51, 79, 90, 153, 154, 165, 226, 227

Muslim Woman, The 5, 6, 35, 36, 44n, 47, 54

Musrepov, Gabit 65, 68

Mute Coolness 180, 182, 184

Mutiny 63–67

My Brother, Silk Road 28, 131, 133, 199, 203, 204, 206

My Name is Kozha 164

Narimanov, Nariman 35, 44n

Narliev, Khodjakuli 13, 16, 17, 19, 20, 24, 89, 94–102, 103, 110, 112, 131

Narymbetov, Satybaldy 67, 169, 171, 173, 178, 193, 223

Nasreddin in Bukhara 12

Nasyrov, Gaziz 132, 208, 209

nation-building 1, 45, 48, 49, 163–74, 187, 197, 233n

Native Dancer 27, 181–82

Naughty Brothers, The 20

Naumenko, Maik 149

Needle, The 2, 21, 22, 147–60, **153**, 166, 167, 169, 182, 188–89

Neorealism 17, 105, 106, 176, 185n, 227

Nepesov, Djuma 90

New Economic Policy (NEP) 43n, 48

New Wave, French 17, 22, 151, 176

New Wave, Kazakh 21, 25, 67, 147, 148, 151, 153, 154, 167, 176, 177, 181, 183, 185n, 188, 219, 224

Night of the Yellow Bull 24, 223

Night Watch 28

Nights of Cabiria 17

Niyazov, Durdy 28

Niyazov, Saparmurat 23, 24, 28, 101–3, 221

Nomad, The 27, 173

Notes of a Railwayman 173

Nugmanov, Rashid 2, 21, 67, 147–60, 166, 169–70, 176, 182, 188–9

Nurmukhambetov, Erlan 178, 184

Oath, The 10, 53, 54

Ochkin, Alexei 164

October 5

Oedipus 132

Okeev, Tolomush 2, 17, 19, 20, 100, 128, 129, 137–46, 199

Omarova, Gulshad (Guka) 27, 172, 173, 182, 193

Omirbaev, Darejan 21–23, 25, 27, 67, 166–67, 169, 170, 176–79, 181, 189–92, 194, 223–24

Ompa 223

Orator, The 25, 224

Orazov, Oraz 28

Orazsiakhedov, Kakov 20

Orientalist, Oriental, Orient 5, 33, 35, 36, 37, 43n, 44n, 47, 54, 91, 94, 98, 99, 109, 233n

Other, The 27, 218

Our Dear Doctor 14

Our House 143

Pain of Love, The 119, 124

Papava, Mikhail 68

Party (Communist) 6, 7, 34, 37, 43, 49, 50, 51, 58, 59, 62, 68n, 83, 91, 120, 121, 123, 124, 144, 166, 174n

Party (Conference on Cinema Affairs) 34, 48

Party (Congress) 6, 64

Passage 131

Passer, Ivan 27, 173

Patchwork Quilt 173, 180

Path of the Burning Wagon 18

Pathé 3

Paustovsky, Konstantin 42

Pechorina, Liudmila 9

Pedestal of Death 7

Perelshtein, Rafail 14, 15, 92

Perestiani, Ivan 3

perestroika 21, 22, 102, 120–22,
124, 125, 130, 139, 148, 149, 152,
166, 170, 171, 224
Place on the Grey Triangular Hat, The
169, 170, 194
Platonov, Andrei 18
Platonov, Andrei 95
Poem about Love 14, 64, 65, **66**, 67
Pokrovsky, Mikhail 52
Politburo 34
Poplavskaya, Irina 128
Poselsky, Yakov 67
post-Soviet 2, 23, 75, 76, 84, 86, 150,
154, 155, 157, 169, 173, 185n,
187, 188, 189, 199, 211, 222–26,
228, 230
Potter, The 177
Poziljonov, Jahongir 27
Poznan, Dmitri 8
Pravov, Ivan 41
Prayer for the Chaste Bird 203
Preobrazhenskaya, Olga 41
Procurator, The 10, 91
Prokofiev, Sergei 12
Proletkino 4, 35,
Pronin, Vasili 14, 74, 143
propaganda 4, 5, 33, 35, 36, 39, 48,
51, 55, 56n, 83, 89, 90, 116, 127,
128, 143, 163, 217
Protazanov, Yakov 12, 90–91
Prut, Iosif 68
Ptushko, Alexander 67
Pudovkin, Vsevolod 11, 67, 68, 90
Pure Coolness 28, 132, 133, 196
Push 181
Pyriev, Ivan 14, 67

Qodiri, Abdullah 49, 56n
Quenching the Thirst 95, 96

Raihan 10, 63, 64
Raizman, Yuli 7, 8, 9, 41, 67, 90
Rakhimov, Abdusalom 16, 119
Rakhimzodi, Saif 23, 122–24
Rakhmatov, Daler 222
Ramazan 51

Ravenous 169
Ray, Satyajit 226
Razumny, Alexander 39, 41, 42,
Razumovsky, Alexander 8
Razykov, Yusup 25, 196, 213, 223–24
Reading of Petrarch, The 133, 134
Red Apple, The 20, 128
Red Army 4, 10, 18, 118, 166
Red Guard 49
Red Poppies of Issyk-Kul, The 20, 129
Régnier, Natacha 132
Renaissance Island 173, 178, 223
Repentance 28
Restless Morning 164
Return to A. 28
Revolution 3, 4, 6, 9, 10, 13, 14, 15,
18, 20, 34, 35, 36, 46, 48, 51, 52,
56n, 58, 59, 62, 65, 98, 117, 127,
129, 164
Rich Guy 27
Rise, The 9, 51
Road, The 177
Romm, Abram 12
Romm, Mikhail 10
Roshal, Grigori 12, 64, 67, 68
Rossellini, Roberto 106, 112
Rough River, Placid Sea 208
Route of Hope, The 133
Rover 222
Rudaki 14, 119, 126n
Ruhnama (Niyazov) 23, 28
Running 134
Running Target 169
Russian Empire 3, 33, 52, 53, 65
Rustam and Suhrab 19, 118
Rustembekov, Erzhan 177–78,
180–81

Sabinsky, Cheslav 35,
Sabirov, Tahir 14, 119
Sadoul, Georges 59, 69n
Sadykov, Bako 123–24
Sagdiev, Rustam 213–17
Saidov, Nosir 222
Salamat, Daniyar 181
Salawat Yulayev 58

Saliev, Erkin 207–8
Salieva, Urkuia 19
Salt for Svanetia 8
Saltanat 14, 143
Saltykov, Nikolai 3
Salykov, Kalykbek 67, 171, 169, 181
Sanzhira 132
Saparov, Usman 24, 75, 81–83, 223
Saratan, see *Village Authorities*
Sarulu, Marat 28, 131, 133, 199, 203
Sarykhanov, Nurmurat 94, 106
Schizo 27, 172, 173, 181, 193
Schnittke, Alfred 128
Second Wife, The 5, 6, 36, 44n, 47, 163
Secret of Karatau, The 38, 41, 61, 64
Secrets of Maqam, The 93
Seidov, Yazgeldy 94
Seille, Guillaume de 133
Seven Hearts 10
Seventh Bullet, The 20, 164, 218
Sevzapkino 4, 35, 46, 89
Sex and Philosophy 26, 226
Shahnameh 19
Shahobiddinov, Ayub 27, 218
Shamahmudov, Shaahmed 74, 76, 86, 87
Shamshiev, Bolotbek 18, 20, 113n, 129, 144
Shanghai 169, 170
Sharip(ov), Bolat 67, 171
Sharipov, Orzumurod 122
Shchors 58
She Defends the Motherland 74
Sheik, The 47
Shepherd, The 196, 213, 223
Shepherd's Son, The 14, 92
Shepitko, Larisa 105, 128, 143
Shinarbaev, Ermek 67, 169, 194
Shklovsky, Viktor 14, 68
Shneiderov, Vladimir 7
Shok and Sher 164
Shozimov, Pulat 115, 116, 117, 126n
Shpigel, Grigori 67
Shub, Esfir 67, 68
Shuga 27
Silence, The 226, 226

Siranov, Kabysh 60, 62, 64, 65, 68n, 69n
Sixth Part of the World, A 7
Sky of Our Childhood, The 2, 17, 128, 129, 137–46 (**139**), 199
Slave Girl, The 18, 95, 96
Socialist Realism 10, 14, 107, 111, 141, 157
Soiunkhanov, Mukhamed 94
Sokurov, Alexander 158
Soliev, Safarbek 123, 124, 222
Soloviev, Sergei 21, 148, 150, 176, 188
Son of Tajikistan, The 74, 117
Son, Time to Get Married 14
Song about Manshuk 19
Song of Happiness 41
Song of Southern Seas 133, **204**
Song of the Steppes, The 38, 41, 60, 61, 63, 64, 67
Songs of Abai 12, 63–67
Soviet Empire 22, 129, 139, 140, 158, 189
Soviet Patriots 92
Sovnarkom 57
Soyuzkinokhronika 39, 57, 69n
Sparrow, The 131
Stains, The 180
Stalin, Iosif 34, 43, 53, 58, 79, 138, 154, 166, 178
Star in the Night 119
State Committee for Cinematography 4, 33, 57, 144
Steppe, The 183
Steppe Express 173
Storm over Asia 18
Stormy Station 131
Stranger, The 169, 170
Strike, The 5
Sturges, John 156
Suleimenov, Olzhas 17, 140, 146n
Suleimenov, Timur 169
Sundance 147, 151
Surzhekey, The Angel of Death 169
Suvorov, Nikolai 67
Swift 178, **179**, 181, 182, 184, 197

Swing, The 24, 131, 182, 190, 199, 200–3, 224

Tachnazarov, Oraz 90
Tahir and Zuhra 12
Tajik Film Concert 12, 117
Tajikfilm 13, 14, 26, 117, 120, 122, 123, 221, 226
Tarantino, Quentin 151, 203
Tarkovsky, Andrei 182
Tashkent – City of Bread 18
Teenager 213
Temenov, Talgat 21, 27, 67, 173
Ten Steps to the East 15
Ten Years of Kazakhstan 44n
Tender Heart 169
Tenderness 17, 218
Terror (Red Terror, Great Terror) 38, 52, 58
Testament of Nine Prophets, The 124
Thaw 17, 19, 74, 75, 81, 94, 102, 129, 139, 146n, 163, 164
These are Horses 140
Thief of Bagdad, The 6, 47
Third Daughter 119
Thirteen 10
Three Brothers 25, 173, 192, 223
Three Songs for Lenin 8
Tikhonov, Nikolai 10
Time of Yellow Grass, The 23, 124
Timoshenko, Semen 12
Tisse, Eduard 67
To Get to Heaven First You Have to Die 222, 224, 230–32, **230**
To the Sounds of the Dombïra 12
Today or Tomorrow 44n
Together with Father 181
Tolchan, Yakov 7
Tolstoy, Leo 27
Toptash 134
Touch, The (Aituarov) 168
Touch, The (Kulbai) 177
Traces Go Beyond the Horizon 164
Trauberg, Leonid 12, 67, 68
Tretiakova, Olga 36, 44n
Trifonov, Yuri 95

True Noon 222
Tsarist 6, 41, 46, 51
Tsoi, Viktor 22, 149, 150, 166, 167, 182, 186n, 188
TsOKS 11, 12, 29n, 57, 58, 62, 67, 68, 74, 105, 140
Tuichiev, Yolkin 213
Tulip Revolution 127
Tulpan 27
Turaev, Anvar 19, 119, 124
Turebaev, Nariman 178, 184
Turin, Viktor 8, 39, 40, 59
Turkmenfilm, aka Ashkhabad Film Factory/Studio, Turkmen(gos)-kino 4, 10, 14, 23, 28, 46, 89, 90, 92, 94, 95, 96, 101, 103
Turksib 8, 39, **40**, 59, 62, 63, 67
Turksib is Open 44n
Tursunov, Ermek 28
Tursunzoda, Mirza 16, 119

Ubukeev, Melis 16, 128
Ulan 20
Umbar 10
Umurzakov, Yeliubai 65
Unexpected Bride, The 213–17, **214**, 218
Urusevsky, Sergei 128
Usmonov, Djamshed 3, 23, 26, 122, 123, 125, 177, 221–33
Usoltsev-Garf, Alexander 10, 53
Uspensky, Viktor 54–5
Utepbergenov, Serikbol 180, 182, 184
Uzbek Film Studio, aka Tashkent Film Studio, Uzbekfilm 15, 25, 27, 35, 50
Uzbekkino 213

Valentino, Rudolph 47
Valikhanov, Chokan 14
Valley of Tears 44n
Valley of the Ancestors, The 129
Vanin, Vasili 67
Vasiliev 'Brothers' 12, 51, 59, 67
Veil, The 6, 36, 49

Venice IFF 13, 30n, 128, 151, 184
Verner, Mikhail 3, 9, 41
Vertov, Dziga 7, 8, 67, 149
VGIK 8, 13, 21, 38, 68, 94, 96, 105, 106, 112, 140, 144, 148, 150, 176, 177, 178, 185n, 188, 226
Village Authorities 28, 131, 132, 199, 207, 208
Visconti, Luchino 106
Viskovsky, Viacheslav 47
Vitkin, Sergei 41
Vladychuk, Alexander 7, 90
Volchek, Boris 67, 96
Volpin, Mikhail 68
Vostokfilm, Vostokkino 2, 8, 33–44, 59–63
VUFKU 11, 38

Walsh, Raoul 6, 47
Wanderer, The 182
Warhol, Andy 149
Wayne, John 20
We are from Kronstadt 59
Wedding Chest, The 132
Well, The 125
When a Woman Saddles a Horse 19, 98, 100
When Emirs Die 9
Where are You, My Zulfia? 16
Where is Your House, Snail? 200
White Army 18
White Gold 7, 90
White Mountains 16, 128
White Ship, The 20, 128, 129
White Sun of the Desert 20, 107
White, White Storks 18
Who is This? 22
Whole Neighbourhood is Talking About It, The 15, 218
Wild East, The 147–60, **158**, 169, 170
Without Fear 20, 218

Woman Between Two Brothers, A 166, 167, **168**
Woman from Afar, The 119
World War I 3, 68n,
World War II (Great Patriotic War) 2, 11, 19, 24, 46, 53, 54, 57, 68, 73–87, 91
Worship of Fire, The 129

Ya-hha 147–60
Yakovlev, Alexander 121
Yarmatov, Kamil 6, 9–11, 13, 15, 18–9, 46, 54–5, 107, 116
Yazhanov, Kurban 94
Yegorov, Mikhail 10, 54
Yenei, Yevgeni 67
Yermolinsky, Sergei 41, 68
Yerofeev, Vladimir 39, 41
You are Not an Orphan 75, 76–78 (**77**), 84, 86, 218
You're my Delight 15
Youth of a Genius 19
Youth of Abai 169
Youth's First Morning 119
Yusupov, Yunus 124
Yusupova, Mairam 23, 123, 124
Yutkevich, Sergei 12

Zamanai 171
Zelim-Khan 41
Zemel, Gennadi 169
Zhambyl 169
Zhan's Diary 177
Zharov, Mikhail 67
Zheksembaeva, Limara 178
Zheliabuzhsky, Yuri 39
Zhenotdel 6, 47, 98
Zhetiruov, Zhanabek 173
Zhosha 181
Zhubanov, Akhmet 65
Zumrad 16, 119